M000287511

The Living Word is without doubt the n
of information about the Bible and its in
possibly want to know is here: statements ....
uments in the preservation and translation of the Bible; tributes by famous
people about the Bible; the presence of the Bible in key historical events ... The
entries cover such an amazing variety that the book becomes a page turner, as
we can barely wait to see what the next entry will place before us. The book is
a triumph of unobtrusive scholarship and research.

> Leland Ryken, Professor of English Emeritus,
> Wheaton College

Diana Severance's *The Living Word* offers a joyful daily tour of the extraordinary role the Bible has played in the life of the church from its New Testament
beginnings until today. The delightful and fascinating readings are selected
and shaped by Diana's substantial scholarship honed as the curator of one of
America's premiere Bible museums. If you love the Bible you will learn again
and again more reasons to do so. And if you don't, you'll discover why so many
do and why you should too.

> Dr. Peter A. Lillback, President,
> Westminster Theological Seminary, Philadelphia

The Living Word is a welcomed invitation to meditate on the Bible, its history, and its influence in our world. The stories and insights in these collected
readings will inform, inspire, and invite reflection. But most important, it will
encourage readers to engage God's Word in new and interesting ways.

> Daniel L. Dreisbach, professor at American University
> and the author of *Reading the Bible with the Founding Fathers*
> (Oxford, 2017).

In this wonderful collection of daily readings, Diana Severance tells the story
of the Bible across time—its challenges and triumphs, its dynamic power and
preservation against all odds. I love this book and commend it warmly to God's
people everywhere.

> Timothy George, Distinguished Professor at Beeson Divinity
> School of Samford University and general editor of the 28-volume
> Reformation Commentary on Scripture.

In this remarkable volume, Diana Severance has provided us with a gold mine of invaluable truths about the primacy and power of the divinely-inspired word of God. Here are 365 daily readings that provide a tour de force on the history-altering, life-changing power of this infallible book that for centuries has impacted the world. You will savor every page of this work, and it will surely increase your love and confidence in the Bible, the greatest book ever written.

STEVEN J. LAWSON, President,
One Passion Ministries; Professor, The Master's Seminary;
Teaching Fellow, Ligonier Ministries

THE LIVING WORD

"... seed was sown on the good soil; and they hear the word and accept it and bear fruit,

thirty, sixty, and a hundredfold." —Mark 4:20

Daily readings on the history, influence and impact of the Bible

DIANA SEVERANCE

KRESS
BIBLICAL
RESOURCES

The Living Word
Daily readings on the history, influence and impact of the Bible
© 2020 Diana Lynn Severance

Unless otherwise indicated, all Scripture quotations are from The ESV® Bible (The Holy Bible, English Standard Version®), copyright © 2001 by Crossway, a publishing ministry of Good News Publishers. Used by permission. All rights reserved.

Published by:

www.kressbiblical.com

ISBN: 978-1-934952-63-4

Cover scripture: New American Standard Bible: 1995 update. (1995). (Mk 4:20). La Habra, CA: The Lockman Foundation.

Some quotations of translated material have been modernized.

CONTENTS

September – mid-19th century

INTRODUCTION

We are told in *Hebrews 4:12* that "The Word of God is alive and powerful ..."
Indeed, the Bible has had a powerful impact and influence in the lives of men
and the affairs of nations. The Bible's influence can also be seen in all areas of
life, including literature, art, science, law, and government. These daily readings tell some of the story of the Bible's history and give examples of ways specific Scriptures have influenced both well-known and little-known individuals
through the centuries. The readings are basically arranged chronologically, from
the first through the twenty-first centuries. Seeing the Bible's influence through
the ages encourages us to read and study the Scriptures daily.

Each reading is followed by a Bible verse about the Word of God, which
can also become a personal prayer, so that the living Word of God molds and
shapes our lives to His honor and glory.

JANUARY 1
A POWERFUL WORD

The opening verses of Genesis introduce us to the power of God's Word. Ten times in the first chapter God speaks, and each spoken Word has powerful results:

1. "And God said, 'Let there be light,' and there was light." (1:3)
2. "And God said, 'Let there be an expanse in the midst of the waters, and let it separate the waters from the waters' … And it was so. And God called the expanse Heaven." (1:6-8)
3. "And God said, 'Let the waters under the heavens be gathered together into one place, and let the dry land appear.' And it was so. God called the dry land Earth." (1:9-10)
4. "And God said, 'Let the earth sprout vegetation, plants yielding seed, and fruit trees bearing fruit in which is their seed … on the earth.' And it was so" (1:11)
5. "And God said, 'Let there be lights in the expanse of the heavens to separate the day from the night. And let them be for signs and for seasons and for days and years, and let them be lights in the expanse of the heavens to give light upon the earth.' And it was so." (1:14-15)
6. "And God said, 'Let the waters swarm with swarms of living creatures, and let birds fly above the earth across the expanse of the heavens." (1:20)
7. "And God said, 'Let the earth bring forth living creatures according to their kinds …' And it was so." (1:24)
8. "Then God said, "Let us make man in our image, after our likeness" … So God created man in his own image, in the image of God he created him; male and female he created them." (1:26-27)

God created the universe and all in it by his powerful Word, and He continues to uphold the universe by the Word of His power. (Hebrews 1:3).

After the creation, God continued to speak, and He gave instructions to the man and woman, giving them responsibility over the creation and provision for their task:

9. "And God said to them, 'be fruitful and multiply and fill the earth and subdue it and have dominion over the fish of the sea and over the birds of the heavens and over every living thing that moves on the earth,'" (1:28)
10. "And God said, 'Behold, I have given you every plant yielding seed that is on the face of all the earth, and every tree with seed in its fruit. You shall have them for food." (1:30)

God continues to speak through the rest of the Scripture and continues to speak through His Word today. His Word continues to have power in the creation and in the lives of His people.

Long ago, at many times and in many ways,
God spoke to our fathers by the prophets,
but in these last days he has spoken to us by his Son,
whom he appointed the heir of all things,
through whom also he created the world.

— Hebrews 1:1-2 —

JANUARY 2
QUESTIONING GOD'S WORD

The universe and all in it were created by the Word of God. God spoke it into existence by the power of His Word. When He created man, He again did so by His Word, saying, "Be fruitful and multiply and fill and subdue it [the earth] and have dominion over the fish of the sea and over the birds of the heavens and over every living thing that moves on the earth." (Genesis 1:28) God placed only one restriction on man. He said, "You may surely eat of every tree of the garden, but of the tree of the knowledge of good and evil you shall not eat, for in the day that you eat of it you shall surely die." (Genesis 2:16-17)

When the serpent came and tempted the woman, he sought to cast doubt on the Word of God, impugning the very character of God. The first question in Scripture is the serpent's questioning of the Word of God, "Did God actually say, 'You shall not eat of any tree in the garden?'" (Genesis 3:1) The question seems innocent enough, but it deceptively places doubts in the woman's mind. By misquoting God's command, God's character is brought into question as well.

In her reply, the woman also misquoted God's Word by not naming the tree of the knowledge of good and evil and by adding they were not to *touch* the tree. After questioning the Word of God, the serpent denied the Word of God when he said "You will not surely die. For God knows that when you eat of it your eyes will be open and you will be like God, knowing good and evil." (3:4) The woman then relied on her own reason, thinking the fruit of the forbidden tree was pleasant to the eye and would be good for food, and she disobeyed God's Word, eating the forbidden fruit. Sin entered the world when God's Word was disobeyed and broken.

The pattern of doubt, skepticism and sin—questioning God's Word and His character, relying on man's reasoning and insight rather than submitting in obedience to God's Word—is found throughout the rest of God's Word, the Bible, and throughout human history. Denying God's Word denigrates God, deifies man, and is the essence of all sin.

Jesus said, "For if you believed Moses,
you would believe me; for he wrote of me.
But if you do not believe his writings,
how will you believe my words?"

— John 5:46-47—

THE UNIQUENESS OF THE BIBLE

The Bible is a unique book, written in a period of 1500 years by over 40 authors with a unified theme of God's redemption. Authors included 3 kings, 3 priests, 1 doctor, 3 shepherds, 1 military general, a couple of fishermen, 2 statesmen, and 1 scribe. Written in three languages, the writings show a diversity of geography and social standing. Almost 3000 people are among the cast of the Bible's story. With 31,000 verses, 700,000 words, and 3.5 million letters, the Bible speaks with one voice. There is one story of humankind, one standard of morality, and one plan of salvation. God is the one author inspiring the Scripture and providing the unity behind the diversity of human authors.

The Bible is a divine work. All Scripture is breathed out by God (II Timothy 3:16). Over 2000 times in the Old Testament we find, "Thus says the Lord." Whenever the New Testament quotes from the Old Testament, it is quoted as God speaking, for whenever Scripture speaks, God speaks.

No other book of antiquity has been as well preserved as the Bible. There are almost 6000 early Greek manuscripts of the New Testament, and 10,000 of the Latin Vulgate, in addition to Syriac and other translations. The earliest fragments of the New Testament are within 50 years of writing, and the entire New Testament can be found in manuscripts within 200 years of writing. In contrast, the earliest manuscripts of Homer are 400 years after his writing; Plato's writings are found in manuscripts 1300 years after his time.

27% of the Bible was prophetic at the time it was written. Some prophecies include the promise Abraham would have a son,[1] Cyrus of Persia would allow the Jews to return to their land[2], the fall of Jerusalem,[3] the Babylonian captivity would last 70 years,[4] and the destruction of Tyre.[5] The greatest fulfillment of prophecy can be seen in the life and ministry of Jesus. No other book in the world has fulfilled prophecies as the Bible has.

Behold, the former things have come to pass,
and new things I now declare;
before they spring forth I tell you of them.

—Isaiah 42:9—

JANUARY 4
THE UNITY OF THE BIBLE

The consistency and unity of the Bible is a powerful argument for its trustworthiness. Erwin Lutzer urged the following considerations about the Bible's unity:

- It evolved over a period of fifteen centuries, written in three different languages. During this period empires rose and fell and cultures came and went, but this did not affect the unity of the Bible. The intricacy of its message and history simply could not have been orchestrated by a man or a group of men.

- It was written by forty different human authors. These came from a variety of occupations: kings, fishermen, tax collectors, shepherds, prophets, and even a physician.

- It would be difficult to find a more diverse collection of writers. They run the gamut from Moses, who was highly educated, to Peter, who was a fisherman. Though they wrote at different periods of world history, their writings dovetail with one another, not superficially, but intricately and brilliantly.

- The books were penned under different circumstances and in different countries and cultures, in Asia, Africa, and Europe. Paul wrote from a dungeon in Rome, James wrote from Jerusalem, Moses from the Sinai and Daniel from Babylon.

- The Bible discusses diverse theological matters, such as the nature of God and His purposes, the characteristics of both good and evil angels, and the nature of man and God's plan of redemption. It would be difficult enough to get ten men to agree on so much as one theological issue, much less forty men agreeing on matters about which others can only speculate.

Imagine, say, a book on medicine written by forty different authors over a period of fifteen centuries. And yet, also imagine that the book is so up-to-date that it can still cure the sick today! Surely we would have to admit that such agreement is remarkable. The Bible treats subjects that are even more controversial and further removed from personal investigation, yet it treats these matters with authority and unity.[6]

The secret things belong to the Lord our God,
but the things that are revealed belong to us and to our children forever,
that we may do all the words of this law.
—Deuteronomy 29:29—

CYRUS, GOD'S ANOINTED

A unique feature of the Bible is its record of God foretelling future events which do come to pass. God tells Isaiah that this is something the idols and false gods cannot do:

> Who is like me? Let him proclaim it … Let him declare what is to come and what will happen …. I am God and there is no other; I am God, and there is none like me, declaring the end from the beginning and from ancient times things not yet done, saying, 'My counsel shall stand and I will accomplish all my purpose.' (Isaiah 44:7-8; 46:9-10)

Isaiah, living and writing in the 7th century B.C., predicts through the "word of the Lord" that the Jewish nation would be taken out of its land into captivity. One hundred years later, Babylon came and took the Jewish people captive in three stages. After a siege, the Jerusalem capital fell to the Babylonians in 586 B.C. Isaiah further prophesied that Babylon itself would be conquered by the Persians, and the Persians would allow the Jews to return to Jerusalem. God even specifically names the Persian king who would let the Jews return to their land. God says

> … of Jerusalem, 'She shall be inhabited,' and of the cities of Judah, 'They shall be built, and I will raise up their ruins' … who says of Cyrus, 'He is my shepherd, and he shall fulfill all my purpose'; saying of Jerusalem, 'She shall be built,' and of the temple, 'Your foundation shall be laid.' (Isaiah 44:26-28)

God further calls Cyrus "his anointed," saying he had grasped his right hand to subdue the nations. He further said of Cyrus:

> I call you by your name, I name you, though you do not know me. I am the Lord and there is no other, besides me there is no God; I equip you, though you do not know me … I am the Lord, and there is no other. (Isaiah 45:5-6)

God told of Cyrus' name and role in returning the Jews to their land about 150 years before the event occurred, about 100 years before the man even lived. There is no other God and no other book which tells the future in such a manner.

Give ear, O my people, to my teaching;
incline your ears to the words of my mouth!
—Psalm 78:1—

JANUARY 6
WHAT JESUS SAYS ABOUT THE SCRIPTURE

The most important reason for believing the Bible is the teaching of Jesus Christ. Jesus affirmed the importance of the Word of God during his temptation in the wilderness. During each temptation, Jesus countered with Scripture, beginning with "Man shall not live by bread alone, but by every word that comes from the mouth of God."[7] In His famous Sermon on the Mount, Jesus claimed to have come to fulfill the Law, "For truly, I say to you, until heaven and earth pass away, not an iota, not a dot, will pass from the Law until all is accomplished."[8] Later, He would proclaim that "it is easier for heaven and earth to pass away than for one dot of the Law to become void."[9] In His dispute with the Jewish leaders, Jesus asserted that "the Scripture cannot be broken."[10] In His prayer after the Passover He prayed to the Father, "Sanctify them in the truth; your word is truth."[11]

Jesus affirmed the entirety of Hebrew Scriptures, and asserted the truth of the historical accounts which are often scoffed at today as myth or legends. as true history accounts often today scoffed at as myths or legends. Jesus recognized Adam and Eve as the beginning of marriage, Noah and the flood as a judgment such as at Jesus' Second Coming, Sodom and Gomorrah as a preview of the final judgment, and Jonah and the great fish as foreshadowing His own resurrection. From the beginning in Genesis to the end of the Hebrew Scriptures, Jesus affirmed the Scripture's authenticity.[12] Jesus also anticipated that the Holy Spirit would provide additional truth after His departure: "When the Spirit of truth comes, he will guide you into all the truth, ... he will take what is mine and declare it to you."[13]

Jesus' testimony to the truthfulness and authority of Scripture certainly encourages us to partake richly of this Word of God.

Therefore we must pay much closer attention to what we have heard,
lest we drift away from it.
—Hebrews 2:1—

THE INSPIRED WORD

J.C. Ryle (1816-1900), a leading evangelical minister in the Church of England, recognized that the inspiration of the Scriptures is

the very keel and foundation of Christianity. If Christians have no divine book to turn to as the warrant of their doctrine and practice, they have no solid ground for present peace or hope, and no right to claim the attention of mankind. They are building on quicksand, and their faith is vain.... If the Bible is not the word of God and inspired, the whole of Christendom for 1800 years has been under an immense delusion ....

But the uniqueness and inspiration of the Bible can be seen in its

extraordinary fullness and richness in the contents ... It throws more light on a vast number of most important subjects than all the other books in the world put together. It boldly handles matters which are beyond the reach of man, when left to himself. It treats of things which are mysterious and invisible—the soul, the world to come, and eternity—depths which man has no line to fathom ... How dim were the views of Socrates, Plato, Cicero, and Seneca! A well-taught Sunday scholar in this day, knows more spiritual truth than all these sages put together.

Ryle noted several areas in which the Bible alone provided truth:

*   The Bible alone gives a reasonable account of *the beginning and end of the globe* on which we live. It starts from the birthday of the sun, moon, stars, and earth ... it foretells the dissolution of all things.

*   The Bible alone gives a *true and faithful account of man*. It does not flatter him as novels do ... It shows him to be a corrupt being under every circumstance ...

*   The Bible alone gives us *true views of God*. By nature man knows nothing clearly or fully about him. All of his conceptions of him are low, groveling and debased. What could be more degraded than the gods of the Canaanites and Egyptians, of Babylon, of Greece, and of Rome? ...

*   By the Bible we know that *God loves sinners*. His gracious promise in the day of Adams's fall; his longsuffering in the time of Noah ... his sending his Son into the world, in due time, to be crucified; his commanding the gospel to be preached to the Gentiles ...

- By the Bible we learn that *God knows all things.* We see him foretelling things hundreds and thousands of years before they take place, and as he foretells, so it comes to pass ...

- The Bible alone teaches us that *God has made a full, perfect, and complete provision for the salvation of fallen man.* It tells of an atonement made for the sin of the world, by the sacrifice and death of God's own Son upon the cross ...

- The Bible alone *explains the state of things that we see in the world around us* ... The amazing inequality of conditions, the poverty and distress, the oppression and persecution, ... the failures of statesmen and legislators ...

In sum, Ryle stated,

In the matter of its contents, the Bible stands entirely alone, and no other book is fit to be named in the same day with it. He that dares to say the Bible is not inspired, let him give a reasonable account of this fact, if he can.[14]

I open my mouth and pant,
because I long for your commandments.
—Psalm 119:131—

PRACTICAL STEPS FOR READING THE BIBLE

Scottish minister Thomas Boston (1676-1732) was noted as a preacher who carefully and warmly exposited the Scriptures. He wrote that the Bible was

> … the best of books. You assume people who have many good books know much, but if you have the Bible then you have the best book in the world. It is the book of the Lord, dictated by unerring infinite wisdom. There is no dross here with the gold; no chaff with the corn. Every word of God is pure. There is nothing for our salvation to be had in other books but what is learned from this. They are but the rivulets that run from this fountain and all shine with light borrowed from the Bible. And it has a blessing annexed to it, a glory and majesty in it, an efficacy with it that no other book has in the same way. Therefore Luther professed he would burn the books he had written rather than allow those books to divert people from reading the Scriptures.

After extolling the Bible's many virtues, Boston gave some practical steps for studying the Scriptures:

1. Keep to a regular plan of reading the Bible so that you may become acquainted with the whole of it.
2. Mark those passages which particularly move your heart and are most applicable to your case.
3. Use the marginal notes in your Bible to compare one Scripture with another so that more obscure passages are explained by others. Keep Christ in view, for the entire Scripture is of Him.
4. Read with reverence and attention to the majesty of God and the divine authority requiring our obedience.
5. Let your main end in reading the scripture be practice and not bare knowledge. (James 1:22)
6. Pray to God and look to his Spirit for understanding as you read. (I Corinthians 2:11)
7. Beware of a fleshly, worldly mind which can come between you and the light of the word, eclipsing its truth.
8. Labor towards godliness, and let the Scriptures speak to your particularly case.
9. Put in practice whatever you learn from the word. [15]

Praise the Lord! Blessed is the man who fears the Lord,
who greatly delights in his commandments!
—Psalm 112:1—

JANUARY 9
THE BOOKS OF THE BIBLE POEM

In Genesis the world was made by God's creative hand;
In Exodus the Hebrews march to gain the Promised Land;
Leviticus contains the law, holy, just, and good,
Numbers records the tribes enrolled, all sons of Abraham's blood.
Moses in Deuteronomy records God's mighty deeds.
Brave Joshua into Canaan's land the host of Israel leads,
In Judges their rebellion oft provokes the Lord to smite,
But Ruth records the faith of one well-pleasing in his sight.
In 1st and 2nd Samuel of Jesse's son we read;
Ten tribes in 1st and 2nd Kings revolted from his seed.
In 1st and 2nd Chronicles we see Judah captive made,
But Ezra leads the remnant back by princely Cyrus' aid.
The city walls of Zion Nehemiah builds again,
While Esther saves her people from the plots of wicked men.
In Job we read how faith will live beneath afflictions' rod,
And David's Psalms are precious songs to every child of God.
The Proverbs, like a goodly string of choicest pearls, appear;
Ecclesiastes teaches men how vain are all things here.
The Song of Solomon exalts sweet Sharon's lovely rose,
While Christ the Saviour and the King the rapt Isaiah shows.
The admonishing Jeremiah apostate Israel warns,
His plaintive Lamentations their awful downfall mourns.
Ezekiel tells in wondrous words the Kingdom's mysteries,
While God's great Kingdom yet to come Daniel in vision sees.
Of judgment and of mercy Hosea loves to tell,
Joel describes the blessed days when God with man will dwell.
Among Tekoa's brethren Amos received his call,
And Obadiah prophesies of Edom's final fall.
Jonah enshrines a wondrous type of Christ, our risen Lord;
Nahum declares, on Nineveh just judgment shall be poured
When Christ our risen Saviour shall come to be adored.
A view of Chaldees' coming doom Habakkuk's vision gives,
While Zephaniah warns the Jews to turn, repent, and live.
Haggai wrote to those who saw the Temple built again,
Zechariah prophesies of Christ's triumphant reign.
Malachi was the last to touch that high prophetic cord;

His final notes sublimely show the coming of the Lord.
Matthew, Mark, Luke, and John the Gospel story give,
Describing how the Saviour was born and died that man may live.
Acts tells how well the apostles preached with signs in every place,
And Paul in Romans proves that man is saved through faith by grace.
The Apostle in Corinthians instructs, exhorts reproves;
Galatians proves that faith in Christ alone the Father approves.
Ephesians and Philippians tell what Christians ought to be;
Colossians bids us live for God and from all sin be free.
In Thessalonians we are taught the Lord will come from heaven,
In Timothy and Titus a shepherd's rule is given.
Philemon marks a brother's love as only brethren know;
Hebrews reveals Christ's priestly works prefigured long ago.
James teaches, without holiness, faith is but vain and dead;
While Peter points the narrow way in which the saints are led.
John in his three epistles on love delights to dwell;
But Jude gives warning terrible of those once who fell.
The revelation prophesies that tremendous day
When all the kingdoms of the earth with noise shall pass away.
'Even so, come Lord Jesus.'[16]   —Author unknown

He which testifies to these things says, "Surely I am coming soon." Amen.
Come, Lord Jesus!
The grace of the Lord Jesus Christ be with all. Amen.
— Revelation 22:20-21—

JANUARY 10
THE FIRST BIBLE TRANSLATION

The Bible is the most frequently translated book in the world, with at least one book of the Bible translated into nearly 3000 languages. The Bible is also the first book known to have been translated, when the Hebrew Scriptures were translated into Greek in the third century B.C. This translation is known as the Septuagint (Latin for "seventy"), from the legend that 72 translators, 6 from each one of the twelve tribes of Israel, worked on the translation independently, and all came up with exactly the same translation! Often this version is identified by "LXX," the Roman numerals for seventy. Another source says that the high priest Eleazar sent translators to Egypt to make the translation at the request of Ptolemy II, ruling Egypt at the time, who wanted the translation for his library at Alexandria. There were many Jews living in Alexandria who were fluent in Greek but no longer familiar with Hebrew.

The Septuagint translation was apparently made over several centuries. The Torah or books of Moses were translated in the third century B.C., while other Hebrew Scriptures were translated over the next two centuries. The Septuagint also came to include some Jewish writings not in the Hebrew Scriptures, such as the *Wisdom of Solomon* and the *Books of Maccabees*. These books were later called the apocrypha or deuterocanonical books.

The Septuagint was read by Greek-speaking Jews of the first and second centuries, and some copies have been found among the Dead Sea Scrolls. Early Christians used the Septuagint, and many of the New Testament quotations of the Jewish Scriptures are from the Septuagint. Many of the early translations of the Christian Scriptures translated the Old Testament from the Septuagint, including the Old Latin, Coptic, Ethiopic, Armenian, Georgian, Slavonic and some Arabic translations. Though Jerome began his Latin translation from the Septuagint, he learned Hebrew and translated from the Hebrew, something Augustine criticized him for. The famous early 4th century Greek codices of the Bible—Codex Sinaiticus, Codex Vaticanus, and Codex Alexandrinus, all have the Septuagint.

For the word of the Lord is upright,
and all his work is done in faithfulness.
—Psalm 33:4—

EARLY MANUSCRIPTS

The name "Bible" comes from the Greek word for "book." Actually a collected library of nearly 70 separate books and letters, the Bible recounts events from the creation of the world to a future eternity, and it is read by more people in the world than any other book. No other book has had such an impact on civilization or people's lives.

The earliest Bible manuscripts were written in Hebrew or Greek on papyrus or parchment scrolls. Though many of the early Bible manuscripts were intentionally destroyed during the years when the early church was persecuted, there are today over 6000 known Biblical fragments or manuscripts. Some manuscripts are from within 50 years of the original writing, making the Bible itself the most well-attested of all ancient books.

There were several ways, besides being written in a different language, that these early manuscripts differed from the Bibles we have today. Of course, there were no chapters and verses; those were added centuries later. And of course, since the printing press was not invented until the 15th century, these were manuscripts—hand-written documents. Since lower-case letters also had not yet developed, all the letters were capitals. There were also no spaces between the words or punctuation marks between sentences. This almost required the words be read aloud rather than silently as we often read today. One scroll could not contain all the Scriptures; it would be too long. So, the Scriptures (or writings) would be a collection of scrolls.

Interestingly, it was the Christians who were the first to extensively use a book format rather than scrolls for their Scriptures. Books were less expensive, since both sides of the papyrus sheet or parchment could be used. Books were very much like pocket notebooks and could be transported more easily and with less notice than scrolls—a definite advantage when the new Christian faith was spreading and subject to persecution. Paul's letters, or the four gospels, easily fit in a small book which could be hidden or concealed if necessary.

Though the format of the early Bible is very different from what we have today, the truth and power of the Word of God continues the same throughout the ages.

Forever, O Lord, your word is firmly fixed in the heavens.
—Psalm 119:89—

JANUARY 12
A PRIESTLY BLESSING

During Gabriel Barkay's excavations of Ketef Hinnom, overlooking the Hinnom Valley in Jerusalem, he found several looted burial caves. In 1979-1980, however, he found an undisturbed burial where ninety-five bodies had been interred. Dating from the first Temple period (7th century B.C.), the site contained pottery and beautiful silver and gold jewelry. Most intriguing were two tiny silver scrolls, with a space so that the little scroll could be threaded and worn. After carefully unrolling the sheets of silver, each was found to contain inscriptions. Though difficult to read, scholars recognized that the Paleo-Hebraic script was the form used around the 7th century B.C. Both scrolls were inscribed with an abbreviated version of the priestly benediction of Numbers 6:24-26, "The Lord bless you and keep you; the Lord make his face to shine upon you and be gracious to you; the Lord lift up his countenance upon you and give you peace." Though some critics had contended that the book of Numbers was written after the exile or Babylonian captivity, the presence of these silver scrolls attests to an earlier date for the writing. The little scrolls were probably amulets, with the priestly blessing being used as a kind of charm to ward off evil.

The silver scrolls "preserve the earliest known citations of Biblical texts ... these plaques not only contain Biblical quotations, but they also provide us with the earliest examples of confessional statements concerning Yahweh."[17]

The words of the Lord are pure words,
like silver refined in a furnace on the ground,
purified seven times.
—Psalm 12:6—

THE DEAD SEA SCROLLS

In 1947, some Bedouin shepherd boys were looking for a lost goat in the area around the Dead Sea. One of the boys threw a rock into a cave, hoping to scare out the goat if it was there, and heard something break. Entering the cave, he found cylindrical clay jars covered with bowl lids. Inside the jars, wrapped in linen cloths, were seven parchment scrolls written in Hebrew and Aramaic. The scrolls included two copies of the biblical book of Isaiah, a commentary on Habakkuk and four scrolls of a sectarian nature. Archaeologists began exploring the region, and eleven more caves were found with ancient manuscripts. Over 230 of the manuscripts discovered are copies of books from the Hebrew Bible, while over 600 other texts include portions of Jewish literature and sectarian texts.

Many recognize the discovery of the scrolls as the most important archaeological find of the century. The Dead Sea Scrolls date from the third century B.C. to the first century A.D. and are one thousand years older than the oldest Hebrew biblical texts previously known. All of the Hebrew biblical books are represented among the scrolls, except the book of Esther (though it is referenced in the other Jewish writings among the scrolls). In comparing the Dead Sea Scroll biblical texts with the later available texts, scholars discovered only about 5% variation, attesting to the preservation of the Scriptures over the millennia. Most of the differences are spelling alterations or obvious slips of the pen.

The Dead Sea Scrolls are important not only for the study of the biblical texts, but also for background to the Second Temple period. They provide information about the Pharisees, Sadducees, and Essenes and Jewish practices at the beginning of the Christian era.

For the earth will be filled with the knowledge of the glory of the Lord
as the waters cover the sea.
—Habakkuk 2:14—

JANUARY 14
JESUS' MOTHER KNEW THE SCRIPTURES

The young woman God chose to be the mother of Jesus was a woman who knew the Scriptures. In many of the paintings of Gabriel's announcement to Mary that she would have a son, Gabriel comes to Mary when she is reading the Scriptures. As Mary takes in the written Word of God, she will conceive the Living Word of God.

The Gospels depict Mary as deeply rooted in the Scriptures. Knowing that bearing a child apart from the normal means of conception was impossible, she yet believed God's Word spoken to her by Gabriel, knowing that with God nothing is impossible.

When Mary meets her cousin Elizabeth in Luke 1:46-55, Mary's song of praise reveals her deep knowledge of Scripture; the song has over thirty Scriptural quotes or allusions:

My soul magnifies the Lord,	*II Samuel 2:1-10; Psa. 34:2*
And my spirit rejoices in God my Savior,	*Psa. 35:9; Hab. 3:18; Isa. 61:10*
For he has looked on the humble estate of his servant,	*Psa. 138:6*
For behold, from now on all generations will call me blessed;	*Psa. 72:17*
For he who is mighty has done great things for me,	*Psa. 89:8; Zeph. 3:17; Psa. 71:19*
and holy is his name.	*Psa. 99:3; 111:9; Isa. 57:15*
And his mercy is for those who fear him	*Deut. 5:10; Psa. 89:1-2; 103:17*
From generation to generation.	
He has shown strength with his arm;	*Psa. 89:10; 98:1; 118:16; Isa. 51:9*
He has scattered the proud in the thoughts of their hearts;	*Dan. 4:37*
He has brought down the mighty from their thrones	
And exalted those of humble estate;	*Psa. 75:7; 107:40; 113:7-8; 147:6*
He has filled the hungry with good things,	*Psa. 34:10; 107:9*
and the rich he has sent empty away.	*Job 22:9*
He has helped his servant Israel,	*Isa. 41:8-9; 44:21; 49:3*
In remembrance of his mercy,	*Psa. 98:3; Mic. 7:20*
as he spoke to our fathers,	*Gen. 17:9; Psa. 132:11*
to Abraham and to his offspring forever.	

---

*... remember the predictions of the holy prophets and the commandment of the
Lord and Savior through your apostles.*
—II Peter 3:2—

JESUS AND THE HEBREW SCRIPTURES

Some contend that the stories in the Old Testament are really myths, legends, and fables, but not records of actual historical events. Jesus, however, thought the Old Testament narratives were reliable accounts of real events and people.[18] He refers to Adam and Eve as the first historical people. (Matt. 19:4-6) Cain's slaying of Abel was the first of a series of historical persecutions of righteous people. (Matt. 23:35) He likened the days before His Second Coming to those before the flood in Noah's day. (Matt. 24:37-38) The judgments which fell on the cities of Tyre, Sidon, and Sodom, would not have occurred if they had seen all the miracles which Jesus performed in the Galilean villages of Chorazin and Bethsaida. (Matt. 11:21-24) The founders of Israel, Abraham, Isaac, and Jacob are also affirmed as historical people (John 8:56; Matt. 8:11), as well as God appearing to Moses in the burning bush. (Mark 12:26-27)

The manna in the wilderness looked forward to Jesus as the true bread come down from Heaven (John 6:32, 49, 58), and the bronze serpent Moses raised in the wilderness was like Christ crucified and raised for the salvation of His people. (John 3:14) Other historical persons from the Old Testament Jesus referenced included David and Solomon (Matt. 12:3, 42), the Queen of Sheba (Matt. 12:42), Elijah and Elisha (Luke 4:25-27), Isaiah (John 12:38-41), and Zechariah (Matt. 23:35). These are not just spiritual illustrations, but real, historical figures.

Importantly, Jesus also referred to Jonah being swallowed by a great fish and thrown up on the shore in three days as a real historical event as well as a type of Jesus' own resurrection after three days in the tomb (Matt. 12:40-41). For Jesus, the Old Testament was God's truth and looked forward to the greater fulfillment in His own person, David's Greater Son.

Do not think that I have come to abolish the Law or the Prophets;
I have not come to abolish them but to fulfill them.
—Matthew 5:17—

JANUARY 16
PROPHECIES FULFILLED IN JESUS

When we think about the Bible's description of Jesus, we usually think of the four Gospel accounts, Matthew, Mark, Luke, and John. Yet the Hebrew Scriptures also speak of Jesus. Early in His ministry Jesus told the Jewish leaders in Jerusalem, "You search the Scriptures because you think that in them you have eternal life; and it is they that bear witness about me."[19] On the day of His resurrection, Jesus had a wonderful conversation with some disciples on the road to Emmaus: "And beginning with Moses and all the Prophets, he interpreted to them in all the Scripture the things concerning himself."[20]

Jesus' birth to a virgin in Bethlehem, as well as His infancy in Egypt and His ministry in Galilee, are all anticipated in the Hebrew Scriptures.[21] So are His ministry in the Temple and His healings and miracles.[22] The events surrounding Jesus' death and resurrection are presaged in some detail, with Isaiah 53 and Psalm 22 describing the suffering as well as the victory of the cross. Some details described include: Jesus was betrayed by a friend for 30 pieces of silver, and the money was used to buy a potter's field;[23] Jesus was forsaken by His disciples and silent before His accusers as He was wounded, bruised, smitten, mocked, and spit upon;[24] He prayed for His persecutors while they cast lots for His clothes;[25] Jesus' hands and feet were pierced as He was crucified between two thieves;[26] He suffered thirst; His side was pierced; He was forsaken by God;[27] no bones were broken before He committed Himself to God;[28] darkness came over the land;[29] buried in a rich man's tomb; He saw no decay, but was raised from the dead.[30] These and more must have been the Scriptures Jesus interpreted to those disciples along the road that first Easter morning.

And beginning with Moses and all the Prophets, he interpreted to them in all the Scriptures the things concerning himself.
—Luke 24:27—

COUNSELING WITH SCRIPTURE

One of the earliest Christian writings we have after the New Testament is a letter written by Clement, Bishop of Rome (d. 99). He was a first-century convert who was taught by Peter and Paul. Some speculate that the Clement mentioned in Philippians 4:3 was the Clement who later became Bishop of Rome.

When strife and division plagued the church at Corinth (again!), Clement wrote a letter encouraging the Corinthians to peace and reconciliation and encouraging them in the truths received from the apostles. Clement's letter is saturated with Scripture and includes at least 150 quotes from the Scriptures. Following are a few of the Scriptures Clement used in his encouragement and counseling of the Corinthians:

"Let the one who boasts, boast in the Lord" (I Corinthians 1:31).

"For with the judgment you pronounce you will be judged, and with the measure you use it will be measured to you" (Matthew 7:2).

"This people honors me with their lips, but their heart is far from me" (Mark. 7:6).

"What no eye has seen, nor ear hard, nor the heart of man imagined, what God has prepared for those who love him" (I Cor. 2:9).

"whoever causes one of these little ones who believe in me to sin, it would be better for him to have a great millstone fastened around his neck and to be drowned in the depth of the sea." (Matthew 18:6).

"For the Lord disciplines the one he loves, and chastises every son whom he receives." (Hebrews 12:6).

In his skillful weaving of scriptural references together, Clement encouraged the Corinthians in their holy calling, to "attend to what is good, pleasing, and acceptable in the sight of Him who formed us."[31]

I have not departed from the commandment of his lips;
I have treasured the words of his mouth more than my portion of food.
—Job 23:12—

JANUARY 18
EXTRA-BIBLICAL STATEMENTS ABOUT JESUS

The New Testament is, of course, the main source of our information concerning the person and work of Jesus of Nazareth. There are a few early extra-biblical references to Jesus and the early Christians, however, which are of interest. When describing how Nero blamed the great fire of Rome on the Christians, the Roman historian Tacitus (c. 56–c. 120 A.D.) corroborated Jesus' death at the hands of Pontius Pilate:

> ... Nero fastened the guilt and inflicted the most exquisite tortures on a class hated for their abominations, called Christians by the populace. Christus, from whom the name had its origin, suffered the extreme penalty during the reign of Tiberius at the hands of one of our procurators, Pontius Pilatus, and a most mischievous superstition, thus checked for the moment, again broke out not only in Judea, the first source of the evil, but even in Rome, where all things hideous and shameful from every part of the world find their centre and become popular.[32]

The Jewish historian Josephus (37–c. 100 A.D.) was descended from the Jewish priests on his father's side and claimed royal descent from his mother. Josephus' *Jewish Antiquities* relied heavily on the Hebrew Scriptures while explaining Jewish history, law, and customs to the Roman world. In a section on the Roman governor Pontius Pilate, Josephus gave the following account of Jesus:

> At this time there was a wise man called Jesus and his conduct was good, and he was known to be virtuous. Many people among the Jews and the other nations became his disciples. Pilate condemned him to be crucified and to die. But those who had become his disciples did not abandon his discipleship. They reported that he had appeared to them three days after his crucifixion and that he was alive. Accordingly, he was perhaps the Messiah, concerning whom the prophets have reported wonders. And the tribe of the Christians, so named after him, has not disappeared to this day.[33]

For since, in the wisdom of God, the world did not know God through wisdom,
it pleased God through the folly of what we preach to save those who believe.
— I Corinthians 1:21—

STONY EVIDENCE

The Scriptures contain the narratives of numerous ancient historical events, and often the broader historical context of the events is given. For example, Luke specifically dates the time of Jesus' birth to the time when Caesar Augustus was Roman Emperor and Quirinius was governor of Syria. During the trials preceding Jesus' crucifixion, two key figures were Pontius Pilate, the Roman governor of Judea, and Caiaphas, the Jewish high priest. Both are mentioned in other written historical records of the period, and both also have some interesting archaeological finds associated with them.

In 1990, when construction was being done on a water park south of the Old City of Jerusalem, bulldozers broke through a roof of a cave which was an ancient burial site. Inside were six ossuaries or bone boxes. (The Jewish practice at the time of Christ was to place the body in a cave or tomb for a year, then gather the bones together and place in ossuaries in the tomb.) One of the limestone ossuaries found was very ornately designed with rosettes. The name "Joseph, son of Caiaphas" is inscribed on the ossuary. Inside were the bones of a man about sixty years old. Many believe this was the high priest at one of Jesus' trials who found Jesus guilty of blasphemy and sent him to Pilate for execution.

In 1961, Italian archaeologists were excavating at the theater in Caesarea Maritima, the provincial capital of Roman Judea. When excavating a stair, they discovered a stone slab with an inscription on it. Apparently, the slab had been a stone marker which was reused as a stair step when the theater was being renovated in the fourth century. Though the inscription is incomplete and cannot be fully read, some words can clearly be seen: Tiberium, Pontius Pilate, Prefect of Judea. Where the slab was originally located is not known, but apparently Pilate had built a building to honor Emperor Tiberius, possibly a temple in his honor.

The insolent have dug pitfalls for me;
they do not live according to your law.
—Psalm 119:85—

JANUARY 20
P⁵²

Traveling in Egypt in 1920, Dr. B.P. Grenfell purchased a collection of ancient papyri for the John Rylands Library at the University of Manchester. The fragments were accessioned, added to the library, and somewhat neglected. In 1934, Colin Roberts, of St. John's College, Oxford, was studying the fragments and on one was able to decipher words from the Gospel of John, from the account of Jesus' trial before Pilate. The fragment, about 3.5" x 2.5," has seven lines of John 18:31-33 on the front and even lines of John 18:37-38 on the back. Since it's written on both sides, the papyrus fragment was from a codex or book, not a scroll (The Christians were among the first to use the codex or book form rather than the scroll.) The larger size of the text suggests this was from a book to be used in congregational reading, with the entire Gospel of John comprising a book of 130 pages. Based on the style of the script, Roberts dated the fragment to the first half of the second century, making it the oldest Biblical manuscript we now have.

Though the amount of Scripture in this little fragment is slight, P⁵² has tremendous significance. As Dr. Bruce Metzger, a prominent New Testament scholar wrote, "Just as Robinson Crusoe, seeing but a single footprint in the sand, concluded that another human being, with two feet was present on the island with him, so P⁵² proves the existence and use of the Fourth Gospel during the first half of the second century in a provincial town along the Nile, far removed from its traditional place of composition."³⁴

John probably wrote his gospel in Ephesus, in what is now Turkey, at the end of the first century. P⁵² shows that within a few years the gospel was circulating in Egypt and being read along the Nile, indicating that the Word of God spread quickly.

… the gospel must first be proclaimed to all nations.
—Mark 13:10—

CHRISTIANITY'S ANCIENT ROOTS

One of the arguments used against Christianity in its earliest days was that it was a new, upstart religion. Justin Martyr (c. 100-c. 167) was an early apologist for the Christian faith who dealt with this issue. Born into a pagan family in Samaria, Justin was well educated in philosophy, especially the philosophy of Plato. One day he conversed with an old man along the seashore who told him about the ancient prophets who were esteemed philosophers, announcing the truth, being filled with the Holy Spirit. Their writings helped in understanding things which philosophers ponder—the beginning and end of all things. They told of the Creator, the Father and God of all, and His Son.

After that conversation, Justin began studying the Scriptures and began to see that Christianity was the true philosophy. He traveled about teaching and wrote several works explaining the Christian faith. His first *Apology* was a formal petition to Emperor Antoninus Pius, defending Christianity against political and ethical charges which had been made against it. A large portion of the work is an account of prophecies found in the ancient Hebrew Scriptures which were fulfilled in Christ.[35]

Justin began with Moses' account of Jacob's prophecy, "The scepter shall not depart from Judah, nor the ruler's staff from between his feet and to him shall be the obedience of the peoples." for Jesus was a descendant of Judah. (Genesis 49:10) He noted the prophecies of Jesus being born of a virgin (Isaiah 7:14) and the ruler being born in Bethlehem (Micah 5:2-3). David's Psalm 22 had no reference to anything in David's life, but looked forward to Jesus' sufferings and death. Justin also quoted the Scripture in Isaiah 53 as looking forward to Jesus' humiliation, while David's Psalm 110 looked forward to Jesus' being seated in majesty at the father's right hand. David had also foretold of the Gospel's spread, "There is no speech, nor are there words, whose voice is not heard. Their voice goes out through all the earth, and their words to the end of the world (Psalm 110:3-4)."

Justin showed from the Scriptures that Christianity was not a new religion, but its seeds were from ancient times. Justin was martyred for his faith some time during the reign of Emperor Marcus Aurelius.

Hear the word of the Lord, you who tremble at his word …
—Isaiah 66:5—

JANUARY 22

THE BIBLE IN THE CATACOMBS

The catacombs of ancient Rome, those underground chambers used for burials in the early days of the church, contain some of the earliest Christian art and provide a window into early Christian understanding of the Bible. Many of the illustrations are scenes from the Old Testament and show God's help for His people. Moses striking the rock and the water flowing out became a picture of baptism and salvation. Jonah is often depicted; Jesus Himself said that Jonah's exit from the great fish after three days prefigured His resurrection after three days in the tomb. (Matthew 12:40) Other Old Testament scenes include Daniel in the lions' den, Noah, Isaac's sacrifice, and the three men in the fiery furnace.

New Testament scenes represented include the feeding of the 5000 and the raising of Lazarus (which is depicted 53 times). The crucifixion and resurrection are not depicted, but Jesus is depicted as the Good Shepherd 114 times, often with a lamb or ram upon his shoulders. Jesus as the Shepherd has rich biblical roots. In Ezekiel 34:23, God promised, "I will set up over them one shepherd, my servant David, and he shall feed them: he shall feed them and be their shepherd." Isaiah similarly looked forward to a future ruler who would "tend his flock like a shepherd; he will gather the lambs in his arms; he will carry them in his bosom, and gently lead those that are with young" (Isaiah 40:11). In Luke 15, Jesus told the parable of a shepherd who looked tirelessly for the one lost sheep out of a flock of one hundred. Though there was joy when the sheep was found, Jesus said that "there will be more joy in heaven over one sinner who repents than over ninety-nine righteous persons who need no repentance." Most poignantly, Jesus described Himself as the good shepherd who lays down his life for the sheep, "No one takes it from me, but I lay it down of my own accord. I have authority to lay it down, and I have authority to take it up again." (John 10:11-18) How appropriate that Christ the Good Shepherd should be so frequently pictured in the ancient catacombs.

... these are written so that you may believe that
Jesus is the Christ, the Son of God,
and that by believing you may have life in his name.
—John 20:31—

IRENAEUS ON THE GOSPELS

Irenaeus, who died about 202 A.D., was from Smyrna, where he had heard Polycarp, a disciple of the Apostle John, preach. Irenaeus defended the apostolic teaching against the Gnostics and other heretical groups, repeatedly quoting the Scriptures. Different groups had favored different gospels, but Irenaeus asserted that the four Gospels we now have in our Bibles were the true Gospels of Scripture. He offered the following argument:

> It is not possible that the Gospels can be either more or fewer in number than they are. For, since there are four zones of the world in which we live, and four principal winds, while the Church is scattered throughout all the world, and the "pillar and ground" (I Timothy 3:15) of the Church is the Gospel and the spirit of life; it is fitting that she should have four pillars, breathing out immortality on every side, and vivifying men afresh. From which fact, it is evident that the Word, the Artificer of all, He that sitteth upon the cherubim, and contains all things, He who was manifested to men, has given us the Gospel under four aspects, but bound together by one Spirit. As also David says, when entreating His manifestation, "Thou that sittest between the cherubim, shine forth." (Psalm 80:1). For the cherubim, too, were four-faced, and their faces were images of the dispensation of the Son of God. For, [as the Scripture] says, "The first living creature was like a lion," (Rev. 4:7) symbolizing His effectual working, His leadership, and royal power; the second [living creature] was like a calf, signifying [His] sacrificial and sacerdotal order; but "the third had, as it were, the face as of a man,"—an evident description of His advent as a human being; "the fourth was like a flying eagle," pointing out the gift of the Spirit hovering with His wings over the Church.

Irenaeus' description of the four Gospels as analogous to the four faces of the cherubs (as described in Ezekiel 1) became a frequent theme throughout the ensuing centuries. Matthew, represented by the face of a man, begins with the human genealogy of Jesus. Mark, represented by the lion as King, begins with a prophetic reference to Isaiah. Luke, represented by the ox, began with the priest Zacharias offering sacrifice to God, and Jesus was indeed our sacrifice. John was represented by an eagle, soaring with the Spirit of God.

> But that these Gospels alone are true and reliable, and admit neither an increase nor diminution of the aforesaid number, I have proved by so many and such [arguments]. For, since God made all things in due proportion and

adaptation, it was fit also that the outward aspect of the Gospel should be well arranged and harmonized.[36]

I warn everyone who hears the words of the prophecy of this book: if anyone adds to them, God will add to him the plagues described in this book, and if anyone takes away from the words of the book of this prophecy, God will take away his share in the tree of life and in the holy city, which are described in this book.
—Revelation 22:19—

THE CANON OF SCRIPTURE

The Bible is a library of 66 books written over a 1500-year period in 3 languages by some 40 authors living in several different countries. A cast of 2930 characters are depicted in 1551 places. How did this amazing collection of writings come about?

As God revealed Himself to the Hebrew prophets, the Jews reverenced the writings of the prophets and carefully preserved them. These writings became the first Scriptures for the Christians, who recognized that they contained promises of the coming of Jesus. Inspired writings from the earliest church were added to the Hebrew writings to make up a canon of Scripture. The Greek word *canon* (very different from the Latin *cannon*—used in warfare!) meant a rule, measuring rod, or standard.

Jesus had told the disciples that when the Holy Spirit came, He would give them additional revelation: "When the Spirit of truth comes, he will guide you into all the truth, for he will not speak on his own authority, but whatever he hears he will speak, and he will declare to you the things that are to come." (John 16:13) This truth given by the Spirit is the New Testament. Peter himself recognized that the letters Paul had written were Scripture. (II Peter 3:15-16)

The canon of Scripture was not established by any church father or church council. As New Testament scholar F.F. Bruce explained, "The New Testament books did not become authoritative for the church because they were formally included in a canonical literature. On the contrary, the church included them in her canon because she already regarded them as divinely inspired."[37]

For the word of the Lord is upright,
and all his work is done in faithfulness.
—Psalm 33:4—

JANUARY 25
TWO TESTAMENTS

The first person to use the terms Old and New Testaments to refer to the Hebrew and Christian Scriptures was Tertullian, the second-century Christian apologist from Carthage. In *Against Praxeas* he referred to the "old scriptures" and the "New Testament."[38] In *Against Marcion*, Tertullian quotes Revelation 1:16, which describes a two-edged sword coming from Jesus' mouth, and says, "This may be understood to be the Divine Word, who is doubly edged with the two testaments of the law and the gospel."[39]

In the fourth century Lactantius, an advisor to Emperor Constantine, noted that

> ... all scripture is divided into two Testaments. That which preceded the advent and passion of Christ—that is, the law and the prophets—is called the Old; but those things which were written after His resurrection are named the New Testament. The Jews make use of the Old, we of the New; but yet they are not discordant, for the New is the fulfilling of the Old, and in both there is the same testator, even Christ ... As the prophet Jeremiah testifies when he speaks such things: "Behold, the days come, saith the Lord, that I will make a new testament to the house of Israel and the house of Judah, not according to the testament which I made to their fathers, in the day that I took them by the hand to bring them out of the land of Egypt." For that which He said above, that He would make a new testament to the house of Judah, shows that the old testament which was given by Moses was not perfect, but that which was to be given by Christ would be complete.[40]

The word "testament" has the same meaning as the word "covenant." Jeremiah was the first to look forward from the old Mosaic covenant to a new covenant, saying that with the new covenant, God would put His law in their hearts. (Jeremiah 31:31-34) At His Last Supper, Jesus said the cup was the new covenant in His blood. (Luke 22:20) Paul noted that he and the other apostles were ministers of a new covenant. (II Corinthians 3:6) The New Testament is the revelation of the new covenant in Christ.

Behold, I have come; in the scroll of the book it is written of me.
—Psalm 40:7—

AN EARLY ATTACK UPON THE SCRIPTURES

Jesus warned that "many false prophets will arise and lead many astray" (Matthew 24:11), and the Apostle John later wrote that every spirit that does not confess that Jesus has come in the flesh is not from God (I John 4:2). One of the earliest of these false teachers was Marcion (c. 86–c. 160), a ship-master from Pontus, around the Black Sea in modern Turkey.

Marcion decided that the God of the Hebrew Scriptures was not the same God as in the New Testament. He taught that the Jewish God was indeed the Creator, but he was a lesser God, a tribal deity of the Jews, in contrast to the universal God of love and compassion of the New Testament. Marcion further denied that Jesus had a real, physical body, leading him to deny the death and bodily resurrection of Jesus as well. In formulating his beliefs, Marcion rejected the Hebrew testament as Scripture. He accepted as Scripture only a modification of the Gospel of Luke (with most of the references to the Hebrew Scriptures removed) and ten of the epistles of Paul, which were also altered to fit Marcion's ideas.

Numerous church leaders, including Irenaeus, Tertullian, and Justin Martyr, spoke out and wrote against Marcion, noting his heretical teachings. Irenaeus wrote of him:

> Whereas also Marcion and his followers have betaken themselves to mutilating the Scriptures, not acknowledging some books at all; and, curtailing the Gospel according to Luke and the Epistles of Paul, they assert that these are alone authentic, which they have themselves thus shortened.[41]

Interestingly, some of Marcion's attacks upon Scripture in the second century sound very similar to some modern criticisms of the Bible.

Hot indignation seizes me because of the wicked,
who forsake your law.
—Psalm 119:53—

JANUARY 27
A SOLDIER'S CHOICE

Marinus was from an illustrious family in Caesarea, Palestine and a man of virtue and wealth. Around 272, the post of centurion became vacant, and Marinus was offered the position. However, when Marinus was about to receive the honor, someone else came before the tribunal and demanded the office for himself, claiming that, according to ancient laws, Marinus must first sacrifice to the emperors. When Marinus confessed to being a Christian who could not sacrifice to the emperors, Achaeus, the judge, gave him three hours for reconsideration.

The bishop in Caesarea, Theotecnus, met Marinus as he left the tribunal, talked with him and led him into the church. Theotecnus placed a copy of the Gospels before Marinus, then pointed to the sword at Marinus' side and told him to choose between the two. Marinus without hesitation reached for the Scripture. Theotecnus told him, "hold fast to God, and strengthened by him mayest thou obtain what thou hast chosen, and go in peace."[42]

Marinus returned to the tribunal and proclaimed his Christian faith more zealously than he had before. Immediately, he was led away and executed. Asterius, a noble of senatorial rank and great wealth, saw Marinus' exemplary faith and his courage in the face of death. After Marinus died, Asterius used his cloak to gather up the head and body of Marinus and buried it. For this, Asterius too suffered death, adding to the numbers of Christian martyrs.

This is my comfort in my affliction,
that your promise gives me life.
—Psalm 119:50—

READING THE SCRIPTURES
IN THE EARLY CHURCH

In his last letter to Timothy, Paul encouraged the young pastor to "devote your-self to the public reading of Scripture, to exhortation, to teaching." (II Timothy 4:13) The public reading of the Scripture was a central part of the worship of the church from its earliest days. This was a continuation of the practice in the Jewish synagogues, which we see in Jesus' reading of the Scriptures in Nazareth. (Luke 4:16-21) Justin Martyr, in describing the weekly worship of the Christians described the centrality of the Scripture reading in the meeting of the church:

> And on the day called Sunday, all who live in cities or in the country gather together to one place, and the memoirs of the apostles or the writings of the prophets are read, as long as time permits; then, when the reader has ceased, the president verbally instructs and exhorts to the imitation of these good things ...[43]

Some became Christians through their own private reading of the Scriptures. Second-century apologists Justin and Tatian replaced their Greek philosophy with Christianity after reading the Hebrew prophets which foretold the coming of the Christ and events of Jesus' life. Tatian found the Hebrew prophets

> ... too old to be compared with the opinions of the Greeks, and too divine to be compared with their errors; and I was led to put faith in these by the unpretending cast of the language, the unartificial character of the writers, the foreknowledge displayed of future events, the excellent quality of the pre-cepts, and the declaration of the government of the universe as centered in one Being. And, my soul being taught of God, I discern that the former class of writings [the philosophy of the Greeks] lead to condemnation, ...[44]

Irenaeus, Tertullian, and other early church writers encouraged the reading and meditating on Scripture, especially on days when there was no regular meet-ing of the church together. Scripture reading was important to spiritual vitality.

If they do not hear Moses and the Prophets,
neither will they be convinced if someone should rise from the dead.
—Luke 16:31—

JANUARY 29
MEDITATING ON THE WORD

Didascalia Apostolorum, written in Syria in the third century, is a summary of teaching on the Christian life and the organization of the church. It opens with admonitions to flee iniquity, not commit adultery, and to bless and love those who curse you. The husband is encouraged to be merciful and gracious with his wife, avoid idleness, and to occupy himself with the Scriptures. He is to meditate on the words of the Lord and learn them. He can learn the Scriptures by being with those who are like-minded, or by sitting at home and reading "the Law, and the Book of Kings and the Prophets and the Gospel" which is the fulfillment of these. He should avoid all heathen books, which are filled with strange sayings and lying prophecies. Why should he read heathen fables when he has the Scriptures?

> For what is wanting to thee in the word of God, that thou shouldst cast thyself upon these fables of the heathen? If thou wouldst read historical narratives, thou hast the Book of Kings; but if wise men and philosophers, thou hast the Prophets, wherein thou shalt find wisdom and understanding more than that of the wise men and philosophers; for they are the words of the one God, the only wise. And if thou wish for songs, thou hast the Psalms of David; but if (thou wouldst read of) the beginning of the world, thou hast the Genesis of the great Moses; and if laws and commandments, thou hast the glorious Law of the Lord God. All strange (writings) therefore, which are contrary (to these), wholly avoid.[45]

Such admonitions indicate that in the third century, individuals could have at least portions of the Scriptures to read privately in their homes. In addition, we know from the second-century writer Justin Martyr that the "memoirs of the apostles or the writings of the prophets" were regularly read in the Sunday worship services, followed by an exposition of what was read. His contemporary Tatian noted that Christian ladies sang spiritual songs and talked about Scripture at their spinning. Though the Scriptures were not as readily available in those early centuries as they are today with printed and digital versions in abundance, hearing, reading, and meditating on the Word was an important part of the Christian life.

My eyes are awake before the watches of the night,
that I may meditate on your promise.
—Psalm 119:148—

DESTROYING AND PRESERVING
THE CHRISTIAN SCRIPTURES

February 23, 303 the Roman Emperor Diocletian issued an edict to destroy all Christian churches and copies of the Scriptures. Any Christians in public office were to be deprived of their positions. Diocletian also required Christians to turn over their sacred books to be burned or to report houses where such books were located. Those who did hand over the books to the authorities were called *traditores*, traitors. Others who refused to turn over Scriptures or continued to confess their Christian faith were called *confessors*. Many were imprisoned and executed, becoming *martyrs* or witnesses for the Gospel. In ensuing edicts, Diocletian required all to sacrifice to the pagan idols. Heralds would go through a town with a roll of the people, calling them out by name to sacrifice in the idol temples. Diocletian's persecution lasted for ten years, with varying intensity in different parts of the Roman Empire. It was Diocletian's intent to eradicate the name of "Christians" and destroy all their Scriptures. It was the last desperate attempt to preserve Roman pagan worship. Diocletian retired to private life in 305. His successor, Galerius, issued an edict of toleration in 311. In it, he admitted that Christians had not been eliminated and allowed them to hold their worship without the government's interference. The next year, in 312, Constantine became emperor in the western empire. In 313 Constantine issued a further edict of toleration, restoring church property. It was the first proclamation of the principle that each man could choose his religion according to his own conscience, without interference from the government.

Whereas Emperor Diocletian sought to destroy the Scriptures, two decades later, in 322, Emperor Constantine asked Eusebius to have scribes prepare 50 copies of the Christian Scriptures on parchment to be used by the churches in Constantinople.

Heaven and earth will pass away,
but my words will not pass away.
—Matthew 25:35—

JANUARY 31
A FOURTH-CENTURY GOSPEL PREACHER

Euplius was a deacon in Catana, Sicily in the 4th century, during the days of Diocletian when copies of the Scriptures were banned. He delighted in reading and sharing the Gospels with others. He carried them with him wherever he went and read them to people on the streets or in the marketplace. All who had the Gospels were to turn them in to be burned. Soldiers arrested Euplius while he was reading the Gospels to a group of bystanders. When brought before the governor, the judge ordered him to read something from the book. Euplius read, "Blessed are they that suffer persecution for justice sake, for theirs is the kingdom of heaven … He that will come after Me, let him take up his cross and follow Me." (Matthew 5:10; 10:38) He explained this was the law of God which had been given by Jesus Christ. With Euplius' confession to being a Christian, the judge delivered him to be tortured.

After some torture, the judge asked if he maintained his confession. Euplius replied, "That which I have said I now repeat. I am a Christian!"[46] The judge demanded Euplius deliver the Gospels to the authorities, but Euplius replied, "Because I am a Christian. I will sooner die than deliver them. In them is eternal life, which is lost by him who would betray what God has entrusted to his keeping." After further tortures, the authorities demanded that Euplius worship Mars, Apollo, and Aesculapius. He replied, "I adore the Father, the Son, and the Holy Spirit, one only God; besides whom there is no God. May your gods find no worshippers! I offer myself a sacrifice to the true God; nor is it possible to change me."

Condemned, Euplius went to his death as to a coronation. He prayed, "Oh Lord Jesus Christ! I give Thee thanks for having granted me strength to confess Thy holy name. Complete, Oh Lord, what Thou has begun, that Thy enemies may be confused." Before his execution, he turned to those who followed him and said, "Brethren, love the Lord with all your hearts; for he never forgets those who love him. He remembers them during life and at the hour of their death, when he sends his angels to lead them to their heavenly country." Euplius had the Gospels around his neck as he was beheaded, August 12, 304.

Remember the word that I said to you: 'A servant is not greater than his master.' If they persecuted me, they will also persecute you. If they kept my word, they will also keep yours.
—John 15:20—

EARLY BIBLE TRANSLATIONS

The Bible is the most translated book in the entire world and the first book we know of which was translated into another language, when the Hebrew Scriptures were translated into Greek in Egypt during the 3rd century B.C. This Greek translation, known as the Septuagint, was widely used among the Jews in the Diaspora and among the early Christians. In Acts 8, this Greek translation was very likely what the Ethiopian eunuch was reading, from Isaiah 53, when Philip met him.

In the second century, Tatian composed the *Diatessaron*, an early harmony of the four gospels in Syriac. This was later used as the lectionary for the Syrian church. By the end of the second century, portions of the Scriptures had also been translated into Chaldee, Old Italic, and Sahidic Coptic, an Egyptian dialect. Jerome prepared his Latin translation in the 4th century. This translation, known as the Vulgate, became the translation used throughout Europe for the next millennium.

Ulfilas, the missionary to the eastern Goths, became the first to develop a written language for a people who only had an oral culture, a process which would often be repeated as Christianity spread. Ulfilas used 27 letters from the Greek and Roman alphabets. By the end of the 5th century, the Scriptures had been translated into Ge'ez, the language of Ethiopia. Also in the 5th century, Mesrop invented the Armenian alphabet and translated the Scriptures for the Armenians, who had become a Christian nation at the beginning of the fourth century. The first sentence Mesrop is said to have written down once the alphabet was developed was from the first chapter of the book of Proverbs, "To know wisdom and instruction; to perceive the words of understanding."

The 9th-century missionaries Cyril and Methodius brought the Gospel to the Slavs in Moravia. Like Ulfilas before them, they developed an alphabet to translate the Scriptures. Known as the Cyrillic alphabet, variations of this alphabet continue to be used in Russia and Slavic lands.

Heaven and earth will pass away,
but my words will not pass away.
—Matthew 24:35—

FEBRUARY 2
IMPORTANCE OF READING THE DIVINE WORD DAILY

The early apostles were devoted to prayer and the ministry of the Word (Acts 6:4), and the Word was always foundational to the Christian life. In the early Church, there was often the daily, public reading of Scriptures. Personal, private reading of the Scriptures was also encouraged.

In the third century, Hippolytus encouraged the Christians to not follow human wisdom, but seek to know what the Father has given us in His Scriptures:

> There is, brethren, one God, the knowledge of whom we gain from the Holy Scriptures, and from no other source. For just as a man, if he wishes to be skilled in the wisdom of this world, will find himself unable to get at it in any other way than by mastering the dogmas of philosophers, so all of us who wish to practice piety will be unable to learn its practice from any other quarter than the oracles of God. Whatever things, then, the Holy scriptures declare, at these let us look; and whatsoever things they teach, these let us learn; and as the Father wills our belief to be, let us believe; and as He wills the Son to be glorified, let us glorify Him, and as He wills the Holy Spirit to be bestowed, let us receive Him.[1]

In *The Apostolic Tradition,* also thought to be by Hippolytus, he wrote that every faithful man and woman should wash their hands and pray to God as soon as they rise from sleep and then go receive some instruction in the Word, if there is teaching that day. If there is no teaching that day, then read the Scriptures to gain an advantage from them.

In the fourth century, in a letter to the Emperor's chamberlain, Bishop Theonas of Alexandria gave detailed advice on how he should conduct his duties in a Christian and godly manner. Theonas concluded:

> Let no day pass by without reading some portion of the sacred Scriptures, ... and giving some space to meditation. And never cast off the habit of reading in the Holy Scriptures; for nothing feeds the soul and enriches the mind so well as those sacred studies do. ... His eternal promises ... in truth surpass all human comprehension and understanding, and shall conduct you into everlasting felicity.[2]

I am yours; save me, for I have sought your precepts.
— Psalm 119:94—

LISTING THE BOOKS OF SCRIPTURE

Lodovico Muratori (1672-1750) was one of the leading Italian historians of his day. At the Ambrosian Library in Milan and later at the Ducal Library in Modena, Muratori collected and published numerous unedited manuscripts from the library archives, contributing greatly to the preservation of the sources of early Italian history. Among his discoveries in the Ambrosian Library is a 7th century Latin fragment of 85 lines originally from the Columbanus monastery at Bobbio Abbey. The manuscript is apparently a translation of a Greek manuscript from the end of the second century (it can be clearly dated by its reference to Pope Pius as being bishop of Rome shortly before this, and he was bishop of Rome from 140-155). The fragment is the earliest known written list of the books of Scripture. The beginning portion that is missing apparently contained a list of the Hebrew Scriptures. The fragment begins with listing the 3rd and 4th gospels as Luke and John (the 1st and 2nd are presumably Matthew and Mark). Also listed are 13 of Paul's Epistles, the Acts of the Apostles, the Epistle of Jude, two epistles bearing the name of John, and the Apocalypse of John. The fragment does not mention the books of Hebrews, James, or the epistles of Peter. The fragment also mentions two works not included in the accepted canon of Scripture—the Apocalypse of Peter and Book of Wisdom.

Two centuries later, in his Easter letter of 367, Bishop Athanasius of Alexandria in Egypt listed "the books included in the Canon and handed down and accredited as Divine." His list corresponds to the books we have in the Bible today. Athanasius wrote, "These are the fountains of salvation that they who thirst may be satisfied with the living words they contain…Let no man add to these, neither let him take ought from these."[3]

Therefore keep the words of this covenant and do them,
that you may prosper in all that you do.
—Deuteronomy 29:9—

FEBRUARY 4

A GOLDEN-TONGUED PREACHER OF THE SCRIPTURE

John of Antioch, born in 349, was an orphan. His father, a high-ranking military officer in the Roman army, died shortly after John's birth. His devout Christian mother Anthusa raised him. He was taught the truths of the Gospel early, and from an early age memorized Scripture. Anthusa gave John the best classical education available, and he became such an eloquent orator that he began to be known as John *Chrysostom*, which means "golden-mouthed" in Greek. He was ordained and served as a priest in Antioch and later as Archbishop in Constantinople. In his sermons, Chrysostom often taught through entire books of the Bible, interpreting the Scripture in a straight-forward manner, not the allegorical interpretation which had taken hold in some parts of the Church of that day. His biblical sermons continue to be profitably read and studied over sixteen centuries later.

Chrysostom encouraged his congregation to listen to the reading of the Scriptures as if hearing God speaking to them, for the Scriptures are God speaking. The Scriptures were not just for monks, but they should be read daily in every home and taught to the children. Only through learning the Scriptures could children be brought up in the chastening and admonition of the Lord. Chrysostom entreated the people:

> Procure books that will be medicines for the soul…get at least the New Testament, the Apostolic Epistles, the Acts, the Gospels for your constant teachers. If grief befalls you, dive into them as into a chest of medicines; take from there comfort for your trouble, be it loss, or death, or bereavement of relations; or rather do not merely dive into them but take them wholly to yourself, keeping them in your mind.[4]

Some claim they have no time for daily reading due to their many business and family responsibilities, but these people especially need the Scriptures to know how to walk through this world's snares and temptations:

> The divine oracles are a treasury of all manner of medicines so that whether it be needful to quench pride, to lull desire to sleep, to tread underfoot the love of money, to despise pain, to inspire confidence, to gain patience, from them one may find abundant resource. … The divine words, indeed, are a treasury containing every sort of remedy, so that whether one needs to put down senseless pride, or to quench the fire of concupiscence or to trample on the love of

riches, or to despise pain, or to cultivate cheerfulness and acquire patience—in them one may find in abundance the means to do so.[5]

Take to heart all the words by which I am warning you today,
that you may command them to your children,
that they may be careful to do all the words of this law.
—Deuteronomy 32:46—

FEBRUARY 5
CODEX SINAITICUS

Codex Sinaiticus is the oldest surviving Greek New Testament and one of two oldest manuscripts of the entire Bible. Dating from the mid-4th century, the book is important not only for the study of biblical manuscripts but also for the history of book-making and bookbinding. The original book's 730 parchment leaves would have required at least 365 large animal skins.

The story of the manuscript's discovery is filled with intrigue and open questions. In 1844, German biblical scholar Constantine Tischendorf visited St. Catherine's Monastery near Mt. Sinai. In a basket he found 129 parchment sheets of a 4th century manuscript of the Greek translation of the Old Testament. Tischendorf took 43 folio leaves back to Germany and gave them to the Saxon government for the library at Leipzig University, where they remain to this day. There's some debate about whether Tischendorf had permission to take the manuscripts.

When Tischendorf returned to the monastery in 1853, no one knew anything about the manuscript's remaining leaves. But in 1859, Tischendorf discovered the much larger manuscript, including 86 Old Testament leaves, the entire New Testament, and two writings from the early church. Tischendorf persuaded St. Catherine's Monastery to give the manuscript to Tsar Alexander II of Russia, who had financed Tischendorf's travels and was patron of the Orthodox Church. In return, the Tsar gave St. Catherine's 7,000 gold rubles. In 1933, when Russia had become Communist and was in great need of cash, Russia sold most of its portion of the manuscript to England for £100,000, funds raised under the leadership of England's Prime Minister and the Archbishop of Canterbury (five leaves did remain in Russia). The volume is in the British Library. In 1975, 12 more leaves and 24 fragments of the manuscript were found during a restoration project at St. Catherine's. Recently a fragment was also found in the binding of another book at the monastery.

In 2005, the holders of the various portions of the manuscript, which include the British Library, the National Library of Russia, Leipzig University Library, and St. Catherine's Monastery, agreed to participate in the Codex Sinaiticus Project. The Project's website, www.codexsinaiticus.com, reflects the use of the most cutting-edge technology to research and study this most important book from the ancient world.

The grass withers, the flower fades, but the word of our God will stand forever.
—Isaiah 40:8—

CODEX VATICANUS

The earliest Bible manuscripts were written in Hebrew and Greek on scrolls made from papyrus, which is made from a plant, or parchment, which is made from animal skins. The Christians were the first to use a book or codex format rather than scrolls for their Scriptures. In fact, they were the first in the ancient world to extensively use books, apparently because the book format made cross referencing the Scriptures easier. Books were also less expensive, for writing could be done on both sides of the material.

Though many of the early Bible manuscripts were intentionally destroyed during the years when the early church was persecuted, there are today over 6000 known Biblical fragments or manuscripts. Among the most important is Codex Vaticanus. Written in Greek on vellum, or calf's skin, the Codex has been in the Vatican library since at least 1475, where it is found in the earliest Vatican Library catalogue. Speculation is that it was brought to Rome about the time of the fall of Constantinople and the Byzantine Empire. The writing of the manuscript is a neat uncial script, using only capital letters, without spaces between words or punctuation marks. Of course, there are no chapters or verses either; those were added centuries later. Six or seven centuries after the manuscript was first made, a scribe carefully reinforced the fading ink.

The script and character of Codex Vaticanus are very similar to the Codex Sinaiticus, now in the British Museum. Because of their similarities, scholars speculate that the two manuscripts originated in the same scriptorium in Egypt in the first half of the fourth century. Possibly they were even among the fifty complete Bibles Constantine commissioned in 331 from Eusebius of Caesarea for the growing number of churches in Constantinople.

The law of the Lord is perfect, reviving the soul;
The testimony of the Lord is sure,
making wise the simple;
—Psalm 19:17—

FEBRUARY 7
AUGUSTINE'S CONVERSION

Born in what is now Algeria in 354, Augustine was a promising young man who excelled in his studies. His mother Monica was a Christian, but his father was a pagan. Augustine didn't take to his mother's religion. He studied philosophy and followed Cicero's exhortation to seek wisdom. When he tried reading the Scriptures, they seemed dull to him. His youthful lusts captivated him, and Augustine took a mistress and fathered an illegitimate son.

After being a professor of rhetoric for three years in Carthage, Augustine decided to move to Rome and then to Milan. There he began attending church merely to hear the eloquence of Bishop Ambrose. Reading the Scripture more, he understood man's lost estate, but his lust and sensuousness warred with the high ideal of Christianity. One day, with his soul in turmoil, Augustine sat under a tree in a garden weeping. He later wrote about it:

> [I was] weeping in the most bitter contrition of my heart, when, lo! I heard from a neighbouring house a voice, as of a boy or girl, I know not, chanting, and oft repeating, "Take up and read; Take up and read." Instantly, my countenance altered, I began to think most intently, whether children were wont in any kind of play to sing such words: nor could I remember ever to have heard the like. So checking the torrent of my tears, I arose; interpreting it to be no other than a command from God, to open the book, and read the first chapter I should find …Eagerly then I returned to the place where Alypius was sitting; for there had I laid the volume of the Apostle, when I arose thence. I seized, opened, and in silence read that section on which my eyes first fell: *Not in rioting and drunkenness, not in chambering and wantonness, not in strife and envying: but put ye on the Lord Jesus Christ, and make not provision for the flesh,* in concupiscence [Romans 13:13-14]. No further would I read; nor needed I: for instantly at the end of this sentence, but a light as it were of serenity infused into my heart, all the darkness of doubt vanished away.[6]

Reading the Scripture in Romans led to Augustine's conversion and complete trust in the Lord. One of the first things Augustine did was go and tell his mother, who jumped for joy and praised the Lord that her prayers for the salvation of her son had been answered. Augustine went on to become a leader in the church, and his numerous writings are still influential today.

Your words were found, and I ate them,
and your words became to me a joy and the delight of my heart.
—Jeremiah 15:16—

THE SCRIPTURES DO NOT ERR

From the earliest days of the Church, it was recognized that the Scriptures were the Word of God. Necessarily, being from God, they were without error. Clement of Rome, writing to the Church of Corinth in the first century, encouraged the Corinthian Christians with numerous warnings and advice supported by Scriptural quotations. He exhorted the Corinthians: "Look carefully into the Scriptures, which are the true utterances of the Holy Spirit. Observe that nothing of an unjust or counterfeit character is written in them."[7] In his *Dialogue with Trypho,* the second-century apologist Justin Martyr asserts that no Scripture ever contradicts another Scripture. If there appears to be a contradiction, there simply must be something the reader does not understand properly.[8]

In the fifth century, Augustine wrote Jerome that of all books, only the Scriptures were "completely free from error." He further noted:

> If in these writings I am perplexed by anything which appears to me opposed to truth, I do not hesitate to suppose that either the manuscript is faulty, or the translator has not caught the meaning of what was said or I myself have failed to understand it. As to all other writings, in reading them, however great the superiority of the authors to myself in sanctity and learning, I do not accept their teaching as true on the mere ground of the opinion being held by them; but only because they have succeeded in convincing my judgment of its truth either by means of these canonical writings themselves, or by arguments addressed to my reason.[9]

From the earliest centuries to the present, the infallibility, inerrancy, and authority of God's Word has been an accepted truth.

Scripture cannot be broken.
— John 10:35—

FEBRUARY 9
AN EARLY LADIES' BIBLE STUDY IN ROME

Descended from the wealthy Roman family of the Marcelli, Marcella (325-410) lived in a palace on the Aventine Hill in Rome. Marcella herself was an ascetic and lived simply. She used her wealth for the furtherance of the Gospel and the help of others. She had a ladies' Bible study in her palace, and her home was frequently a place for prayer and psalm-singing. When Jerome came to Rome in 382, Marcella sought him out to deepen her understanding of the Scriptures. She was full of questions—What were the meanings of the Hebrew words *Allelulia, Amen, Selah?* Why weren't these words translated? What were the *ephod* and *teraphim?* What were the Hebrew names for God? What was the sin against the Holy Spirit? Even after Jerome left Rome and was living in Palestine, Marcella wrote letters to him filled with questions about Biblical interpretation. Marcella also had a group of scribes working in her home to copy the Scriptures. People knew that if they wanted a copy of the Scriptures, they could come to Marcella. Her home was a kind of 4th-century Bible society. If anyone in Rome, including priests or church officials, had questions about Scripture, they came to Marcella.

When she was eighty-five, in August 410, the Goths came to Marcella's home demanding gold. When she told them that she had none and pointed out to them her simple dress, they thought she was hiding her wealth and severely whipped her. She died a few days later. Many in Rome were richer in the Scriptures because of her.

My zeal consumes me, because my foes forget your words.
—Psalm 119:139—

THE VULGATE BIBLE

A discussion of Christian theology today among English-speaking peoples would be almost impossible without referring to "justification," "propitiation," "regeneration," or "Scripture"—all words which came into the English language from Jerome's Latin translation of the Bible. We also acquired Greek words such as "apostle," "evangel," and "baptism" via Jerome's translation, one of the most influential translations of the Scriptures of all time.

There were several different translations of the Christian Scriptures, or portions thereof, circulating in the Roman Empire of the fourth century. As early as the second century, North African Christians had translations of the Scriptures available in provincial Latin. Other translations into Latin were made over the years, with varying degrees of accuracy and readability. Damasus, Bishop of Rome, wanted a standardized Latin version of the Gospels and Psalms which could be used in all of the churches. In 382 he commissioned Jerome, the leading Christian scholar of the day, to revise the Old Latin Scriptures and provide an accurate translation. Jerome began his revision in Rome while he was Damasus' Secretary, completing the Gospels shortly before Damasus' death in 384. Jerome then revised the Latin Psalter from the Septuagint, or Greek translation of the Hebrew Scriptures. After he left Rome and went to live in Palestine, Jerome improved this revision using Origin's translation and early Biblical manuscripts. When the New Testament writers quoted Scripture, they usually quoted the Septuagint. The Septuagint became so revered among Christians that some, such as Augustine, considered that translation inspired. However, Jerome, one of the few Christian scholars of the fourth century who even knew Hebrew, thought it was necessary to go back to the Hebrew Scriptures. He made his third translation of the Psalms into Latin from the Hebrew. This was not well received, since people were more familiar with the versions from the Septuagint. As Jerome noted, "So great is the force of established usage that even acknowledged corruptions of text please the greater part, for they prefer to have their copies pretty rather than correct."[10] Though Jerome's translation of the psalms from the Hebrew never was highly accepted, the remainder of his translation of the Scriptures from early Hebrew and Greek manuscripts became the accepted Scripture of the western church. His translation was not in elegant Ciceronian Latin but in the common literary Latin of his day. His version became known as the Vulgate, or translation for the public, and was the Bible used throughout Europe for a millennium. Though they have never been completely catalogued, it is estimated that about 8000 Vulgate manuscripts are in existence today. When John Wycliffe and his followers first translated the Bible into English in the fourteenth century, they translated from the Latin Vulgate. When Johann Gutenberg chose the first book to be printed with his new invention of moveable type, he chose to print Jerome's Vulgate Bible.

Open my eyes,
that I may behold wondrous things out of your law.
—Psalm 119:18—

WORDS ABOUT THE WORD, FROM THE 4TH—16TH CENTURIES

Throughout the ages, Christians have testified to the foundational importance of the Scriptures to their faith. Here are samples from past centuries:[11]

Jerome (331-420), translator: "Read again and again the divine Scriptures; … let the holy book never be out of your hands. Learn, that you may teach."

Augustine of Hippo (354-430), great theologian: "Night does not extinguish the stars, so this world's iniquity does not obscure the minds of believers clinging to the firmament of holy Scripture."

John Chrysostom (347-407), Bishop of Constantinople and greatest preacher of the Greek church: "There is nothing in the Scriptures which can be considered unimportant; there is not a single sentence of which does not deserve to be meditated on, for it is not the word of man, but of the Holy Spirit, and the least syllable of it contains a hidden treasure."

Gregory the Great (550-604), Pope: "As the word of God exercises the understanding of the wise, so does it nourish the simple. It furnishes what may be fed to the little ones; it contains that which higher minds admire. It is a river both shallow and deep, in which the lamb may have footing and the elephant may swim."

Martin Luther (1483-1546), German Reformer who translated the Bible into German: "We must make a great difference between God's word and the word of man. Man's word is a little sound which flies into the air, and soon vanishes; but the word of God is greater than heaven and earth, yes, it is greater than death and hell, for it is the power of God, and remains everlastingly. Therefore, we ought to learn God's word diligently, and we must know certainly and believe that God Himself speaks with us."

Thomas Cranmer (1489-1556), Archbishop of Canterbury: "The Holy Ghost has so ordered and regulated the Scriptures, that in them publicans, fishers, and shepherds may find their edification as well as great doctors their learning."

What value and characteristics do these earlier Christians see in the Bible?

Of his own will he brought us forth by the word of truth,
that we should be a kind of firstfruits of his creatures.
—James 1:18—

FEBRUARY 12
LECTIO DIVINA

Reading the Scripture was part of the Christian life from the earliest days of the Church. The Scriptures were read both in public meetings of the Church and in private settings. But the reading of the Scriptures was not just a ritual to be performed; the Scriptures were to penetrate the heart and transform the reader or hearer. A method of reading the Scriptures was encouraged by the early church fathers Origin, Ambrose, and Augustine, among others, which has come to be known as *Lectio Divina*, Latin for "divine reading." In the 6th and 12th centuries, the monastic leaders Benedict and Bernard of Clairvaux incorporated *Lectio Divina* into their monastic rules. John Calvin and Puritan leaders continued to encourage the practice.

Lectio Divina basically includes four steps. The first is *lectio*, the reading or hearing of the Scriptures. A passage of Scripture is read several times, as if reading a letter from a loving Father. Read the Scripture as if personally written to you, noticing specific words or themes which particularly touch you. Read the passage with the heart as well as the mind. The second step is *meditatio*, or meditation. This is not eastern or New Age meditation, seeking to empty yourself. Instead, it is reflecting on what the words of Scripture meant to the original audience and how they might apply to your life. How is the passage of Scripture relevant to where you are in your spiritual life? The third step is *oratio*, prayer. When we read Scripture, God speaks to us; when we pray, we speak to God. Through both, God and man talk together. The final step of *lectio divina* is *contemplatio* or contemplation. Here the Christian enjoys intimacy with God and commits to living out the truth in His Word.

...the word of God increased and multiplied.
—Acts 12 24—

TAKING AN OATH ON THE BIBLE

Bibles have been used in oath-taking since the time of Augustine in the 5th century. European and British coronation oaths were regularly taken on a Bible. Though the Americans did not intend to establish a monarchy, George Washington recognized that oath-taking was a religious act and that the solemnity of the Presidential oath required a Bible. Before taking his oath in becoming President, Washington asked for a Bible to be brought upon which he could take the oath. Each President since has similarly taken the Presidential oath on a Bible.

Placing one's hand on the Bible is a way of symbolically recognizing a higher standard than oneself bearing witness to the integrity of one's words. For this reason, until recently, many legal authorities held that the testimony of an atheist could not be trusted and was invalid because he did not recognize a higher authority. Renowned Harvard legal scholar Simon Greenleaf (1783-1853) wrote in his *Treatise on the Law of Evidences* that one class of people incompetent to testify as witnesses were those

> who are insensible to the obligations of an oath, from defect of religious sentiment and belief. The very nature of an oath, it being a religious and most solemn appeal to God, as the Judge of all men, presupposes that the witness believes in the existence of an omniscient Supreme Being, who is 'the rewarder of truth and avenger of falsehood'; and that, by such a formal appeal, the conscience of the witness is affected. Without this belief, the person cannot be subject to that sanction, which the law deems an indispensable test of truth …Atheists, therefore, and all infidels, that is, those who profess no religion that can bind their consciences to speak truth, are rejected as incompetent to testify as witnesses.[12]

I keep your precepts and testimonies,
for all my ways are before you.
—Psalm 119:116—

FEBRUARY 14
FISHERMEN, PUBLICANS, AND TENT-MAKERS

The fifth-century theologian and biblical commentator Theodoret looked back over the previous centuries and contrasted the writings of the Christian Scriptures with those of the Greek philosophers:

> I will compare the most celebrated lawgivers of the Greeks with our Fishermen [Peter and John], Publicans [Matthew], and Tent-makers [Paul]; and show the difference between them. The laws of the former were forgotten, soon after the death of those who enacted them, but the laws delivered by Fishermen have flourished and prevailed, ... received not only by Greeks and Romans, but also by Scythians, Persians, and other barbarians. The heralds of truth were not, indeed, masters of the Greek eloquence; but, filled with wisdom, they have carried the divine doctrine to all nations, and have filled the whole world with writings, containing instructions concerning religion and virtue. All men, leaving the dreams and speculations of Philosophers, now nourish themselves with the doctrines of Fishermen and Publicans, and study the writings of a tent-maker. The seven wise men of Greece are forgotten, nor do the Greeks themselves certainly know their names; but Matthew, Bartholomew, and James, Moses, David, and Isaiah, with the other prophets and Apostles, are known to all men, as well as the names of their own children. Whom did Xenophanes, Parmenides, Pythagoras, and Anaxagoras, or Speusippus leave as their successors in Philosophy? What city follows the laws of Plato's republic? ...
>
> Nor are our doctrines understood only by those who preside in the churches, but by smiths, wool-combers, tailors, and artificers of all sorts, by women and maidservants. [Both city and country people] understand, and are able to discourse concerning our doctrines; they practice virtue, and shun vicious actions ... Greeks, Romans, Barbarians, acknowledge a crucified Saviour.
>
> These ... have brought all nations, and men of all sorts, to receive the Laws of a crucified man; and that not by arms, soldiers, or Persian violence, but by reasonings and arguments, showing the usefulness of those laws, people whom Augustus and the whole power of the Roman Empire could not induce to receive their laws, venerate the writings of Peter, Paul, John, Matthew, Luke, and Mark as if they had been sent down from heaven"[13]

... they received the word with all readiness of mind,
and searched the scriptures daily, whether those things were so.
— Acts 17:11—

MISSIONARY TO THE IRISH

In his *Confession* describing his life, the missionary to the Irish begins, "I, Patrick, a sinner, a most simple countryman, the least of all the faithful and most contemptible to many, had for father the deacon Calpurnius, son of the late Potitus, a priest." Raised in a Christian family in Britain in the 5th century, Patrick had little personal interest in Christianity until he was about sixteen, when he was captured by pirates and taken as a slave to Ireland. For six years he was a slave caring for animals. He began spending much time in prayer and recalling the Christian truths he had heard growing up. One day he managed to escape and found his way to a ship headed to Britain. Once home among his family again, Patrick felt called to return to Ireland and share the Gospel of Christ with the Irish.

In his *Confession*, Patrick repeatedly asserts his unworthiness for the calling, yet knew that God would give him the strength and the gift to carry out his missionary work. Patrick quotes numerous Scriptures which encouraged him in his work, beginning with "Call upon me in the day of trouble; I will deliver you, and you shall glorify me." (Psalm 50:15) He knew that the prayers of the Spirit and of Jesus (Romans 8:26; I John 2:1) had enabled him to accomplish his mission among the Irish. He offered his soul a living sacrifice (Romans 12:1) so that he might be a light bringing "salvation to the uttermost ends of the earth." (Isaiah 49:6) Following Christ as a fisher of men (Matt. 4:9), Patrick looked forward to the day when "Many shall come from east and west and shall sit at table with Abraham, and Isaac and Jacob." (Matthew 8:11) He knew "This Gospel of the Kingdom shall be preached throughout the whole world as a witness to all nations, and then the end of the world shall come." (Matthew 24:14)

Patrick recognized that he was an unlearned sinner, and that his entire mission was not from him, but through the gift and grace of God.

(Which now is made manifest by the scriptures of the prophets,
according to the precept of the eternal God, for the obedience of faith,)
known among all nations;
—Romans 16:26—

FEBRUARY 16
THE JOURNEYS OF *CODEX AMIATINUS*

The double monastery of Wearmouth-Jarrow in Northumbria was an important center for Anglo-Saxon Christianity. It was here that the Benedictine monk Bede was educated, worked, and produced his *Ecclesiastical History of the English People* as well as his works of biblical scholarship. Ceolfrith (642-716) was abbot of the monasteries and did much to build up their libraries as centers of scholarship. On a trip to Rome in 678, Ceolfrith and Abbot Benedict Biscop acquired numerous books for the monastic libraries, including the *Codex Grandior*, a large Latin Bible that had been made for Cassiodorus' monastery of Vivarium.

The books brought back to England doubled the size of the Wearmouth-Jarrow libraries, and the two monasteries themselves became important producers of manuscripts. In 692, Ceolfrith ordered 3 copies of the *Codex Grandior* made—one for the monastery at Wearmouth, one for Jarrow, and the other intended as a present for the pope.

In 716, Ceolfrith, in declining health, began his journey to Rome with one of the immense Bibles produced at the monastery. The volume, written by seven scribes, was impressive, measuring 19 ¼ inches high, 13 ⅜ inches wide, and 7 inches thick, and weighing over 75 pounds. With over 1000 pages, 1500 head of cattle would have been needed to produce the vellum! Ceolfrith died before reaching Rome, but his companions continued on and made the presentation to the pope, who wrote the Wearmouth-Jarrow monks a letter of appreciation for the fine gift. By the 9th century, the book was in an Abbey in Mount Amiata, Tuscany, and began to be called Codex Amiatinus. Today Codex Amiatinus is in the Laurentian Library in Florence, Italy.

Codex Amiatinus is the oldest surviving Latin Vulgate manuscript of the Bible and was the principal reference for Pope Sixtus V's new edition of the Vulgate in 1587. Ceolfrith's gift traveled a long distance and continued to be read and studied centuries after it had left England.

I will keep your law continually forever and ever.
—Psalm 119:44—

THE BOOK OF KELLS

Some of the most prominent publishers of Bibles in early America were Irish immigrants—Matthew Carey, Isaiah Thomas, and Isaac Collins. The Irish, however, had been prominent in Bible production centuries earlier. In the sixth century, Irish monasteries were important centers of Christian learning, and Irish missionary monks spread the gospel of Christ and the Christian Scriptures throughout the still-pagan parts of Europe. The most famous Bible produced by these Irish monks is the Book of Kells. The intricately-decorated manuscript of the four gospels was produced in the ninth century by monks on the island of Iona, off the west coast of Scotland. When the Vikings attacked the island and killed sixty-eight monks, the remaining monks of Iona moved to Kells, Ireland, taking their precious manuscripts, including their decorated gospels, with them. The manuscript, ever since known as the Book of Kells, was later moved to Dublin for safekeeping. For over 350 years, the Book of Kells has been housed in the Trinity College Library in Dublin.

The Book of Kells consists of 340 leaves of vellum with the Latin texts of the four gospels written in a Celtic script. On almost every page are brilliant illuminations in the richest colors. Some of the dyes for the decorations were imported from as far away as the Middle East. The care taken in producing the beautiful one-of-a-kind manuscript of the four gospels was the monks' way of showing not only their devotion, but the value placed on the Word of God. The manuscript reminds us of the rarity of copies of the Scripture in that earlier day. The monks of Iona could not imagine a day when every person could have his or her own individual copy of the Bible.

The law of thy mouth is better unto me
than thousands of gold and silver pieces.
—Psalm 119:72—

FEBRUARY 18
KING ALFRED, LAWS, AND THE BIBLE

The 9th-century King Alfred has been given the title of "the Great" for his wise rule over the Anglo-Saxon kingdom of Wessex. He successfully defended England from the invading Danes while also reorganizing government administration. He was a great advocate of education in the English language (which would be Old English to us), translating important classical and Christian works, including the first fifty psalms from the Bible. Later historians, even more than his contemporaries, recognized Alfred as a wise Christian ruler.

Among his important acts was the promulgation of a law code. Alfred's prologue, which makes up one fifth of the law code, is Alfred's reflections on Christian law, laying out a biblical foundation of the law. Alfred began with an Old English translation of Exodus 20-23, containing Moses' ten commandments and precepts of moral and civil law. Alfred then quoted, again in an Old English translation, Jesus' statement from the Sermon on the Mount, that he had come not to abolish the law but to fulfill it (Matthew 5:17) and noted that Jesus taught mercy and gentleness. He then translated Acts 15:12-19, the letter of the Jerusalem council which showed that the Gospel was to go to the Gentiles, who were freed from an obligation to the Mosaic law. Alfred observed that whoever keeps the law of charity does not need a law book to guide him. Alfred concluded the prologue with the Golden Rule—that a man should not judge another except as he would want himself to be judged. Laws were to be applied in a spirit of mercy, fairness, and kindness.

Alfred's legal prologue is a reflection on God's law from Mt. Sinai, to Jesus' Sermon on the Mount, through the early church and its use of the Golden Rule with Gentile converts. Alfred's law code and his government were to be obedient to the principles of Scripture.

The law was given by Moses;
grace and truth came through Jesus Christ.
—John 1:17—

THE MASORETES AND
JEWISH SCRIBAL TRADITION

The sacred Scriptures and the traditions of the Jewish people were preserved by scribes called *sopherim*. Their title comes from the word *sofer*, which means to count. The scribes counted all the letters of the Torah as a way of ensuring the accuracy of the manuscripts they copied. The *sopherim* had numerous regulations to govern their work, including the following:

- The skins used in parchment must be from only clean animals.

- A column of a scroll was to have at least forty-eight lines and no more than sixty lines, with each line consisting of thirty letters.

- The ink was to be black, prepared from a special recipe.

- The scribe could write no word or letter from memory; he was to copy from an existing manuscript.

- A space of a hair was to be between each consonant and a space of a consonant between each word.

- Before copying the scroll, the scribe was to wash himself and be in Jewish dress.

The Masoretes were one of the most important groups of Hebrew scribes. They worked from about 500-1000 A.D., primarily in Tiberias in Palestine and in Babylon. They reverenced the Hebrew Scriptures and did much to preserve their accuracy. Hebrew is a consonantal script, without vowels. The Masoretes added vowel points to the script to preserve the correct reading of the text. The name "Masorete" comes from the *masora*, the critical and explanatory notes which were placed alongside the text. Many of these were the numbers important for the scribal counting—such as, in the Torah there are 5840 verses, 97,856 words, and 400,945 letters.

My sheep hear my voice, and I know them, and they follow me.
I give them eternal life, and they will never perish,
and no one will snatch them out of my hand.
—John 10:27-28—

FEBRUARY 20

TRAIL OF A HEBREW MANUSCRIPT

The Hebrew Scriptures are known as the *Tanakh*, an acronym for the three sections of the Hebrew Scriptures: *Torah* (the 5 books of Moses), *Nevi'im* (the prophets) and the *Ketuvim* (the writings). The oldest complete manuscript of the *Tanakh* is the Leningrad Codex. Written on parchment in Cairo in 1009 A.D., the manuscript follows the Masoretic text, including the vowel points, cantillation signs, and annotations or masora. It is unusual in that the entire manuscript, including the Masoretic markings, was done by one scribe, Samuel ben Jacob. The manuscript was obtained by collector Abraham Firkovichin in the 1830s and taken to Odessa, Ukraine. In 1867, it was placed in the Imperial library in St. Petersburg, which became Leningrad in 1924 after the Russian Revolution. The Leningrad Codex (*Codex* means it is in book form, rather than a scroll) became the basis for the 1937 *Biblia Hebraica* and of later printed *Tanakh*.

The Leningrad Codex is a copy of the Aleppo Codex, which is a century older. The Aleppo Codex was written in Tiberias, the center of the Masoretic scribes, under the supervision of Aaron ben Moses ben Asher. The manuscript was in a synagogue in Jerusalem, but during the First Crusade, the synagogue was plundered; the codex was taken to Egypt, where Jews paid a ransom for it. In Egypt, it was carefully preserved and consulted by the Jewish scholar Maimonides. At this time, the Leningrad Codex was copied in Cairo from the Aleppo codex. In the 15th century, the codex was brought to Aleppo, Syria, where it remained for five hundred years and acquired its name, Aleppo Codex. In 1947, riots against the United Nations Partition Plan for Palestine spread throughout the region, and the synagogue where the Aleppo codex was kept was burned. For a time, the whereabouts of the Codex were unknown, but in 1958 the Codex was smuggled out of Syria and taken to Israel. It currently is on display in the Israel's Shrine of the Book. However, only 295 of the original 487 leaves remain.

They have almost made an end of me on earth,
but I have not forsaken your precepts.
—Psalm 119:87— '

THE WALDENSIANS AND A BANNED BIBLE

In the 12th century in France, a Christian movement arose to follow the Bible strictly. Called the Waldensians, after a leading merchant, Peter Waldo, they encouraged lay preaching and voluntary poverty. Waldo was the first to translate the Bible into a modern tongue since the Latin Vulgate, when he translated the Bible into Romaunt, the vernacular of east-central France, western Switzerland, and northwestern Italy. Though the church barred lay preaching, the Waldensians met in small groups for Bible reading and sermons. They saw the Roman church as corrupt and marked by greed; they rejected Roman teachings on the mass, transubstantiation, purgatory, and the worship of saints and relics.

The lay preachers memorized large portions of Scripture. Many learned by heart Matthew, John, the Epistles and much of the writings of David, Solomon and the prophets. Each member of a group would memorize different portions of Scripture and recite them to each other in worship.

In 1229 the Church Council in Toulouse forbade vernacular translations of the Bible. Heretics were to be sought out in the parishes, and any non-Latin translations of the Bible were to be destroyed. The Council proclaimed, "We prohibit also that the laity should be permitted to have the books of the Old and the New Testament; unless anyone from the motives of devotion should wish to have the Psalter or the Breviary for divine offices or the hours of the blessed Virgin; but we most strictly forbid their having any translation of these books." (i.e. they were only to be permitted in Latin.).

In spite of persecution, the Waldensians continued to hold their meetings and Bible services in the coming centuries. With the coming of the Reformation, many became part of the new Reformed Churches.

... if anyone loves me, he will keep my word, and my Father will love him,
and we will come to him and make our home with him.
Whoever does not love me does not keep my words.
—John 14:23—

FEBRUARY 22
THE VAUDOIS BIBLE

At a time when the Church was accumulating more wealth and worldly power, Peter Waldo and his followers, called the Waldensians or the Vaodois, sought to live lives of poverty and simplicity, following the Bible rather than religious traditions. Waldo was the first to translate the Bible into French, translating from the Latin Vulgate. In a day when the Bible in the common language of the people was scarce, the Waldensians became known for their knowledge and trust of the Scriptures. "The Vaudois Teacher" by the poet John Greenleaf Whittier (1807-1892), depicts the value the Waldensians placed on the Bible, the "Pearl of Great Price":

O lady fair, these silks of mine are beautiful and rare ...
The richest web of the Indian loom which beauty's queen might wear;
And my pearls are pure as thine own fair neck with whose radiant light they vie;
I have brought them many a weary way ... will my gentle lady buy?

The lady smiled on the worn old man through the dark and clustering curls
Which veiled her brow, as she bent to view his silks and glittering pearls.
And she placed their price in the old man's hand and lightly turned away,
But she paused at the wanderer's earnest call... "My gentle lady stay!"

O Lady fair, I have yet a gem which a purer lustre flings,
Than the diamond flash of the jewelled crown on the lofty brow of kings;
A wonderful pearl of exceeding price, whose virtue shall not decay,
Whose light shall be as a spell to thee and a blessing on thy way."

The lady glanced at the mirroring steel where her form of grace was seen,
Where her eyes shone clear, and her dark locks waved their clasping pearl between:
"Bring forth thy pearl of exceeding worth then, traveler gray and old,
And name the price of thy precious gem, and my pages shall count thy gold."

The cloud went off the pilgrim's brow, as a small and meager book,
Unchased with gold or gem of cost, from his folding robe he took.
"Here, lady fair, is the pearl of price, may it prove as such to thee!
Nay, keep thy gold ... I ask it not, for the Word of God is free."

The hoary traveler went his way, but the gift he left behind
Hath had its pure and perfect work on that highborn maiden's mind,
And she hath turned from the pride of sin to the lowliness of truth,
And given her human heart to God in its beautiful hour of youth.

And she hath left the old gray halls where evil faith had power,
The courtly knights of her father's train, and the maidens of her bower;
And she hath gone to the Vaudois vales by lordly feet untrod,
Where the poor and needy of the earth are rich in the perfect love of God.[14]

... the rules of the Lord are true, and righteous altogether.
More to be desired are they than gold, even much fine gold.
—Psalm 19:11—

FEBRUARY 23
THE KING AND THE LAW

The reign of King John of England (1166-1216) was tumultuous. Wars with France were unsuccessful and led to England's loss of its Angevin lands on the continent. Because of the expenses of the war, King John increased taxation. The English barons, resenting the King's financial policies as well as his arbitrary rule, rebelled. Stephen Langton, the Archbishop of Canterbury, negotiated the disputes between the barons and the King, culminating in a document now known as the Magna Carta, or Great Charter, agreed to by the King at Runnymede, June 15, 1215.

Archbishop Stephen Langton (1150-1228), a key author of the charter, had studied at the University of Paris and lectured on theology for thirty years. He was a student of the Bible and wrote commentaries on every book of the Bible. In studying the Old Testament Scriptures, Langton especially noted that the King was under the law of God. Kings were to copy out the law of God so they would have a personal copy (Deut. 17:18). When Samuel anointed Saul king, he wrote the rights and duties of the king in a book kept in the temple (I Samuel 10:24-25). Justice was to be dispensed with due process, not at the arbitrary rule of the King:

> You shall appoint judges and officers in all your towns that the Lord your God is giving you, according to your tribes, and they shall judge the people with righteous judgment. You shall not pervert justice. You shall not show partiality, and you shall not accept a bribe, for a bribe blinds the eyes of the wise and subverts the cause of the righteous. Justice, and only justice, you shall follow ... (Deut. 16:18-20).

Langton incorporated these biblical principles of governance into the Magna Carta, which is often cited as a foundation document in English and American law: The law was to be written, not at the whim of the rulers; even the king was to obey the law; there was to be no punishment or justice without the due process of law.

Princes persecute me without cause,
but my heart stands in awe of your words.
—Psalm 119:161—

BIBLIA PAUPERUM

Biblia Pauperum was a "Bible" designed for use by poor priests, or traveling Franciscans, in teaching the people. The books were first produced in manuscript in the 13th century, but by the 15th century they were being printed as block books. Block books, printed from carved wood blocks, usually consisted of about 50 leaves. Each leaf consisted of both pictures and text, all carved from one wood block.

The *Biblia Pauperum* was a summary of the most important events of the Old and New Testaments. The New Testament event was illustrated at the center of the page. Illustrations of an Old Testament event which prefigured the New Testament event were placed on each side. At the bottom and top of the page were double windows for the prophets, with words from their writings inscribed as coming from them. A summary of the scenes was placed at the top of the page. The entire page was organized to encourage meditation on the unified truths of Scripture.

An example is the New Testament scene at the center of the page of the women meeting an angel at the empty tomb when they came to embalm Jesus' body (Luke 23:55-24:7). The left-hand Old Testament scene has Rueben (Genesis 37:29) looking for Joseph after his brothers threw him into the well. On the right, the bride from the Song of Solomon is looking for her bridegroom (Song of Songs 5:6). Words of the two top prophets are from Isaiah 55:6 ("Seek ye the Lord, while he may be found, call ye upon him while he is near.") and Psalm 105:3 ("Glory in his holy name: let the heart of them rejoice, that seek the Lord.") The words from the two bottom prophets are from Micah 7:7 ("I will wait for the God of my salvation: my God will hear me") and Genesis 49:18 (I have waited for thy salvation, O Lord.") The entire page, then causes the viewer to reflect on the importance of seeking the Lord and the salvation that comes from waiting on Him.

... if you receive my words and treasure up my commandments with you,
making your ear attentive to wisdom ...
if you seek it like silver and search for it as hidden treasures,
then you will understand the fear of the Lord
and find the knowledge of God.
—Proverbs 2: 1-5—

FEBRUARY 25
JOHN WYCLIF

There was no rest for Wyclif's bones after he died of a stroke in 1384. He was decently buried, but 30 years later the Church Council of Constance condemned his teachings and ordered his bones to be dug up and burned!

John Wyclif had been a leading scholar at Oxford and a chaplain to the King of England. He boldly criticized the corruption of the clergy of his day, the unseemly wealth of the church hierarchy, and the priests' distortion of the truth found in the Bible. If the people were to know God's truth, he believed the Bible should be available for them to read in their own language. The Roman Church, however, believed the Bible could only be understood by the elite and in the Latin Vulgate translation.

Wyclif wrote that "The New Testament is full of authority, and open to the understanding of simple men, as to the points that be most needful to salvation. …Christ did not write His laws on tables, or on parchment. But in the hearts of men…the Holy Ghost teaches us the meaning of Scripture as Christ opened its sense to His Apostles."[15] Christ and His apostles explained the Scriptures in the language spoken by the people. Shouldn't the modern disciples of Christ also be allowed the Scriptures in their own language?

If the people of England were to know the truth, they must have the Bible in English. Under Wyclif's direction, the entire Bible was translated from Latin into English for the first time. Before the printing press was invented, manuscript copies of Wyclif's Bible brought the truth to England, though this English Bible was repeatedly condemned and burned by the authorities. 600 years later, Wyclif's translation of John 3:36 still sounds familiar:

> He that believeth in the son: hath everlasting life—but he that is unbelieveful to the same shall not see everlasting life—but the wrath of God dwelleth on him.

Historian John Foxe, in his *Book of Martyrs* (1500's) described the importance of Wyclif and this first English translation of the Bible when he said,

> though they digged up his body, burnt his bones, and drowned his ashes, yet the Word of God and the truth of his doctrine, with the fruit and success thereof, they could not burn; which yet to this day … doth remain.[16]

Oh how I love your law! It is my meditation all the day.
—Psalm 119:97—

AUTHORITY OF SCRIPTURE AND THE CONSTITUTIONS OF OXFORD

Jerome's Latin translation of the Bible in the fourth century was the Bible used throughout the Middle Ages. Latin was the scholarly language of the era, understood by the elite, but not by ordinary people. Fearing that lay people reading the Bible would result in heresies, the 1229 Council of Toulouse forbade the laity read vernacular translations of the Bible.

14th-century, Oxford scholar John Wycliffe wanted the Bible to be understood by laymen as well as the clergy:

> The chief cause, beyond doubt, of the existing state of things is our want of faith in Holy Scripture. We do not sincerely believe in the Lord Jesus Christ, or we should abide by the authority of His Word, … It is the will of the Holy Spirit that … the books of the Old and New Law should be *read* and *studied*, … We ought to believe in the authority of no man, unless he say the Word of God. It is impossible that any word or deed of the Christian should be of equal authority with Holy Scripture. The right understanding of Holy Scripture is being taught to us by the Holy Ghost just as the Scriptures were opened to the Apostles by Christ …

> The whole Scripture is *one word of God*; also the whole Law of Christ is *one perfect word* proceeding from the mouth of God; …If God's word is the life of the world, and every word of God is the life of the human soul, how may any Antichrist, for dread of God, take it away from us that be Christian men, and thus suffer the people to die for hunger in heresy and blasphemy of men's laws, that corrupteth and slayeth the soul?[17]

But in 1408, a synod in Oxford passed an act stating that:

> The translation of the text of Holy Scriptures out of one tongue into another is a dangerous thing…therefore we enact and ordain that no one henceforth do by his own authority translate any text of Holy Scripture into the English tongue.[18]

The synod banned the reading of any of Wycliffe's works under pain of excommunication and punishment as a heretic (death). Many were executed, and William Tyndale had to leave England to translate the Bible into English.

But Jesus answered them, 'You are wrong, because you know
neither the Scriptures nor the power of God.'
—Matthew 22:29—

FEBRUARY 27
WENCESLAUS IV AND A GERMAN BIBLE

Many have heard of "Good King Wenceslas" from the English Christmas carol. There really was a King Wenceslaus, in fact, several of them. The first was a Duke in Bohemia in the 10th century, later canonized as a saint. This is the "Good King Wenceslaus" of the carol. Later, beginning in the thirteenth century, there was a series of kings of Bohemia named Wenceslaus. Wenceslaus IV (1361-1419) became King of Bohemia by inheritance and the German King by election. In Bohemia during Wenceslaus IV's time, there was the beginning of a reformation of the church and a renewed emphasis on the Scriptures. Preachers such as Konrad von Waldhausen, Milcz von Kremsier and Matthias von Janow all preached against the corruptions of the medieval church and preached from the Bible in the vernacular (common language of the people).

When Wencesluas's sister, Anne of Bohemia, became the wife of King Richard II of England, she brought with her to England copies of the gospels in Bohemian, English, and Latin, which she read daily. John Wycliffe, who translated the Bible into English, praised Anne for her reading of the Scriptures, and when Wycliffe was taken before the authorities for his criticisms of the church, Anne defended and protected him. These events were precursors to the preaching of Jan Hus in Bohemia and the later Reformation under Martin Luther in Germany.

Wenceslaus IV's father, Charles IV, had prohibited any vernacular translations of the Scriptures. Yet one of the earliest translations of the Bible into German was begun under Wenceslaus IV, directly against his father's orders and 150 years before Luther's German translation. The Bible was not completed before Wenceslaus' death and includes only the Old Testament. There are sumptuous illustrations for each chapter, through the book of Nehemiah. The Wenceslaus Bible is a beautiful testimony to the growing importance of the Scriptures at the Bohemian court, and a forerunner of the vernacular Bibles spawned by the Reformation.

In the way of your testimonies I delight as much as in all riches.
—Psalm 119:14—

THE GUTENBERG BIBLE

As a millennium ended in 2000, many agreed that the "Man of the Millennium" had been Johann Gutenberg (c. 1400-1468). Before him, all books were written by hand, one copy at a time. A long book, such as a Bible, would take months or even years to complete. Most people never owned a book.

Gutenberg developed two parts to the technology of printing—the press itself and moveable metal type. The idea for the press probably developed from the wine presses then in use. Gutenberg experimented for some time before he successfully developed the molds for casting the metal type, with the reverse design of the individual letters. The printing process Gutenberg developed remained virtually unchanged for 350 years: a compositor set the text letter-by-letter in a wooden bed; a pressman used round padded dabbers to coat the type with ink; moistened paper was placed into a hinged framework which was rolled over the type; and the pressman pulled the handle that moved the screw downward, pressing the flat platen, thus imprinting the text on the paper. The press could print 200 pages per day with this process, and the scribe's work for one day could be accomplished in a few minutes.

The first complete book printed with Gutenberg's new invention was the most important book—the Bible. Gutenberg worked on this masterpiece in Mainz, Germany, between 1452 and 1455. He printed about 180 Latin Vulgate Bibles. Thirty-five of them were on vellum; the rest were on the finest linen paper from Italy. The letters were cast to produce lettering such as could only previously be done by the most accomplished scribe. The Gutenberg Bibles are beautiful, and the 48 copies or portions which remain today retain much of their original splendor. Fourteen copies of the Gutenberg Bible are located in the United States, five of which are complete.

Producing such a vast number of Bibles in such a short time was unprecedented. Now people throughout Europe could read a page which was exactly the same as another in Europe. Within fifty years, printing presses in 240 European cities had printed 30,000 editions for a total of 10 million books. One half of these books were religious, and three fourths of them were in Latin.

Gutenberg's invention increased both the accuracy and the availability of texts and made possible the growth of literacy and learning. The Reformation begun by Martin Luther depended on the word and the printed Scriptures. Gutenberg's invention truly changed the course of history.

The Lord is faithful in all his words and kind in all his works!
—Psalm 145:13—

FEBRUARY 29
CAXTON AND THE *GOLDEN LEGEND*

The Golden Legend (*Legenda Aurea*), originally entitled *Legenda Sanctorum,* was a collection of the lives of the saints compiled by Jacobus de Voragine, Archbishop of Genoa, around 1260-80. Over the centuries, the content expanded, and it became a medieval best-seller. An estimated thousand manuscript copies are still in existence. Besides the lives of the saints, the book came to include sermons for feast days and Scriptures to be read with them. It became a service book for liturgy as well as a book used for private devotions. When printing was invented, around 1450, editions of *Legenda Aurea* were printed in every major European language, as well as Latin

In 1476, twenty-five years after Gutenberg's printing of the Vulgate Bible, William Caxton introduced printing to England. One of his early books was *The Golden Legend*, which he first printed in 1483. Translating the text from copies of the French and Latin, he omitted some of the saints in Voragine's version, while adding some English and Irish worthies, such as Thomas à Becket of Canterbury. Caxton's *The Golden Legend* was a massive volume of almost 900 pages, lavishly illustrated with woodcuts. Old and New Testament stories were illustrated with 51 full page illustrations, as well as many smaller illustrations. The stories from the Bible were frequently nothing but the quotation of Scripture in English. However, the English Scriptures had been banned since the 1408 Constitutions of Oxford, implemented in opposition to John Wycliffe's translation of the Scriptures into English. In the ensuing decades, people were executed for having any portion of the Scriptures in English or even teaching their children the Scriptures in English.

The Golden Legend includes many fantastic stories alongside of the Scriptures. Nevertheless, Caxton's inclusion of the Scriptures in *The Golden Legend* did make the Scriptures available to a wider audience, though against the law. Comparison of Caxton's Scriptures with Wycliffe' translation suggest that Caxton had a copy of Wycliffe's Bible. It would be another fifty years before a Bible in English was no longer banned and the Bible in English could circulate freely, without being hidden in fantastic legends.

My soul longs for your salvation; I hope in your word.
—Psalm 119:81—

MARCH 1
CHRISTOPHER COLUMBUS

Every school child used to know the little ditty, "In 1492 Columbus sailed the ocean blue." Christopher Columbus' determination in sailing west to reach the Indies in spite of ridicule, delays and opposition was also well-known. Did you know, though, that Columbus found inspiration in the Bible for his exploration? In a letter to his sponsors, King Ferdinand and Queen Isabella of Spain, Columbus wrote,

> I found our Lord well-disposed toward my heart's desire, and he gave me the spirit of intelligence for the task … He … consoled me through the holy and sacred Scripture … encouraging me to proceed, and continually, without ceasing for a moment, the [Scriptures] inflame me with a great sense of urgency.[1]

From his diligent study of the Bible, Columbus concluded that Christ would come and establish His kingdom once all the nations had heard the gospel. By bringing the gospel to lands where the truth was not known, Columbus felt he was advancing the coming of Christ's Kingdom. He wrote out key Bible passages speaking of all nations coming to the Lord in a "book of prophecies." Many of the passages were from the psalms and Isaiah such as:

Psalm 95: "The Lord reigns, let the earth be glad;
Let the distant shores rejoice."
Psalm 105: "Give thanks to the Lord, call on his name;
Make known among the nations what he has done.
He is the Lord our God;
His judgments are in all the earth."
Isaiah 12: "Make known among the nations what he has done;
and proclaim that his name is exalted.
Sing to the Lord, for he has done glorious things;
let this be known to all the world."

Columbus' given name, Christopher, meant "Christ-bearer," and he thought his destiny was to bear the message of Christ to the uttermost parts of the earth.

… the earth shall be full of the knowledge of the Lord
as the waters cover the sea.
—Isaiah 11:9—

MARCH 2

SAVONAROLA: A REFORMER FOR CHRISTIAN VIRTUE

In the fifteenth century, Florence was one of the most prosperous cities in Europe. The wealthy Medici family provided credit and banking for many European monarchs as well as the papacy. Patronage of the Medicis supported Florentine Renaissance artists whose works continue to adorn the city today. But when Dominican friar Girolamo Savonarola (1452-1498) looked at the city, he saw rampant despotic rule, the poor exploited, the clergy corrupt, and immorality rampant. He eloquently preached for reform in the Church as well as in the Florentine government. Pope Alexander VI banned Savonarola from preaching, and when he continued, the Pope excommunicated him.

While under excommunication, he wrote *The Triumph of the Cross,* examining the cross's victory over sin and death and the nature of a true Christian. In it, Savonarola wrote:

> the teaching of the Holy Scripture has more efficacy than has any other doctrine, in enlightening and consoling men, and in inclining them to live virtuously. For the preachers who discourse only on philosophical subjects, and pay great attention to oratorical effect, produce scarcely any fruit among their Christian hearers. Whereas our forefathers, who in past times confined themselves to the simple preaching of the Holy Scriptures, were able to fill their hearers with Divine love, enabling them to rejoice in affliction and even in martyrdom. I speak also from personal experience. For, when at one time … my habit was to discourse on subtle points of philosophy, I found that the people who heard me were inattentive. But as soon as I devoted myself to the exposition of the Bible, I beheld all eyes riveted upon me, and my audience so intent upon my words, that they might have been carved out of stone…when I set aside theological questions and confined myself to explaining Holy Scripture; my hearers received much more light, and my preaching bore more fruit, in the conversion of men to Christ and to a perfect life. For Holy Scripture contains that marvelous doctrine, which, more surely than a two-edged sword, pierces men's heart with love, which has adorned the world with virtue, and has overthrown idolatry, superstition, and numberless errors. This proves that it can proceed from none but God.[2]

Yet, on May 23, 1498, Savonarola was hanged and burned as a heretic.

Righteous are you, O Lord, and right are your rules.
—Psalm 119:137—

ERASMUS AND THE FIRST PRINTED
GREEK NEW TESTAMENT

Recognized throughout Europe as the greatest scholar of his day, Erasmus believed all Christians should have their lives transformed through the true "philosophy of Christ." He dedicated his life to the study and publishing of the Bible and the writings from the earliest centuries of the Church.

In 1499, Erasmus went to England where in Oxford he met John Colet, later to be Dean of St. Paul's Cathedral in London. Colet was lecturing on the epistles of Paul, favoring a historical, grammatical interpretation of Scripture rather than the allegorical, mystical methods of the medieval scholastics. With Colet's encouragement, Erasmus began an intensive study of Greek while writing what became a four-volume commentary on Paul's epistle to the Romans, published in 1502.

Erasmus believed the corrupt and dead Church of his day could be spiritually transformed by a return to its roots in the Bible. With the encouragement of Johann Froben, a printer in Basel, Switzerland, Erasmus printed the first Greek New Testament, accompanied by his Latin translation, which corrected errors in the Latin Vulgate. Erasmus called his Greek text *Novum Instrumentum*, believing the Greek text with his new Latin translation accompanying it was a new instrument for the revival of Christian spirituality, going back to the biblical source of the faith.

Erasmus' Greek Text went through five printings, with Erasmus making revisions and improvements in each edition. His work became the basis for numerous common translations of the Scriptures. Martin Luther's German translation and William Tyndale's English translation were both based on Erasmus' Greek text.

In contrast with medieval scholastic philosophy, which only the educated could comprehend, Erasmus believed the philosophy of Christ was for everyone. His publication of the Greek text, editions of biblical commentaries of the Church fathers, and his own paraphrases and commentaries on the Bible all were to revive a knowledge of Christ which would transform individual lives.

Blessed are you, O Lord; teach me your statutes!
—Psalm 119:12—

MARCH 4
ERASMUS' *PARAPHRASES OF THE NEW TESTAMENT*

The 16th-century humanist scholar Erasmus sought to develop a "philosophy of Christ" from the Bible, not from Aristotle as the scholastics did. Many of Erasmus' publications were directed towards this end. In 1516, he printed the Greek New Testament with critical annotations and his new Latin translation; he edited editions of commentaries by the Church Fathers; he issued commentaries on Romans, the Psalms, and the Sermon on the Mount; and he published paraphrases of every New Testament book except Revelation.

The *Paraphrases of the New Testament* was a commentary on Scriptures gleaned from the early Church fathers. It was part of Erasmus' effort to provide the Scriptures for all the people. Composed in Latin between 1517 and 1524, the work was quickly translated into many European languages. Swiss Reformers Heinrich Bullinger and John Calvin both referenced Erasmus' *Paraphrases* in their own commentaries.

Queen Catherine Parr, the last wife of Henry VIII, sponsored the translation of the *Paraphrases* into English. Queen Catherine had a Bible available in her royal apartments for anyone to read and held regular Bible studies with those in her court. Fluent in Latin, French, and Italian as well as English, the Queen helped with the translation of the paraphrases of the Gospel of Matthew and the Acts of the Apostles. Princess Mary, later Queen Mary I, translated the paraphrase of the Gospel of John.

In 1547, Kind Edward VI ordered a copy of Erasmus' *Paraphrases* be placed in every church in England, making this virtually the authorized commentary for the Church. However, when Mary came to the throne, she returned the Church of England to Catholicism and ordered all copies of the *Paraphrases* destroyed.

Blessed are those who hear the word of God and keep it.
—Luke 11:28—

MARTIN LUTHER AND THE JUSTICE OF GOD

Martin Luther's father hoped his son would become a lawyer. But Martin was concerned more with the justice of God than that of the law courts. How could he ever become right with a jealous God? The very idea of the justice of God terrified him. One day, caught in a terrifying thunderstorm, Luther vowed to become a monk—and he became a most fastidious one—endless praying, fasting, confessions, and flagellations , but no peace with God.

When Luther (1483-1546) was assigned to teach the Bible in the new University of Wittenberg, he began to study the Scriptures. Luther first taught the Psalms, and then the book of Romans, all the while wrestling with how he, a sinner, could stand before a righteous God. Especially meaningful to him was Romans 1:16-17, "For I am not ashamed of the gospel, for it is the power of God for salvation to everyone who believes, to the Jew first and also to the Greek. For in it the righteousness of God is revealed from faith to faith, as it is written, 'The righteous shall live by faith.'" As Luther explained,

> *I greatly longed to understand Paul's epistle to the Romans and nothing stood in the way but that one expression "the justice of God," because I took it to mean that justice whereby God is just and deals justly in punishing the unjust.* My situation was that, although an impeccable monk, I stood before God as a sinner troubled in conscience, and I had no confidence that my merit would assuage Him. Therefore I did not love a just and angry God, but rather hated and murmured against Him. Yet I clung to the dear Paul and had a great yearning to know what he meant.
>
> Night and day I pondered until I saw the connection between the justice of God and the statement that "the just shall live by faith." Then I grasped that the justice of God is that righteousness by which through grace and sheer mercy God justifies us through faith. Thereupon I felt myself to be reborn and to have gone through open doors into paradise. The whole of Scripture took on a new meaning, and whereas before "the justice of God" had filled me with hate, now it became to me inexpressibly sweet in greater love. This passage of Paul became to me a gate to heaven ...
>
> If you have a true faith that Christ is your savior, then at once you have a gracious God, for faith leads you in and opens up God's heart and will, that you should see pure grace and overflowing love. That it is to behold God in faith that you should look upon his fatherly, friendly heart, in which there is no anger nor ungraciousness. He who sees God as angry does not see him rightly but looks only on a curtain, as if a dark cloud had been drawn across his face.[3]

Luther's understanding of justification by faith brought about a Reformation in the Church.

In God, whose word I praise, in the Lord, whose word I praise,
In God I trust; I shall not be afraid. What can man do to me?
— Psalm 56:10-11—

SOLA SCRIPTURA

During the Reformation, as the foundations of the Christian faith were explored, one of the key terms that emerged was *Sola Scriptura.*[4]

Sola Scriptura means that the Scriptures are the ultimate authority for faith and practice. When Scripture speaks, God speaks, and we should listen. Scripture is authoritative because God is its author. All other authorities, whether creeds, church councils, or tradition, are under the authority of Scripture. Scripture is the supreme authority, speaking truth for everything we need in salvation and to follow Christ. Because the Scripture is God speaking, God's Word, it is true, trustworthy, and without error.

The Enlightenment began an attack on Scripture by denying the possibility of supernatural revelation from God. Truth, the Enlightenment thinkers thought, could be attained through human reason. Later, pragmatists said that truth is relative and depends on the social situation of the time. Postmodernists continued the attack on truth, seeing all truth as relative. *Sola Scriptura* counters these attacks on the truth by proclaiming the authority of the Scripture as God's revelation to man.

All your commandments are sure ...
—Psalm 119:86—

MARCH 7
FORMATTING THE BIBLE

Our Bibles look quite different from those in earlier centuries. The word Bible comes from the Greek *biblia*, meaning books, for the Scriptures are a collection of books. Indeed, through the centuries the Bible often was a multi-volume work, a *Bibliotheca*, or library of books.

In the late twelfth century, theologians at the University of Paris began designing Bibles in a single book, made possible by a smaller script and a lighter weight paper. These "Paris Bibles" were commercially produced manuscript Bibles designed for individual use, unlike the larger Bibles used in monasteries and churches. They were especially useful to the traveling friars in their preaching and evangelism. Each page of text was in two columns, a tradition of Bible formatting carried over from the earlier manuscript scrolls.

The Hebrews had markings in the manuscripts of their Scriptures for the sections to be read in the synagogue. In the 4th century, Eusebius of Caesarea divided the 4 Gospels into sections and designed a table to show the parallel passages of the last three Gospels with the Gospel of Matthew, creating a harmony of the Gospels. Throughout the Middle Ages, these "Eusebian canons" were usually placed before the Gospels and were highly decorated.

Stephen Langton (c. 1150-1228), later Archbishop of Canterbury, made chapter divisions in the Bible while teaching at the University of Paris in 1204-1205. These were adopted by the producers of the Paris Bibles and are the chapter divisions we use today. The Paris Bibles also included subject headings at the top of each page.

Various people had made verse divisions of the Scriptures, but none were widely adopted until printer and Bible scholar Robert Estienne printed verse divisions in his 1551 edition of the Greek text. These divisions were then used in a 1553 French Bible and a 1555 Vulgate. In 1557, Estienne's verse divisions were first used in an English New Testament printed in Geneva. These verse divisions continued to be used in the Geneva Bible of 1560 and have become standard today.

Chapter and verse divisions make it easier to reference passages , but they are not part of the original text. Some publishers recently have begun printing Bibles without them, making the text easier to read without distractions.

I will never forget your precepts, for by them you have given me life.
—Psalm 119:93—

MARCH 8

MARTIN LUTHER'S GERMAN
BIBLE TRANSLATION

In 1517, Martin Luther opened a debate within the Church on the validity of indulgences, by which the Church offered early release from suffering in Purgatory. Central to the debate was the authority of Scripture in determining truth. Luther believed, "A simple layman armed with Scripture is to be believed above a pope or cardinal without it."[5] When called before the Emperor to recant his views, Luther famously replied,

> Unless I am convinced by the testimony of the Scriptures or by clear reason (for I do not trust either in the pope or in the councils alone, since it is well known that they have often erred and contradicted themselves), I am bound by the Scriptures ... and my conscience is captive to the Word of God.[6]

Though Luther had been given a safe conduct to appear before the Emperor at the Diet of Worms, he and his works were condemned at the Diet. To protect Luther, the Elector of Saxony kidnapped him and took him to the Wartburg Castle, where Luther remained in hiding for a year, disguised as Knight George. While there Luther translated the New Testament from Greek into German in seven weeks. His translation was the first vernacular translation from the original Greek since Jerome's Latin Vulgate translation 1000 years earlier. Luther's translation is still the standard German translation.

At Wartburg, Luther also translated the Psalms, published in 1522. Returning to Wittenberg, he worked with a team of scholars to finish translating the Old Testament from Hebrew. They sought to translate the Scripture into the kind of German spoken in the home and in the marketplace, helping people understand the Bible. Johann Cochlaeus, one of Luther's opponents, noted that in his day, "Even shoemakers and women and every kind of unlearned person, whoever of them…had somehow learned German letters, read it most eagerly as the font of all truth. And by reading and rereading it they committed it to memory and so carried the book around with them in their bosoms."[7]

And these words that I command you today shall be on your heart.
You shall teach them diligently to your children,
and shall talk of them when you sit in your house,
and when you walk by the way, and when you lie down, and when you rise.
—Deuteronomy 6:6-7—

MARCH 9
WHO SHOULD READ THE SCRIPTURE?

In the early centuries of the church, the Scriptures were translated into numerous languages. But in the West, the Latin Vulgate increasingly came to be viewed as authorized Scripture. When the brothers Cyril and Methodius began work among the Slavs in the 800's and translated the liturgy and Scriptures into Slavonic, some church authorities opposed it, but Pope John VIII approved their work and the use of the Scriptures among the Slavic people.

By 1079, however, Pope Gregory VII prohibited reciting the liturgy or the Scriptures in Slavonic. He said that if the Scriptures were available to ordinary men in their native language, they would become disrespected and falsely understood. In 1199, Pope Innocent III, concerned about the Waldensians in France, prohibited lay people from discussing the Scriptures together or reading them in their native language. He held that even the wise and literate cannot completely comprehend the Scriptures; giving them to the common people would be like casting pearls before swine! In 1229, the Synod of Toulouse forbade any translation not approved by papal or synodal action. In 1408, the English Archbishop Arundel forbade Wycliffe's English translation; in 1589, Archbishop Bertholdt of Mainz forbade the circulation of the German Bible. In the 16th century, however, Erasmus boldly wrote that the Scriptures should be in the language of the people:

> I utterly dissent from those who are unwilling that the sacred Scriptures should be read by the unlearned translated into their own vulgar tongue, as though the strength of the Christian religion consisted in men's ignorance of it. ... Christ wished his mysteries to be published as openly as possible. I wish that even the weakest woman should read the Gospel and the epistles of Paul. And I wish they were translated into all languages, so that they might be read and understood. ... I long that the husbandman could sing portions of them to himself as he follows the plow, that the weaver should hum them to the tune of his shuttle, that the traveler should beguile with their stories the tedium of his journey.[8]

The Protestant Reformation, with its foundation in Scripture, encouraged the translation of Scripture into the language of the people. Luther's German translation of the Scriptures is sometimes called his greatest gift to the German people, and Tyndale's English translation is foundational to later translations, and especially the King James Bible.

When I told of my ways, you answered me; teach me your statutes!
—Psalm 119:26—

SPEAKING BOLDLY FOR THE SCRIPTURES

When Argula von Grumbach (1492-1554) was ten, her father gave her a beautiful German Bible. He encouraged her to read it, but the Franciscan preachers said reading it would just confuse her. At sixteen, she became lady-in-waiting to Duchess Kunigunde of Bavaria. At the Duchess' court, Argula met John von Staupitz, who had counselled Martin Luther on salvation by grace through Christ's sacrifice on the cross. Argula was persuaded that the Scriptures were the source of truth and began studying the Bible in earnest. She read many of Martin Luther's writings and even began corresponding with him. However, Bavarian authorities had forbidden Luther's works.

When Arsacius Seehofer, an eighteen-year-old student at the University of Ingelstadt, visited Wittenberg and brought back some of Luther's writings, he was arrested and charged with heresy. He could have been executed, but the court allowed him to be confined to a monastery if he recanted, which he did. In 1523, Argula wrote an extensive letter to the University of Ingelstadt authorities protesting the action against Seehofer. Argula's letter itself shows her familiarity with the Scriptures, for she has at least 80 biblical references.

Argula saw the arrest and trial of Seehofer as an attack on Scripture itself:

> How in God's name can you and your university expect to prevail when you deploy such foolish violence against the word of God; when you force someone to hold the holy Gospel in their hands for the very purpose of denying it as you did in the case of Arsacius Seehofer? When you confront him with an oath and declaration such as this, and use imprisonment and even the threat of the stake to force him to deny Christ and his word?

She wrote that the University was standing for the foolish wisdom of man, as Paul described in I Corinthians. Argula exclaimed, "Ah, but what a joy it is when the Spirit of God teaches us and gives us understanding—God be praised—so that I came to see the genuine light shining out."

Argula's letter and defense of the Scriptures was printed in a pamphlet form and became a best seller!

... for the sake of your tradition you have made void the word of God.
—Matthew 15:6—

MARCH 11
A FAMED ARTIST'S GIFT TO THE CITY COUNCIL

Nuremberg artist Albrecht Dürer (1471-1528) has been recognized as the greatest artist of the Northern Renaissance. Though he worked in numerous media, his woodcuts transformed printmaking and first gained him fame. Dürer moved away from the color-book style of woodcuts, using line and shading to add dimension to his work. In 1498, Dürer produced a series of 15 woodcuts of the Apocalypse, the book of Revelation, which were widely acclaimed. The series was not printed in a Bible, but with the Biblical text on the back of the prints. Many people expected the end of the world in 1500, and the timing of the publication of Dürer's prints met a receptive audience.

Dürer became a follower of Martin Luther, especially valuing his focus on the Scriptures. After Nuremberg became a Protestant city in 1525, Dürer painted two large panels of John and Peter, Paul and Mark for the Nuremberg City Council. Each pair of evangelists was holding a copy of the Scriptures. Underneath the panels were quotations from the Scriptures in Luther's translation. The Scripture quotations warned against false teachers and prophets (II Peter 2:1-3; I John 4:1-3) rampant immorality (II Timothy 3:1-7) and religious hypocrites (Mark 12: 38-40). The painting was Dürer's personal testimony to his biblically grounded Christianity as well as an encouragement for the Nuremberg City Council to keep faithful to the Scriptures and not stray into errors of belief or practice. Dürer wrote to the council,

> All worldly rulers in these dangerous times should give good heed that they receive not human misguidance for the Word of God, for God will have nothing added to His Word nor taken away from it. Hear therefore these four excellent men, Peter, John, Paul, and Mark and their warning.[9]

You shall not add to the word that
I command you, nor take from it,
that you may keep the commandments
of the Lord your God that I command you.
—Deuteronomy 4:2—

VALUE OF THE WORD

Jacques Lefèvre (1455-1536) was a devout French philosopher and academic who prayed long prayers before the images of the saints. Around 1507, he was writing the life stories of saints and found a Bible in the Sorbonne library. He thought it might help him in his writing. Though he didn't find the lives of the saints in the Bible, he discovered for the first time the beauty of the Scripture and of Jesus Christ:

> The Scriptures seemed to give off a perfume whose sweetness was beyond all compare, beside them all human studies are a fog and shadow. Since their study has been neglected, the monasteries have fallen into ruin, piety is dead, and true religion has snuffed out.[10]

Lefèvre began to devote himself to the study of the Scriptures. In 1508 he wrote a Latin commentary of the Psalms which Luther used in his early studies of the Psalms. In 1512, Lefèvre wrote a commentary on the Pauline epistles. As he studied the Scripture, Lefèvre realized that for true reform to take place, the people needed the Scriptures in their own language. In 1523, Lefèvre published his French translation of the New Testament. It is the basis of all later French translations. His translation of the entire Bible was published in 1530. Lefèvre now realized that the Scripture was the source of true knowledge of Jesus:

> Know that men and their doctrines are worth nothing, unless they be confirmed and supported by the Word of God. And Jesus Christ is everything; He is wholly human and wholly divine; and no man is worth anything without Him; and no word of man has any value, except in His Word.[11]

Many of Lefèvre's works were banned by the Sorbonne, and he fled from France for a time because of persecution. One of his students at the University of Paris had been G. Farel, who later founded Reformed churches in Switzerland and persuaded John Calvin to remain in Geneva. When Calvin had fled France, he visited Lefèvre on his way into exile. Calvin had many questions, which elderly Lefèvre endeavored to answer. He also encouraged Calvin, telling him God would use him in establishing Christ's kingdom in France.

Many are my persecutors and mine enemies;
yet do I not decline from thy testimonies.
—Psalm119:137—

MARCH 13

CALVIN AND THE PSALMS

John Calvin (1509-1564) called the Psalms, "An Anatomy of All the Parts of the Soul" because the Psalms reflect every human emotion. In the Psalms he believed the Holy Spirit had "drawn to the life all the griefs, sorrows, fears, doubts, hopes, cares, perplexities, in short, all the distracting emotions with which the minds of men tend to be agitated."[12] In other parts of the Bible, God spoke to men, but in the Psalms the prophets spoke to God, and drew later readers to examine their own souls. The Book of Psalms is unique:

> There is no other book in which there is to be found more express and magnificent commendations, both of the unparalleled liberality of God towards his Church, and of all his works; there is no other book in which there is recorded so many deliverances, nor one in which the evidences and experiences of the fatherly providence and solicitude which God exercises towards us, are celebrated with such splendour of diction, and yet with the strictest adherence to truth; in short, there is no other book in which we are more perfectly taught the right manner of praising God, or in which we are more powerfully stirred up to the performance of this religious exercise.[13]

To Calvin, the Psalms teach much about prayer. Reading the Psalms awakens people "to a sense of their maladies, and at the same time, instructed in seeking remedies for their cure."[14] Psalms are the best guide for prayer.

Calvin encouraged the Christian singing of the Psalms, and by 1539, had a psalter published in Strassbourg. He tried his hand at poetic paraphrases of the Psalms, but also incorporated the French Psalm translations of Clement Marot into the Geneva Psalters. The singing of Psalms has characterized the reformed churches under Calvin's influence, including those in America.

Influenced by Calvin's emphasis on the singing of Psalms, Puritan ministers in Massachusetts made a versification of the psalms in English in 1640. This *Bay Psalm Book* was the first English book printed in America.

Oh sing to the Lord a new song; sing to the Lord, all the earth!
Sing to the Lord, bless his name;
tell of his salvation from day to day.
Declare his glory among the nations,
his marvelous works among all the peoples!
—Psalm 96:1-3—

THOMAS BILNEY'S CONVERSION THROUGH READING THE SCRIPTURES

Thomas Bilney (1495-1531) was a graduate of Trinity Hall, Cambridge, and had taken holy orders in 1519. Some time later he came to faith in Christ by reading Erasmus' Greek/Latin text of the New Testament. The first sentence he read was I Timothy 1:15, "This is a faithful saying, and worthy of all acceptance, that Christ Jesus came into the world to save sinners of whom I am chief." Bilney responded with joy:

> I felt a marvelous comfort and quietness … After this, the Scripture began to be more pleasant unto me than the honey or the honeycomb; wherein I learned that all my labours, my fasting and watching, all the redemption of masses and pardons, being done without truth in Christ, who alone saveth his people from their sins, these I say, I learned to be nothing else but even … a hasty and swift running out of the right way.[15]

Bilney began to study the Scriptures. He began a Bible study in Cambridge and prayed for the light of Scripture to come to England. Bilney influenced many other young men in the Scriptures, including Matthew Parker, future Archbishop of Canterbury, and Hugh Latimer. He boldly began preaching in the open air against the mediation and veneration of the saints, and the spiritual efficacy of pilgrimages. In 1531, he was arrested for heresy and condemned to death in Norwich. The evening before his execution, friends marveled at his cheerfulness. At one point, Bilney put his finger into a candle's flame, "trying his flesh;" he recalled Isaiah 43:2, "When thou walkest through the fire, thou shalt not be burned neither shall the flame kindle upon thee."

On his way to the stake, Bilney recited Psalm 143, repeating twice "Enter not into judgment with your servant, for no one living is righteous before you," and especially calling out, "I stretch out my hands to you; my soul thirsts for you like a parched land." Bilney died on August 19, 1531, one of the first martyrs of the English church. In later sermons, Hugh Latimer repeatedly noted that Bilney died for the Word of God.

You make known to me the path of life;
in your presence there is fulness of joy;
at your right hand are pleasures forevermore.
—Psalm 16:11—

MARCH 15

WILLIAM TYNDALE

"Lord, Open the King of England's eyes." That was William Tyndale's dying prayer before he was strangled and burned at the stake in 1536. What was Tyndale's crime? What did he want the King to see?

William Tyndale's (1494-1536) passion was to translate the Bible from the Greek and Hebrew into English. He wanted the Bible in English so that even the poorest ploughboy would be able to read the Scriptures for himself. The problem was—it was against the law to translate the Bible into English! When John Wyclif made the first English translation of the Bible in 1382, the Church leaders were not pleased. They issued the Constitutions of Oxford specifically forbidding anyone reading such a book "on pain of ex-communication." People reading the Bible in common English, rather than in the Latin of the educated elite, could be punished with forfeiture of their goods, cattle, land, and even their life. William Tyndale, however, was convinced even the common people should be able to read the Scriptures, and he sought permission from the church authorities to make his English translation. When permission was refused, Tyndale went to Europe, living in Germany and Holland as he diligently translated the New Testament. He also learned Hebrew and began a translation of the Old Testament. In 1526, the first printed English New Testaments were smuggled into England. The king and church authorities were furious. Spies were sent to the continent to search for Tyndale. He was hunted down until, betrayed by an assumed friend, he was arrested in 1535. He was tried and found guilty of heresy (for embracing the teachings of the condemned Martin Luther). Even as he faced death, he prayed for the King's eyes to be opened to the need for a Bible the English people could read.

Tyndale's dying prayer was soon answered. Within a year after Tyndale's death, King Henry VIII ordered a copy of the English Bible be placed in every church in England. Tyndale's work lived on in many later translations. 85% of the long-lived King James translation is the work of William Tyndale.

In 1994, the British Library bought one of three surviving copies of Tyndale's 1526 New Testament, printed in Worms. Paying a little over £ 1 million for the volume, the Library called it "the most important book in the English language."[16]

Even though princes sit plotting against me,
your servant will meditate on your statutes.
—Psalm 119:23—

ADVICE ON READING THE SCRIPTURE
FROM THE FIRST PRINTED ENGLISH BIBLE

In 1535, Miles Coverdale (1486-1569) published the first complete translation of the Bible into English. With the growing persecution of church reformers under King Henry VIII, in 1528, Coverdale had fled to the continent. There he met William Tyndale and assisted him in his revisions of his New Testament translation which had been first published in 1525. Coverdale also worked on translating the Old Testament from the Latin and Martin Luther's German translation, since Coverdale knew little Hebrew. Coverdale dedicated his Bible, which incorporated much of Tyndale's New Testament, to King Henry. Coverdale's extensive prologue to his Bible offered advice on how to read and interpret the Scriptures and apply them to various aspects of everyday life.

Coverdale urged the reader of Scripture to consider the context—to whom the words were spoken and the circumstances surrounding them:

> For there are some things which are done and written, to the intent that we should do likewise, as when Abraham believes God, is obedient unto his word, and defends Lot his kinsman from violent wrong. There are some things also which are written, to the intent that we should avoid such like. As when David lies with Urias' wife, and causes him to be slain … when you read scripture, be wise …; and when you come to such strange manners of speaking and dark sentences, … as are hid from your understanding, commit them unto God or to the gift of his holy spirit in those who are better learned than you …. Sit down at the Lord's feet and read his words, and, as Moses teaches the Jews [Deut. 6] take them into your heart, and let your talking and communication be of them when you sit in your house, or go by the way, when you lie down, and when you rise up. And above all things fashion your life and conversation according to the doctrine of the holy ghost therein, that you may be a partaker of the good promises of God in the Bible and be heir of his blessing Christ. In whom if you put your trust, and are an unfeigned reader or hearer of his word with your heart, you will find sweetness therein … take these words of scripture into your heart, and be not only an outward hearer, but a doer thereafter [James 1:22], and practice yourself therein, that you may feel in your heart, the sweet promises for your consolation in all trouble, and for the sure establishing of your hope in Christ.[17]

Make Your face shine upon Your servant, And teach me Your statutes.
—Psalm 119:135—

 THE LIVING WORD | 84

MARCH 17
AN ANSWER TO TYNDALE'S PRAYER

In 1534, John Rogers (1505-1555) left England for Antwerp to become chaplain to the English merchants there. In Antwerp, Rogers met William Tyndale, the translator of the New Testament from the Greek into English. When Tyndale was executed for heresy in 1536, his dying prayer was for the King to allow the Bible in England. Within a year after Tyndale's death, King Henry VIII allowed a Bible in England. This Bible, "set forth with the King's most gracious license," was the work of John Rogers.

Rogers used the previously printed New Testament and five books of Moses, and the book of Jonah translated by Tyndale, as well as Tyndale's unpublished translation of the historical books through II Chronicles. For the rest of the Old Testament, Rogers used Coverdale's translation, amended by his own reference to the German and Latin. Printed in Antwerp in 1537, the title page said this was the translation of "Thomas Matthew." Perhaps this was the alias Rogers or Tyndale used in Antwerp, or perhaps this was a pseudonym combination of the names of two apostles, to disguise this as Tyndale's work (which was banned at the time in England).

When Edward VI became King, and Protestantism was more favored in England, Rogers returned to London, where he was a powerful preacher. However, early in the reign of Queen Mary he was arrested and imprisoned. Though offered pardon if he recanted, Rogers refused, saying, "That which I have preached I will seal with my blood." Rogers' wife and eleven children lined the path as he went to his execution. There he saw his youngest child for the first time. The French ambassador described the scene "as if he had been led to a wedding." Rogers became the first of many martyrs under Queen Mary. He went to the flames reciting Psalm 51.

The insolent utterly deride me,
but I do not turn away from your law.
—Psalm 119:51—

CALVIN AND THE GENEVA BIBLE

John Calvin's cousin, Pierre Robert Olivetan (1506-1538), was chosen by the Waldensians to translate the Bible into French from the original Greek and Hebrew. When Olivetan's Bible was published in 1535, the newly converted John Calvin wrote a Latin preface to the New Testament. Beginning with Creation, Calvin traced the working of God in history through the redemption brought by Jesus Christ. The point of the entire Scripture was "truly to know Jesus Christ, and the infinite riches that are comprised in him and are offered to us by him from God the Father. If one were to sift thoroughly the Law and the Prophets, he would not find a single word which would not draw and bring us to him." In the Scripture "is enclosed all the wisdom which men can understand, and ought to learn in this life which no angel, or man, dead or living, may add to or take away from." [18] Calvin concluded his preface by praising the Bible in the vernacular language and excoriating the rulers and bishops who tried to keep the Scriptures from the people.

Four years later, in 1539, Calvin published the first edition of his most influential work, *The Institutes of the Christian Religion*. He revised and greatly expanded the *Institutes* in the next 20 years, always emphasizing the Bible's authority. He wrote, "My object in this work is to prepare and train students of sacred theology for the study of the Word of God that they might have an easy access into it and be able to proceed in it without hindrance." [19]

After his move to Geneva, Calvin was actively involved in revisions to Olivetan's French Bible. English exiles worked on the English Geneva Bible, borrowing much from the user-friendly French editions. They translated Calvin's New Testament preface, "Christ is the End of the Law," and placed it as the preface to the Geneva New Testament published in 1557. They included book introductions, chapter summaries, and theological and textual notes in the margin, and illustrations and diagrams. Many of the notes were taken from Calvin's commentaries. Calvin's stamp and influence were clearly evident in the Geneva Bible, the version used by Shakespeare, John Bunyan, the Pilgrims, Puritans, and early colonists in America at Jamestown and Plymouth.

---

beginning with Moses and all the Prophets he [Jesus] interpreted to them in all the Scriptures the things concerning himself.
—Luke 24:27—

MARCH 19
FIRST PRINTED BIBLICAL COMMENTARY

The first Biblical commentary ever printed was that of Nicholas de Lyra (1270-1349) in 1541. Nicholas' Latin commentary was widely copied in manuscript form before going through numerous editions in printed format. The large volumes had the Scriptural text in the upper middle of the page, and two columns of surrounding commentary in a different script or font. The commentary also included six illustrations to help understand the text, including depictions of Noah's ark, the Ark of the Covenant, the Temple in Jerusalem, and Ezekiel's opening vision of the glory of the Lord.

Nicholas was a Franciscan and professor at the Sorbonne in France. He believed that Scripture should be interpreted in a literal sense, according to the author's original, plain meaning. During the medieval period, allegorical and mystical interpretations of the Scripture prevailed and often obscured the literal meaning of a passage. Nicholas also sought to remove corruptions and copyist errors which had crept into the Latin Vulgate Bible, especially in the Old Testament. He sought out Hebrew manuscripts which he could compare and use to correct the accepted Vulgate text.

Nicholas de Lyra had an important influence on Martin Luther and the Reformation, reflected in the couplet, "Si Lyra non lyrasset, Luterhus non saltasset." (If Lyra had not played his lyre, Luther would not have danced.) Luther frequently quoted Nicholas in his own works and in his *Table Talk*. He praised Nicholas for his knowledge of Hebrew and warned against allegorizing of Scripture:

> For this reason I like Lyra and rank him among the best, because throughout he carefully adheres to, and concerns himself with, the historical account…A fine soul: a good Hebraist and a true Christian.[20]

I hasten and do not delay to keep your commandments.
—Psalm 119:160—

THOMAS CRANMER AND THE GREAT BIBLE

A central tourist site in Oxford, England is the Martyrs' Memorial, a Victorian monument honoring three 16th-century leaders of the English Reformation who under Queen Mary were burned at the stake for their faith. Hugh Latimer and Nicholas Ridley met their fiery deaths together in October 1555. Thomas Cranmer, Archbishop of Canterbury, followed them to the flames on March 21, 1556.

Thomas Cranmer's influence and legacy continued long after the flames which consumed his body had died. As one of the prime architects of the Reformation in the Church of England, Cranmer elevated the position of the Scriptures in the life of the Church. When he became Archbishop in 1533, possessing a portion of the Scriptures in English was still illegal. In 1538, King Henry VIII required every church in England to buy a Bible and to place it "some convenient place" for everyone to read. In the midst of the political and religious turmoil during the reign of King Henry VIII and Henry's heir, King Edward, Cranmer encouraged the dissemination of the Scriptures. With his encouragement, in 1539, what became known as the Great Bible, because of its large size, was published.

Cranmer's Preface to the Great Bible encouraged the individual's personal, daily reading of the Scripture. He quoted extensively from the fourth-century church father John Chrysostom to show that reading of the Bible by the individual Christian was a practice encouraged in the early church. In the *Articles of Religion for the Church*, Cranmer clearly stated the sufficiency "of the holy Scriptures for salvation" and asserted that "it is not lawful for the church to ordain anything that is contrary to God's written Word." In *The Book of Common Prayer*, Cranmer made the English Scriptures the basis and foundation of the Church's worship. Two thirds of *The Book of Common Prayer* comes from the Scriptures. Cranmer provided a pattern of daily Scripture reading in which readers read through the book of Psalms each month and the entire Bible every two years. Cranmer taught that "to a Christian man, there can be nothing neither more necessary or profitable, than the knowledge of holy scripture, forasmuch as in it is contained God's true word, setting forth his glory and also man's duty."[21]

I cling to your testimonies, O Lord; let me not be put to shame!
—Psalm 119:31—

MARCH 21

CRANMER ON READING THE BIBLE

The 1540 second edition of the Great Bible, and numerous Bibles following, included a Preface by Archbishop Thomas Cranmer. It addressed two main issues—the benefits of individuals reading the Scriptures and a warning to those who spent their time in endless disputes about the Scriptures. In a country which had forbidden the personal reading of the Scriptures for generations, Cranmer took the bold step of exhorting the people to read the Scriptures daily. His exhortation and practical admonitions showed a pastor's heart. He wrote that being too busy for the Scriptures because of one's work in government, or household duties, or caring for the children, or time needed for business is no excuse. Those most distracted by the affairs of the world are most in need of the Scriptures! Cranmer wrote that in the Scriptures can be found the medicine and remedy for many grievous wounds and ailments. If your wife provokes you to anger, your child causes you sorrow, your enemies lie in wait for you, your friend (or so you thought) envies you, your neighbor picks quarrels with you, your mate undermines you, your lord threatens you, poverty is painful to you, you mourn the loss of a beloved, prosperity exalts you, or adversity brings you low, the Scriptures contain the needed treatment. In the Scriptures are the salves for cares, tribulations and temptations. The reading of the Scriptures also protects against sin.

In the second part of his Preface, Cranmer cautioned people to read the Scriptures with the fear of God in their hearts. The Scriptures are not to be used for endless disputations or read with philosophical sophistry. Endless talk about the Scriptures is no substitute for a holy life transformed through the power of God's Word:

> ... Every man that comes to the reading of this holy book, ought to bring with him first and foremost this fear of almighty God, and then next, a firm and stable purpose to reform his own self according thereunto, and so to continue, proceed and prosper from time to time, showing himself to be a sober and fruitful hearer and learner; which, if he do, he shall prove at the length well able to teach. Though not with his mouth, yet with his living and good example, which is sure the most lively and effective form and manner of teaching.

Today, nearly 500 years after his death, Cranmer's words on the importance of the Scripture continue to challenge us.

Blessed are those who keep his testimonies,
who seek him with their whole heart ...
—Psalm 119:2—

AN EXHORTATION TO STUDY THE HOLY SCRIPTURE

By 1541, more than 9000 copies of the Great Bible had been printed. The 1541 edition of the Great Bible has a beautifully designed page of biblical encouragements to Bible study. The list was taken from the 1537 Matthews Bible, prepared by John Rogers (spelling has been modernized):

Christ unto the people. — John 5
Search the Scriptures: For they are they that testify of me.

Paul to Timothy — II Timothy 3
All Scripture given by inspiration of God is profitable to teach, to improve, to amend and to instruct in righteousness, that the man of God may be perfect and prepared to all good works.

The same to the Romans — Romans 4
What things so ever are written, are written for our learning: that we through patience and comfort of the Scripture might have hope.

Solomon — Proverbs 30
All the word of God is pure and clean, it is a shield unto them that put their trust in him. Put nothing unto his words, lest he reprove thee and thou be found a liar.

Moses to the people — Deut. 12
Ye shall not do every man what seems him good in his own eyes. But whatsoever I command you, that take heed to do: and put nought thereto, nor take ought there from.

The Lord unto Joshua — Joshua 1
Let not the book of this law depart out of thy mouth. But record therein day and night, that thou may be circumspect to do according to all that is written therein. For then shall thou make thy way prosperous, and then shall thou have understanding. Turn therefore neither to the right hand, nor to the left: that thou may have understanding in all that thou takes in hand.

The same to the people — Exodus 18
And thou shall show thy son at that time, saying: This is done because of that which the Lord did unto me when I came out of Egypt. Therefore it shall be a sign unto thee upon they hand, and a remembrance between thine eyes, that the Lord's law may be in thy mouth. For with a strong hand the Lord brought thee out of Egypt.

Moses — Deut. 31

See that thou read this law before all Israel in their years. Gather the people together, both men, women, and children, and strangers that are in thy cities, that they may hear, learn, and fear the Lord your God, to keep all the words of his law.

I long for your salvation, O Lord, and your law is my delight.
—Psalm 119:174—

READING THE BIBLE IN ST. PAUL'S CATHEDRAL

After English Bibles had been forbidden for over a century, in 1537, King Henry VIII allowed them in England. Though copies of Tyndale's New Testament had been burned in front of St. Paul's Cathedral as a forbidden book, a decade later, by 1538, it was required that there be an English Bible in every church in England! Miles Coverdale prepared the edition authorized by the King. William Tyndale's translation was used for the New Testament and the portions of the Old Testament he had completed. Coverdale translated the remaining of the Old Testament from the Latin and German versions. The 1539 authorized Bible came to be known as the Great Bible because of its size. The large Bible was often chained to a lectern in church and made available for any to read.

Bishop Bonner, however, became concerned when some would read the Bible aloud during the church service and disrupt the sermon. King Henry then decreed that no one "shall openly read the bible or New Testament in the English tongue in any churches or chapels or elsewhere with any loud or high voice, and specially during the time of divine service, but quietly and reverently read the bible and New Testament by themselves secretly at all times and places convenient."[22] Henry also forbade lower classes from reading the book, saying it was for noblemen and ladies of quality to read quietly alone, not to others.

In 1542, Bishop Bonner arrested John Porter for reading and expounding the Bible in St. Paul's Cathedral in London. He was sent to Newgate prison, where he was secured to the wall with a collar of iron while his legs and arms were secured with irons. Within days he was found dead. John Foxe wrote of his sad case as an example of someone martyred for reading the Scriptures.

They read from the book, from the Law of God, clearly,
and they gave the sense, so that the people understood the reading.
—Nehemiah 8:8—

MARCH 24
TRUE AND PERFECT JOY FOUND IN THE SCRIPTURES

Marguerite de Navarre (1492-1549), Queen of Navarre, was known in her own day for her kind, gentle spirit, her intellectual acumen, and her charitable works. A favorite sister of King Francis I of France, Marguerite corresponded with leaders throughout Europe, from Erasmus to Calvin. She longed for a Reformation in the church in France and protected those suffering persecution for their biblical faith. In the preface to a work of short stories called *Heptameron*, Marguerite wrote of her love of Scriptures:

> You ask me, my children, to do a very difficult thing—to invent a diversion that will drive away your *ennuis* [boredom]. I have been seeking all my life to effect this, but I have found only *one* remedy, which is *reading the Holy Scriptures*. By perusing them, my mind experiences its true and perfect joy; and from this pleasure of the mind, proceed the repose and health of the body. If you desire me to tell you what I do, to be so cheerful and so well, at my advanced age, it is because as soon as I get up, I read these sacred books. There I see and contemplate the will of God, who sent his Son to us on earth, to preach that Holy Word; and to announce the sweet tidings, that he promises to pardon our sins and extinguish our debts, by giving us his Son, who loved us, and who suffered and died for our sakes. This idea so delights me, that I take up the Psalms, and sing them with my heart; and pronounce with my tongue, as humbly as possible, the fine hymns which the Holy Spirit inspired David, and the sacred authors. The pleasure I receive from this exercise, so transports me, that I consider all the evils that may happen to me in the day, to be real blessings; for I place Him in my heart, by faith, who endured more misery for me. Before I sup, I retire in the same manner, to give my soul a congenial lesson. At night, I review all that I have done in the day; I implore pardon for my faults; I thank my God for his favors; and I lie down in his love, in his fear, and in his peace, my soul being free from every worldly anxiety. Lo! My dear children, what has, for a *long* while, made me so happy. I have sought everywhere else, but have found nothing but this, so solid and so satisfying—and if you will give an hour every morning to such reading, and say your prayers devoutly…, you will perceive in this solitude those charms which will attend you in every city. Indeed, whoever knows God, will find the most beautiful things in Him; but without Him what is there that will not become offensive and disagreeable? You must believe what I say, if you wish to have a safe and pleasant life.[23]

Let your steadfast love comfort me according to your promise to your servant.
—Psalm 119:76—

LADY JANE GREY'S GREEK NEW TESTAMENT

The beginning of the Reformation in England was a period filled with political and religious drama lived out by seemingly larger-than-life personalities. Young King Edward VI, knowing he was dying, tried to keep the crown in Protestant hands by naming his cousin Jane Grey (1537-1554) his successor. Jane was an extremely well-educated young lady with strong Protestant convictions. She knew Latin, Greek, and Hebrew, and corresponded with leading Reformers on the continent. The people, however, did not accept Jane as queen and saw Henry VIII's daughter Mary, and sister of Edward, as the rightful successor. After nine days, Jane stepped down as queen. When Jane's father was involved in a rebellion, Queen Mary decided Jane must be executed; Mary sent her chaplain to Jane to try to convert her to Catholicism, but Jane was firm in her beliefs, answering the chaplain with Scriptures.

The day before her execution, Jane gave her Greek New Testament to her sister Katherine. At the back of the Testament, she wrote a letter in which she expressed her Christian convictions and hope:

> I have sent you, my dear sister Katherine, a book, which although it be not outwardly trimmed with gold, or the curious embroidery of the artfulest needles, yet inwardly it is more worth than all the precious mines which the vast world can boast of: it is the book, my only best, and best loved sister, of the law of the Lord: it is the Testament and last will, which he bequeathed unto us wretches and wretched sinners, which shall lead you to the path of eternal joy: and if you with a good mind read it, and with an earnest desire follow it, no doubt it shall bring you to an immortal and everlasting life: it will teach you to live, and learn you to die: it shall win you more, and endow you with greater felicity ... Farewell once again, my beloved sister, and put your only trust in God, who only must help you. Amen. Your loving Sister[24]

Before Jane was beheaded on February 12, 1554, she recited Psalm 51. Here are the first two verses from Coverdale's translation:

> Haue mercy vpon me (o God) after thy goodnes, & acordinge vnto thy greate mercies, do away myne offences.
> Wash me well fro my wickednesse, & clense me fro my synne.

I love your commandments above gold, above fine gold.
—Psalm 119:127—

MARCH 26
CONVERTED BY READING THE WORD

Franciscus Junius (1545-1602) was born into a noble French family. At thirteen he began the study of law and later pursued his love of the classics in Lyon. Reading Cicero and Epicurus, Franciscus was increasingly attracted to atheism, which caused his father much consternation. However, through reading the Scriptures, Francisco's heart was turned to Christ. As he tells the story:

> My father, who was frequently reading the New Testament, and had long observed with grief the progress I had made in infidelity, had put that book into my way in his library, in order to attract my attention, if it pleased God to bless his design, though without giving me the least intimation of it. This New Testament thus providentially laid before me, I open, deeply engaged in other thoughts. At the very first view, the most august chapter of John, the evangelist and apostle, 'In the beginning was the Word,' etc., presents itself to me. I read part of the chapter, and reading, am so affected with it, that I am suddenly struck with the divinity of the argument, and the majesty and authority of the composition, as very far surpassing the highest flights of human eloquence. My body shuddered; my mind was overwhelmed, and I was so agitated the whole day that I scarcely knew who I was. Thou didst remember me, O Lord my God, according to thy boundless mercy, and dost receive the lost sheep into thy flock! From that day that God worked so mightily in me by the power of his Spirit, I began to have less relish for all other studies and pursuits and bent myself with greater ardor and attention to everything which had relation to God.[25]

To his father's delight, Franciscus changed his course of studies and went to Geneva, where he studied under John Calvin and Theodore Beza. Later, Franciscus became minister at Antwerp and then went to Heidelberg, where he and Emmanuel Tremellius completed a Latin translation of the Bible. It was read and studied by many Reformation scholars. Later, he was a diplomat. In his closing years, Franciscus was professor of theology at the University of Leiden. There he wrote several important theological works, including *The Mosaic Polity*, which analyzed the Mosaic Law and the relationship between the church and the state. Junius noted that the Mosaic laws could be classified as moral, judicial, and ceremonial, with varying contemporary applications, an analysis followed by many later commentaries.

I will also speak of your testimonies before kings and shall not be put to shame …
—Psalm 119: 46—

A NINETEEN-YEAR-OLD
MARTYR FOR THE SCRIPTURES

When Mary Tudor became queen in 1553, one of her goals was to reverse the Reformation in England and restore the Catholic faith. At Easter, an order required all in London to receive communion at a mass. Nineteen-year-old William Hunter, an apprentice to a London silk weaver, refused. They threatened to bring him to the bishop of London. Fearing reprisal, Hunter's master dismissed him. Hunter returned to his family in Brentwood. A few weeks later, he went into the local chapel and found a Bible on the desk, which he began reading. A priest came in and reprimanded him for, commenting, "It was never merry world since the Bible came abroad in English." Hunter replied,

> Not so, for God's sake: for it is God's book, and of which every one that hath grace may learn to know both what things please God, and also what displeaseth him… I pray God that we may have the blessed Bible amongst us continuously.[26]

Hunter was brought before the magistrate and asked to affirm that the bread and wine of communion was the true body and blood of Christ. William could not in good conscience affirm that. Though Jesus said the bread was his body, he could not have two bodies as he in his body then gave the bread to the disciples to eat. This was a figure of speech, similar to Jesus saying he was the door or the vine, though he wasn't a literal door or vine.

Hunter was sent to Bishop Bonner in London for further examination and imprisonment. He was in prison there for 9 months and was brought before the Bishop five times for interrogation. The Bishop wanted him to recant and promised him he would make him a freeman in the city and give him forty pounds in good money to set up a business, or he would make him steward of his house, for he really liked Hunter. William answered,

> I thank you for your great offers: notwithstanding, my Lord, if you cannot persuade my conscience with Scriptures, I cannot find in my heart to turn from God for the love of the world; for I count all things worldly but loss and dung, in respect of the love of Christ.

Hunter recited Psalm 84 as he was burned at the stake for his faith on March 27, 1555.

O Lord of hosts, blessed is the one who trusts in you!
—Psalm 84:12—

MARCH 28

BIBLE TRANSLATIONS ENHANCE THE ENGLISH LANGUAGE

The first recorded use of many of the words used in ordinary English today can be found in the early translations of the Bible into English. When John Wycliffe translated the Bible into English from Jerome's Latin Vulgate in the fourteenth century, he enlarged the English language by adapting many Latin words into his English Bible. The words treasure and mystery, glory and horror, female and sex all owe their English usage to Wycliffe's Bible.

Tyndale, translating from the Hebrew and Greek in the 16th century, did not borrow as much from the Latin as did Wycliffe. He did coin words from the Dutch and Germanic sources (after all, he did his translation work while in those two countries) as well as French. Beautiful and ungodly were such words. Many of Tyndale's coined words were compound words, such as fisherman, castaway and busybody.

Both Wycliffe's and Tyndale's translations include phrases which readily entered the language with their Bible translations –phrases like a city on a hill, my brother's keeper, ye of little faith, salt of the earth, and thirty pieces of silver. Numerous other phrases first found in Bible translations have become part of colloquial speech, including the following:

thorn in the flesh	I Corinthians 12:7
as old as Methusalah	Genesis 5:27
as old as the hills	Job 15:7
patience of Job	Job 19:20
at his wit's end	Psalm 107:27
written in stone	Exodus 31:18
handwriting on the wall	Daniel 5:5-6
go the extra mile	Matthew 5:41

We can pray and work to speak in such a way that our words are echoes of our own reading of the Bible, and not merely accidental echoes of what people read in the past.

I have stored up our word in my heart,
that I might not sin against you.
—Psalm 119:11—

THE PSALMS FOR SINGING

One of the fruits of the Reformation was the return of congregational singing to the church. John Calvin especially encouraged the singing of the Biblical psalms, writing that there were no better songs suitable for singing than those which had been written by the Holy Spirit in the book of Psalms. Metrical versions of the psalms soon appeared throughout Europe. A French Genevan Psalter was first published in 1539; a Dutch metrical Psalter appeared in 1566; a German translation was made in 1573. John Daye published the first English Psalter in 1562. This Psalter came to be known as "Sternhold and Hopkins," for its main contributors, Thomas Sternhold and John Hopkins. Sternhold, a courtier at the courts of King Henry VIII and his son Edward had been the first to make an English metrical version of the psalms. Here is Sternhold's version of Psalm 1:

The man is blest that hath not lent
   to wicked men his ear,
Nor led his life as sinners do,
   nor sat in scorner's chair.

But in the law of God the Lord
   doth set his whole delight,
And in the same doth exercise
   himself both day and night.

He shall be like a tree that is
   planted the rivers nigh,
Which in due season bringeth forth
   its fruit abundantly;

Whose leaf shall never fade nor fall,
   but flourishing shall stand:

E'en so all things shall prosper well
   that this man takes in hand.

As for ungodly men, with them
   it shall be nothing so;
But as the chaff, which by the wind
   is driven to and fro.

Therefore the wicked men shall not
   in judgment stand upright,
Nor in th' assembly of the just
   shall sinners come in sight.

For why? The way of godly men
   unto the Lord is known:
Whereas the way of wicked men
   shall quite be overthrown.

… be filled with the Spirit, addressing one another in psalms and hymns and spiritual songs, singing and making melody to the Lord with your heart.
—Ephesians 5:18-10—

MARCH 30
A QUEEN STRENGTHENED BY SCRIPTURE

The reign of Queen Elizabeth I (1533-1603) is remembered as a glorious one in England's history, but the life of the young Elizabeth was filled with difficulties and dangers. When she was four, Elizabeth's father, King Henry VIII, had her mother, Anne Boleyn, beheaded and Elizabeth was declared illegitimate. When Elizabeth's half-sister later became Queen Mary I, Elizabeth was for a time imprisoned in the Tower of London and later placed under house arrest. Elizabeth, however, had a firm Christian faith and had grown under the Bible studies that Queen Catherine Parr held in the palace. Elizabeth placed her trust in the Lord and found comfort in the Scriptures. When Mary died, and Elizabeth learned she would be queen, she quoted Psalm 118:23, "This is the Lord's doing; it is marvelous in our eyes." She looked to the Scriptures for wisdom in her reign and prayed

> O Lord God, Father everlasting, which reignest over the kingdoms of men and givest them at Thy pleasure which of Thy great mercy has chosen me Thy servant and handmaid to feed Thy people and Thine inheritance; so teach me, I humbly beseech Thee, Thy Word and so strengthen me with Thy grace that I may feed Thy people with a faithful and a true heart, and rule them prudently with power, O Lord ... Grant me, O Lord, a listening ear to hear Thee and a hungry soul to long after Thy Word. Endue me with Thy heavenly Spirit. Give me Thy Spirit of wisdom that I may understand Thee. Give me Thy Spirit of truth, that I may know Thee ...

> Since all things in this world, both heaven and earth, shall pass and perish and Thy Word alone endureth forever, engraft, O most Gracious Lord Christ, this Thy Word of grace and life so in my heart that from hence forth I neither follow after feigned comforts in worldly power, neither distract my mind to transitory pleasures, nor occupy my thoughts in vain delights, but that carefully seeking Thee where Thou showest Thyself in Thy Word, I may surely find Thee to my comfort and everlastingly enjoy Thee to my salvation.

> Create therefore in me, O Lord, a new heart and so renew my spirit within me that Thy law may be my study, Thy truth my delight, Thy Church my care, Thy people my crown, Thy righteousness my pleasure ... Thy gospel my kingdom, and Thy salvation my bliss and my glory .... Which, O merciful Father grant for the merit of Thy Son Jesus Christ, to whom with the Holy Ghost be rendered all praise and glory forever, amen.[27]

When I think on my ways, I turn my feet to your testimonies;
—Psalm 119:59—

THE PLEASANT FIELDS OF HOLY SCRIPTURE

The reign of England's Queen Elizabeth I, who reigned 1558-1603, is sometimes called a golden age in England's history. It was an age of exploration and expansion, with Francis Drake sailing around the world and the first English colonies being established in America. There was a renaissance in art and literature, with the flourishing of Shakespeare. Elizabeth was also able to keep a relative peace as compared with the political and religious turmoil of earlier reigns.

Throughout her long life, Scripture frequently provided strength to Elizabeth. She had been taught Scripture as a child and could read the Scriptures in Latin, Greek, and French, as well as English. As a teenager, she translated religious works into other languages, including some by John Calvin. Her writings throughout her life reflect Scripture. When imprisoned in the Tower of London under Mary, her prayers reflected Matthew 6:25, "do not be anxious about your life, what you will eat or what you will drink, nor about your body, what you will put on." When she later learned Mary had died and she would become queen, she quoted Psalm 118:23, "This is the Lord's doing; it is marvelous in our eyes." As ruler, she looked to King Solomon and followed him in praying for an understanding mind to govern the people. (I Kings 3:9) When the Spanish Armada went down to defeat, Elizabeth saw England's deliverance comparable to the Israelites deliverance from Pharaoh in walking across the dry bed of the Red Sea.[28]

Elizabeth reflected her love of Scriptures when she wrote,

I walk many times in the pleasant fields of the Holy Scriptures, where I pluck the goodlisome herbs of sentences by pruning, eat them by reading, digest them by musing, and lay them up, at length in the high seat of memory by gathering them together, so that, having tasted their sweetness, I may less perceive the bitterness of life.[29]

Let my cry come before you, O Lord;
give me understanding according to your word!
—Psalm 119:169—

APRIL 1
THE BEAR BIBLE

Casidoro de Reina (1520-1594) was a devout monk in the San Isidro Monastery in Seville. After becoming acquainted with the Waldenseans and the writings of Luther and the Reformers, the Superior of the monastery, de Reina, and several of the other monks accepted the biblical teaching of justification by faith. When the Spanish Inquisition became suspicious of the teachings in the monastery, Reina and ten other monks fled to Frankfurt. The Inquistion still threatened, so Reina fled to London, where he briefly pastored a church of Spanish refugees, and then to Antwerp, and back to Frankfurt!

While in London, Reina began a translation of the Bible into Spanish. Published in Switzerland in 1569, Reina's translation was the first complete Bible printed in Spanish. The first Spanish Bible translated from the Greek and the Hebrew, Reina's Bible forms the basis of all later Spanish trans-lations. Printed by the Bavarian printer Mattias Appiarius, whose name means "bee-keeper," the title page has an engraving of a bear trying to reach a container of honeycombs in a tree. Some saw this as a pictorial allusion to Psalm 119: 103, "How sweet are your words to my taste, sweeter than honey to my mouth."

In 1551, the Inquisition had prohibited the translation of the Bible into Castilian romance or any other vulgar tongue. Under the Inquisitions decree, many of Reina's Bibles were confiscated, destroyed, and never made it to Spain. However, Reina's translation was widely used by Spanish refugees in other lands.

Whoever belongs to God hears what God says.
The reason you do not hear is that you do not belong to God.
—John 8:47—

THE FIRST AND LAST ANCHOR

In his dying days, John Knox (c. 1513-1572), who helped establish the Reformation in Scotland, asked for Scriptures to be read to him. He asked for readings from the Psalms and Isaiah 53, the moving Scripture that looks forward to Jesus being "wounded for our transgressions" and "crushed for our iniquities." He also asked for reading from I Corinthians 15, on the meaning of Jesus' resurrection. Then he asked his wife to read him from John 17, where "I cast my first ancre [anchor]."[1] This prayer of Jesus addressed the Father on behalf of not only the disciples, but believers down through the ages: "I do not ask for these only, but also for those who will believe in me through their word, that they may all be one ..." (John 17:20). Knox was deeply moved when he first realized Jesus had actually been praying for him, as well as all future believers. In Jesus' prayer, Knox understood that salvation is by God's grace; justification is by faith and in Christ, for Jesus prayed, "I have manifested your name to the people whom you gave me out of the world, yours they were, and you gave them to me, and they have kept your word." (John 17:7)

The Scripture which had been Knox's "first anchor" also was important, thirty years later, as his last anchor in death. After hearing John 17, Knox said, "Is not that a comfortable chapter?" Six hours later, Knox breathed his last on earth, to enter the presence of his Savior.

Let your steadfast love come to me, O Lord,
your salvation according to your promise;
—Psalm 119:41—

APRIL 3
FIRST ENGLISH BIBLE IN AMERICA

Though sailors have the reputation for being a rowdy lot, during the days of English exploration in the sixteenth century, daily prayers and psalm singing were regular features of life aboard ship. In 1579, while Sir Francis Drake was overhauling his ship the *Golden Hind* on California's coast before sailing further around the world, the natives were friendly and curious. They had never seen Europeans before. Three days after they arrived, however, the English witnessed a mutilation rite that so horrified Drake he ordered his friends to prayers. All the Englishmen lifted their eyes and hands to Heaven to show the natives where God was. They also sang some psalms and began reading the Scriptures. The natives gathered around attentively and were greatly affected. This was America's first encounter with the English Bible. Amazingly, the English thought that reading the Bible in English to natives who understood no English could still be effective.

Five years after Drake's stopover in California, Thomas Harriot sailed with Sir Walter Raleigh and established the colony of Roanoke, Virginia. In 1588, Harriot wrote the first English treatise on the new world, entitled Brief and True Report. In his report, Harriot described his explorations of the land along Chesapeake Bay, noting that:

> Many times and in every town where I came, according as I was able, I made declaration of the contents of the bible, that therein was set forth the true and only God, and his mighty works, that therein was contained the true doctrine of salvation through Christ ... and although I told them the book materially and of itself was not of any such virtue, as I thought they did conceive, but only the doctrine therein contained; yet would many be glad to touch it, to embrace it, to kiss it, to hold it to their breasts and heads, and stroke over all their body with it, to show their hungry desire of that knowledge which was spoken of.[2]

Other early accounts also indicate that even before the natives could clearly understand the words and meaning of the Bible, they had a respect and awe for the Bible. By the manner and actions of the Englishmen themselves, they could tell the Bible was a special, holy book.

You search the Scriptures because you think that in them you have eternal life;
and it is they that bear witness about me ...
—John 5:39—

MORE WORDS ABOUT THE WORD, FROM THE 16TH THROUGH 18TH CENTURIES

In these words about the Scripture from centuries ago, what importance is ascribed to Scripture?

Thomas Cooper (1517-1594), Vice-Chancellor of Oxford and Bishop of Lincoln and Winchester: "What ground shall our faith have if we leave the word of God?[3]

Martin Chemnitz (1522-1586), Lutheran theologian: "It is through the word that Christ deals with us; it is through the word that He offers Himself and His blessings to us and imparts Himself to our souls."

Richard Hooker (1554-1600), English Puritan: "The general end both of Old and New Testaments is one; the difference between them consisting in this, that the Old did make wise by teaching salvation through Christ that should come, the New by teaching that Christ the Saviour is come; and that Jesus, whom the Jews did crucify, and whom God did raise from the dead, is He."

Joseph Caryl (1602-1672), English Puritan: "He doth not say, the word was a light unto his eyes, but a light unto his feet. The word is a light to the eyes: that is, it shineth to the understanding; yet the word is sometimes a light unto our feet when it is not a light unto our eye; that is, God will have us to go where we cannot see our way."

John Milton (1608-1674), English poet: "We reverence the martyrs, but rely only upon the Scriptures."

Matthew Hale (1609-1676), Chief Justice of England, to his children: "Every morning read seriously and reverently a portion of the Holy Scriptures, and acquaint yourselves with the history and doctrine thereof. It is a book full of light and wisdom, will make you wise to eternal life, and furnish you with directions and principles to guide and order your life safely and prudently. There is no book like the Bible for excellent learning wisdom, and use.[4]

Massillon (1663-1742), Bishop of Clermont: "On the histories which have been left us by men, we see nothing but the agency of man. They are men who obtain the victories, who take towns, who subdue kingdoms, who dethrone sovereigns, to elevate themselves to the supreme power. God appears in no part; men are the sole actors of all these things. But in the history of the holy Books, it is God alone who performs the whole. God alone causes kings to reign, places them upon their thrones, or deposes them again. It is God alone who opposes the enemy, who sacks towns, who disposes of kingdoms and empires, who gives peace or excites war. God alone appears in sacred history: it is He, I may so speak, who is the sole hero. The kings and conquerors of the earth appear but as the ministers of His will. In short, these divine books unfold the ways of Providence. God, who conceals Himself in the other events recorded in our histories, seems to reveal Himself in these and it is in this book alone that we ought to learn to read the other histories which men have left us."

Robert Boyle (1626-1691), scientist: "I use the Scripture, not as an arsenal to be resorted to only for arms and weapons to defend this part, or to defeat its enemies, but as a matchless temple, where I delight to be to contemplate the beauty the symmetry, and the magnificence of the structure, and to increase my awe and to excite my devotion to the Deity there preached and adored."

William Romaine (1714-1795), English evangelical: "In books I converse with men, in the Bible I converse with God."

... put away all filthiness and rampant wickedness
and receive with meekness the implanted word,
which is able to save your souls.
—James 1:21—

THE INCOMPARABLE TREASURE
OF THE HOLY SCRIPTURES

The Geneva Bible was the most-used Bible for the earliest English settlers in America. Most Geneva Bible printings after 1578 had the following poem and prayer.

Of the Incomparable Treasure of the Holy Scriptures,
with a prayer for the true use of the same

Isa. 12:3 & 49:10	Here is the Spring where waters flow,
Rev. 21:16 & 22:17	to quench our heat of sin;
Jer. 33:15	Here is the Tree where truth doth grow,
Psa. 119:160	to lead our lives therein:
Rev. 2:7 & 22:2	Here is the Judge that stints the strife,
	when men's devices fail:
John 6:35	Here is the Bread that feeds the life,
	that death cannot assail.
Luke 2:10	The tidings of Salvation dear,
	comes to our ears from hence:
	The Fortress of our Faith is here,
Eph. 6:16	and shield of our defence.
	Then be not like the hog, that hath
Mal. 7:6	a pearl at his desire,
	And takes more pleasure of the trough
II Pet. 2:22	and wallowing in the mire.
	Read not this book, in any case,
	but with a single eye:
	Read not, but first desire God's grace,
Psa. 119:27, 73	to understand thereby.
	Pray still in faith, with this respect,
Jude 20	to fructify therein,
	That knowledge may bring this effect,
Psa. 119:11	to mortify thy sin.
	Then happy thou, in all thy life,
John 1:8	whatso to thee befalls:
Psa. 1:1,2	Yea, double happy shalt thou be,
Psa. 94:12, 13	when God by death thee calls.

O gracious God and most merciful Father, which hast vouchsafed us the rich and precious jewel of thy holy Word, assist us with thy Spirit, that it may be written in our heart to our everlasting comfort, to reform us, to renew us according to thine own image, to build us up, and edify us into the perfect building of thy Christ, sanctifying and increasing in us all heavenly virtues. Grant this, O heavenly Father, for Jesus Christ's sake. Amen

Behold, I long for your precepts; in your righteousness give me life.
—Psalm 119: 40—

LIVING BY FAITH IN THE WORD OF GOD

In his work on *How to Live*, Elizabethan Puritan William Perkins (1558–1602) examined the implications of Habakkuk 2:4, "the just shall live by his faith." He saw that living by faith requires knowing and trusting God's Word:

> For this is the first and principal honor of God to believe him upon his bare Word; and thereby to make a confession of the truth of God; This the devil knew right well; and therefore the first thing that he sought to overthrow in *Adam* was his faith in God's Word: and the scope of the first temptation, ... [of] Christ, was to overthrow that faith & confidence he had in his Father, saying, *If thou be the Son of God, command that these stones be made bread...*
>
> That this obedience, which we give to God by trusting his very Word, may be right obedience, it must have fixed conditions. First of all, it must be *absolute*: for we must (as it were) shut up our own eyes, and simply without any more ado trust God upon his bare and naked Word, and suffer ourselves to be led by it. ... God must be trusted, though that which be faith be against reason and experience. Thus, *Abraham* believed God *against* all human hope. *Rom.* 4.18. The second condition is, that this obedience must be *sincere* for we must trust God's word for itself, because it is God's word ... They which are as the stony ground, receive God's Word and rejoice in it: and yet afterward in time of temptation go awry. The reason is, because they *receive the Word, and rejoice in it*, not properly for itself, but in respect of honor, profit, or pleasure, which they look to reap thereby .... The third condition is, that we must trust God not in part but *in his whole Word*: and therefore many fail in their faith, that are content to trust him in his promise of mercy and salvation, but choose not to believe him in his commandments and threats. The fourth condition is, that we must trust God in his Word, *with all our hearts*, that it may deep root and be an *ingrafted Word*. It is not sufficient for us to have a taste of the good Word of God, and to receive it with joy, unless we thoroughly & soundly build and rely ourselves upon it. The fifth condition is, that this trusting of God must be with an *honest heart*, that is, with a heart which there is a distinct purpose not to sin, but in all things to do the will of God. The good hearers are they which receive the Word *with an honest and good heart*, Luke *8.15*. ... in the Word three things are to be known, *Precepts* or commandments, because they teach obedience; *threatenings*, because they restrain disobedience; *promises*, because they serve to confirm us in our obedience.[5]

Then they believed his words; they sang his praise.
—Psalm 106:12—

APRIL 7

THE BIBLE IN JAMESTOWN, THE FIRST PERMANENT ENGLISH SETTLEMENT IN AMERICA

In 1607, 144 men aboard the *Susan Constant*, the *Godspeed*, and the *Discovery* sailed from England to America with a 3-fold mandate from the sponsoring London Company: find gold and precious metals; discover a water route to the Pacific; and bring the Christian gospel to the natives.

When the Jamestown colony was established, two English Bible versions or translations were brought to the colony—the Bishops Bible and the Geneva Bible. Captain Argoll told of a trading expedition along the coast in 1610 during which a native chief came aboard the ship to warm himself by the ship's fire. The chief watched an Englishman reading a Bible as if he would like to do the same. Captain Argoll turned to the illustration of creation at the front of the Bishops Bible and explained the Bible's account of creation to the chief. The records of the London Company frequently included Scripture quotations. These all are from the Geneva Bible, the translation popular with the English Puritans. John Rolfe, who later married Pocahontas, was probably a reader of the Geneva Bible. In his letter to Sir Thomas Dale on whether he should marry Pocahontas, Rolfe included Biblical references which shaped his thinking on the issue. Pocahontas herself was instructed in the Christian faith by Rev. Whitaker, who regularly quoted the Geneva Bible in his letters and sermons. This would have been the English Bible with which Pocahontas was familiar.

Put false ways far from me and graciously teach me your law!
—Psalm 119:29—

SHAKESPEARE AND THE BIBLE

As one of the world's greatest writers, William Shakespeare (1564-1616) touched on every human emotion and portrayed every possible personality, often using Biblical quotations and allusions in developing his characters. *Hamlet* and *Othello* each have 50-60 conscious Biblical references, while other plays have somewhat less. A conservative count is that there are 1200 Biblical references in Shakespeare's plays. Jesus' parable of the prodigal son is Shakespeare's most frequent Biblical reference, while the story of brothers Cain and Abel is the second most quoted, appearing more than 25 times. Some scholars think Shakespeare must have had the opening chapters of Genesis memorized, because they are referenced so frequently in his plays.

In Shakespeare's day, people were familiar with the Bible from the regular reading of the Bible in the church services. Following the schedule in the Anglican Book of Common Prayer, the New Testament was read three times a year and the Old Testament once. The Bible version Shakespeare consistently used was the Geneva Bible, the Bible much loved by the Puritans and followers of the Reformation. Shakespeare would have used the Geneva Bible in the Stratford Grammar school, where he was assigned passages to translate into Latin and back again into English.

Sometimes Shakespeare refers to a specific Scripture. When Horatio counsels Hamlet to call off a duel with Laertes, Hamlet intends to continue on, saying, "There is a special providence in the fall of a sparrow," alluding to Jesus' words in Matthew 10:29-31. At other times, Shakespeare associates one of his characters with a biblical figure. Lady Macbeth washing her hands to clear herself of the murder of Duncan is reminiscent of Pilate washing his hands to remove any guilt of Jesus' condemnation. Macbeth consulting the witch is reminiscent of King Saul consulting the witch of Endor.

Shakespeare's biblical references and allusions added depth to his plays. His audience was steeped in the biblical text, and the drama was enriched and deepened by these biblical references.

I am your servant; give me understanding,
that I may know your testimonies!
—Psalm 119:125—

APRIL 9
THE BIBLE AND LITERATURE

The Bible has influenced the culture and life of the people wherever it has gone. This can be seen in English literature. Every play of Shakespeare's contains biblical quotes and allusions throughout. For example, the title of his play "Measure for Measure" is taken from Matthew 7:2, "with what measure ye mete, it shall be measured to you." The play explores the themes of law and grace, justice and mercy.

John Steinbeck's novel *East of Eden* similarly takes its title from the Bible. Genesis 4:16 says, "And Cain went out from the presence of the Lord, and dwelt in the land of Nod, on the east of Eden." Steinbeck took the story of Adam, Eve, Cain, and Abel and placed it in the Edenic fields of pre-World War I California.

Dante's *Divine Comedy* is an epic journey through Hell, Purgatory, and Paradise which shows what sin does to the human soul and how God's mercy frees us from sin. Milton's *Paradise Lost* is a poetic retelling of the fall of Satan and the fall of man, a dramatic reenactment of this cosmic conflict. For both poets, Scripture provided the framework of much of their thought.

In earlier times, if a family owned two books, they would be the Bible and John Bunyan's *Pilgrim's Progress*. Bunyan's allegory of the Christian's journey to the Heavenly City is immersed in Scripture. Charles Spurgeon said of Bunyan:

> Read anything of his, and you will see that it is almost like reading the Bible itself. He had read it till his very soul was saturated with Scripture; and, though his writings are charmingly full of poetry, yet he cannot give us his *Pilgrim's Progress*—that sweetest of all prose poems—without continually making us feel and say, "Why, this man is a living Bible!" Prick him anywhere—his blood is Bibline, the very essence of the Bible flows from him. He cannot speak without quoting a text, for his very soul is full of the Word of God.[6]

Your testimonies are my heritage forever,
for they are the joy of my heart.
—Psalm 119:111—

THE HAMPTON COURT CONFERENCE AND THE KING JAMES VERSION

There was great hope and anticipation in England when King James VI of Scotland prepared to become King James I of England. As the King moved south into England on the way to his coronation, he was presented with a petition signed by over 1000 Puritans requesting many religious reforms. The Puritans also wanted a uniform translation of the Bible used in all the churches. To consider these requests James called a conference to be held at his Hampton Court Palace. Though most of the Puritan requests were denied, the Hampton Court Conference did agree to a new Bible translation. On January 17, 1604, a motion was carried "… that a translation be made of the whole Bible, as consonant as can be to the original Hebrew and Greek …, to be used in all Churches of England in time of divine service."[7]

The Hampton Court Conference appointed fifty-four scholars to produce a new translation. The scholars included Anglicans, Puritans, linguists, theologians, clergy and laymen. This was a national undertaking without any special interest group in control, and the scholars were able to build upon a century of Bible translation work in England, revising the earlier translations from the Hebrew and Greek texts.

Amazingly, the King James Version is the product of committees. The translators were organized into six committees or companies—two each at Westminster, University of Oxford, and University of Cambridge. The work of the three committees was reviewed by a final committee which read the translation aloud, contributing to the eloquent language and later influence of the work.

By 1611 the translation was complete. This King James Version became a major influence in forming the Christianity and molding the language of English-speaking people around the world for four centuries; its influence continues to this day.

All Scripture is breathed out by God and profitable for teaching,
for reproof, for correction, and for training in righteousness …
— II Timothy 3:16—

APRIL 11
THE KING JAMES BIBLE

The 1611 King James Bible included a Dedication to King James and a preface giving the history and method of the Bible translation as well as encouraging the study of the Scriptures. The work of translating the Scriptures was described as something

> That openeth the window, to let in the light; that breaketh the shell, that we may eat the kernel; that putteth aside the curtain, that we might look into the most Holy place; that removeth the cover of the well, that we may come by the water ... Indeed without translation into the vulgar [common] tongue [language], the unlearned are but like children at Jacob's well (which is deep) without a bucket or something to draw with.

No one in 1611 could have imagined the global importance the English language would have 400 years later—neither King James who authorized the new translation of the Bible into English nor the 54 translators themselves. When the King James Version was first published in 1611, there were four million English speaking people, almost all living on the island nation of Great Britain, at the edge of Europe. Today, 400 years later, English is a global language with two billion English-speaking people and 70 nations with English as the majority language. Wherever English speakers have gone on the globe—and into space—they have taken with them the King James Version of the Bible.

The King James Version continued to be the most prominent English Bible translation for well over 350 years and remains an important translation in use today. However, two factors have led to the need for contemporary Bible translations. First, over the centuries, the English language has changed both in the spelling and meaning of words, making the King James Bible difficult for many to understand. Second, discoveries of Greek and Hebrew manuscripts centuries older than those used by the King James translators allow scholars to translate from a more accurate Biblical text.

I will delight in your statutes;
I will not forget your word.
—Psalm 119:16—

HIDING THE WORD IN YOUR HEART

Throughout the Scriptures we are given examples of people who trusted God's promises in their lives. Hebrews 11 is an entire chapter noting those who walked by faith in God's Word. In 1618, Puritan clergyman Nicholas Byfield (1579-1622) published *The Promises: or a Treatise Showing a Godly Christian May Support His Heart with Comfort Against all the Distresses Which by Reason of Any Afflictions or Temptations Can Befall Him in This Life* (those old titles tell you everything about the book!). In this work, Byfield encouraged the memorization of Scripture and gave pointers for trusting the promises of the Word of God:

> First, when we come to the promises, we must renounce our own merits, and all opinion of our own worthiness, and acknowledge from our hearts that all the grace we find in the promises is in and through Jesus Christ. All the promises are yes and amen through Him, and only in Him.

> Second, when we have the promises laid open before us, we must believe them and apply them to ourselves or else they will do us no good.

> Third, we must be further careful to "hide them in our hearts" [Psalm 119:11], and to commit them to memory, that we may be often thinking of them, and musing upon them. It will not serve the turn that we have them written in the Bible, or in our notebooks, but we must get them written in our hearts too. We must be at pains to acquaint ourselves distinctly with them, and to fill our heads with stores of them.

> Fourth, when anything ails us, we must flee to God for refuge and cast the "anchor of our hope" [Heb. 6:18] upon them that God Himself may see that our hearts are bent to trust upon His Word.

> Fifth, we must never cast away our confidence in them, but wait with patience and not limit God to the time, or manner, or means of accomplishment, but hold fast to God, as Scripture says in many places, especially Heb. 10:36 and Rom. 4:22.

> Sixth, in short, we must look to it that we are not slothful and idle, and such as will not be at pains to study and commit to memory, and rest upon these glorious comforts; but we must follow them which through faith and patience did inherit the promises (Heb. 6:22).[8]

The law of his God is in his heart; his steps do not slip.
— Psalm 37:31—

APRIL 13

PURITANS ON THE BIBLE

After Henry VIII separated England from the Roman Church, establishing himself as the head of the Church of England, many desired more reforms in the Church of England, following the ideas of Martin Luther and John Calvin on the continent. Those who wanted to purify the Church of England of unbiblical practices and teachings became known as Puritans. The Puritans not only greatly influenced the course of England during the 16th and 17th centuries, but also America, where many Puritans immigrated. Foundational to Puritan ideas was that the Scripture is the rule for life, applicable to every area of private and public life. Following are some statements about the Scriptures by leading Puritans:

John Cotton: "FEED upon the WORD." "Let not a day ordinarily pass wherein you will not read some portion of it." "The rule according to which conscience is to proceed is what God has revealed in the Sacred Scriptures"

Richard Baxter: "Love, reverence, read, study, obey and stick close to the Scripture"

John Owen: "Pin not your faith upon men's opinions; the Bible is the touchstone." "The whole authority of the Scripture ... depends solely on its divine original...The Scripture hath all its authority from its Author." The Bible is "a stable, infallible revelation of [God's] mind and will."

Thomas Watson: "Think in every line that God is speaking to you."

John Eliot: "The writings of the Bible are the very words of God."

Edward Reynolds: The entire Bible is "written by the Spirit of truth, which cannot lie nor deceive."

Samuel Rutherford: "The Word of God is infallible."

Richard Sibbes: "There is not anything or any condition that befalls a Christian in this life but there is a general rule in the Scripture for it, and this rule is quickened by example, because it is a practical knowledge."

Thomas Cartwright: The Bible "contains the direction of ... whatever things can fall into any part of man's life."

William Perkins: The Bible "comprehendeth many holy sciences ... ethics ... economics (a doctrine of governing a family) ... politics (a doctrine of the right administration of a common weal) ... academy (the doctrine of governing schools well)."

Increase Mather: "But though we ought to reverence the blessed Bible above all other books, yet we may not worship it, but the author of it only."[9]

Lord, to whom shall we go? You have the words of eternal life…
—John 6:68—

APRIL 14

READING SCRIPTURES LIKE THE PURITANS

J.I. Packer likened the 16th- and 17th-century Puritans to California redwoods—as the redwoods tower over all other trees with massive, strong trunks, many of which have been burned and survived the fires, "so the mature holiness and seasoned fortitude of the great Puritans shine before us, overtopping the stature of the majority of Christians in most eras."[10] Most important to the Puritan believer was the Bible, the very words of God to man. To ignore or neglect God's written words was the greatest insult to God,

> conversely, there could be no truer act of homage to him than to prize it and pore over it, and then to live out and give out its teaching. Intense veneration for Scripture, as the living word of the living God, and a devoted concern to know and do all that it prescribes, was Puritanism's hallmark.[11]

Packer noted six principles which characterized the Puritans' interpretation of the Scriptures. First, the Puritans interpreted the Scriptures literally and naturally, not allegorically as had the medieval theologians. Secondly, since Scripture was the product of one divine mind, it was consistent and harmonious; Scripture should be interpreted with Scripture. Thirdly, Scripture is a book about God and should be interpreted from a God-centered standpoint. Fourthly, since Christ is the true subject of all Scripture, it should be read as bearing witness to Christ. Fifthly, as a book of spiritual experience, Scripture should be interpreted practically. Finally, Scripture should be interpreted with a faithful application. In keeping with these principles, when reading the Scriptures, six questions should be asked of each passage:

1. What do these words actually mean?
2. What light do other Scriptures throw on this text?
3. What truths does it teach about God, and about man in relation to God?
4. How are these truths related to the saving work of Christ, and what light does the gospel of Christ throw upon them?
5. What experiences do these truths delineate, or explain, or seek to create or cure? For what practical purpose do they stand in Scripture?
6. How do they apply to myself and others in our own actual situation? To what present human condition do they speak, and what are they telling us to believe and do?[12]

I delight to do your will, O my God;
your law is within my heart. —Psalm 40:8—

TEACHER OF ALL TRUTH

When the French philosopher Voltaire spoke about Francis Bacon to a French audience in 1733, he called him the "Father of the Scientific Method," and so Bacon has often been called. Francis Bacon (1561-1626) encouraged scientific studies through close observation and inductive reasoning, rather than Aristotelean philosophical speculation. Bacon believed the close observation of nature is an important way to better understand God's creation. He said that there are two books which revealed God—Scripture and the book of nature. In a detailed personal confession, Bacon wrote that he believed that

> Jesus, the Lord, became in the flesh a sacrifice and a sacrifice for sin; a satisfaction and price paid to the justice of God; a meriter of Glory and Kingdom; a pattern of all righteousness; a preacher of the Word, which Himself was; a finisher of the ceremonies; a cornerstone to remove the separation between Jew and Gentile; an intercessor for the Church; a Lord of nature in His miracles; a conqueror of death and the power of darkness in His resurrection; and that He fulfilled the whole counsel of God, performing all His sacred offices, and anointing on earth, accomplishing the whole work of redemption and restitution of man to a state superior to the angels, whereas the state of man by creation was inferior; and reconciled and established all things according to the eternal will of the Father.

He further believed that

> … the Word of God, whereby His will is revealed, continued in revelation and tradition with Moses; and that the Scriptures were from Moses' time to the time of the Apostles and Evangelists; in whose ages, after the coming of the Holy Ghost, the teacher of all truth, the book of Scripture was shut and closed, so as to receive no new addition, and the Church hath no power after the Scriptures to teach or command anything contrary to the written Word.[13]

The wise men shall be put to shame;
they shall be dismayed and taken;
behold, they have rejected the word of the Lord,
so what wisdom is in them?
—Jeremiah 8:9—

APRIL 16
THE PILGRIMS' BIBLE

Eight large paintings in the rotunda of the U.S. Capitol depict key events in the early history of America. One of the paintings is "Embarkation of the Pilgrims" by Robert Weir. The Pilgrims are shown kneeling on the deck of their ship in 1620, as they depart for America from Holland. William Brewster holds an open Bible, while Pastor John Robinson leads all in prayer. The open Bible was the Geneva Bible, favored by the Pilgrims and early Puritans.

That Bible had its roots in persecution. After Mary Tudor became Queen of England in 1553, she initiated persecution against those who would not follow Roman Catholicism. Hundreds of English Protestants fled to the continent for safety, many settling in Geneva, Switzerland. Under the leadership of William Farel and John Calvin, Geneva had become an intellectual and spiritual center for European Protestants. One of the English exiles was William Whittingham, a Hebrew and Greek scholar from Oxford. Whittingham and others began a completely revised translation of the English Bible. At the same time back in England, almost three hundred Protestants were executed by "Bloody" Mary. When Mary died in 1558, there was much joy, and many of the Geneva exiles returned to England. The new Bible translation begun in Geneva was published in 1560 and dedicated to the new Queen Elizabeth.

The Geneva Bible was unique among English Bibles in several ways. It was the first to be translated from the Greek and Hebrew. It was the first to be printed in Roman letters rather than in heavy Gothic black letter. It was the first to have numbered verses. It was also the first to use italics for words the translators added because of English idiom, but which were not in the original. Published in a smaller size (6 ½" x 9 ¾") and for a moderate price, it was designed to be read by ordinary individuals. Notes were added to explain difficult passages. Additional study aides were included at the back of the Bible.

Sometimes the Geneva Bible is called "the Breeches Bible" because Genesis 3:7 is translated "and they sewed fig tree leaves together and made themselves breeches." 150 editions of the Geneva Bible were printed between 1560 and 1644, and for three quarters of a century it was the household Bible of a large section of English-speaking Protestants. It was the version used by Shakespeare, John Bunyan, and the earliest settlers to America. In England and America, the Geneva Bible helped form a Christianity which made a permanent impact on Anglo-American culture.

Your word is a lamp to my feet and a light to my path.
—Psalm 119:105—

A PILGRIM LEARNING HEBREW

Most of what we know about the 17ᵗʰ century settlement of the Pilgrims in Plymouth, Massachusetts comes from *Of Plymouth Plantation*, the history written by Governor William Bradford (1590-1657), who came over on the *Mayflower* and was the long-time governor of the colony. In his narrative of the establishment of Plymouth, Bradford provides an account of God's Providence throughout the colony's many trials as well as successes. Scripture references, quoted from the Geneva Bible, are woven throughout.

After Plymouth became part of the Massachusetts Bay Colony, Bradford's priceless historical manuscript was kept in the tower of the Old South Meeting House in Boston. When British troops occupied Boston during the American Revolution, the manuscript disappeared. For a century, no one knew its whereabouts. Finally, the missing manuscript was discovered in the library of the Bishop of London and was eventually returned to the Governor of Massachusetts in 1897.

Interestingly, on the blank fly leaves before the historical narrative of the colony are eight pages of Hebrew, mostly a Hebrew-English vocabulary of over 1000 Hebrew words plus 25 passages in biblical Hebrew. At the beginning of these notes Bradford movingly wrote:

> Though I am growne aged, yet I have had a longing desire to see with my own eyes, something of that most ancient language, and holy tongue, in which the Law, and oracles of God, were writen; and in which God, and angels, spake to the holy patriarchs, of old time; and what names were given to things, from the creation. And though I canote attaine to much herein, yet I am refreshed, to have seen some glimpse hereof; (as Moses saw the Land of Canan afar of) my aime and desire is, to see how the words, and phrases lye in the holy texts; and to discerne somewhat of the same for my owne contente.[14]

He declares his word to Jacob, his statutes and rules to Israel.
He has not dealt thus with any other nation; they do not know his rules.
—Psalm 147:19-20—

APRIL 18

THE HEAVENS DECLARE HIS GLORY

As a boy, Johannes Kepler (1571-1630) was fascinated by the great comet of 1577 and the lunar eclipse of 1580. As he matured, he increasingly glorified God for His creation. Kepler began studying theology, intending to become a Lutheran minister. But at age 23, he was offered a position teaching mathematics and astronomy. He accepted, intending to continue his ministerial training later. Kepler believed Providence moved him into scientific studies for God's glory. Eventually, Kepler developed laws of planetary motion. These were foundational to Isaac Newton's later description of gravity.

Kepler believed that God created the world in an intelligible plan, according to mathematical laws, which man can uncover by his reason. One of many Biblical references and praises to God in Kepler's *The Secret of the Universe (Mysterium Cosmographicum)* is a virtual paraphrase of Psalm 8:

> Great God, Creator of the Universe, and our eternal power, how great thy fame in every corner of the whole wide world! How great thy glory, which flies wondrously above the far flung ramparts of the heavens with rushing wings! ... Yes, to believe thy Godhead is within this spacious sphere, let me look up astonished at thy achievement of this mighty heaven, the work of the great Craftsman, miracles of thy strong hand; ... see how the Moon varies her path, her toils, how many stars thy hand has scattered over that boundless field. Great Builder of the Universe, what plea of the poor, humble, small inhabitant of this so tiny plot compelled thy care for his harsh troubles? Yet thou dost look down on his unworthiness, carry him up on high, a little lower than the gods, bestow great honors on him, crown his head nobly with diadem, appoint him king over the tokens of thy handiwork. Thou makest all that is above his head, the great spheres with their motions, bow before His genius. All creatures of the Earth ... by thy command he ... Great God, Creator of the Universe, and our eternal power, how great thy fame in every corner of the whole wide world.[15]

Kepler wrote,

> I declare hereby ... that I establish and build the foundation of my faith, by which I am emboldened to serve God, my Creator, in this world and to reach blessedness forever, exclusively on the most clear sayings of the written word of God, known for all times, in their original language.[16]

I remember your name in the night, O Lord, and keep your law.
—Psalm 119:55—

A CITY ON A HILL

In 1630, a fleet of eleven ships left England, carrying Puritans to America. They chose the hazards and difficulties of establishing a home in the New World rather than the growing political and religious oppression under King Charles. John Winthrop was a leader of this first wave of Puritan immigrants. On the voyage over, he gave an address summarizing their hopes, dreams, and aspirations. Weaving Scripture throughout his address, Winthrop said they were a city on a hill; that God was making a covenant with them. Winthrop urged them to love their neighbor, to care for posterity, and to love one another. He ended by exhorting the Puritans to follow the Lord's ways and not seek to "embrace this present world … , seeking great things for ourselves and our posterity." To avoid a breach of the covenant they had with God, Winthrop advised:

> Now the only way to avoid this shipwreck, and to provide for our posterity, is to follow the counsel of Micah, *to do justly, to love mercy, to walk humbly with our God.* [Micah 6:8] For this end, we must be knit together, in this work, as one man. We must entertain each other in brotherly affection. … We must delight in each other; make other's condition our own; rejoice together, labor and suffer together, always having before our eyes our commission and community in the work, as members of the same body. So shall we *keep the unity of the spirit in the bond of peace.* [Ephesians 4:3] The Lord will be our God, and delight to dwell among us, as his own people, and will command a blessing upon us in all our ways. So that we shall see much more of his wisdom, power, goodness, and truth, than formerly we have seen…when he shall make us a praise and a glory, that men shall say of succeeding plantations, 'The Lord make it likely that of *New England.*' For we must consider that we shall be as a City upon a hill. The eyes of all people are upon us [Matthew 5:15-16] … I shall shut up this discourse with that exhortation of Moses, that faithful servant of the Lord, in his last farewell to Israel (Deut. 30). *Beloved, there is now set before us life and good, Death and evil, in that we are commanded this day to love the Lord our God, and to love one another, to walk in his ways, and to keep his Commandments and his Ordinance and his Laws, and the articles of our Covenant with him…*let us choose life that we, and our seed may live, by obeying His voice and cleaving to Him, for He is our life and our prosperity.[17]

Oh that they had such a heart as this always,
to fear me and to keep all my commandments,
that it might go well with them and with their descendants forever!
—Deuteronomy 5:29—

APRIL 20

THE SAINTS SURE AND PERPETUAL GUIDE

Robert Bolton (1572-1631) was a scholar and preacher whose writings are very practical. In *The Saints Sure and Perpetual Guide*, he wrote on the many facets of the Scripture's importance:

> There is nothing proposed and handled in the Word of God, but things of greatest weight, and highest excellency: As, the infinite majesty, power, and mercy of God; the unspeakable love and strange sufferings of the Son of God, for our sakes; the mighty and miraculous working of the holy Spirit upon the souls of men. There is nothing in this treasury, but Orient Pearls, and rich Jewels; as promises of grace, spiritual comfort, confusion of sin, the triumph of godliness, refreshing of wearied souls, the beauty of Angels, the holiness of Saints, the state of Heaven, salvation of sinners, and everlasting life. What Swine are they, that neglecting these precious Pearls, root only in the Earth, wallow in worldly pleasures, feed upon vanities, transitory trash, and vanishing riches, which in their greatest need will *take them to their wings, like an Eagle, and fly into the Heavens?* Besides, the Word of God is only able to prepare us for true happiness in this world, and to possess us of it, in the world to come. It only begets in us a true, ... and universal holiness; *without which, none shall ever see the face of God,* or the glory of Heaven: for it is impossible, hereafter to live the life of glory and blessedness in Heaven, if we live not here the life of grace and sincerity in all our ways. It is called the *immortal Seed,* because it regenerates and renews us both in our Spirits, Souls and Bodies: *in our Spirits;* that is, in judgment, memory, & conscience: *in our Souls;* that is, in our will and affections: *in our Bodies;* that is, in every member. If the Prince of this world hath not blinded the eyes of our minds, ... that we be not reprobates, as concerning salvation, it only is able to enlighten our understandings, to rectify our wills, to sanctify our hearts, to mortify our affections, to set *David's Door* before our *lips, that we offend not with our tongues* [Psalm 141:3]; to set *Job's Door* before our eyes, *that they behold not vanity* [Job 31:1]; to manacle our hands & feet with the cords and bands of God's Law, that they do not walk or work wickedly: nay, and it is able to furnish and supply us with ... spiritual strength, to continue in all these good things, and in a godly course unto the end ... As before, this holy Word did translate us from the darkness of sin, into the light of grace; it can now much more easily, with joy and triumph, bring us, from the light of grace, to the light of immortality, and everlasting pleasures at God's right hand.[18]

How sweet are your words to my taste,
sweeter than honey to my mouth!
—Psalm 119:103—

SEARCH THE SCRIPTURES

When explaining the pattern of prayer found in the Lord's Prayer, William Gouge (1578-1653), minister in Black-Friars London, noted that the third petition in the Lord's Prayer, "thy will be done on earth as it is in Heaven," leads us to search the Scriptures. For, how else could we know the will of God to do it?

We ought to *search the Scripture* that we may know the will of God. For in them is the will of God contained. This is that searching to which knowledge and understanding is promised (Prov. 2:4-5). And for our better help therein, we ought diligently to frequent the Ministry of God's Word: as it is noted of the converted Jews, that they *continued steadfastly in the Apostles doctrine* (Acts 2:42)*:* whereby is declared that they were diligent and constant hearers of the Apostles, and also faithful professors and practisers of their doctrine. The former was the cause of the latter. The preaching of the Word is a great help to bring us to do the will of God: and that is in a double respect. First, because the will of God is thereby the more clearly, distinctly, and fully opened unto us. Secondly, because it is a means sanctified of God to breed credence to the truth of that which is revealed, and assistance therein: yea, and to bow our will, heart, and affections to yield thereto, and to be settled thereupon. In this respect saith the wisdom of God, which is especially set forth in the preaching of his Word, *Blessed is the man that heareth me: watching daily at my gates, waiting at the posts of my doors* (Proverbs 8:34).

We ought to *hide God's Word in our heart* (Psalm 119:11), we may not carelessly *let it slip.* So will all the fruit and benefit of our reading and hearing be lost, as meat or physicke [medicine] that is vomited up so soon as it is taken (Heb. 2:1). But by retaining God's Word in mind and memory, we shall be provoked the more to do God's will, and kept from transgressing it: to which purpose the Psalmist saith, *Thy word have I hid in mine heart, that I might not sin against thee* (Psa. 119:11*).* Wherefore *let the word of Christ dwell in you richly* (Col. 3:16).[19]

> *I will run in the way of your commandments*
> *when you enlarge my heart!*
> *—Psalm 119:32—*

APRIL 22
REMBRANDT: PAINTING THE SCRIPTURES

Rembrandt von Rijn, born July 15, 1606, was one of Europe's greatest paint-ers and certainly one of the most prominent Dutch painters of all times. Art patrons of 17th-century Holland favored paintings which instructed as well as pleased the eye. What painting could be more instructive than one based upon the Scriptures? It is not surprising then that more of Rembrandt's works were based on biblical texts than any other subject. Out of his enormous artistic production (about 600 paintings, 300 etches, and 1500 drawings), about 850 of Rembrandt's known works are from the Bible. Over 600 of his drawings of Biblical subjects survive. Many of these are on the backs of letters or bills and seem to be his personal meditations on Biblical subjects. In his paintings, Rembrandt showed ordinary people transformed by contact with God and Christ.

By the use of light, Rembrandt often concentrated on the inner thoughts and feelings of his subjects rather than simply their outer actions. Rembrandt's biblical paintings span the breadth of Scripture. Many are from Genesis, focus-ing on the faith displayed by the patriarchs. Heroes such as Samson, Saul, David, and Daniel, as well as the heroines Ruth and Esther are movingly portrayed. Jesus' birth, including the adoration of the shepherds, the adoration of the magi, and the flight into Egypt, were portrayed numerous times. Rembrandt painted a series of works on Jesus' parable of the Prodigal Son, showing the son squandering his inheritance, living among the pigs, and returning to his father. Rembrandt also portrayed the story of the Good Samaritan.

Numerous scenes of Jesus' Passion, from the Last Supper through His crucifixion and resurrection, are depicted. Rembrandt also did several works on the two disciples meeting Jesus on the road to Emmaus. In his *Raising of the Cross*, Rembrandt placed himself in a painter's beret at the foot of Jesus on the cross. Rembrandt recognized he was among those sinners for whom Jesus died.

I will meditate on thy precepts and have respect unto thy ways.
—Psalm 119:15—

A SCIENTIST AND BIBLE SCHOLAR

When he was thirteen, Robert Boyle (1627-91) woke in a fright during a furious storm and as the lightning flashed outside. Wondering if the day of judgment had come, the young Boyle also considered if his soul was ready for that day. Then and there, he resolved to live a life dedicated to serving Christ, a resolution he kept for the fifty years remaining in his life.

Boyle's family had great wealth, and he used it, as well as his time and talents, for the cause of Christ. He was a noted inventor, chemist, and physicist and a founder of the Royal Society. He knew Hebrew, Greek, Chaldee, and Syriac, and was a diligent Bible student. He also promoted Bible translations among many peoples, from Asia to North America, and personally financed the printing of Bibles in Malay, Irish, and Turkish. He wrote forty books on both scientific and theological subjects. The following are selections from his *Some Considerations Touching the Style of the Holy Scriptures*:

> The books of Scripture illustrate and expound each other; Genesis and the Apocalypse are in some things reciprocal commentaries; as in the mariner's compass the needle's extremity, though it seem to point purposely but at the north, doth yet at the same time discover both east and west, so do some texts of scripture guide us to the intelligence of others from 'which they are widely distant in the Bible, and seem so in the sense.[20]

> All is not Scripture that is in the Scripture; many wicked persons are introduced whose sayings the Holy Ghost does not adopt, but barely registers, nor does the Scripture affirm that which they said was true, but that it is true they said it. [21]

> When I find anything enjoined in Scripture, I then leave roving, and see where to cast anchor; I think it my part, without disputing thereon, to obey His orders; and acquiesce more in that imperious 'Thus saith the Lord' than in a whole dialogue of Plato, or an epistle of Seneca. I love to build my ethics as well as my creed upon the Rock; and esteeming nothing but the true, proper, and strict sense of the Scripture, and what is convincingly deducible from it, to be obligatory either as to faith or practice, it is no wonder if I study God's will most in that Book wherein alone I think it revealed.[22]

Everyone then who hears these words of mine and does them
will be like a wise man who built his house on the rock.
—Matthew 7:24—

THE BAY PSALM BOOK

The first book printed in America was a portion of Scripture—the book of Psalms. The Puritans of colonial New England were a singing people who included music in all their social gatherings. In church worship, the Puritans believed the Biblical Psalms were the best songs to sing.

New England's leaders concluded that earlier metrical versions of the psalms did not faithfully express the meaning of the original Hebrew. They sought to produce a psalter that was a more accurate translation as well as singable. A committee of approximately thirty clergymen prepared metrical English versions of the psalms. Translators included John Eliot, missionary to the Indians, and Massachusetts founders Richard Mather and John Cotton. The translators conscientiously avoided paraphrasing or adding to the psalms. Though the poetry is sometimes crude, the psalms are at least readily singable with a few set tunes. Psalm 23 began

> The Lord to me a shepherd is,
>   want therefore shall not I.
> He in the folds of tender grass,
>   doth cause me down to lie:
> To waters calm me gently leads
>   restore my soul doth he:
> He doth in paths of righteousness:
>   For his names sake lead me.

The Puritans imported a printing press from Holland for the printing of this first book in America. *The New England Psalm Book,* also called *The Bay Psalm Book,* went through several revisions and remained in use for over one hundred years. Independent congregations in England and Scotland also used the *Bay Psalm Book.* Portions were even incorporated into the Scottish Psalter.

My tongue will sing of your word,
for all your commandments are right.
—*Psalm 119:172*—

CALMING THE STORM

Many recognize John Owen (1616-1683) as the greatest pastor-theologian of the Puritan era. Born the year Shakespeare died and four years before the Pilgrims came to America, Owen lived at the center of the Puritan 17th century. Owen became noted as a theologian, was administrator at Christ Church, Oxford, and chaplain to Oliver Cromwell. With a warm pastoral heart, he was a prolific author of theological works which are still read and studied today.

Owen's father was a Puritan pastor, and Owen himself was a committed Puritan from his youth. Yet, he was often in spiritual distress, with no assurance that he belonged to Christ. One Sunday in 1642, when Owen was twenty-six, he and his cousin went to hear the noted Puritan preacher Edmund Calamy. When Calamy wasn't preaching that Sunday, the cousin wanted to leave, but Owen wanted to stay. The preacher was a country preacher of no renown, but his sermon on Jesus' words to the disciples after calming the storm, "Why are you afraid, O you of little faith?" (Matt. 8:26) brought a calm peace and assurance to Owen. His struggle with depression undoubtedly gave him a concern for others who had no peace with God, and Owen in his writings frequently referred to Jesus' calming words after the storm.

When the conscience of the believer asserts he is a child of God by faith, his own failings might cause him to doubt his acceptance with God. It is then, Owen wrote, the Spirit brings comfort to the soul through the promises of the Word:

> When the Lord Jesus at one word stilled the raging of the sea and wind, all that were with him knew that there was Divine power at hand, Matt. viii.25-27. And when the Holy Ghost by one word stills the tumults and the storms that are raised in the soul, giving an immediate calm and security, the soul knows his divine power, and rejoices in his presence... his bringing the promises of Christ to remembrance, glorifying him in our hearts, shedding abroad the love of God in us as to our spiritual estate and condition, sealing us to the day of redemption (being the earnest of our inheritance), anointing us with privileges as to their consolation, confirming our adoption, and being present with us in our supplications. Here is the wisdom of faith.[23]

Plead my cause and redeem me;
give me life according to your promise!
—Psalm 119:154—

APRIL 26
THE SOULDIERS POCKET BIBLE

The practice of distributing Bibles to soldiers in the field began with Oliver Cromwell during the 17th-century English Civil War. Cromwell insisted that his soldiers be "religious men" and "refrain from pillage and disorder, drunkenness and impiety." Since an entire Bible was too large for a soldier to conveniently carry, in 1643, *The Souldiers Pocket Bible* was distributed in Cromwell's Army. This was a 4½" x 7" book of 16 pages containing a collection of Scriptures "useful for any Christian to meditate upon, now in this miserable time of war." The verses were organized under headings such as "A Soldier must not do wickedly," "A Soldier must pray before he goes to fight," and "A Soldier must consider that sometimes God's people have the worst in battle as well as God's enemies."

In 1854, a Massachusetts antiquarian collector, George Livermore, found a copy of the 1643 *The Souldiers Pocket Bible* among a collection of pamphlets he bought. With the outbreak of the American Civil War, he reprinted 100 copies for private distribution. The American Tract Society soon reprinted copies of this Cromwellian pocket Bible for Union soldiers, replacing the Geneva Bible translation with the King James when citing verses. Printed on the title page was Oliver Cromwell's famous battle cry to his troops, "Trust in the Lord and keep your powder dry." The American Tract Society republished *The Soldier's Pocket Bible* in the Spanish American War and distributed 126,000 to soldiers in World War I. The World War I edition had a manuscript facsimile in handwriting:

Sagamore Hill   June 1st 1917
This is worth reading,
Comrade and friend.
Theodore Roosevelt

And take the helmet of salvation, and the sword of the Spirit,
which is the word of God!
—Ephesians 6:17—

WESTMINSTER ON SCRIPTURE

As part of the Reformation of the Church of England, in 1643, the English Parliament called for an assembly of clergymen to provide an exposition from Scripture of Christian theology for the Church. Over a period of five years, the group met at Westminster Abbey, producing a confession of faith and a Larger and Shorter Catechism. The Westminster Confession was later modified and adopted by various Congregationalists, Baptists, and Presbyterians and continues to be an important reference for Christian doctrine.

The first chapter was on the subject "Of the Holy Scripture:"

Although the light of nature and the works of creation and providence do so far manifest the goodness, wisdom, and power of God, as to leave men unexcusable,[24] yet are they not sufficient to give that knowledge of God, and of his will, which is necessary unto salvation.[25] Therefore it pleased the Lord, at sundry times, and in divers manners, to reveal himself, and to declare that his will unto his church,[26] and afterwards, for the better preserving and propagating of the truth, and for the more sure establishment and comfort of the church against the corruption of the flesh, and the malice of Satan and of the world, to commit the same wholly unto writing[27] which maketh the Holy Scripture to be most necessary, those former ways of God's revealing his will unto his people being now ceased.

After listing the books of the Scripture and explaining why the Apocrypha was not Scripture, the Confession continued:

The authority of the Holy Scripture, for which it ought to be believed, and obeyed, dependeth not upon the testimony of any man or church; but wholly upon God (who is truth itself) the author thereof: and therefore it is to be received, because it is the Word of God.[28]

… the rules of the Lord are true, and righteous altogether.
More to be desired are they than gold, even much fine gold; sweeter also than
honey and drippings of the honeycomb.
—Psalm 19:9-10—

APRIL 28
UNDERSTANDING THE SCRIPTURE

The *Westminster Confession* opens its exposition of the Christian faith with a chapter on the Scripture. Recognizing Scripture's majestic scope, its revelation of the way of salvation, its perfections, and its evidence as being the Word of God, the *Confession* recognized "Our full persuasion and assurance of the infallible truth and divine authority thereof, is from the inward word of the Holy Spirit bearing witness by and with the Word in our hearts."[29]

Though the whole counsel of God needed for man is in Scripture, the illumination of the Spirit is necessary for a right understanding:

> The whole counsel of God concerning all things necessary for his own glory, man's salvation, faith and life, is either expressly set down in Scripture, or by good and necessary consequence may be deduced from Scripture: unto which nothing at any time is to be added, whether by new revelations of the Spirit, or traditions of men.[30] Nevertheless, we acknowledge the inward illumination of the Spirit of God to be necessary for the saving understanding of such things as are revealed in the Word:[31]

The proper path in some cases can be deduced from nature or from prudence, following the "general rules of the Word." Not everything in Scripture is plain and clear to all,[32] but

> Those things which are necessary to be known, believed, and observed for salvation, are so clearly propounded, and opened in some place of Scripture or other, that not only the learned, but the unlearned, in a due use of the ordinary means, may attain unto a sufficient understanding of them.[33]

If something is unclear in Scripture, search for another Scripture which speaks more clearly. The Scripture should be the supreme judge of all religion, never the opinions of ancient writers nor the doctrines of men.[34]

For this commandment that I command you today is not too hard for you, neither is it far off....' But the word is very near you. It is in your mouth and in your heart, so that you can do it.
—Deuteronomy 30:11-14—

WORD AND WORSHIP

The Scriptures were central to the worship services of the Puritans. In addition to a call to worship (from Scripture) and prayers, there were Old Testament and New Testament readings, the singing of metrical psalms, and an exegetical sermon from the Scriptures, one or two hours long. The Westminster Confession's section on public worship begins with:

> Reading of the word in the congregation, being part of the public worship of God, (wherein we acknowledge our dependence upon him, and subjection to him), and one mean sanctified by him for the edifying of his people, is to be performed by the pastors and teachers .... All the canonical books of the Old and New Testament (But none of those which are commonly called *Apocrypha*) shall be publicly read in the vulgar tongue [i.e. common language], out of the best allowed translation, distinctly, that all may hear and understand.
>
> How large a portion shall be read at once, is left to the wisdom of the minister; but it is convenient, that ordinarily one chapter of each testament be read at every meeting; and sometimes more, where the chapters be short, or the coherence of matter requireth it.
>
> It is requisite that all the canonical books be read over in order, that the people may be better acquainted with the whole body of the scriptures; and ordinarily, where the reading in either Testament endeth on one Lord's day, it is to begin the next.
>
> We commend also the more frequent reading of such scriptures as he that readeth shall think best for edification of his hearers, as the book of Psalms, and such like.
>
> When the minister who readeth shall judge it necessary to expound any part of what is read, let it not be done until the whole chapter or psalm be ended; and regard is always to be had unto the time, that neither preaching, nor other ordinances by straitened, or rendered tedious. ...
>
> Beside public reading of the holy scriptures, every person that can read, is to be exhorted to read the scriptures privately (and all others that cannot read, if not disabled by age or otherwise, are likewise exhorted to learn to read,) and to have a Bible.[35]

Keep steady my steps according to your promise,
and let no iniquity get dominion over me.
— Psalm 119:133—

APRIL 30

A CHRISTIAN LAWYER

One of the founders of International Law was Dutch jurist Hugo Grotius (1583-1645). Grotius's understanding of international law had a theological foundation, for he saw the world, its peoples, and nations as all part of God's creation and thus under the natural law God had placed in His creation. This natural law is consistent with the revealed law found in Scriptures. The moral precepts of the Ten Commandments found in the Old Testament were confirmed by Christ and still valid. Natural law and revelation cannot contradict each other, for both are from God. Grotius thought that at the foundation of all law is Jesus' commandment, "as you wish that others would to you, do so to them" (Luke 6:31). All men came from the same parents, so it is wrong for any man to intend mischief to other men. Grotius also wrote in support of freedom of the seas and free trade, recognizing the importance of missionary work and the free spread of the Gospel. Grotius concluded the prologue to his foundational work *On the Rights of War and Peace,* "… if I have said anything which is at variance with sound piety, with good morals, with holy scripture, with the unity of the Christian Church, with truth in any form;—let that be as unsaid."[36]

Grotius also wrote one of the first works of Christian apologetics of the modern era, *On the Truth of the Christian Religion,* refuting skeptical critics of Christianity and defending the truth of Scripture. Originally intended as a handbook for Dutch sailors to the Far East, it was soon translated into English, French, German, and Arabic and continues to be read and studied. Grotius showed the reliability and authenticity of the Scriptures as a foundation for the Christian faith.

… and many nations shall come, and say:
'Come, let us go up to the mountain of the Lord,
to the house of the God of Jacob,
that he may teach us his ways
and that we may walk in his paths.'
For out of Zion shall go forth the law,
and the word of the Lord from Jerusalem.
—Micah 4:2—

ANNALS OF THE WORLD

James Ussher (1581-1656) was a leading scholar of his day. A professor and administrator of Trinity College Dublin, he authored 27 books, including histories of the early British and Irish churches. Ussher also became Archbishop of Armagh, the highest official of the Church of Ireland. He is most remembered today for his dating of Biblical and ancient events in his *Annals of the World.*

In the 16th and 17th centuries, many scholars (including Martin Luther and Isaac Newton) made ancient and Biblical chronology a focus of study. Joseph Scaliger (1540-1609) collected every chronological reference in ancient and Latin works and published a chronology of the ancient world in 1583. All of these studies recognized that the Jewish people were the only ancient people who, through their Bible, had a unified history in years, going back to the creation of the world. Centuries before, the early Christians and Josephus, the ancient Jewish historian, noted the uniqueness of the biblical narrative in their arguments for the truthfulness of the Jewish and Christian faiths. The Bible became the framework for understanding all of history.

Ussher began constructing his chronology by simply adding up the ages of the Biblical Patriarchs when they begot their first son. He assumed that the genealogies of Scripture were continuous and complete; later scholars recognized the possibility of the incompleteness of the genealogies and gaps in the chronological records. The Babylonian captivity of Israel was the first Biblical event Ussher was able to connect with datable events from another culture. The key datable event for Ussher was the death of the Babylonian King Nebuchadnezzar, which could be correlated with the exile of King Joachin (II Kings 25:27). In correlating Biblical events with known secular history, Ussher used various ancient calendar systems and also Johann Kepler's astronomical tables to help correlate events with the Julian calendar.

In 1675, a London bookseller began printing Ussher's dates for Biblical events in his Bibles. By the 1700's, Ussher's dates were regularly printed in Bibles; many thought Ussher's dates were part of the Scriptures themselves.

Make me understand the way of your precepts,
and I will meditate on your wondrous works.
— Psalm 119:27—

MAY 2
GOD'S EPISTLE TO US

In his work *Divine Optics, or a Treatise of the Eye discovering the Vices and Virtues thereof,* Puritan Robert Dingley (1619-1660) made a case for the importance of reading the Scriptures:

> The Scriptures are God's epistle to us. Christ has honored reading with His own example. For coming to Nazareth, as His custom was, He stood up and read the Scriptures. And the same Christ has charged us that we also search the Scriptures; and for so doing the Bereans were styled noble. Sabellicus says that the Virgin Mary spent the third part of her time in reading the Scriptures. Timothy was trained up in them from a child, and so was Origen. And although the Word preached is the ordinary means of conversion, yet some have been converted in reading of the Scriptures, as Augustine and Fulgentius. Junius was converted by reading the first chapter of John. Reading the Scriptures shuts out worldly cares, dulls carnal delights, and enflames divine love. It steers the judgment, clears the memory, cheers the conscience, and sweetly composes the affections. Let your eyes be upon the Scriptures daily, they will make you perfect in the doctrines of faith and the rules of life ... The Rabbis say that on every syllable and tittle of the law hangs a mountain of sense and holy doctrine. It is a dreadful thing that so many slight and neglect reading of the Scripture ... Those of highest attainments and endowments may find much delight in the Word, for in the Scriptures we find variety of learning, that the eyes of no reader depart unsatisfied. There are histories for the historian, philosophy for the philosophical, ethics for the moralist, mysteries for the artist, and tongues for the linguist. There is food for elephants, food for lambs, milk for babes, and meat for adults. Let us then delight to have our eyes in the Scriptures into which angels pry; read, though you understand not; in God's time a Philip comes to the eunuch [Acts 8:30]. Mingle meditations and prayers with your reading; confer with the judicious, which are dead by their comments, but are living by their conference. Finally, live up to the light you have received; so shall you mind, understand, remember, and delight in the Scriptures, above thousands of gold and silver.[1]

My eyes shed streams of tears,
because people do not keep your law.
—Psalm 119: 136—

SCRIPTURE LIGHT THE MOST SURE LIGHT

In 1656, Puritan minister William Bridge (1600-1670) preached a sermon on II Peter 1:19, "We have also a more sure word of prophecy, whereunto ye do well that ye take heed, as unto a light that shineth in a dark place, until the day dawn, and the day star arise in your hearts." In his sermon Bridge noted that the light of Scripture is most needed in dark times:

> "Scripture light is our great and most sure light, whereunto we shall do well that we take heed, and that especially in our dark times and places." Though a good man may be in a dark place, state, or condition, God has "not left him without Scripture light to walk by." [2]

> There are many false lights in the world, but Scripture light is the true light. The proper work of light is to make manifest: "They will not come to the light (saith our Saviour) lest their deeds be made manifest." Now the light of the Scripture doth manifest things unto us; it is by James compared to a looking-glass. When you look upon a looking-glass, you see three things, the glass, yourself, and all the other things, persons, tools or pictures that are in the room. So in looking in the Scripture, this great looking-glass, you see ... God ..., and Christ ...; there also you see yourself, and your own dirty face; there also you see the creatures that are in the room with you, and their emptiness .... This is that manifesting light under Christ, that is true light indeed .... in Scripture knowledge, the more light you have, and the more you know, the more you will lift your hands and ..., at your own ignorance and God's grace ....

> Other false lights do lead men into fens and bogs; but we have a more sure and safe light, and the more it falls upon your eye, the more your eye is preserved .... this is that light which doth bring men to rest; for when a man knows what shall be his portion forever, then his heart is at rest, and not before. Now it is only the Scripture, and the light thereof, which under Christ doth discover and manifest that unto men ... This is that satisfying light which doth bring unto rest.[3]

Scripture is the best light in the world, far surpassing other lights men follow, such as experience, dreams, astrology, visions, reason, or "the law and light within."

My eyes long for your salvation
and for the fulfillment of your righteous promise.
—Psalm 119:123—

MAY 4

PRAISE FOR THE WRITTEN WORD

Edmund Calamy (1600-1666) was the fourth generation in a line of English ministers. He was active in the Westminster Assembly, which wrote the Westminster Confession and Catechism. He also edited *The Souldier's Pocket Bible*, an anthology of Bible passages especially meaningful to soldiers during the time of the English Civil War. *The Godly Man's Ark,* a selection of sermons first published in 1658, included praise for the written Word of God:

> Let us bless God, not only for revealing His will in His Word, but for revealing it by writing. Before the time of Moses, God disclosed His will by immediate revelations from heaven. But we have a surer word of prophecy (II Peter 1:19). Surer than a voice from heaven, for the devil (says the apostle) transforms himself into an angel of light. He has his apparitions and revelations…and in imitation of God, he appears to his disciples and makes them believe that it is God that appears, and not the devil…if God should … [today] disclose His way of worship and His divine will by revelations, how easily would men be deceived and mistake diabolical delusions for divine revelations. Therefore let us bless God for the written Word, which is surer safer …. There are some that are apt to think that if an angel should come from heaven and reveal God's will to them, it would work more upon them [who think an angelic revelation would affect them more] … than the written Word, but I would have these men to study the conference between Abraham and Dives [the rich man] (Luke 16:27-31). "They have Moses and the prophets"; if they will not profit by them, neither would they profit by any that should come out of hell or down from heaven to them, for it is the same God that speaks by His written Word, and by a voice from heaven. The difference is only in the outward clothing; and therefore if God's speaking by writing will not amend us, no more will God's speaking by a voice. O Bless God exceedingly for the written Word! Let us cleave close to it and not expect any revelations from heaven of new truths, but say with the apostle (Gal. 1:8-9): "But though we, or an angel from heaven, preach any other gospel unto you than that which we have preached unto you, let him be accursed."

> Let us prize the Word of God above gold, yes, above fine gold. Let us read it diligently, reverently, praying to God to give us the same Spirit that wrote it to enable us to understand it, and conscientiously to practice it, Let us make it the joy and rejoicing of our heart; and, as it is in the text, let us make it our delight … it will keep you from perishing in the time of your greatest affliction; it will comfort you when you have most need of it … when all outward

comforts and creatures fail. It will be food to strengthen your weak faith—medicine to cure the remainder of corruption; ... to revive your drooping spirits and fainting souls; it will make you more than conquerors over all temptations and distresses.[4]

This blessing has fallen to me, that I have kept your precepts.
—Psalm 119:56—

MAY 5
JESUS ACCOMPLISHES
WHAT THE PROPHETS WROTE

One of the earliest calculating machines was developed by the 19-year-old mathematical genius Blaise Pascal (1621-1662). The teenage Pascal developed the machine, which could do addition and subtraction and was called the Pascaline, to help his father calculate his taxes. When computers were developed, one of the early programming languages was named Pascal in honor of the 17th-century Frenchman. Pascal went on to make important contributions in both mathematics and physics. He also wrote important works examining and defending the Christian faith, most notable being *Pensées*. He wrote of the importance of the Scriptures and Jesus Christ to man's understanding of God and himself:

> We know God only through Jesus Christ. Without this Mediator, is taken away all communication with God; through Jesus Christ we know God. All those who have pretended to know God, and prove him without Jesus Christ, have only impotent proofs. But, to prove Jesus Christ we have the prophecies which are good and valid proofs. And those prophecies, being fulfilled, and truly proved by the event, indicate the certainty of these truths, and therefore the truth of the divinity of Jesus Christ. In Him, and by Him, then, we know God. Otherwise, and without Scripture, without original sin, without a necessary Mediator, we can not absolutely prove God, nor teach a good doctrine and sound morals. But by Jesus Christ and in Jesus Christ, we prove God and teach doctrine and morals. Jesus Christ, then, is the true God of men. Not only do we know God only through Jesus Christ, but we know ourselves only through Jesus Christ. We know life, death, only through Jesus Christ. Except by Jesus Christ we know not what life is, what our death is, what God is, what we ourselves are. Thus, without Scripture, which has only Jesus Christ for its object, we know nothing, and we see not only obscurity and confusion in the nature of God, and in nature herself. Without Jesus Christ, man must be in sin and misery; with Jesus Christ, man is exempt from sin and misery. In Him is all our virtue, and all our felicity. Out of Him, there is nothing but sin, misery, error, darkness, death, and despair.[5]

And taking the twelve, he [Jesus] said to them, "See, we are going up to Jerusalem, and everything that is written about the Son of Man by the prophets will be accomplished."
—Luke 18:31—

JOHN ELIOT'S ALGONQUIAN BIBLE

The first seal of the Massachusetts Bay Colony shows a Native American surrounded by the words from Acts 16:9, "Come and help us." One of the purposes the Puritans had in coming to America was to follow that missionary call and bring the Gospel to the New World. John Eliot (1604-1690), who came to Massachusetts in 1631, became known as the "Apostle to the Indians" for his missionary work.

Eliot was pastor of the church in Roxbury, outside of Boston. He also had a passion for the Native Americans to come to know the Gospel of Christ. He spent three to four days at a time in their villages, trying to learn their language. By 1646, Eliot was preaching to the Indians in their own language. He began by describing the glorious power, goodness, and greatness of God as seen in His creation. He then explained the Ten Commandments to the Indians, pointing out what God required of them and the punishment which would come from breaking His law. All this was to prepare the Indians for the Gospel message: God loved them and sent Jesus Christ to die for their sins. Eliot always took time to answer the Indians' questions after he preached. One question they had was, "How could God hear the Indian prayers when He was used to hearing English prayers?"

Eliot realized the Indians needed a Bible in their own language. The Native Americans did not have a written language, and Eliot spent ten years developing a written language for the Algonquians, writing Indian grammars and then translating the Scriptures themselves. Eliot kept people in England informed of his missionary endeavors, and in 1649 Parliament authorized the Society for the Propagation of the Gospel in New England to help support his translation work. The Society paid for the printing of Eliot's translation of the Bible into the Massachusetts language. Published in 1663, not only was this the first Bible published in America, it was the first Bible printed with a distinctly missionary purpose.

The earth is the Lord's and the fullness thereof,
the world and those who dwell therein...
—Psalm 24:1—

MAY 7

COMFORT IN TIMES OF PERSECUTION

Many of Marion Fairlie's friends tried to discourage her from marrying William Veitch in 1664. Veitch was a nonconforming minister and part of the Scottish Covenanters. In 1660, King Charles II had returned the Stuarts to the throne, and the Commonwealth begun by Cromwell came to an end. With all the political and religious turmoil in Scotland surrounding these events, persecution and hardship seemed likely if Marion married William. Marion, however, decided to trust God and join with William in marriage.

After only two years of marriage, persecution began. William was part of the Covenanters' resistance to the king's forces at Pentland Hills and was declared guilty of treason and worthy of death. He found safety in England, and Marion followed with their two sons some years later. Having lost all their land in Scotland, Marion prayed that God would supply them with food and clothes in England. One night, a group of dragoons broke into the house and captured William and took him to Edinburgh on charges of high treason. During the break-in, several Scriptures came to Marion's mind to give her peace. Mark 7:37 taught her that God had "done all things well" and that men could do nothing that God did not permit. She had perfect peace trusting the Lord and not fearing what men could do (Psalm 56:11). In the months ahead, Marion continued to turn to the Scriptures for comfort. Psalm 43:5 told her, "Why are you cast down, O my soul, and why are you in turmoil within me? Hope in God, for I shall again praise him, my salvation and my God." She could rest totally in God, that He would do what He had appointed for her (Job 23:14). William was released after several months in prison. After spending some years in exile in Holland, Marion and William and their family returned to Scotland, and William became minister of Dumfries. The fifty-eight years of Marion and William's marriage saw many difficulties and trials, but the promises of God in the Scriptures always provided strength and peace.

How long must your servant endure?
When will you judge those who persecute me?
—Psalm 119:84—

THE TREASURE OF THE WORD

In 1665, George Swinnock (1627-1673) a Puritan pastor, published *The Christian Man's Calling*, examining the character and nature of the life of a Christian. Here is an excerpt:

> The Word of God is a spring of living water, a deep mine of costly treasure, a table furnished with all sorts of food, a garden of variety of pleasant fruits, and the church's charter, containing all her privileges and deeds, manifesting her title to this possession. This Word contains pious precepts for the Christian's reformation and precious promises for consolation. If the saint is afflicted, it can hold his head above water and keep him from sinking when the billows go over his soul. There are cordials [medicines] in it rich enough to revive the most fainting spirit. If the saint is assaulted, the Word is armor ..., with which he may defend himself manfully, and wound his foes mortally. If the soul is unholy, this Word can sanctify it: "You are clean through the word which I have spoken to you" (John 15:3). This water can wash out all spots and stains. If the soul is an heir of hell, this Word can save it: "From a child you have known the holy Scriptures, which are able to make you wise to salvation" (II Timothy. 3:15). Other writings may make a man wise to admiration, but this only can make him wise to salvation.

> This word, which is of such unspeakable worth, God has deposited as a special treasure into the hands of the children of men, that they might "obey his will, and know the just one." And, reader, it is your duty to search and study this book. When kings send out their proclamations, ... they expect that all should take notice ..., and give them the reading and hearing. What an affront do you offer to the King of the whole world, if you turn your back upon his word!...

> But reader, if you are a child of God, I doubt not but you delight to look at your Father's will, and weigh every word in it, as knowing that in his testament there is a great charge committed, and a great legacy bequeathed, to thee. It is your daily companion and counselor; you dare not go without your pleasant medicine, being liable every day to faint; nor without your weapons, being called every hour to fight. The Scriptures are the light by which you walk, and the tools with which you work. ... "Let the word of Christ dwell in you richly," Col. 3:16. ... Do not leave your Bible, as some do, at church .... Let ... it be an inhabitant, one that accompanies you to bed and board and with whom you converse continually as your familiar and intimate friend. Make your heart ... by the assiduous reading and hearing the Scriptures, ... the library of Jesus Christ.[6]

I trust in your word. —Psalm 119:42—

MAY 9

THE SCRIPTURE AND TRUE RELIGION

Recognized as one of the greatest of English poets and writers, John Milton (1608-1674) was also a Christian involved in the public events of his day. Writing pamphlets favoring the Puritan and Parliamentary cause in the English Civil War, Milton went into hiding and even was briefly imprisoned at the Restoration because of his previous support of Cromwell and the Parliament. But it is certainly Milton's poetry that makes him memorable today. His *Paradise Lost, Paradise Regained, Samson Agonistes,* and *On the Morning of Christ's Nativity* are clearly based on the Bible, but other works as well are permeated with biblical references. Milton recognized that the Bible must be the basis for all true religion:

> True religion is the true worship and service of God, learnt and believed from the Word of God only. No man or angel can know how God would be worshipped and served, unless God reveal it; he hath revealed and taught it us in the Holy Scriptures by inspired ministers, and in the Gospel by his own Son, and his Apostles, with strictest command to reject all other traditions or additions whatsoever. According to that of St. Paul, "Though we, or an angel from heaven, preach any other gospel unto you, than that which we have preached unto you, let him be anathema or accursed." [Galatians 1:8] And, Deut. iv:2: "Ye shall not add to the word which I command you, neither shall ye diminish aught from it." Rev. xxii:18, 19: "If any man shall add," &c. "If any man shall take away from the words," &c. With good and religious reason therefore, all Protestant churches, with one consent. And particularly the Church of England in her Thirty-nine Articles, art. 6th, 19th, 20th, and 21st, and elsewhere, maintain these two points, as the main principles of true religion that the rule of true religion is the Word of God only; and that their faith ought not to be an implicit faith, that is, to believe, though as the church believes, against or without express authority of Scripture.[7]

In the way of your testimonies
I delight as much as in all riches.
—Psalm 119:14—

143 | *THE LIVING WORD*

THE WORD OF GOD IN WRITING

Sir Matthew Hale (1660-1671) was a noted English jurist who served in Parliament and became Chief Justice of the King's Bench. His *Analysis of the Common Law* was the first published history of English Law and strongly influenced William Blackstone's magisterial *Commentaries on the Laws of England*. Hale also wrote works on moral and religious issues which reflect not only his Christian faith but the logic of his legal mind.

In *Contemplations Moral and Divine*, Hale wrote that God gave the Scriptures as a guide for man to fulfill his created purpose of glorifying God. Why are they written? Before Moses, oral communication from father to son was sufficient. In part, the great ages of the first men made this reasonable:

> For *Adam*, the first man, lives about twenty years after *Methuselah*, the eighth from *Adam* was born; and *Methuselah* lived almost an hundred years after *Shem* was born; and *Shem* lived about sixty years after *Isaac* was born. So that in these three men, *Adam, Methuselah,* and *Shem*, all truths of God for above two thousand years were preserved and delivered over. [8]

When men's lives became shorter and God began to work with Israel among the nations, God wrote his law on the Tablets of Stone, and Moses wrote the first five books of Scripture. The histories and prophecies of the Old Testament and the Gospel of the New Testament were written as well. By having these in writing, they could be better preserved from being corrupted and could be "better dispersed and communicated to all mankind."

Hale gave several evidences that these writings are the Word of God. Though written by many different men over many ages, the Scriptures all speak the same truth. Men, unaided, could not have produced their prophecies of the Babylonian captivity, the Persian and Grecian kingdoms, "the birth and death of Christ, the final destruction of *Jerusalem*, the dispersion of the *Jews*, the conversion of the *Gentiles* ... '" The Scriptures contain hugely important matters about God's will and about how we can have peace with God, things which could never be discovered but by God's special revelation.

Let your mercy come to me, that I may live;
for your law is my delight.
—Psalm 119:77—

MAY 11
GROWING IN THE WORD

The Scripture is often described as necessary spiritual food. In His temptation in the wilderness, Jesus quoted Deuteronomy 8:3, "man shall not live by bread alone, but by every word that comes from the mouth of God." In the midst of his suffering, Job told his friends he had not departed from the commandments of the Lord, "I have treasured the words of his mouth more than my portion of food." (Job 23:12). Scripture is the necessary food for spiritual growth, even for young Christians. Puritan pastor Ralph Venning (1621-1673) described the importance of the milk of the Word to a growing Christian:

> Milk is the food of babes; and therefore it is necessary that we come to know what this milk is...In the general, all the Word of God (the gospel) is called "milk." "As new-born babes desire the sincere milk of the word, that you may grow thereby" (I Peter 2:2). This milk is for growth; the Word is not only for begetting, as in I Peter 1:23, but for nourishing and bringing up also, even to a perfect stature (Ephesians 4:11-16). It is observable that Peter does not speak merely of the Word written in the Bible, but of the Word preached. But then this Word preached must be the sincere milk of the Word, not mixed with and corrupted by the devices of invention, glosses, and comments; this the Apostle Paul disclaims against: "We are not as many, who are corrupt, or deal deceitfully with the word of God, but as of sincerity, but as of God, in the sight of God we speak in Christ (II Corinthians 2:17) ... As the Word must not be mixed with and corrupted by false doctrine and base ends, so this milk must not be made luscious and fulsome with the sugar and honey of men's wisdom and eloquence, for this the Apostle no less disowns and disallows ... So then it is not a sound of words, but sound and sincere doctrine or milk of the Word by which we grow and thrive.[10]

Like newborn infants, long for the pure spiritual milk,
that by it you may grow up into salvation—
—I Peter 2:2—

CAPTIVE IN THE WILDERNESS

On February 10, 1675, in the middle of King Philip's War, a group of native Americans attacked the settlement of Lancaster in the Massachusetts Bay Colony, burning houses and capturing many of the colonists, including Mary Rowlandson and her three children. As the captives were marched away from the settlement, Mary and six-year-old Sarah were separated from the older two children. Both Mary and Sarah were wounded, and Sarah died 9 days into the march. Traveling northwest, stopping at various Indian villages along the way, occasionally Mary would meet up with her daughter and son from the other group of captives. After one raid, a native had among his booty a Bible, which he let Mary read. In the Scriptures she took great comfort. The first Scripture she read was Deuteronomy 28, about the curses upon Israel for their departure from the Lord. Sorrowful as that was, there was great comfort when she read Deuteronomy 30:1-7, about the blessings received upon repentance. Numerous other Scriptures brought comfort in the coming weeks:

> Wait for the Lord; be strong, and let your heart take courage; wait for the Lord! (Psalm 27:14)

> Thus says the Lord: Keep your voice from weeping, and your eyes from tears, for there is a reward for your work, declares the Lord, and they shall come back from the land of the enemy. There is hope for your future. (Jeremiah 31:16-17)

As they crossed rivers, wading through them, Isaiah 43:2 took on special meaning, "When you pass through the waters, I will be with you; and through the rivers, they shall not overwhelm you."

Mary believed the suffering the colonists endured at the hands of their captors was a discipline to cause them to repent and turn to the Lord (Psalm 81:13-14). She had renewed hope from Psalm 118;17-18, "I shall not die, but I shall live, and recount the deeds of the Lord. The Lord has disciplined me severely, but he has not given me over to death."

After eleven weeks in captivity, Mary and her children were released. She returned to her husband, and they set up a new home in Boston. Mary later wrote an account of her captivity, filled with the Scriptures which strengthened her and recounting the sovereignty and goodness of God throughout her ordeal. She concluded her narrative,

I have learned to look beyond present and smaller troubles, and to be quieted under them As Moses said, 'Stand still and see the salvation of the Lord." (Exodus 14:13)[11]

Give your servant a pledge of good; let not the insolent oppress me.
—Psalm 119:122—

PILGRIM'S PROGRESS

Do you know the name of the book the Chinese communist government printed as an example of western culture which sold out its initial printing of 200,000 copies in three days? It was John Bunyan's *Pilgrim's Progress*, first published in England on February 18, 1678. Even in its own day, *Pilgrim's Progress* was a runaway best seller, and it has continued to be a steady seller for over three centuries. The book has not only edified English-speaking Christians, but it has been translated into numerous European, Asian, and African languages and dialects. This is often the book missionaries translate after they've completed a translation of the Bible into a new language.

Pilgrim's Progress continues to be read by Christians of all nationalities because of its graphic, universal description of the Christian life. Christians throughout the world appreciate the burdensome weight of sin and the joy which comes with sin's forgiveness at the cross. All those on the narrow road to the Heavenly City have gone through times of despondency, doubting, loss, and frivolity, places which Bunyan vividly characterized as the Slough of Despond, Doubting Castle, Valley of Shadow, and Vanity Fair.

John Bunyan wrote his allegory of the Christian life while imprisoned for preaching the Gospel without a license. Though an uneducated laborer, Bunyan knew the Bible thoroughly. In the margins of his story he placed the Scripture references which were the background for Christian's pilgrimage adventure.

If you've never read *Pilgrim's Progress*, or if it's been a while since you have, refresh your soul by reading this Christian classic and best-seller published over three hundred years ago. Reading the Bible references in the margin will enhance your appreciation for this wonderful work.

I am a sojourner on the earth;
hide not your commandments from me!
—Psalm 119:19—

A BEST SELLER, AFTER THE BIBLE

Though the Bible is indubitably the best-selling book of all time, John Bunyan's *Pilgrim's Progress* must be in second place . Bunyan's allegorical story of Christian's pilgrimage from the City of Destruction to the Celestial City begins with a man clothed in rags, a great burden on his back and a book in his hand. The rags are a reference to Isaiah 64:6—"we are all as an unclean thing, and all our righteousness are as filthy rags;" the burden on his back represent his grievous sins; and the book in his hand is the Bible.

Charles Spurgeon first read Bunyan's work as a boy, discovering it in his grandparents' library. By the time of his death, he said he had read the work at least 100 times. References to Bunyan can be found throughout Spurgeon's sermons and writings, and he encouraged Christians:

> Read anything of his [Bunyan's], and you will see that it is almost like reading the Bible itself. He had read it till his very soul was saturated with Scripture; and, though his writings are charmingly full of poetry, yet he cannot give us his *Pilgrim's Progress*—that sweetest of all prose poems—without continually making us feel and say, "Why, this man is a living Bible!" Prick him anywhere his blood is Bibline, the very essence of the Bible flows from him. He cannot speak without quoting a text, for his very soul is full of the Word of God. I commend his example to you, beloved.[12]

Spurgeon never tired of *Pilgrim's Progress*, for it was compiled of Scriptures. Its story of the Christian pilgrimage could be a tool in counseling others in their spiritual walk. In 1854, as a young pastor, when Spurgeon heard of Susannah Thompson's concern about her spiritual state, he sent her a copy of *The Pilgrim's Progress* with the note "Miss Thompson, with desires for her progress in a blessed pilgrimage, from C.H. Spurgeon." Susannah's spiritual progress led to her marriage to Charles Spurgeon in 1856.

Teach me your way, O Lord, that I may walk in your truth;
unite my heart to fear your name.
—Psalm 86:11—

HEARING THE WORD

In his *A Christian's Walk and Work on Earth until he attain to Heaven,* Christopher Ness (1621-1705) wrote of the treasure we have in the Bible:

> That you have the Word of God to read and hear, you must prize as a precious privilege, and praise the Lord for it with your heart, lips, and life. God has deposited a rich treasure with you in lending you His Word and gospel. You might have been begging drops of mercy in hell at this time, when behold God offers you oceans of grace on earth in His Word and gospel. ... It was a special favor and vouchsafement [or guarantee] to Israel, that God committed to them the lively (and life-giving) oracles (Rom. 3:2). It is truly a choice talent, a matter of great trust, to know your Master's will. There is much in that of Luke 12:48; "Unto whomsoever much is given, of him shall much be required." The poor pagan world lay under a long night of darkness (having only the twinkling starlight of the fallen nature) wherein they wander woefully ... Their starlight indeed leaves them inexcusable (Rom. 1:20), but cannot lead them to the star of Jacob, the bright Morning Star, nor to life and salvation (Acts 4:12).[13]

Only by the Word of God, not unaided human reason, is the truth and grace of God in Christ and our salvation made known.

My soul is consumed with longing for your rules at all times.
—Psalm 119: 20—

MAY 16

THE WORD OF GOD:
A PATTERN FOR OUR LIVES

Victorian Preacher Charles Spurgeon considered Thomas Watson's *The Ten Commandments* "One of the most precious of the peerless works of the Puritans." In his exposition of God's moral law, Watson (c. 1620-1686) extolled the reverence and esteem the Christian should have for the Scriptures:

> Let us have a reverend esteem of every part of Scripture. "More to be desired are they than gold." Psalm 19:10. Value the book of God above all other books. It is a golden epistle, written by the Holy Spirit, and sent to us from heaven. ... The Scripture is a spiritual looking-glass, to dress our souls by. It shows us more than we can see by the light of natural conscience. This may discover gross sins; but the glass of the Word shows us heart-sins, vain thoughts, unbelief, etc. It not only shows us our spots—but washes them away. The Scripture is an armory, out of which we may fetch spiritual artillery to fight against Satan. When our Saviour was tempted by the devil, he fetched armor and weapons from Scripture; "it is written!" Matt. 4:4, 7. The holy Scripture is a ... medicine for the soul; it gives a recipe to cure deadness of heart, Psalm 119:50; pride, 1 Pet. 5:5; and infidelity, John 3:36. It is a garden of remedies, where we may gather a herb or antidote to expel the poison of sin. The leaves of Scripture, like the leaves of the tree of life, are for the "healing of the nations." Rev. 22:2. Should not this cause a reverential esteem of the Word? ...

> If we would have the written Word effectual to our souls, let us peruse it with "intenseness of mind." "Search the Scriptures." John 5:39. The Greek word signifies to search as for a "vein of silver." The Bereans "searched the Scriptures daily." Acts 17:11. The word signifies to make a meticulous and critical search. Apollo was mighty in the Scriptures. Acts 18:24. Some gallop over a chapter in haste—and get no good by it. If we would have the Word effectual and saving, we must mind and observe every passage of Scripture. That we may be diligent in the perusal of Scripture, consider that the Scripture is "the only standard of conduct"—the rule and platform by which we are to square our lives. It contains in it all things needful to salvation; what duties we are to do, and what sins we are to avoid. Psalm 19:7. God gave Moses a pattern how he would have the tabernacle made; and he was to go exactly according to the pattern. Exodus 25:9. The Word is the pattern God has given us in writing, for modeling our lives. How careful, therefore, should we be in pursuing and looking over this pattern! ...

When we read the holy Scriptures—let us look up to God for a blessing. Let us beg the Spirit of wisdom and revelation, that we may see the "deep things of God." Eph. 1:17, 1 Cor. 2:10. Ask God, that the same Spirit that wrote the Scripture would enable us to understand it. Pray that God would give us the "savor of his knowledge," that we may relish a sweetness in the Word we read. 2 Cor. 2:14. David tasted it as "sweeter than the honeycomb." Psalm 19:10. Let us pray that God would not only give us his Word as a rule of holiness— but his grace as a principle of holiness![14]

His divine power has granted to us all things that pertain to life and godliness, through the knowledge of him who called us to his own glory and excellence, by which he has granted to us his precious and very great promises.
—II Peter 1:3-4—

MAY 17
A LOVER OF THE WORD

An early chapter in Puritan Thomas Watson's (c. 1620-1686) work *The Godly Man Pictured* is "A Godly Man is a Lover of the Word." Watson delineates how the godly man loves the counseling part of the Word which provides direction for his life. He loves the threatening part of the Word which threatens against sin and evil; he loves the consolatory part of the Word with its comforting promises.

The godly man demonstrates his love for the Scriptures in several ways. He diligently reads the Word, as the noble Bereans "searched the Scriptures daily." (Acts 17:1) "The Word is our Magna Carta for heaven; we should be daily reading over this charter. The Word shows what is truth and what is error. It is the field where the pearl of price is hidden. How we should dig for this pearl!" The godly man meditates on the Scripture throughout the day (Psalm 119:97). His mind is steeped in the Scriptures: "By meditation, he sucks from this sweet flower and ruminates on holy truths in his mind."

The godly man delights in the Scripture; it is his recreation (Jer. 15:16). He hides the Word in his heart as a treasure that should not be stolen. He defends it so it cannot be taken from him. The Word is most precious and preferred before food (Job 23:12), riches (Psalm 119:72), and worldly honor. The godly man talks of the Word as a treasure full of beauty and sweetness. His life is conformed to the Word: "The Word is his compass, by which he sets his life, the balance in which he weighs his actions."

The godly man loves the Word preached:

The Scriptures are the precious spices; the preaching of the Word is the beating of these spices, which causes a wonderful fragrance and delight... the preaching of the Word is called "the power of God to salvation" (Rom. 1:16). By this Christ is said (now) to speak to us from heaven (Heb. 12:25). This ministry of the Word is to be preferred before the ministry of angels.[15]

Deal with your servant according to your steadfast love,
and teach me your statutes.
—Psalm 119:124—

ENCOURAGEMENT TO
READ THE SCRIPTURES

In the years following the Reformation, daily Scripture reading became an important spiritual exercise. Puritan Thomas Gouge (1605-1681) noted that there were treasures in the Scripture which could not be found in any other work: "All the abstruse Learning, and Mysteries of other Books and Writings, are but straw and stubble, yea, dross and dung, in comparison of the precious Pearls in this." Antiquity had nothing comparable to this Word of Truth, which begins with the beginning of the World. Scripture alone

> … declares what is truly profitable, and most advantageous to our best good, our spiritual welfare. They show us, as what is true Riches, and true honour; so likewise the means how to attain thereunto…as there is not a condition into which a Child of God can fall, but there is a Direction and Rule in the Word, in some measure suitable thereunto; so that there is not an affliction into which a Child of God can fall, but there is a promise in the Word, in some measure, suitable thereunto. God has opened his Heart unto us in the Word and reached out many sweet and gracious Promises for us to lay hold on, and whereon to stay ourselves in our several straights and exigencies. To the burdened we find God has promised ease and rest, *Matt. 11:28.* Comfort to those who mourn, *Matt. 5:4.* Assistance and deliverance to them who are tempted, *I Cor. 10:13.* Yes, many, many Promises has God made of preservation and protection from Evil and of a comfortable supply of all Blessings, both Temporal and Spiritual, which by Faith we may, and ought to apply unto ourselves.[16]

Hear then the parable of the sower: When anyone hears the word of the
kingdom and does not understand it, the evil one comes and snatches
away what has been sown in his heart. This is what was sown along the path.
As for what was sown on rocky ground, this is the one who hears the word and
immediately receives it with joy, yet he has no root in himself, but endures for a
while, and when tribulation or persecution arises on account of the word,
immediately he falls away. As for what was sown among thorns, this is the one
who hears the word, but the cares of the world and the deceitfulness of riches choke
the word, and it proves unfruitful. As for what was sown on good soil, this is the
one who hears the word and understands it. He indeed bears fruit and yields,
in one case a hundredfold, in another sixty, and in another thirty.
—Matthew 13:18-23—

MAY 19

DIRECTIONS FOR READING THE SCRIPTURES

As printed English Scriptures became more available, daily home Bible reading increased. Puritan pastor Thomas Gouge (1605-1681) laid out some directions, noting that Jesus commanded us to "search the Scriptures" (John 5:39).

Rules and Directions before reading:

1. Go about it with all holy reverence, as in the sight and presence of God, believing it to be the Word of God ... Say to yourself, *I will hearken what the Lord will speak unto me therein.*

2. Quicken and rouse up yourself to all possible attention ... As Children will rouse up themselves at reading of their Father's will, out of an expectation of some Portion or Legacy bequeathed them, so you ought to rouse up yourself to the reading of the Word, in regard of the many rich and precious Legacies which our Saviour hath bequeathed unto you ...

3. Lift up your heart in prayer unto God ... to open the Eyes of your Understanding, that you may rightly conceive his Word; so for Wisdom to apply, Memory to retain, Faith to believe, and Grace to practice what you shall read ...

Rules and Directions in reading:

1. Read the holy lives and actions of God's Children, not only as ... History, but as patterns of imitation. For, for this end are they recorded unto us, ... Rom. 15:4. *Whatever things were written aforetime, were written for our learning* ... Labour to adorn your profession with those graces and Ornaments, and to be inwardly and outwardly endued with like Virtues.

2. In reading the Promises and Threatenings, the Exhortations and Admonitions, and other parts of the scripture: So apply them to yourself, as if God by name had delivered the same unto you; Whereby the Word will become very profitable unto you ...

Rules and Directions after the reading of the word:

1. Seriously meditate on what you have read, that so you may... the better remember, and understand the same: For Meditation is a special means to help, as our Memory, so our Understanding...indeed, how is it possible the Word you read should do thee good, when you never think of it after you have read it?

2. Labour to work something of that you have read upon your heart and give not over 'till you have found the affections of your Soul warmed thereby.[17]

The earth, O Lord, is full of your steadfast love; teach me your statutes!
—Psalm 119:64—

THE WORD FOR THE MIND,
THE HEART, AND THE WILL

The Puritans were not only concerned with knowing the Bible, with having the mind saturated with the Scriptures, but they desired to have the Scriptures reach the affections[18] and will. They believed that by meditating on the Word, the Word can reach the heart and affect the will. Meditation on the Scriptures "begins in the understanding, endeth in the affection; it begins in the brain, ascends to the heart; begins on earth, ascends to heaven."[19] In meditation, the individual reflects upon the Word to evaluate his own soul, "to see how the matter stands between God, and my own soul."[20] This involves looking backwards to see what has been your behavior to God and man as well as looking forward to consider what needs to be done.

The Puritans saw meditating on the Scriptures as essential to true piety. The Scriptures must not merely be read or heard, but digested, which is the process of meditation: "The word feeds meditation, and meditation feeds prayer ... Meditation must follow hearing and precede prayer ... What we take in by the word we digest by meditation and let out by prayer."[21]

Puritan Thomas Brooks reminded his readers:

Remember, it is not hasty reading—but serious meditation upon holy and heavenly truths, that make them prove sweet and profitable to the soul. It is not the bee's touching of the flower, which gathers honey, but her abiding for a time upon the flower, which draws out the sweet. It is not he who reads most—but he who meditates most, who will prove the choicest, sweetest, wisest and strongest Christian.[22]

I have not forgotten your statutes.
—Psalm 119:83—

MAY 21
JESUS AS KING OF THE CHURCH

The years 1680-1688 in Scotland became known as The Killing Time. When Charles II became King, he sought to remove the presbyteries and synods of the Church of Scotland and establish an Episcopal church government for Scotland as in England. Everyone was required to take an oath of allegiance to Charles as King of Scotland and head of the church. Those who refused were imprisoned, and many were executed. At least 18,000 Scots suffered during this period for their Christian convictions.

Two women in Wigtown refused to take the oath of allegiance—eighteen-year-old Margaret Wilson and sixty-three-year-old Margaraet Maclauchlan. They contended that Jesus Christ, not the King, was head of the Church. Both were arrested, and on May 11, 1685, were tied to posts in the Solway Frith, where the incoming tides would engulf them. As the waters came up, Margaret sang from Psalm 25:

> Let not the errors of my youth,
>   Nor sins remembered be:
> In mercy for thy goodness' sake,
>   O Lord, remember me.
> The Lord is good and gracious,
>   He upright is also:
> He therefore sinners will instruct
>   In ways that they should go.

Before the waters totally engulfed her, she recited the words of Romans 8, "For I am persuaded, that neither death, nor life, nor angels, nor principalities, nor powers, nor things present, nor things to come, Nor height, nor depth, nor any other creature, shall be able to separate us from the love of God, which is in Christ Jesus our Lord."

May my heart be blameless in your statutes,
that I may not be put to shame!
—Psalm 119:80—

THE BIBLE AND GOVERNMENT

The English colonists in America held the Bible to be an important foundation for their laws and government. Laws in Massachusetts and Connecticut recognized that "the open contempt of God's Word, and messengers thereof is the desolating sin of civil states" and protected the preaching of the Scriptures, punishing any who would interfere with the preaching of God's Word.[23] In Connecticut, the oath taken by the magistrates concluded with the words, "will further the execution of Justice for the time aforesaid, according to the righteous rule of God's word; so help me God."[24] In New Hampshire, if any Christian "shall speak contemptuously of the holy Scripture, or of the holy penmen thereof," such person or persons shall be punished by fine or corporeal punishment.[25] In New Haven, the law of God as given to Moses was the basis of the moral law of the colony. A Virginia law of 1699 disqualified anyone from public office who "shall deny the Christian religion to be true, or the holy scriptures of Old and New Testament to be of divine authority."[26]

John Adams wrote that if a nation adopted the Bible as its law book, it would be a Utopia:

> Suppose a nation in some distant region should take the Bible for their only law-book, and every member should regulate his conduct by the precepts there exhibited! Every member would be obliged, in conscience, to temperance and frugality and industry, to justice and kindness and charity towards his fellow men; and to piety, love, and reverence towards Almighty God. In this commonwealth, no one would impair his health by gluttony, drunkenness, or lust; no man would sacrifice his most precious time to cards or any other trifling and mean amusement; no man would steal, or lie, or in any way defraud his neighbor, but would live in peace and good will with all men; no man would blaspheme his Maker or profane his worship; but a rational and manly, a sincere and unaffected piety and devotion would reign in all hearts. What a Utopia; what a Paradise would this region be![27]

Give attention to me, my people, and give ear to me, my nation; for a law will go out from me, and I will set my justice for a light to the peoples.
—Isaiah 51:4—

MAY 23

THE BIBLE IN EDUCATION

In America, the Bible has had an important place in education since the colonial days. Literacy was high among the American colonists, primarily because reading the Bible was considered so important. Massachusetts passed a school law in 1647 to ensure all children be taught to read and write, primarily so they could read the Bible. Sometimes this is called the "Old Deluder" law because of the law's explanation of the need for such schools—"It being one chief project of the old deluder, Satan, to keep men from the knowledge of the Scripture..."[28]

The New England Primer, first published in 1690, and used by generations of New Englanders, taught the youngest children the alphabet and basic spelling. The *Primer* taught these elemental principles of reading within a Biblical framework. The alphabet was taught in couplets such as

> In **A**dam's Fall We sinned all.
> The **B**ible Mind Heaven to find.
> **C**hrist Crucify'd For sinner dy'd

Higher education too had the Bible at its foundation. The 1636 Harvard rules for students directed, "Every one shall so exercise himself in reading the Scriptures twice a day that he shall be ready to give such an account of the proficiency thereof." Early Harvard rules also stated that "the only foundation of all sound knowledge and learning" is Jesus Christ.[29] Yale, founded in 1699, similarly required, "The Scriptures ... morning and evening are to be read by the students at times of prayer in the school."[30]

Let your heart hold fast my words;
keep my commandments, and live.
Get wisdom; get insight; do not forget,
and do not turn away from the words of my mouth.
Do not forsake her, and she will keep you;
love her, and she will guard you.
—Proverbs 4:4-6—

CONVERSION TO THE WORD OF GOD

Philip Henry (1631-1696), father of famed Bible commentator Matthew Henry, was a minister who as a child had the later Kings Charles II and James II as playmates. His diaries and letters provide a detailed account of the religious and political life of the period, as well as reflections from his personal life. He once memorized Psalm 119, the longest psalm in the Bible and the one which references the Scripture or word of God in all but 5 of its 176 verses.[31] Henry recommended meditating on one verse of the psalm each morning. In that way, the entire psalm will be pondered twice a year, and that "will bring you to be in love with all the rest of the scripture .... All grace grows, as love to the word of God grows."

Reflecting on Psalm 119:59, "I think on my ways, I turn my feet to your testimonies," Henry observed:

> ... that the great turn to be made in heart and life is *from* all other things *to* the word of God. Conversion turns us to the word of God, as our touch-stone, to examine ourselves, our state, our ways, spirits, doctrines, worships, customs; as our glass [mirror} to dress by, James 1; as our rule to walk and work by, Galatians 6:16; as our water, to wash us, Psalm 119:9; as our fire, to warm us, Luke 24; as our food, to nourish us, Job 23:12; as our sword to fight with, Ephesians 6; as our counselor, in all our doubts, Psalm 119:24; as our cordial, to comfort us; as our heritage, to enrich us.

> Noticing the *exceeding great and precious promises* of the divine word, ... Those good things, which are only convenient for us, are not absolutely promised as degrees of grace, comforts, externals.

> To every command there is a promise—Deuteronomy 10:16; compare 30:6; Ezekiel 18:31; compare 30:26; the command finds us work; the promise finds us strength. The purposes of God are his concealed promises; the promises, his revealed purposes.[32]

Since we have these promises, beloved,
let us cleanse ourselves from every defilement of body and spirit,
bringing holiness to completion in the fear of God.
—II Corinthians 7:1—

MAY 25
FEARFULLY AND WONDERFULLY MADE

John Ray (1627-1705) is often considered the "Father of Natural History" in Britain. He was one of several parson-naturalists in the seventeenth and eighteenth centuries, clergy who studied God's creation to better understand God's wisdom and power. Ray was especially interested in studying plants, though his work came to include studies of animals as well. He travelled throughout England and Europe observing different plants and animals, keeping detailed records of his observations. His classification system of plants was based on close observation and led him to develop a definition of species that Linnaeus later built upon in developing his taxonomy. A Fellow of the Royal Society, Ray's studies not only focused on classification of species, but also on form and function of organisms, a correlation which Ray argued necessitated an omniscient Creator.

In 1691 Ray published *The Wisdom of God Manifested in the Works of the Creation*, examining the created order from the stars through the plant and animal worlds, down to the lowliest insects, all manifesting God's wisdom and power in creation. Ray concluded his work by a look at the human body, calling on his readers to thank God for the marvelous bodies God has given them, recognizing we are all "fearfully and wonderfully made" (Psalm 139:14). He noted that if God made the body, He should "have the Service of it," encouraging his readers to "present your Bodies a living Sacrifice, Holy, acceptable of God." (Romans 12:1). Ray then went through the various parts of the body and how they are to be a sacrifice. The eye is to behold no evil and the tongue to speak no filthy word or the hand to do anything unlawful, but rather they should all be used in doing good. Ray cited and elaborated on numerous Scriptures encouraging the proper use of the eyes, tongue, and hands for God's use and glory. If the body is to be to God's glory, how much more the soul! As the body needs food, so does the soul; the soul should feed on Scripture (I Peter 2:2; Hebrews 5:12; I Corinthians 2:3). We should look to the Good Physician to cure the Soul in sickness (Matt. 9:12). The Soul should be clothed with righteousness, virtue, and good works (I Peter 5:5; Rev. 19:8; Matt. 23:11). Finally, the soul is to be defended by wearing the spiritual armor (Ephesians 5:13-14).

I hate and abhor falsehood, but I love your law.
—Psalm 119:163—

BY DAY AND BY NIGHT

Evangelical preachers George Whitefield, John Wesley, and Charles Spurgeon all recommended the Bible commentaries of Matthew Henry (1662-1714), and Henry's works continue to be great tools in Bible study today. The commentaries reflect Henry's exegetical style of preaching, which closely followed the literal interpretation of the Scriptures, as well as a devotional application of the Scriptures.

In his commentary on Psalm 1, Henry considered the importance of submitting to and delighting in the Word of God: "All who are well pleased that there is a God must be well pleased that there is a Bible, a revelation of God, of his will, and of the only way to happiness in him." A godly man maintains an intimate acquaintance with God through his daily meditation on the Word:

> To meditate in God's word is to discourse with ourselves concerning the great things contained in it, with a close application of mind, a fixedness of thought, till we be suitably affected with those things and experience the savour and power of them in our hearts. This we must do day and night; we must have a constant habitual regard to the word of God as the rule of our actions and the spring of our comforts, and we must have it in our thoughts, accordingly, upon every occasion that occurs, whether night or day. No time is amiss for meditating on the word of God, nor is any time unseasonable for those visits. We must not only set ourselves to meditate on God's word morning and evening, at the entrance of the day and of the night, but these thoughts should be interwoven with the business and converse of every day and with the repose and slumbers of every night. When I awake I am still with thee.[33]

The Lord gives the word.
—Psalm 68:11—

MAY 27
PRAYING THE SCRIPTURES

Matthew Henry's famed commentaries on the entire Scripture were actually never completed by him, but completed by others after his death. Henry had interrupted his commentary work to write a book on prayer, modeling how prayers can be enriched by praying the scriptures. The Puritans called this "pleading the promises." As God has made promises to His people, so we honor Him by conforming our prayers to the Scriptures. Henry's work, titled *A Method for Prayer with Scripture Expressions Proper to Be Used under Each Head* included Scriptural prayers for every possible need and occasion. Among them, was a prayer of thanksgiving for the Scriptures themselves:

> *Thank the Lord for recording his eternal Word in the written form of Scripture, and for preserving his Word in its purity and entirety up to the present day.*

> We wonder at the privilege we have to search the Scriptures, your holy Word, for in them we come to possess eternal life. We see clearly that all Scripture is given by inspiration of God, that it testifies of Christ, and is profitable for doctrine, for reproof, for correction, and for instruction in righteousness. *John 5:39; II Timothy 3:16.*

> We understand that everything recorded in the scriptures in earlier days was written to instruct us who live today. Enable us to live in hope through the patience and encouragement that comes through the Scriptures. With our whole hearts we embrace the prophetic word which is now made even more certain, as a light shining in a dark place, for the vision of your glory does not come to us as the words of a book sealed shut. Instead, we hear and read about our amazing works in our own mother tongue. *Rom. 15:4; II Peter 1:19; Isaiah 29:11; Acts 2:11.*

> Father, though many prophets and kings longed to see the truths about your wondrous way of redemption they were not able to do so. But we thank you, Lord of heaven and earth, that these saving realities that remained hidden from the wise and prudent are now clearly revealed to simple babes like us. Father, we praise you, for that was what seemed good in your sight. *Luke 10:21, 24.*[34]

I keep your precepts with all my heart.
—Psalm 119:69—

THE CREATOR'S POWER DISPLAYED

Joseph Addison (1672-1719), son of an Anglican minister and Dean of Lichfield, held numerous government positions during his life: Member of Parliament, Under Secretary of State, secretary to the Lord Lieutenant of Ireland, and member of the Irish House of Commons. But Addison is most remembered, along with his friend Richard Steele, as publisher of the magazine *The Tattler* and the daily newspaper *The Spectator*. The publications promoted family and morality and polite conversation on a wide variety of topics. Several issues of *The Spectator* included hymns by Addison. The issue for August 23, 1712, included an essay on reasonably strengthening and confirming faith. Addison quoted Psalm 19:1, "The heavens declare the glory of God," and then concluded with the following ode:

The spacious firmament on high,
with all the blue ethereal sky
and spangled heavens, a shining
    frame,
their great Original proclaim,
the unwearied sun from day to day
does his Creator's power display,
and publishes to every land
the work of an almighty hand.

Soon as the evening shades prevail
the moon takes up the wonderous tale,
and nightly to the listening earth
repeats the story of her birth;

whilst all the stars that round her burn,
and all the planets in their turn,
confirm the tidings as they roll,
and spread the truth from pole to pole.

What though in solemn silence all
move round the dark terrestrial ball;
what though not real voice nor sound
amid their radiant orbs be found;
in reason's ear they all rejoice,
for ever singing as they shine,
'The hand that made us is divine.'[35]

Addison's hymn was included in numerous hymnals in ensuing centuries, set to a tune from Haydn's *Creation*.

Day to day pours out speech,
and night to night reveals knowledge.
There is no speech, nor are there words,
whose voice is not heard.
—Psalm 19:2-3—

MAY 29

HUNGARIAN STRUGGLE FOR THE BIBLE

The Bible was first translated into Hungarian in 1439, under the influence of the teaching of John Hus, the Czech Reformer. However, religious wars throughout the 17th century at times restricted the availability of the Scriptures. The Austrian rulers, under the influence of the Jesuits, strongly opposed the Protestants. Hungarian Bibles could not be printed in Hungary, but had to be printed elsewhere and brought into the country. Nevertheless, Pastor Komaromi, a Hebrew scholar, made a new Hungarian translation in 1681, to make the language more understandable to the people.

Debrecen, the second largest city in Hungary after Budapest, was a center of Reformation teaching, with important reformed colleges and schools. In 1718, the city of Debrecen, at great expense, ordered 4000 Bibles printed in Leyden. However, the Jesuits persuaded the King to seize the shipment, and the Bibles were brought to the Jesuit house at Kassa. The council and citizens of Debrecen, after much lobbying, were able to convince King Charles III to issue a royal edict freeing the Bibles on June 29, 1723. The Jesuits, however, had the Bishop of Eger carry the Bibles to his palace, where he threw them into a damp cellar. There they remained until November 1, 1754 when the bishop had them burned before a large crowd in the court of his palace. A few copies had been hidden in the Prussian ambassador's house in Varso and were brought to Debreco in 1789, over 70 years after the town had ordered them.

In spite of opposition over the centuries, the Reformed Church in Debrecen remains. The Reformed Theological University, founded in 1538, was the only Reformed theological school that remained open in Hungary under communist rule.

Hot indignation seizes me because of the wicked,
who forsake your law.
—Psalm 119:53—

ROBINSON CRUSOE: A STORY OF REDEMPTION

Daniel Defoe (1660-1731) grew up in a family of Presbyterian dissenters, who dissented from England's established church. From his youth he was well instructed in the Bible, and many thought he would enter the ministry. But Defoe became a merchant, while also writing numerous pamphlets, essays, and poems on important issues of the day. When Queen Anne penalized Dissenters, Defoe was arrested and spent time in the pillory and in prison.

In 1719, in his late fifties, Defoe published *Robinson Crusoe*, which many consider the first English novel. The story of Crusoe's rebellion against his parents, taking to sea, and being shipwrecked on a desert island for twenty-eight years is an adventuresome framework for a narrative of a man's struggles with faith. Helpless and alone on the island, Crusoe began to see God's hand of Providence in preserving him during the shipwreck and pondered his past wickedness. He began reading a Bible he had rescued from the ship:

> I was earnestly begging God to give me repentance, when it happened providentially, the very day, that reading the Scripture, I came to these words: "He is exalted a Prince and a Saviour to give repentance and to give remission," I threw down the book; and with my heart as well as my hands lifted to heaven, in a kind of ecstasy of joy I cried out aloud, "Jesus. Thou Son of David! Jesus! Thou exalted Prince and Saviour! Give me repentance! ... I prayed ... with a true Scripture view of hope, founded on the encouragement of the Word of God.[36]

Crusoe later rescued a native South American from cannibals and began instructing him in the Scriptures. Crusoe reflected on the effect of God's Word in their lives:

> How infinite and inexpressible a blessing it is that the knowledge of God, and of the doctrine of salvation by Christ Jesus, is so plainly laid down in the Word of God, so easy to be received and understood, that, as the bare reading the scripture made me capable of understanding enough of my duty to carry me directly on to the great work of sincere repentance for my sins, and of laying hold of Saviour for life and salvation ... so the plain instruction sufficiently served to the enlightening of this savage creature and bringing him to be such a Christian as I have known few equals to him in my life.

Deal bountifully with your servant, that I may live and keep your word.
—Psalm 119:17—

MAY 31
A GUIDE TO STUDYING THE SCRIPTURE

Auguste Hermann Francke (1663-1727) was a scholar, theologian, pastor, and philanthropist in Germany. He became chair of Greek and oriental languages at the new University of Halle, organized by Frederick III of Brandenburg, and pastored a church while serving as professor. Francke established a public charity school which became a model for instruction and orphanages around the world. A careful student of the Scriptures, Francke wrote numerous books. One of the most influential was *A Guide to the Reading and Study of the Holy Scriptures*. He wrote that one must

carefully guard himself that in his reading he does not have any false motive, or unrighteous purpose in his heart. For the scribes and Pharisees also used to read the Holy Scriptures but were not the better for it. They supposed that in the Scriptures they had eternal life, but they would not come to Christ, that they might have life. Now it is a false motive and a wrong purpose, when one reads the Scriptures as a mere perfunctory performance .... There are many men who congratulate themselves on their diligent reading of God's word, whose whole spirit and life are wholly out of harmony with God's word. It is also a wrong motive, when one examines the Scriptures only with the idea of becoming learned ... for the sake of gratifying one's own selfishness and vanity. ... They busy themselves more about unprofitable questions or deep secrets in the Scripture rather than first laying a good foundation in repentance and faith. But where one has these or other wrong motives in his heart, when he reads the Scriptures ... he is in danger of the uttermost damnation, even though he have learned the entire Bible by heart. Let the learner, therefore, bring to the reading of the Scriptures a truly teachable heart, that is, an upright and sincere desire that through the Scriptures he may believe and live as it may be revealed to him from God himself. In short, when you read the Scriptures, you must have only the one upright purpose, to become a faithful and devout Christian. A learner of this kind, before he reads the Bible should pray to God, not with the lips only but with a truly devout heart: thou eternal and living God, how can we sufficiently thank thee that thou has so graciously revealed to us in thy Word thy holy will, that through it we may learn how to become devout and blessed believers! So grant to me thy Holy Spirit, that He may open mine eyes to behold marvelous things out of thy law; that through thy word He may create and increase faith in my heart, and mightily control my will.[37]

... no prophecy of Scripture comes from someone's own interpretation. For no prophecy was ever produced by the will of man, but men spoke from God as they were carried along by the Holy Spirit. —II Peter 1:20-21—

ALL MEN ARE CREATED EQUAL

One of the men who greatly influenced the thought of the United States' Founding Fathers was John Locke (1632-1704). Many of the ideas in the Declaration of Independence can be traced back to Locke: all men are created equal and have certain natural rights, such as life and liberty; governments are formed to protect people's rights. Under Locke's social contract theory, individuals surrender some of their freedoms to protect their rights, or, as the Declaration stated, governments derive their authority from the "consent of the governed."

Locke derived many of his seminal ideas from Scripture. Basic to understanding human nature was that both man and woman are created equal by God. Rules such as the 10 commandments, the Golden Rule and the teachings of Jesus and Paul are moral guides. God's deliverance of the Israelites from bondage in Egypt shows the importance of freedom as a theme in Scripture.

The last fifteen years of his life, Locke devoted almost totally to the study of the Scriptures. His *Paraphrase and Notes on the Epistles of St. Paul* reflects his careful study of the New Testament. In the study of morality, Locke wrote that "there are books enough writ both by ancient and modern philosophers; but the morality of the gospel doth so exceed them all, that, to give a man a full knowledge of true morality, I shall send him to no other book, but the New Testament."[1] When asked what was the surest way to gain a true knowledge of Christianity, Locke replied, "Let him study the Holy Scriptures, especially the New Testament. It has God for its author Salvation for its end; and Truth, without any mixture of error, for its matter."[2]

Your hands have made and fashioned me;
give me understanding that I may learn your commandments.
—Psalm 119:73—

JUNE 2
THE ONLY WISE GOD

Jonathan Edwards (1703-1758) was the son and grandson of ministers. the only son in a family of eleven children, so it was almost assumed that he would become a minister. When he was about nine, Edwards was taken up in the "remarkable awakening" in his father's congregation. He became concerned about his salvation and prayed five times a day. He talked with other boys about religion, and they even built a booth in a swamp, where they could retire for prayer. After time, however, these religious concerns wore off.

Edwards entered Yale College at age 13. He continued his early interest in science and also became acquainted with Locke's philosophy. In his last year in college, Edwards had pleurisy and was close to dying. Becoming very uneasy about his readiness for death, he renewed his religious devotion. Soon after his recovery, this new interest in religion again wore off. Edwards had many objections, doubts, and inward struggles about the goodness of God's sovereignty in His creation. But one day, Scripture changed that:

> The first that I remember that ever I found anything of that sort of inward, sweet delight in God and divine things, that I have lived much in since, was on reading those words, *I Timothy 1:17*, "Now unto the King eternal, immortal, invisible, the only wise God, be honor and glory forever and ever, Amen." As I read the words, there came into my soul, and was as it were diffused through it, a sense of the glory of the divine being; … quite different from anything ever experienced before. Never any words of Scripture seemed to me as these words did. I thought … how excellent a Being, that was; and how happy I should be, if I might enjoy that God, and be wrapt up to God in heaven, and be as it were swallowed up in him. I kept saying, and as it were singing over these words of Scripture to myself; and went to prayer, to pray to God that I might enjoy him; and prayed in a manner quite different from what I used to do; with a new sort of affection. … I began to have a new kind of apprehensions and ideas of Christ, and the work of redemption, and the glorious way of salvation by him. I had an inward, sweet, sense of these things, that at times came into my heart; … my mind was greatly engaged, to spend my time in reading and meditating on Christ; and the beauty and excellency of his person, and the lovely way of salvation, by free grace in him.[3]

Edwards' delight in God's beauty and excellencies remained, and he became a leading minister and theologian.

But you are near, O Lord, and all your commandments are true.
—Psalm 119:151—

BACH'S BIBLE

A catalog of musician Johann Sebastian Bach's estate listed a library of 80 theological works, but by 1900, all had disappeared. In 1934, Pastor C.G. Riedel attended a Conference of The Lutheran Church—Missouri Synod in Frankenmuth, Michigan, staying at the farm home of Leonard Reichle, his cousin. When Reichle showed him a German commentary Bible his father had bought in Philadelphia in 1847, Pastor Riedel saw something the Reichle family had never noticed—the signature "J.S. Bach, 1733" in the corner of the title page. Reichle brought down the two companion volumes of this same Bible. Each had the same signature and date. Could this have been signed by J.S. Bach 200 years earlier? A tracing of the signature was sent to Hans Preuss in Germany, who verified the signature's authenticity.

Dealers often persuaded needy immigrants to sell their books at very low prices. Efforts to trace the book-sellers of Bach's Bible and to discover if other books from Bach's library made it to America were unsuccessful. In 1938, Leonard Reichle presented the three-volume Bach Bible to the library of Concordia Seminary in St. Louis.

Bach's Bible, originally published in three volumes in 1681-1682, consists of Luther's German Bible translation and a commentary written by Abraham Calov (1612-1686). Much of Calov's commentary is quotes from Luther's works. In the Bible, each verse of Scripture is in large bold type, followed by Calov's commentary in a smaller font. Since Bach purchased the Bible in 1773, others must have owned it previously. Scientific analysis of the ink and handwriting has identified 348 markings, underlinings and marginal notes by Bach's own hand. These were made for Bach's private use, and they offer a glimpse into Bach's spiritual life. Several of the notes are grammatical corrections in the text or additions where verses were missing from Calov's text—showing Bach's knowledge and close attention to the Scriptures. Beside I Chronicles 25 Bach wrote "This chapter is the true foundation of all God-pleasing church music." It is well known that Bach wrote "SDG," for "Soli Deo Gloria"—"only to the glory of God"—on many of his musical manuscripts. With that same spirit, Bach wrote in his Bible at II Chronicles 5:12-13, "In devotional music, God is always present with His Grace."

Let the word of Christ dwell in you richly, teaching and admonishing one
another in all wisdom, singing psalms and hymns and spiritual songs,
with thankfulness in your hearts to God.
—Colossians 3:16—

JUNE 4
YOU MUST BE BORN AGAIN

The most well-known figure in colonial America was the British evangelist George Whitefield (1714-1770). Whitefield had a commanding presence and a dramatic, powerful voice which in themselves were captivating. Before his conversion, he had a passion for the theater, and he brought his talent for acting into his sermons, re-enacting the Bible stories. Whitefield brought the message of the Gospel outside the church, first preaching in the open air to miners outside Bristol. Whitefield's melodic voice was so powerful that he preached at one time to a crowd of nearly 100,000, without any amplification.

In addition to preaching throughout England and Scotland, Whitefield made seven trips to America and preached throughout the colonies, from Georgia to Maine. Throughout his preaching, John 3:3 was his central text, "Verily, verily, I say unto thee, except a man be born again, he cannot see the kingdom of God." He preached on this verse over three hundred times, for he saw this as the universal need. This is the revelation of God without which there is no salvation.

A woman once asked Whitefield why he so often preached that you must be born again. Whitefield simply answered, "Because, you must be born again!" A person could no more bring himself to a spiritual rebirth than he ever brought about his physical birth: "The sinner can no more raise himself from the deadness of sin than Lazarus, dead four days, until Jesus came and cried out, 'Lazarus, come forth.'"[4] A dead sinner is made a new creature in Christ, is born again, through the power and work of the Holy Spirit, not by any works of his own.

Great is your mercy, O Lord;
give me life according to your rules.
—Psalm 119:156—

CHRIST IN THE PSALMS

Isaac Watts (1674-1748) was a precocious child who learned to read early, was learning Latin at age four, and went on to learn Greek, Hebrew, and French as well. His family were Dissenters from the Church of England, and his father had been imprisoned twice for his religious views. Watts became a pastor at a chapel in London, though ill health caused him to relinquish his pulpit. He then worked as a tutor and wrote extensively. His book on *Logic* was used in the universities. Most memorable, however, are Watts' over 600 hymns. In his poetic paraphrase of the psalms, Watts sought to have David speak "the language of a Christian:"

> Where the psalmist describes religion by the fear of God, I have often joined faith and love to it. Where he speaks of the pardon of sin through the mercies of God, I have added the merits of a Savior. Where he talks of sacrificing goats or bullocks, I rather choose to mention the sacrifice of Christ, the lamb of God. Where he promises abundance of wealth, honor, and long life, I have changed some of these typical blessings for grace, glory, and life eternal, which are brought in by the light of the Gospel, and promised in the New Testament.[5]

This method can be seen in Watts' rendering of Psalm 2:

Why did the nations join to slay
    The Lord's anointed Son?
Why did they cast his laws away,
    And tread his gospel down?

The Lord that sits above the skies,
    Derides their rage below;
He speaks with vengeance in his eyes,
    And strikes their spirits through.

"I call him my Eternal Son,
    "And raise him from the dead;
"I make my holy hill his throne,
    "And wide his kingdom spread.

"Ask me, my Son, and then enjoy
    "The utmost heathen lands:
"Thy rod of iron shall destroy
    "The rebel that withstands."

Be wise, ye rulers of the earth,
    Obey th' anointed Lord,
Adore the King of heav'nly birth,
    And tremble at his word.

With humble love address his throne;
    For if he frown, ye die:
Those are secure, and those alone,
    Who on his grace rely.[6]

Did not our hearts burn within us
while he talked to us on the road,
while he opened to us the Scriptures?
—Luke 24:32—

JUNE 6
THE CALL OF WISDOM

Hymn writer Isaac Watts not only put the psalms in English verse so that David could "sing like a Christian," but he composed hymns from other portions of Scriptures as well. One such hymn versified the call of Wisdom in Proverbs 8:

Shall wisdom cry aloud,
And not her speech be heard?
The voice of God's eternal Word,
Deserves it no regard?

"I was the chief delight,
His everlasting Son,
Before the first of all His works,
Creation was begun.

"Before the flying clouds.
Before the solid land,
Before the fields, before the floods,
I dwelt at His right hand.

"When he adorned the skies,
And built them, I was there,
To order where the sun should rise,
And marshal every star.

"When he poured out the sea,
And spread the flowing deep,
I gave the flood a firm decree
In its own bounds to keep.

"Upon the empty air
The earth was balanced well.
With joy I saw the mansion where
The sons of men should dwell.

"My busy thoughts at first
On their salvation ran,
Ere sin was born, or Adam's dust
Was fashioned to a man.

"Then come, receive my grace,
Ye children, and be wise;
Happy the man that keeps my ways;
The man that shuns them dies."[7]

For I am the Lord; I will speak the word that I will speak,
and it will be performed.
—Ezekiel 12:25—

THE HOLY SCRIPTURES

Being the very Word of God, the Bible provides hope in the face of fear and guilt as well as solace in time of grief. The Scriptures provide wisdom when reason fails. This pearl of great price helps us see Jesus and leads to the very presence of God. Hymn writer Isaac Watts expressed this beautifully in his hymn, "The Holy Scriptures:"

> Laden with guilt, and full of fears,
>   I fly to thee, my Lord,
> And not a glimpse of hope appears
>   But in thy written word.
>
> The volume of my Father's grace
>   Does all my griefs assuage;
> Here I behold my Savior's face,
>   Almost in every page.
>
> Here consecrated water flows,
>   To quench my thirst of sin;
> Here the fair tree of knowledge grows;
>   Nor danger dwells therein.
>
> This is the field where hidden lies
>   The pearl of price unknown;
> The merchant is divinely wise
>   Who makes the pearl his own.
>
> This is the judge that ends the strife,
>   Where wit and reason fail;
> My guide to everlasting life,
>   Through all this gloomy vale.
>
> Oh, may Thy counsels, mighty God,
>   My roving feet command;
> Nor I forsake the happy road,
>   That leads to Thy right hand.[8]

Depart from me, you evildoers, that I may keep the commandments of my God.
—Psalm 119:115—

JUNE 8
A BOOK FROM YOUTH TO OLD AGE

Isaac Watts (1674-1748), recognized as the "Father of English Hymnody," not only versified the psalms, to make, as he said, David sing as a Christian, but he wrote hymns which expressed the Christian experience. Many continue in use today, including, "Joy to the World," "Our God Our Help in Ages Past" and "When I Survey the Wondrous Cross." Watts wrote several hymns about the Bible. One focused on the importance of the Bible for young people:

In another, he wrote of God's revelation both in nature and in the Scriptures:

How shall the young secure their
    hearts,
    And guard their lives from sin?
Thy word the choicest rules imparts
    To keep the conscience clean.

When once it enters to the mind,
    It spreads such light abroad,
The meanest souls instruction find,
    And raise their thoughts to God.

'Tis like the sun, a heavenly light,
    That guides us all the day;
And through the dangers of the night
    A lamp to lead our way.[9]

The Bible is incomparable, suitable for youth and useful into old age.

The starry heavens thy rule obey,
    The earth maintains her place;
And these thy servants night and day
    Thy skill and power express.

But still thy law and gospel, Lord,
    Have lessons more divine;
Not earth stands firmer than thy word,
    Nor stars so nobly shine.

Let all the heathen writers join
    To form one perfect book:
Great God, if once compared with
    thine,
How mean their writings look!

Not the most perfect rules they gave,
    Could show one sin forgiven,
Nor lead a step beyond the grave;
    But then conduct to heaven.

Thy word is everlasting truth;
    How pure is every page!
That holy book shall guide our youth,
    And well support our age.[10]

If your law had not been my delight,
I would have perished in my affliction.
—Psalm 119:92—

PRAYERS BEFORE STUDYING

Isaac Watts (1674-1748), best known as a hymn writer and author of *Psalms of David*, (first printed in America by Benjamin Franklin in 1729!) also was very interested in education and wrote a number of works encouraging learning. His *Logic, or The Right Use of Reason in the Enquiry after Truth* encouraged critical thinking and became a standard text at Oxford, Cambridge, Harvard, and Yale. He supplemented this with *The Improvement of the Mind*, which laid out the different rules and methods for learning. Watts noted that "He, that trusteth in his own heart is a fool" (Proverbs 28:26) and advised the student "to trust in the Lord with all our heart, and not to lean to our own understandings, nor to be wise in our own eyes" (Proverbs 3:5-6). He encouraged students to pray before studying:

> Offer up, therefore, your daily requests to God, the father of lights, that he would bless all your attempts in reading, study and conversation. Think with yourself, how easily and how insensibly, by one turn of thought he can lead you into a large scene of useful ideas. He can teach you to lay hold on a clue, which may guide your thoughts with safety and ease, through all the difficulties of an intricate subject. Think, how easily the Author of your being can direct your motions, by his providence, so a word striking the ear, or a sudden turn of fancy, shall conduct you to a train of happy sentiments.... Implore constantly his divine grace, to point your inclination to proper studies, and to fix your heart there.[11]

Joseph Emerson, who edited Watts' work in the nineteenth century, included a possible prayer for use before studying the Scriptures:

> O God of nature and of grace; Father of angels and of saints, I bless thee for the light of sun, moon, and stars. But more especially would I praise thee, for the light of redemption, the light that beams forth from the face of Jesus, that glows on the pages of thy holy word. To this holy word, may I ever take heed, as to a light shining in a dark place, O Lord, I beseech thee to show me thy glory; teach me wondrous things out of thy law; open my understanding, that I may understand the Scriptures; quicken my memory, to return thy truth; and my heart, to obey it; that by thy word and Spirit, I may be trained for everlasting life, through Jesus Christ to whom be honor, praise, dominion and glory forever. Amen.[12]

Hear instruction and be wise, and do not neglect it.
—Proverbs 8:33—

JUNE 10
A HEART FOR THE WORD

Jonathan Edwards (1703-1758) is recognized by many as one of the leading American theologians and preachers of all times. A staunch Puritan, Edwards was forefront in the revival known as The Great Awakening which shaped the American colonies before the American Revolution. For Edwards, as for Puritans in general, the Word of God was central to preaching and the Christian life. Edwards expressed his passion for the Scriptures in his "Personal Narrative" describing his spiritual life:

> Oftentimes in reading it, every word seemed to touch my heart. I felt an harmony between something in my heart, and those sweet and powerful words. I seemed often to see so much light, exhibited by every sentence, and such a refreshing ravishing food communicated, that I could not get along in reading. Used oftentimes to dwell long on one sentence, to see the wonders contained in it; and yet almost every sentence seemed to be full of wonders.

Edwards would sometimes become so engrossed in his reading and study of the Scriptures that he would skip dinner rather than break away from his study.

Edwards stressed that the Bible is for every person, not just the clergy. The treasure of Scripture should be searched by the "learned and unlearned, young and old, men and women." The most brilliant scholar can never exhaust the Scripture. The subject of God is inexhaustible, for God is "infinite, and there is no end to the glory of her perfections." The great part of a Christian's life should be applying his heart and mind to the Scripture; he should search the Scriptures as if digging in a mine of gold. A person who has a Bible and does not look into it, "is like a man that has a box full of silver and gold, and don't know it, don't observe that it is anything more than a vessel filled with common stones. As long as it is thus with him, he'll be never the better for his treasure."[13]

Salvation is far from the wicked,
for they do not seek your statutes.
—Psalm 119:155—

CONVERSATIONS WITH GOD

The famed Puritan preacher Jonathan Edwards wrote that a conversation between God and mankind is "maintained by God's word on his part, and prayers on ours."[14] God speaks to us in His Word, and we speak to Him through our prayers. All Scripture is important, with no trivial points or speculations to be found in them. We should pay close heed to the Scriptures:

> It shows a wicked contempt in a child, when he is no way careful to retain the counsels and admonitions given him by a father. How much more when men thus treat the infinitely great God, when he in a solemn manner directs himself to us and gives his holy counsels and instructions.[15]

Edwards encouraged diligent Scripture reading:

> Be assiduous in reading the holy Scriptures. This is the fountain whence all knowledge in divinity must be derived. Therefore let not this treasure lie by you neglected. Every man of common understanding who can read, may, if he please, become well acquainted with the Scriptures. And what an excellent attainment would this be!… When you read, observe what you read. Observe how things come in. Take notice of the drift of the discourse, and compare one scripture with another. For the Scriptures, by the harmony of the different parts of it, cast great light upon itself. We are expressly directed by Christ to "search the scriptures" [John 5:39], which evidently intends something more than a mere cursory reading.[16]

Without the Scriptures,

> … men would undoubtedly forever be at a loss what God expects from us and what we may expect from him; what we are to depend upon as to our concern with God, and what ground we are to go upon in our conduct and proceedings that relate to him; what end we are to aim at and what rule we are to be directed by, and what good and what harm is to be expected from a right or wrong conduct. Yea, without a revelation, men would be greatly at a loss concerning God …[17]

The Scriptures make possible our conversation with God.

Therefore all Your precepts concerning all things
I consider to be right; I hate every false way.
—Psalm 119:128—

JUNE 12
MESSIAH

The Enlightenment of the eighteenth century elevated human reason in opposition to supernatural revelation. Enlightenment ideas spawned Deism, which believed in a Supreme Being and Creator, but thought he was aloof and had no interactions in the affairs of men. The divine revelation of the Scriptures and the actions of Providence in history were both rejected by the Deists. Charles Jennens (1700-1773), a wealthy Englishman and devout Christian, was deeply concerned with the inroads Deism were making into the church. He thought the suicide of his brother after his rejection of the Christian faith was due in part to the skepticism induced by Deistic writers.

Jennens had a love and understanding of music and became a close friend of the composer George Frederic Handel (1685-1759). Jennens brought the first piano to England, on which Handel performed. He wrote several libretti for Handel, including *Saul, L'Allegro, il Penseroso, Belshazzar,* and probably assembled the Scripture citations used in Handel's *Israel in Egypt.* When Jennens prepared the libretto for *Messiah,* 60% of the story of Jesus was taken from Old Testament Scriptures, especially from Isaiah, Haggai and Malachi. That in His life and death Jesus fulfilled numerous Hebrew prophecies was a powerful refutation of Deism.

When Handel set Jennens' libretto to music, he amazingly completed the entire composition in 24 days. His servant brought him meals on a tray, but then would often find the meals uneaten as Handel was so consumed with his composition. Often Handel was enraptured by the Scripture and the scenes described. After completing the *Messiah*, Handel wrote, "S.D.G." at the bottom—"Soli Deo Gloria," "to God alone the glory." Wherever *Messiah* has been performed, the prophetic words of Scripture and the story of Jesus are powerfully proclaimed.

And the Word became flesh and dwelt among us, and we have seen
his glory, glory as of the only Son from the Father,
full of grace and truth.
—John 1:14—

SAUER BIBLE

Christoph Sauer (1695-1759) has been called a "One-man Bible Society," yet when he immigrated to Pennsylvania from Germany in 1724, he had little idea he would become a major publisher of Bibles. Soon after establishing his medical practice in Germantown, Christoph became concerned that the Germans lacked morally uplifting reading material in their own language. He began importing Bibles and religious books and encouraged Bible societies in Germany to donate Bibles to distribute among the poor. Some interested Christians sent over a large number of religious books as well as a printing press and type for printing German religious books in America. When the man who was sent over to undertake the work proved incapable, Christoph Sauer took over the business, bringing in workmen from Germany, and launching his own publishing business. He printed the first German almanac published in America, which continued to be published for forty years. In 1739, he began publishing the first religious newspaper in America and soon began publication of a German religious quarterly.

Recognizing the need for more of the German settlers to own a Bible, he began plans for the enormous undertaking of publishing a German Bible. A font of German type was donated by a type-founder in Frankfurt, Germany. Christoph erected a mill for making his own paper and ink. He also did his own binding and cast any extra type he needed. It took three years to print and bind 1200 copies. In 1743, Christoph Sauer issued the first European language Bible published in America. The Bible was Martin Luther's German translation. As Sauer wrote in the preface, the Bible was published without notes because the Holy Spirit in the heart of the Christian will reveal the meaning of the Scripture if one asks God for wisdom. Sauer did include Scriptural cross-references, however, believing that one passage of Scripture can help explain another.

If anyone could not afford to buy a Bible, Christoph gave it to him. He lived his life following the motto on the wall of his printing shop, "To the glory of God and my neighbor's good."

The sum of your word is truth,
and every one of your righteous rules endures forever.
—Psalm 119:160—

JUNE 14
AMAZING GRACE

For over fifty years, John Newton (1725-1807) marked the anniversary of March 10, 1748 with special prayer and thanksgiving, as the day of his conversion, when "the Lord sent from on high and delivered me out of deep waters." [18] Newton's mother, a devout Christian, began to train him in Christian truth, but she died when he was only six. Newton went to sea at age 11 with his father, a shipmaster. Later, he was impressed into the Royal Navy and then was on ships in the African slave trade. He was debauched and profane; despised by the other sailors. Once he was left on the African coast and became a slave himself. A sea captain friend of his father's (who had since died) found him and rescued him.

After his rescue, as the ship was returning to England, it was caught in an enormous storm and was in danger of sinking. As the ship filled with water, Newton called out to God for mercy. He had not thought of God's mercy in many years. At one point during the storm, Newton was tied to the helm so he could steer the ship through the winds and waves. During that time, he thought about his spiritual condition and began to pray. During a break in the storm, he found a Bible and began to read. Newton read Luke 11:13—"if you then, who are evil, know how to give good gifts to your children, how much more will the heavenly Father give the Holy Spirit to those who ask him!" He took this promise to heart and prayed that the Holy Spirit would guide his understanding of the Scriptures. Jesus' parables of the fig tree and especially the prodigal son (Luke 13:6-9; 15:11-31) also deeply affected him:

> I thought that had never been so nearly exemplified as by myself. And then, the goodness of the Father in receiving, nay, in running to meet such a son, and this, intended only, to illustrate the Lord's goodness to returning sinners!— ... I continued much in prayer. I had a satisfactory evidence in my own mind of the truth of the Gospel as considered in itself, and of its exact suitableness to answer all my needs. I saw, that, by the way they were pointed out, God might declare not his mercy only, but his justice also in the pardon of sin on account of the obedience and sufferings of Jesus Christ .... I stood in need of an *Almighty* Saviour, and such a one I found described in the New Testament. [19]

John Newton was indeed born again. He became an influential pastor and the author of many hymns, the most well-known being "Amazing Grace."

Follow the pattern of sound words that you have heard from me, in the faith and love that are in Christ Jesus. By the Holy Spirit who dwells within us, guard the good deposit entrusted to you.
—II Timothy 1:13-14—

JUNE 15
QUENCHING THE SPIRITUAL THIRST

In 1749, two years after missionary David Brainerd's death at age 29, Jonathan Edwards published a biography of Brainerd based largely on his diary. Edwards' *An Account of the Life of the late Reverend Mr. David Brainerd* has never been out of print since then! It is the most-reprinted of Jonathan Edwards' works, and has influenced many for missionary work. Methodist founder John Wesley thought every preacher should read it carefully. William Carey, called the "Father of Modern Missions," was inspired to his own missionary work in India by Brainerd's in America. Henry Martyn, missionary to Persia, was deeply moved by Brainerd's devotion and resolved to follow his missionary example. Brainerd's life impacted many other pastors, missionaries and evangelists, including Robert McCheyne, David Livingston, Andrew Murray, Frederick Schwartz, and John Eliot.

Born into a Puritan home in Connecticut, David Brainerd (1718-1747) was orphaned at age 14. Brainerd read Jesus' words, "If any man thirst, let him come unto me and drink." (Matt. 11:28) What did that mean? How was he supposed to come to Christ? Brainerd was irritated that he did not know how to follow that command. Then, on the Sunday evening of July 12, 1739, Brainerd was walking alone when, as he later wrote,

> the way of salvation opened to me with infinite wisdom, suitableness, and excellency, that I wondered I should every think of any other way of salvation; was amazed that I had not dropped my own contrivances, and complied with this lovely, blessed, and excellent way before. If I could have been saved by my own duties, or any other way that I had formerly contrived, my whole soul would now have refused. I wondered, that all the world did not see and comply with this way of salvation, entirely by the *righteousness of Christ*.[20]

He realized that Jesus' words, "If any man thirst," implied a world filled with people with a spiritual thirst. He longed to tell the world of Jesus' offer. He began working as a missionary among the native Americans near his home. Though often weak with tuberculosis, he tirelessly proclaimed Christ. Many rejoiced and believed. Brainerd's consuming desire was the conversion of the heathen, to bring them the living water of salvation which had so refreshed his own soul. His example has inspired many across the centuries.

You are my hiding place and my shield; I hope in your word.
—Psalm 119:114—

PRAYER BEFORE READING
THE SCRIPTURES

William Burkitt (1650-1703) was a vicar and lecturer in Dedham, England. About 1700 he published in two volumes his *Expository Notes on the New Testament,* which went through numerous editions. The subtitle of the work gives Burkitt's purpose: *Expository Notes, with practical Observations, on the New Testament of Our Lord Jesus Christ. Wherein the sacred Text is at Large Recited, The Sense Explained, and the Instructive Example of the Blessed Jesus, and His Holy Apostles, to our Imitation Recommended. The Whole Designed to Encourage the Reading of the Scriptures in Private families and to Render the Daily Perusal of Them Profitable and Delightful* (long titles were really in vogue in that day!). This was a work especially designed to aid families in their Bible reading together.

In 1770, the father of James Madison (fourth President of the United States) ordered William Burkitt's *Expository Notes on the Bible* for the family's library. While a student at the College of New Jersey, James Madison carefully studied Burkitt's commentary, and Madison's notes from his Bible studies are among the James Madison papers in the National Archives. Matthew Henry said that Burkitt's *Notes* were the inspiration for his own famous commentary, and Charles Spurgeon recommended Burkitt's work.

In his *Notes,* Burkitt included the following prayer before reading the Scriptures:

ALMIGHTY God and merciful Father, who hast appointed thy word to be a light to our feet, and a lamp to our paths, and caused all holy scriptures to be written for our learning; grant us the assistance of thy Holy Spirit, that we may in such ways read, mark, learn, and inwardly digest them, that by patience and comfort of thy holy word, we may embrace, and ever hold fast the blessed hope of everlasting life, which thou hast given us in our Saviour Jesus Christ. And seeing of thy tender love to mankind, thou hast given thy dear and only Son to be unto us both a sacrifice for sin, and also an example of Godly life, give us grace that we may always most thankfully receive this his inestimable benefit, and also daily endeavour ourselves to follow the blessed steps of his most holy life; who liveth and reigneth with Thee and the holy Ghost, ever one God, world without end. Amen.

My son, keep my words and treasure up my commandments with you;
keep my commandments and live; keep my teaching as the apple of your eye.
—Proverbs 7:1-2—

JUNE 17
THE TEN COMMANDMENTS

The son of Puritan preacher Henry Erskine and the younger brother of prominent preacher Ebenezer Erskine, Ralph Erskine (1685-1752) was a noted minister in his own right. A minister at Dunfermline for forty years, Ralph Erskine was a powerful preacher, and numerous volumes of his sermons were published during his lifetime. Erskine also wrote poetical paraphrases of large portions of Scripture, volumes which continued to be published after his death. Among these poetical paraphrases is his poem on "The Ten Commandments":

1. No God but me thou shalt adore,
   I am thy God alone.
2. No image frame to bow before,
   But idols all dethrone.
3. God's glorious name take not in vain,
   For be rever'd he will.
4. His sacred Sabbath don't profane,
   Mind it is holy still.
5. To parents render due respect,
   This may thy life prolong.
6. All murder shun and malice check,
   To no man's life do wrong.
7. From thoughts of whoredom base abstain,
   From words and actions vile.
8. Shun theft and all unlawful gain,
   Nor gather wealth by guile.
9. False witness flee, and sland'ring spite,
   Nor willful lies invent.
10. Don't covet what's thy neighbour's right,
    Nor harbor discontent.[21]

My mother and brothers are those who hear God's word
and put it into practice.
—Luke 8:21—

THE BIBLE AND JOHNSON'S DICTIONARY

In 1755, Samuel Johnson (1709-1784) published his *A Dictionary of the English Language*. Though there had been many earlier English dictionaries, Johnson's became the standard for completeness and an example for later dictionaries to follow on how entries in dictionaries should be written. Johnson included notes and examples on word usage and was not averse to including humor in his examples. Johnson's definition of "Bible" gives an example of his work:

> BI′ BLE.*n.s.*[from βίϐλιον, a book; called, by way of excellence, The Book.] The sacred volume in which are contained the revelations of God.

> If we pass from the apostolic to the next ages of the church, the primitive Christians looked on their *bibles* as their most important treasure. *Government of the Tongue,* § 3.

> We must take heed how we accustom ourselves to a slight and irreverent use of the name of God, and of the phrases and expressions of the holy *bible*, which ought not to be applied upon every slight occasion. *Tilliotson, sermon* i.

> In questions of natural religion, we should confirm and improve, or connect our reasonings, by the divine assistance of the *bible. Watt's Logick*[22]

Johnson was familiar with the Bible from his youth, and regularly read through the Bible every year. He had a small pocket–size New Testament which he always had with him. Besides reading his English Bible, Johnson studied the Scriptures in the original Greek as well as in Latin. In his 60s, when he thought he had become well acquainted with the Scriptures, he began reading them in other languages as well.

If we receive the testimony of men,
the testimony of God is greater,
for this is the testimony of God
that he has borne concerning his Son.
—I John 5:9—

JUNE 19

DELIGHTING IN GOD'S WORD

Augustus Toplady (1740-1778) was a minister who is now best remembered for his hymn "Rock of Ages." He was 16 and visiting in Ireland when he heard a layman preaching in a barn on Ephesians 2:13, "Ye who were sometimes far off are made nigh by the blood of Christ," and he came to faith in Christ. Toplady later wrote:

> Strange that I, who had so long sat under the means of grace in England, should be brought nigh to God in an obscure part of Ireland, amidst a handful of God's people met together in a barn, and under the ministry of one who could hardly spell his name! Surely it was the Lord's doing and is marvelous! The excellency of such power must be of God and cannot be of man. The regenerating Spirit breathes not only on whom, but likewise, when, where, and as he listeth.[23]

From the early days of his conversion, Toplady wrote poems and hymns on Christian truth and doctrine. In 1759, he published a collection of poems written in the early years of his conversion, before he was eighteen. Among them was a poem on Psalm 119:40-49:

1 Let thy loving mercy, Lord,
  Come also unto me;
Now according to thy word.
  My present Saviour be:
Unbelievers then no more
  Shall against my hope
  blaspheme:
Forc'd to own, "The mighty pow'r
  Of God hath rescu'd him."

2 In thy word my trust I place,
  And humbly urge my claim.
'Til I of thy saving grace,
  A living witness am;
Give me, Lord, thyself to know,
  Then in me thy word fulfill,
To walk in all things here below,
  According to thy will.

3 Seeking now in steadfast faith,
  I wait a word from thee:
Bring my feet into the path
  Of perfect liberty:
Then, when I the path have found,
  Un-asham'd thy truth I'll shew:
Kings shall hear the joyful sound,
  And seek salvation too.

4 My delight is in thy word
  Which I have lov'd of old,
Dearer is thy promise, Lord,
  To me than mines of gold:
Up to thee my hands I lift,
  'Till I of thy grace receive;
Give the never changing gift,
  Thy full redemption give.[24]

I hold my life in my hand continually, but I do not forget your law.
—Psalm 119:109—

THEODOSIA

Anne Steele (1717-1778) came from a line of English Puritans, and from an early age she had a devotion to the things of Christ, a piety expressed in her poems and essays. An invalid from childhood, Anne was often confined to her room in pain and weakness. Yet, from her pen came an outpouring of spiritual poems and hymns. Under the name "Theodosia," meaning God's gift, in 1760 Anne published *Poems on Subjects Chiefly Devotional*. Among the poems was one on "The Excellency and Sufficiency of the Holy Scriptures" which was published in numerous later hymnals:

> Father of Mercies, in thy Word
> > What endless Glory shines!
> For ever be thy Name ador'd
> > For these celestial Lines.
>
> Here, may the wretched Sons of Want
> > Exhaustless Riches find;
> Riches, above what Earth can grant,
> > And lasting as the Mind.
>
> Here, the fair Tree of Knowledge grows,
> > And yields a free Repast.
> Sublimer Sweets than Nature knows
> > Invite the longing Taste.
>
> Here the Redeemer's welcome Voice
> > Spreads heavenly Peace around;
> And Life, and everlasting Joys
> > Attend the blissful Sound.
>
> O may these heavenly Pages be
> > My ever dear Delight;
> And still new Beauties may I see,
> > And still increasing Light!
>
> Divine Instructor, gracious Lord,
> > Be thou for ever near,
> Teach me to love thy sacred Word,
> > And view my Savior there.[25]

Let my soul live and praise you, and let your rules help me.
—Psalm 119:175—

JUNE 21
LAWS OF NATURE AND NATURE'S GOD

During the American Revolution and for decades after, the standard law book was William Blackstone's four volume *Commentaries on the Laws of England,* first published in 1765. In his masterful work, which is still quoted in legal and even Supreme Court decisions, Blackstone (1723-1780) saw God as the source of all law.

Even as a youth, Blackstone was a voracious reader. By the time he was seven he had read the entire Bible, Bunyan's *Pilgrim's Progress,* and much of Milton. The biblical foundation of his legal outlook was established at an early age. He wrote that man, as a creature, is dependent on the laws of his Creator and should conform to the Creator's will, called the Law of Nature:

> For as God, when He created matter, and endued it with a principle of mobility, established certain rules for the perpetual direction of that motion, so, when He created man, and endued him with free will to conduct himself in all parts of life, He laid down certain immutable laws of human nature, whereby that free will is in some degree regulated and restrained, and gave him also the faculty of reason to discover and purport of those laws.

These natural laws the Creator allows to be discovered by man's reason and are true throughout the globe and at all times. No human laws contrary to the natural law are of any validity.

In His Providence and compassion "to the frailty, the imperfection, and the blindness of human reason," God has also been pleased

> ... at sundry times and in divers manners, to discover and enforce its laws by an immediate and direct revelation. The doctrines thus delivered we called the revealed or divine law, and they are to be found only in the Holy Scriptures. These precepts, when revealed are found upon comparison to be really a part of the original law of nature, as they tend in all their consequences to man's felicity.

But man's reason could not discern these because of his sin and corruption. The moral system of the revealed law of Scriptures is superior to the law of nature, for the revealed law is declared by God Himself, uncorrupted by man's imaginings.

Blackstone asserted that all human laws rest on the foundation of the law of nature and the law of revelation. No human laws should contradict these.[26]

With my lips I declare all the rules of your mouth.
—Psalm 119:13—

PROCLAIM LIBERTY THROUGHOUT THE LAND

The Liberty Bell, often pictured on stamps and coins, has become an iconic symbol of the United States. When Pennsylvania was founded in 1682, William Penn brought a bell to the city to give notice of proclamations or warnings of danger. In 1751, when a new bell tower was being built in the Pennsylvania State House, the Pennsylvania Provincial Assembly commissioned a better-quality bell from a foundry in London. The bell would commemorate the 50th anniversary of the "Pennsylvania Charter of Privileges" of 1701. The Pennsylvania Charter laid out the basic principles of the rule of law and affirmed civil and religious liberties. The inscription on the bell was to read "By order of the Assembly of the Provinces of Pennsylvania for the State House in the City of Philadelphia, 1752."

In honor of the 50th anniversary of the Charter of Privileges of Pennsylvania, the inscription chosen for the top of the bell was from Leviticus 25:10 "Proclaim Liberty throughout all the Land unto all the inhabitants thereof." The biblical text further explains that the 50th year "shall be a jubilee unto you; and you shall return every man unto his family." During the Jubilee year, debts were forgiven, a reminder of the liberty God grants His people.

Just before the British captured Philadelphia in 1777, the State House Bell was moved to Allentown, Pennsylvania and hidden in a church. This would prevent the British melting the bell down to make cannons! The bell returned to Philadelphia in 1778. Because of its inscription for liberty, in the 19th century, the bell came to be known as the Liberty Bell and became a symbol for the abolitionists. Some time around the 1840s, the bell began to crack; repairs were unsuccessful, and the bell has not rung since 1846. Though silent, the Liberty Bell, now a revered symbol, still proclaims liberty throughout the land.

Remember your word to your servant,
in which you have made me hope.
—Psalm 119:49—

JUNE 23
THE FOUNDING FATHERS
AND THE SCRIPTURE

As the colonial leaders at the time of the American Revolution wrestled with their new-found independence and organized a government for the new nation, they frequently looked to the Scripture for insight and guidance. Some passages were especially referenced. Jethro's advice to Moses when overwhelmed with governing the people seemed especially wise. Moses was to set the laws of God before the people but was also to "look for able men from all the people, men who fear God, who are trustworthy and hate a bribe, and place such men over the people as chiefs of thousands, of hundreds, of fifties, and of tens. And let them judge the people at all times." (Exodus 18:21-22).[27] The kind of federalism instituted among the tribes of Israel seemed quite suited to the thirteen colonies brought into a union of one government.

Other Scriptures were repeatedly referenced as giving guidance to the new government. "Righteousness exalts a nation, but sin is a reproach to any people." (Proverbs 14:34) taught the importance of morality among the people in giving a firm foundation to the nation, a theme echoed by all leaders of the early government. Righteous rulers were important for the government's success, "When the righteous increase, the people rejoice, but when the wicked rule, the people groan. By Justice a king builds up the land, but he who exacts gifts tears it down." (Proverbs 29:2,4)

From its earliest days, Congress approved special days of thanksgiving and prayer on notable occasions. This was an example they took from the Scriptures, especially the day of thanksgiving and celebration at the dedication of Solomon's temple. (I Kings 8; II Chronicles 5-7)[28]

The God of Israel has spoken; the Rock of Israel has said to me:
When one rules justly over men, ruling in the fear of God,
he dawns on them like the morning light...
—II Samuel 23:4-5—

A WRITER OF PSALMS AND SIGNER OF THE DECLARATION OF INDEPENDENCE

A little-known American Founding Father with numerous accomplishments was Francis Hopkinson (1737-1791). A native of Philadelphia, Hopkinson was among the first class at the College of Philadelphia. He was an organist and choir leader at Christ Church, where he put many of the psalms to music. He became a customs collector, but resigned in 1776 to become a delegate to the Continental Congress, where he signed the Declaration of Independence. Under the new government, he helped ratify the Constitution in Pennsylvania and was appointed to the U.S. District Court for Pennsylvania.

Hopkinson wrote poems, satirical pamphlets, popular songs, and the first American cantata (*America Independent*). He claimed to be the "first Native of the United States who has produced a musical composition."[29]

In the 1760s, the Dutch Congregation of New York asked Hopkinson to translate the psalms into English which could be sung to traditional Dutch Reformed church tunes. This *Psalms of David,* published in 1765, was the first book with musical notes printed in America. The type for the music was imported from Amsterdam. Here's his translation of the opening of Psalm 1:

How blest is he, who ne'er consents to walk,
By ill Advice, nor dares to stand and talk
In Sinners' Way, their Vice and Cause maintaining
Nor sits with Scorners, Thus divine profaning:
But in God's sacred Law takes great Delight,
Still reads by Day and meditates by Night.

Like some fair Tree, fix'd by the River's Side,
Which bends with Fruit and spreads its Foliage wide;
So shall he flourish, Heav'n his Cause defending,
And sweet Success his good Designs attending;
In vain the Tempest strives to shake his Leaf,
The Sun of Joy breaks thro' the Clouds of Grief.[30]

Truly, truly, I say to you, whoever hears my word and believes him who sent me has eternal life. He does not come into judgment, but has passed from death to life.
—John 5:24—

JUNE 25
FRANCIS ASBURY PREACHING IN AMERICA

On November 24, 1771, Methodist Francis Asbury began preaching in America. His tireless ministry over the next forty-five years would firmly establish the Methodist church in America.

Born in England in 1745, Francis Asbury was fourteen when he heard a travelling preacher. He was amazed to see preaching without a sermon book, praying without a prayer book, and men and women on their knees shouting Amens. They seemed to have a more joyful type of religion than the cold ceremonialism that Asbury had previously known in church. Asbury began having meetings in his own house and became a local preacher himself. At 21, he was accepted at the Wesleyan Conference in London and volunteered as a missionary to America. He wrote in his journal that he was going to the New World to live for God and to bring others to Him

Arriving in America in 1771, Asbury spent a few days preparing for his work. He prayed, read his Bible and John Wesley's sermons. Then he set out on his amazing ministry as a rugged travelling preacher with a rigid schedule. He rose at 4 A.M. for two hours of prayer and meditation. As he rode his horse, he read and studied. Every 4 months he read through the Bible, and he knew the New Testament by heart. He preached at least every other day, stressing the sinner's need for redemption in Jesus Christ. Asbury had an overwhelming sense of responsibility for America—and he would remain to minister there until his death in 1816. As the American frontier expanded, Asbury found himself travelling territory the size of western Europe. He covered so much ground that he was recognized by more Americans than even the President of the young United States.

... preach the word; be ready in season and out of season;
reprove, rebuke, and exhort, with complete patience and teaching.
—II Timothy 4:2—

THE BIBLE'S INFLUENCE IN
AMERICA'S FOUNDING

Leaders of the American Revolution and the founders of the United States knew they were embarking on a new venture and a new beginning in government that was unique in the history of the world. They studied and pondered governments from ancient times to the present, seeking to fathom what the best government for this new nation should be. They read ancient accounts of government in Greece and Rome and classical commentaries on politics. They studied the English common law, the political thinkers of the Puritan era and the Glorious Revolution in England, as well as Enlightenment thinkers such as John Locke and Baron de Montesquieu.

A comprehensive analysis of the American political writings published between 1760 and 1805 yielded some surprising results.[31] One third of the citations were from the Bible, and the Bible was more frequently cited than any other writing, followed by citations from Charles-Louise Montesquieu and William Blackstone. The most frequently cited book of the Bible was Deuteronomy, which details God's covenant with Israel and the organization of the nation. The Bible was an intimate part of the education and thinking of the day and influenced the Founding Fathers as they fashioned a new government for their new country. As historian Daniel Dreisbach noted:

> … the Bible was the most authoritative, accessible, and familiar book in eighteenth-century America, and it was an important source that Americans studied for insights into law, politics, civil government, and many other activities of human society. The Bible was thought to offer valuable insights into human nature, political authority, and other matters of importance to political theory. Moreover, the moral instruction found in Scripture was thought to nurture the civic virtues a people require for self-government.[32]

Be careful to obey all these words that I command you,
that it may go well with you and with your children after you forever,
when you do what is good and right in the sight of the Lord your God.
—Deuteronomy 12:28—

JUNE 27
CONSOLED BY SCRIPTURE

June 1774, Abigail Adams (1744-1818) stood on a hill near her home in Braintree, Massachusetts, with little seven-year-old John Quincy by her side, watching and hearing the cannon fire of the Battle of Bunker Hill ten miles away. She was distressed for days, especially on learning that their dear friend Dr. Joseph Warren had been killed in the fighting. The day after the battle, Abigail wrote husband John, who was in Philadelphia representing Massachusetts at the Continental Congress. Scripture had been a part of her life since childhood, and in describing the battle, she thought in Scriptural terms:

> "The race is not to the swift, nor the battle to the strong; but the God of Israel is he that giveth strength and power unto his people. Trust in him at all times; ye people, pour out your hearts before him. God is a refuge for us.' Charlestown is laid in ashes.[33]

When John was away in Europe, Abigail encouraged them both with Scripture. Often she didn't know just where he was, but she knew that he was

> at all times and in all places under the protecting care and guardianship of that Being who not only clothes the lilies of the field and hears the young ravens when they cry, but hath said, 'Of how much more worth are ye than many sparrows;' and this confidence, which the world cannot deprive me of, is my food by day and my rest by night and was all my consolation.[34]

Years later, when John Adams became President of the United States, Abigail used Solomon's prayer when he became King, writing to her husband,

> And now, O Lord my God, thou hast made thy servant ruler over the people. Give unto him an understanding heart, that he may know how to go out and come in before this great people; that he may discern between good and bad. For who is able to judge this, thy so great a people?' were the words of a royal sovereign; and not less applicable to him who is invested with the Chief magistracy of a nation, though he wears not the crown nor the robes of royalty. My thoughts and my meditations are with you, though personally absent; and my petitions to Heaven are that 'the things which make for peace may not be hidden from your eyes.'…[35]

I am a companion of all them that fear thee,
and of them that keep thy precepts.
—Psalm 119:63—

FIRST PRAYER IN CONGRESS

In early September 1774, delegates from throughout the North American colonies began to assemble in Carpenter's Hall, Philadelphia, to consider the Intolerable Acts the British Parliament had imposed on the colonies. They elected a president and secretary and established rules for the Congress. A motion was made that the meetings should begin with prayer, and the first prayer in Congress was held the following morning, September 7. Rev. Jacob Duche, Episcopal clergyman at Philadelphia's Christ Church, led in prayer and read the psalm for the day from *The Book of Common Prayer*.

John Adams was quite moved by the prayer and Scripture reading and described the whole scene to his wife Abigail. He wrote that Rev. Duche prayed "with such fervor, such Ardor, such Earnestness and Pathos, and in Language so elegant and sublime—for America, for the Congress, for the Province of Massachusetts Bay, and especially the Town of Boston. It has an excellent Effect upon every Body here."[36] Just the day before, the Congress heard a rumor that the British had cannonaded Boston. Everyone was deeply moved when the Psalm was read, and John encouraged Abigail and the family to read Psalm 35 together. The entire psalm seemed to encourage the struggling colonists in their confrontation with England. It reads in part:

> Plead *my* cause, O LORD, with them that strive with me: fight against them that fight against me. Take hold of shield and buckler, and stand up for mine help. Draw out also the spear, and stop *the way* against them that persecute me: say unto my soul, I *am* thy salvation. Let them be confounded and put to shame that seek after my soul: let them be turned back and brought to confusion that devise my hurt. Let them be as chaff before the wind: and let the angel of the LORD chase *them*. Let their way be dark and slippery: and let the angel of the LORD persecute them. For without cause have they hid for me their net *in* a pit, *which* without cause they have digged for my soul. Let destruction come upon him at unawares and let his net that he hath hid catch himself: into that very destruction let him fall. And my soul shall be joyful in the LORD: it shall rejoice in his salvation ...

In God, whose word I praise, in God I trust;
I shall not be afraid.
What can flesh do to me?
—Psalm 56:4—

JUNE 29
PATRICK HENRY'S "LIBERTY OR DEATH" SPEECH

One month before the shots were fired at Lexington and Concord on April 19, 1775, Patrick Henry delivered an electrifying speech in the Virginia Convention. His famous words were laced with Biblical imagery and references. Following is his speech, with the Bible references included:

> Sir, we are not weak if we make a proper use of those means which the God of nature hath placed in our power. The millions of people, armed in the holy cause of liberty, and in such a country as that which we possess [cf. Deuteronomy 3:12] are invincible by any force which our enemy can send against us. Besides, sir, we shall not fight our battles alone. There is a just God [Isaiah 45:21] who presides over the destinies of nations and who will raise up friends to fight our battles for us [II Chronicles 32:8]. The battle, sir, is not to the strong alone [Ecclesiastes 9:11]; it is to the vigilant, the active, the brave. Besides, sir, we have no election. If we were base enough to desire it, it is now too late to retire from the contest. There is no retreat but in submission and slavery! Our chains are forged! Their clanking may be heard on the plains of Boston! The war is inevitable—and let it come! I repeat it sir, let it come. It is in vain, sir, to extenuate the matter. Gentlemen may cry, Peace, Peace—but there is no peace [Jeremiah 6:14; 8:11]. The war is actually begun! The next gale that sweeps from the north will bring to our ears [cf. phraseology of Acts 17:20] the clash of resounding arms! Our brethren are already in the field! Why stand we here idle [Matthew 20:6]. What is it that gentlemen wish? What would they have? Is life so dear [Acts 20:24] or peace so sweet, as to be purchased at the price of chains and slavery? Forbid it, Almighty God! I know not what course others may take; but as for me, give me liberty or give me death [Joshua 24:15].[37]

In giving his speech, Henry didn't leaf through his Bible to see what verses he could us in his remarks. The biblical phraseology and references came naturally to the fore, since he was saturated with biblical reading and truth, as were many of the generation of the Revolution.

For the commandment is a lamp and the teaching a light,
And the reproofs of discipline are the way of life.
—Proverbs 6:23—

THE DOMINION OF PROVIDENCE

Psalm 76 celebrates Zion's deliverance from a foreign invader, rejoicing in the Lord breaking the weapons of war formed against His people. The actual victory being celebrated is not given, but many have thought it was Jerusalem's deliverance from Sennacherib's invading army, when one night the angel of the Lord struck down 185,000 of the Assyrian army (II Kings 19:35). John Knox Witherspoon (1723-1794) took this setting for the psalm when he preached his powerful sermon, "The Dominion of Providence over the Passions of Men" in Princeton in May 1776.

Witherspoon, a descendant of the Scottish preacher John Knox, came to New Jersey in 1768 as President of the Presbyterian College of New Jersey, which later became Princeton University. He increased the school's academic rigor and financial standing. When the American struggle against England intensified after 1774, Witherspoon was especially concerned about the potential for British increasing authority over the Church and became more involved in political affairs. His May 1776 sermon on "The Dominion of Providence over the Passions of Men" was printed and circulated widely. The text for his sermon was Psalm 76:10, "surely the Wrath of Man shall praise thee; the remainder of Wrath shall thou restrain." While Witherspoon saw the psalm as a victory hymn after the deliverance from Sennacherib, he used the psalm to anticipate American success in the conflict with Britain. He developed the theme that God in His Providence rules over all his creatures in things great and small and works through even evil and calamity to achieve His purposes. Applied to the American colonies, he said that

> the plague of war, the ambition of mistaken princes, the cunning and cruelty of oppressive and corrupt ministers, and even the inhumanity of brutal soldiers, however dreadful, shall finally promote the glory of God, and in the mean time, while the storm continues, his mercy and kindness shall appear in prescribing bounds to their rage and fury.[38]

Witherspoon went on to represent New Jersey in the Second Continental Congress and signed both the Declaration of Independence and the Articles of Confederation. He was President of Princeton until his death in 1794.

Your words have upheld him who was stumbling,
and you have made firm the feeble knees.
—Job 4:4—

JULY 1
FREEDOM FROM TYRANNY

The title page of the Geneva Bible featured the scene of the Israelites preparing to cross the Red Sea. Pharaoh's army is in pursuit, and Moses, with the pillar of cloud overhead, raises his rod to part the waters. The picture is surrounded by Scripture quotes:

- "Great is the trouble of the righteous, but the Lord delivers him out of them all." Psalm 34:19

- "Fear not, stand still and beholde the salvation of the Lord which he will shew to you this day." Exodus 14:13

- "The Lord shal fight for you: therefore holde you your peace." Exodus 14:14

The scene and Scriptures were especially meaningful to the 16th-century English exiles in Geneva. Many had fled England and settled in Geneva to avoid the persecutions under the reign of Queen Mary. It was there scholars in the community translated the first English Bible translated from the Greek and Hebrew, which became known as the Geneva Bible. The title page with its references and picture of the Exodus symbolized the longings of the English exiles in Geneva—a longing to return to their own land and be free from the oppression of a tyrannical ruler.

After the approval of the American Declaration of Independence in 1776, Benjamin Franklin and Thomas Jefferson recommended a design for a state seal for the new United States. Their design was very similar to the Geneva Bible's illustration of the Israelites preparing to cross the Red Sea and undoubtedly came to them from the title page to the Geneva Bible: Pharaoh's army is in pursuit while Moses with the pillar of cloud overhead has his rod upraised to part the sea. Many in the young United States saw parallels between their war for freedom against Great Britain and Israel's deliverance from Egyptian tyranny. The encircling motto for Jefferson and Franklin's seal was "Rebellion to Tyrants is Obedience to God."

Even though princes sit plotting against me,
your servant will meditate on your statutes.
—Psalm 119:22—

The country was in a crisis. Enemy forces had taken over New York and would soon threaten the national capital. Of great concern to Congress was the shortage of Bibles in the land. The year? 1777.

The Chaplain of Congress, Patrick Allison, had brought the issue to Congress' attention. The authority to print the King James Version of the Bible resided with the King of England, and the British had not allowed the printing of English Bibles in colonial America. All English Bibles in America had to be imported. The War for Independence disrupted normal shipping, and Americans were beginning to feel a shortage of Bibles by the fall of 1777. A special Committee of Congress considered the problem, and on September 11 reported,

> The use of the Bible is so universal and its importance so great that your committee refers the above to the consideration of Congress, and if Congress shall not think it expedient to order the importation of types and paper, the committee recommends that Congress will order the Committee of Commerce to import 20,000 Bibles from Holland, Scotland, or else-where, into the different parts of the States of the Union. Whereupon it was resolved accordingly to direct said Committee of Commerce to import 20,000 copies of the Bible.[1]

The British occupied Philadelphia, forcing Congress to flee, before action was taken on the resolution. It is noteworthy today, however, that the Continental Congress thought that it was properly within its jurisdiction to purchase a supply of Bibles for the people.

"Behold, the days are coming," declares the Lord God,
"when I will send a famine on the land— not a famine of bread,
nor a thirst for water, but of hearing the words of the Lord."
—Amos 8:11—

JULY 3
GEORGE WASHINGTON AND THE SCRIPTURES

George Washington's father died when George was eleven. On his death-bed, Augustine Washington gave his son three books on prayer. Mary Ball Washington, now a single mother, educated her five children at home. Among the books she used in George's education were *The Sufficiency of a Standing Revelation, The Wisdom of God Manifested in the Works of Creation,* and Matthew Hale's *Contemplations, Moral and Divine.*

When Washington married Martha Custis, they daily had evening devotions together, reading a chapter and a psalm from the family Bible and kneeling in prayer. Martha's maid would sometimes sing a hymn in the evening gathering. George Washington's writings are replete with Scriptural allusions and references. In his circular to the states in 1783, when he resigned his position as commander of the army, he noted that having the Scripture, the Divine revelation, was one of the highest blessings for Americans:

> The foundation of our Empire was not laid in the gloomy age of Ignorance and Superstition, but at an Epoch when the rights of mankind were better understood and more clearly defined, than at any former period, the researches of the human mind, after social happiness, having been carried to a great extent, the Treasures of knowledge acquired by the labors of Philosophers, Sages and Legislatures, through a long succession of years, are laid open for our use, and their collected wisdom may be happily applied in the Establishment of our forms of Government, the free cultivation of Letters, the unbounded extension of Commerce...and above all, the pure and benign light of Revelation, have had a meliorating influence on mankind and increased the blessings of Society.

Washington concluded his circular with the prayer that God

> would most graciously be pleased to dispose us all, to do Justice, to love mercy, and to demean ourselves with that Charity (Micah 6:8), humility, and pacific temper of mind, which were the Characteristics of the Divine Author of our blessed Religion, and without an humble imitation of whose example in these things, we can never hope to be a happy Nation.[2]

Blessed are those whose way is blameless,
who walk in the law of the Lord!
—Psalm 119:1—

BENJAMIN FRANKLIN'S BIBLICAL HERITAGE

Benjamin Franklin wrote in his *Autobiography* that his ancestors were Bible readers since the earliest days of the English Reformation. Under Queen Mary ("Bloody Mary" ruled 1553-1559), Protestants were persecuted. Hundreds were executed for their faith. Franklin wrote that his ancestors

> had got an English Bible, and to conceal and secure it, it was fastened open with tapes under and within the cover of a joint-stool. When my great-great-grandfather read it to his family, he turned up the joint-stool upon his knees, turning over the leaves then under the tapes. One of the children stood at the door to give notice if he saw the apparitor coming, who was an officer of the spiritual court. In that case the stool was turned down again upon its feet, when the Bible remained concealed under it as before.[3]

Benjamin Franklin's upbringing was rich in Bible reading and teaching. Franklin fondly remembered his father playing the violin and singing psalms in the evening in a "clear, pleasing voice." Though Franklin departed from this Christian upbringing, the knowledge of the Scripture he learned in his youth remained with him and continued to influence him to the end of his life. Franklin became famous for his *Poor Richard's Almanac*, whose proverbs sounded so Solomonic that many today erroneously think "God helps those who help themselves" is a Bible verse.

When he became a printer, Franklin printed important Christian works, including sermons and the hymns of Isaac Watts. When evangelist George Whitefield visited America, Franklin loved to hear him preach and was the official printer of Whitefield's works in America, though he never could accept Jesus Christ or the gospel Whitefield preached.

At the 1787 Constitutional Convention, at age 81, Franklin called for prayer at the Convention, again referencing the Bible in his speech:

> God governs in the affairs of man. And if a sparrow cannot fall to the ground without his notice, is it probable that an empire can rise without His aid? We have been assured in the Sacred Writings that except the Lord build the house, they labor in vain that build it. I firmly believe this. I also believe that, without His concurring aid, we shall succeed in this political building no better than the builders of Babel.[4]

Righteousness exalts a nation, but sin is a reproach to any people.
—Proverbs 14:34—

JULY 5
PRAISE FOR DIVINE
REVELATION OF SCRIPTURE

There are many ways to describe the divine revelation of Scripture. The Word of God is a guide, lighting our path and pointing us to Heaven. The Scriptures enliven the soul by showing us God's love. Its teachings instruct us in the truth as well as comfort us. To have the Scriptures is indeed a blessing which should cause us to offer praise to their Giver. Baptist hymn-writer Anne Steele (1717-1778) put these thoughts into the following hymn:

> When Israel through the desert passed,
> A fiery pillar went before
> To guide them through the dreary waste
> And lessen the fatigues they bore.
>
> Such is the glorious word of God;
> 'Tis for our light and guidance given;
> It sheds a luster all abroad.
> And points the path to bliss and heaven.
>
> It fills the soul with sweet delight,
> And quickens its inactive powers;
> It sets our wandering footsteps right,
> Displays his love and kindles ours.
>
> Its promises rejoice our hearts;
> Its doctrines are divinely true;
> Knowledge and pleasure it imparts;
> It comforts and instructs us too.
>
> Ye favored lands, blest with this word.
> All ye who feel its saving power,
> Unite your tongues to praise the Lord,
> And his distinguished grace adore.[5]

Turn to me and be gracious to me,
as is your way with those who love your name.
—Psalm 119:132—

JOHN BROWN'S SELF-INTERPRETING BIBLE

It seems that a new Bible version hits the market every few months. Either the translation is new (e.g. literal, free paraphrase, contemporary, gender inclusive), the format is different (e.g. leather- bound, paperback, CD, magazine), or the notes are designed for a targeted audience (e.g. women, African-Americans, seniors, cowboys). One of the most long-lived Bible versions is John Brown's *Self-Interpreting Bible*, first published in Scotland in 1778.

John Brown was born in Scotland in 1722, orphaned at an early age, and taught himself Latin and Greek while tending sheep. Later he studied for the ministry and learned Hebrew. For 36 years he was pastor of the church in Haddington, Scotland. He designed his annotated Bible to be practical and helpful for people who wanted to know the Scripture but did not have the time or skill for deep, personal studies. Brown's notes were designed to make the biblical text more understandable and focused on translation issues or historical background. The notes for each section were followed by "reflections" which applied the Scripture to the heart. Throughout his work, Brown emphasized that the goal of Scripture is to promote holiness and virtue and to glorify God. He believed the Scripture references were the most important part of his Bible. By using Scripture to comment and explain Scripture, Brown believed the Holy Spirit Himself became the commentator, and the reader would discover "the truth for himself in God's own light."

John Brown believed the collection of parallel Scriptures included in his *Self-Interpreting Bible* was his most useful and important contribution. In the introduction to his Bible he wrote:

> In these ... we have a delightful view of the Harmony of the scripture, and multiplied Proofs of every article of our Christian faith; ... Herein the serious inquirer has the Spirit of God for his director, the lovely oracles of God for his commentary. He has the pleasure of discovering the truth for himself in God's own light. ...and, while we are thus occupied in comparing the several texts, we may humbly expect that the Holy Ghost will illuminate all with his glory and apply all to the heart.

This God—his way is perfect; the word of the Lord proves true;
he is a shield for all those who take refuge in him.
—Psalm 18:30—

JULY 7

THE NATURE OF THE BIBLE'S REVELATION

In a sermon preached in his parish of Olney, the 18th-century pastor John Newton described the nature and importance of the Bible's revelation as well as the necessity of reading the Scriptures prayerfully:

> The Spirit of God teaches and enlightens by his word as the instrument. There is no revelation from him, but what is … derived from the scriptures …. The scriptures are the appointed rule and test, by which all our searches and discoveries, all our acquisitions in religious knowledge must be tried. To set a high value upon the word of God, all that is necessary to make you wise to salvation is there, and there only. In this precious book you may find a direction for every doubt, a solution for every difficulty, a promise suited to every circumstance you can be in. … There you may be informed of your disease by sin, and the remedy provided by grace. You may be instructed to know yourselves, to know God and Jesus Christ, in the knowledge of whom standeth eternal life. The wonders of redeeming love, the glories of the Redeemer's person, the happiness of the redeemed people, the power of faith, and the beauty of holiness, are here represented to the life. Nothing is wanting to make life useful and comfortable, death safe and desirable, and to bring down something of heaven upon earth. But this true wisdom can be found nowhere else. If you wander from the scriptures, in pursuit either of present peace, or future hope, your search will end in disappointment. This is the fountain of living waters: if you forsake it, and give the preference to broken cisterns of your own devising, they will fail you when you most need them. Rejoice, therefore, that such a treasure is put into your hand; but rejoice with trembling. Remember this is not all you want: unless God likewise gives you a heart to use it aright, your privilege will only aggravate your guilt and misery.
>
> Therefore remember, the necessity of prayer. For though the things of nearest consequence to you are in the Bible, and you should read it over and over, till you commit the whole book to your memory, yet you will not understand or discern the truth as it is in Jesus, unless the Lord the Spirit shews it to you. … Without him all the fancied advantages of superior capacity learning, criticism, and books, will prove as useless as spectacles to the blind. The great encouragement is, that this infallible Spirit, so necessary to guide us into the way of peace, is promised to all who sincerely ask it. This Spirit Jesus is exalted to bestow; and he has said, "Whosoever cometh to me, I will in no wise cast him out." Therefore water your reading with frequent prayer.[6]

Stablish thy word unto thy servant, who is devoted to thy fear.
—Psalm 119:38—

THOMAS SCOTT ON THE AUTHENTICITY OF THE SCRIPTURES

In recent years there have been books, TV specials, and news articles which claim that the books of the New Testament were brought together as Scriptures in the fourth century or so. Some contend there were other ancient writings, such as those of the Gnostics, which reflected early Christianity more than the books we have in the New Testament. Thomas Scott (1747-1821), an 18th century skeptic who became a Christian through the influence of John Newton, published an influential 6-volume commentary on the Bible in which he ably refutes such aspersions on the early acceptance of the New Testament Scriptures by the church. In his commentary's "Introduction to the New Testament," Scott wrote,

> The several books, which now form the New Testament, were early received by the Christian church, as of divine authority. The greatest part of them are quoted by the most ancient Christian writers, and appealed to, as the standard of truth. A vast proportion of the New Testament might be collected from writers who lived in the first two centuries. They formed catalogues of the several books and wrote comments on them: both the orthodox and the heretics appealed to them; lectures on several parts of them are still extant nay, the enemies of Christianity uniformly mention them, as the authentic books of Christians. So that there is the most complete proof, that all the books, now collected in the New Testament, were received, and read in the assemblies of Christians, before the end of the second century …

> It should also be observed, that no other books were received by the primitive Church, as a part of divine revelation. Very many other compositions were sent forth, bearing the names of the apostles or primitive teachers, but on careful examination, all except those which now form the New Testament, were rejected as spurious. And this shows, with what scrupulous caution, the canon of Scripture was fixed. The four Gospels were very early received, as the writings of the evangelists whose names they bear. They are mentioned distinctly by the fathers of the second century as "books well known by the name of Gospels, and as such were read by Christians, at their assemblies every Lord's day." (Whitby) Several other Gospels were published, and some gained a temporary credit, but they are either not mentioned in the approved writings of the primitive Christians, or mentioned with disapprobation.

That which was from the beginning, which we have heard, which we have seen with our eyes, which we looked upon and gave touched with our hands, concerning the word of life—the life was made manifest, and we have seen it, and testify to it and proclaim to you the eternal life, which was with the Father and was made manifest to us—that which we have seen and heard we proclaim also to you, so that you too may have fellowship with the father and with his Son Jesus Christ.
—I John 1:1-3—

HYMNS AND SPIRITUAL SONGS

One of the fruits of the 18th-century Evangelical Revival was the production of a hymnody rich in doctrine and Scriptural references. Charles Wesley (1707-1788), among the founders of Methodism, wrote over 6000 hymns, many of them still in use today. The hymns themselves were a way of teaching the truths of the Scriptures. One of Wesley's most popular hymns was "And can it be, that I should gain?" Notice the numerous Scriptural allusions on which the hymn is based[7]:

And can it be, that I should gain	
An interest in the Saviour's blood!	*Eph. 1:7, 14*
Died he for me?—who caused his pain!	*Gal. 2:20*
For me—who him to death pursued.	*Acts 9:4-5*
Amazing love! How can it be	*Isa. 29:14, I Jn. 3:1*
That thou, my God, shouldst die for me?	*Mk. 15:39, Gal. 2:20*
He left his Father's throne above,	*Jn. 6:38, Rev. 22:3*
So free, so infinite his grace!	*I Cor. 8:9*
Emptied himself of all but love,	*Phil. 2:7*
And bled for Adam's helpless race:	*Rom. 5:12, 14; Rev. 5:9*
'Tis mercy all, immense and free!	*Psa. 145:9, Rom. 11:32*
For O my God! It found out me!	*Acts 9:15; Gal. 1:15-16*
Long my imprisoned spirit lay,	*Acts 12:4-6, Jn. 8:34*
Fast bound in sin and nature's night:	*Rom. 6:17; I Cor. 2:14*
Thine eye diffused a quickening ray;	*Jn. 1:4*
I woke; the dungeon flamed with light;	*Acts 12:7-8*
My chains fell off, my heart was free,	*Psa. 119:32, Zech. 9:12*
I rose, went forth, and followed thee.	*Jn. 8:36, Rom. 6:18*
No condemnation now I dread,	*Rom. 8:1*
Jesus, and all in him is mine:	*Rom. 8:32*
Alive in him, my living Head,	*I Cor. 15:22, Col. 1:18*
And clothed in righteousness divine,	*Isa. 61:10*
Bold I approach the eternal throne,	*Eph. 3:12, Heb. 10:19-22*
And claim the crown, through Christ, my own.	*II Tim. 4:8*

Your statutes have been my songs in the house of my sojourning.
— Psalm 119:54—

JULY 10

REVELATION IN SCRIPTURE

Charles Wesley's hymns are rich in doctrinal, biblical truth. These two speak of God's revelation of salvation which human reason can't discern.[8]

Come, O thou Prophet of the Lord,	Deut. 18:15, Acts 3:22
Thou great Interpreter divine,	Luke 24:27
Explain thine own transmitted word,	Jn. 16:13-15
To teach and to inspire is thine;	Lk. 24:32; Jn. 14:26
Thou only canst thyself reveal,	II Pet. 1:20
Open the book, and loose the seal.	Rev. 5:5
What'er the ancient prophets spoke	II Pet. 1:21
Concerning thee, O Christ, make known;	
Chief subject of the sacred book,	Jn. 5:39, 46
Thou fillest all, and thou alone;	Eph. 1:23, 4:10
Yet there our Lord we cannot see,	I Cor. 12:3
Unless thy Spirit lend the key.	Lk. 11:52. Jn. 16:14
Now, Jesus, now the veil remove,	II Cor. 3:13-14
The folly of our darkened heart;	Rom. 1:21
Unfold the wonders of thy love,	Psa.119:18
The knowledge of thyself impart;	Eph. 4:13
Our ear, our inmost soul, we bow,	Prov. 22:17, Micah .6:6
Speak, Lord, thy servants hearken now.	I Sam. 3:10

Come, divine Interpreter,	Jn. 16:13-14
Bring me eyes thy book to read,	Acts 8:30-31
Ears the mystic words to hear,	
Words which did from thee proceed,	II Tim. 3:15, II Pet. 1:21
Words that endless bliss impart,	Psalm 119:111, Isa. 51;11
Kept in an obedient heart.	Rom. 6:17
All who read, or hear, are blessed,	Rev. 1:3
If thy plain commands we do;	James 1:25
Of thy kingdom here possessed,	Lk. 12:32
Thee we shall in glory view;	I Jn. 3:2, Rev. 22:4
When thou come'st on earth to abide,	Mk. 13:26, Rev. 1:7, Acts 1:11
Reign triumphant at thy side.	Matt. 19:28; Rev. 20:4

Long have I known from your testimonies
that you have founded them forever. —Psalm 119:152—

THE WORD QUICK AND POWERFUL

John Newton (1725-1807) was captain of a British ship in the African slave trade who lived a profane life until he came to belief in Christ for his salvation. He later gave up slave trading and began to seriously study the Scriptures, learning Hebrew, Greek, and Syriac to better understand the Bible. Newton became Anglican pastor in Olney, where his preaching was so popular the church had to be enlarged for the congregation. Newton regularly wrote hymns to correspond with his sermons. "Amazing Grace" and "Glorious Things of Thee Are Spoken" remain his most famous hymns, but his entire collection of hymns was published as *The Olney Hymns*. Many of the hymns are upon particular passages of Scripture Newton preached upon. Following is the hymn he wrote on Hebrews 4:12,13:

The word of Christ, our Lord,
With whom we have to do;
Is sharper than a two-edg'd sword,
To pierce the sinner thro'!

Swift as the light'nings blaze
When awful thunders roll,
It fills the conscience with amaze,
And penetrates the soul.

No heart can be conceal'd
From his all-piercing eyes;
Each thought and purpose stands
reveal'd,
Naked, without disguise.

He sees his peoples fears,
He notes their mournful cry;

He counts their sighs and falling
tears,
And helps them from on high.

Tho' feeble is their good,
It has his kind regard;
Yea, all they would do, if they
could,[9]
Shall find a sure reward.

He sees the wicked too,
And will repay them soon,
For all the evil deeds they do,
And all they would have done.[10]

Since all our secret ways
Are mark'd and known by thee;
Afford us, Lord, thy light of grace
That we ourselves may see.[11]

Hold me up, that I may be safe
and have regard for your statutes continually!
—Psalm 119:117—

THE WORD MORE PRECIOUS THAN GOLD

Among 18th-century pastor John Newton's *Olney Hymns* is this one on the preciousness of the Bible:

Precious Bible! what a treasure
Does the word of God afford?
All I want for life or pleasure,
FOOD and MED'CINE, SHIELD
and SWORD:
    Let the world account me poor,
    Having this I need no more.

FOOD to which the world's a
    stranger,
Here my hungry soul enjoys
Of excess there is no danger,
Though it fills, it never cloys:
    On a dying CHRIST I feed,
    He is meat and drink indeed.

When my faith is faint and sickly,
Or when Satan wounds my mind,
Cordials, to revive me quickly,
Healing MED'CINES here I find:
    To the promises I flee,
    Each affords a remedy.

In the hour of dark temptation
Satan cannot make me yield;
For the word of consolation
Is to me a mighty SHIELD
    While the scripture–truths are
    sure,
    From his malice I'm secure.

Vain his threats to overcome me,
When I take the Spirit's SWORD;
Then with ease I drive him from me.
Satan trembles at the word:
    'Tis a sword for conquest made,
    Keen the edge, and strong the
    blade.

Shall I envy then the miser
Doting on his golden store?
Sure I am, or should be, wiser,
I am Rich, 'tis he is Poor:
    JESUS gives me in his word,
    FOOD and MED'CINE,
    SHIELD and SWORD.[12]

I will meditate on your precepts.
—Psalm 119:78—

THE LIGHT AND GLORY OF THE WORD

Eighteenth-century pastor John Newton's hymns were often written to complement his sermons. One of his hymns is *The Light and Glory of the Word*:

The Spirit breathes upon the word,
  And brings the truth to sight;
Precepts and promises afford
  A sanctifying light.

A glory gilds the sacred page,
  Majestic like the sun
It gives a light to every age,
  It gives, but borrows none.

The hand that gave it, still supplies
  The gracious light and heat;
His truths upon the nations rise,
  They rise, but never set.

Let everlasting thanks be thine
  For such a bright display,
As makes a world of darkness shine
  With beams of heav'nly day.

My soul rejoices to pursue
  The steps of him I love;
Till glory breaks upon my view
  In brighter worlds above.[13]

I hasten and do not delay
to keep your commandments.
—Psalm 119:60—

JULY 14
A PRAYER FOR POWER
ON THE MEANS OF GRACE

In his "Prayer for Power on the Means of Grace," John Newton prayed for God's power be with the preacher as he proclaimed God's Word, and that God would open the ears of the congregation to hear the Word. He especially prayed that this would be true for the young people in the congregation:

O Thou, at whose almighty Word
The glorious light from darkness
    sprung,
The quickening influence afford,
And clothe with power the
    preacher's tongue.

Though 'tis Thy truth he hopes
    to speak,
He cannot give the hearing ear;
'Tis Thine the stubborn heart to
    break,
And make the careless sinner fear.

As when of old the water flowed
Forth from the rock at Thy
    command,[14]
Moses in vain had waved his rod,
Without Thy wonder-working hand.

As when the walls of Jericho,[15]
Down to the earth at once were cast,

It was Thy power that brought
    them low,
And not the trumpet's feeble blast.

Thus we would in the means be
    found,
And thus on Thee alone depend,
To make the gospel's joyful sound
Effectual to the promised end.

Now, while we hear thy Word
    of grace,
Let self and pride before it fall;
And rocky hearts dissolve apace,
In streams of sorrow at Thy call.

On all our youth assembled here,
The unction of Thy Spirit pour:
Nor let them lose another year,
Lest Thou shouldst strive and call
    no more.[16]

... I love your testimonies.
—Psalm 119:119—

HIEROGLYPHIC BIBLES

In 1782, the first *A Curious Hieroglyphic Bible* was printed in London. (In that day, "curious" meant carefully made, not strange or odd.) The little book contained 126 pages with an illustrated Bible verse on each page, from the beginning of creation in Genesis 1:1 through the New Jerusalem in Revelation 21:2. The verses were printed as a rebus, with some of the words represented by pictures. The bottom of the page contained the entire verse printed out, with the pictured word italicized. The *Hieroglyphic Bible* was a fun way for children to learn Bible stories and learn to read at the same time. The chosen verses became a survey of the entire story of Redemption and gave the children an early acquaintance with the important truths of the Bible.

Often the hieroglyphic Bibles also included the poem "A Treasure of the Holy Scriptures" and a Prayer for the True Use of the Holy Scriptures found in the Geneva Bible (see April 5), as well as a short account of the lives of the evangelists.

Hieroglyphic Bibles were popular in colonial America as well as England; they continued to be printed well into the 19th century. By presenting the Bible in this entertaining way, it was hoped the hieroglyphic Bible would be

> ... an instructive companion of childhood's leisure hour. And when leisure hour, after leisure hour, shall have cheerily rolled away, in delightful intercourse with *childhood's* Bible, easy and natural will be the transition to *youth's* and *manhood's* Bible: and many a youthful heart, it is hoped, will be ready to exclaim—"O how I love thy law! It is my meditation all the day." (Psalm 119:97)[17]

Consider how I love thy precepts: quicken me, O Lord,
according to thy lovingkindness.
—Psalm 119:159

JULY 16
THE AITKEN BIBLE—
BIBLE OF THE REVOLUTION

During the colonial period in America, the King licensed the printing of Bibles, and no Bibles were printed in America; all had to be imported. With the disruption of trade in the days leading up to the American Revolution, by 1777 there was a shortage of Bibles in the colonies. Congress was considering financing the importation of Bibles, but the approaching British troops caused Congress to flee Philadelphia, and no action was taken.

Philadelphia printer Robert Aitken, however, took steps to remedy the problem. Aitken had published the *Journals of Congress* for the First Continental Congress and narrowly escaped arrest by the British. Along with Richard Bache, Ben Franklin's son-in-law, Robert Aitken published the *Philadelphia Magazine*. In 1777 he managed to obtain type and paper to publish a small New Testament. He printed three more editions in 1778, 1779 and 1781, one of them specifically for use in the schools.

In January 1781, Aitken asked Congress' approval and support for printing a complete Bible. Chaplains of Congress inspected and approved the work Aitken had done, and Congress passed a resolution approving "the pious and laudable undertaking of Mr. Aitken, as subservient to the interest of religion," and recommending "this edition of the Bible to the inhabitants of the United States."[18]

Though 10,000 were published, copies of Aitken's "Bible of the Revolution" are very rare today, with more copies of Gutenberg's Bible remaining than Aitken's! Its rarity also is marked because it remains the only printed Bible ever specifically approved by Congress.

Every word of God proves true;
he is a shield to those who take refuge in him.
—Proverbs 30:5—

MATTHEW CAREY

Matthew Carey became the leading printer of Bibles in the young United States. His life is a story of courage, conviction, and determination. Born in Ireland in 1760, Carey was dropped by a nurse when an infant and remained crippled for life. Though he had little formal education, he was fluent in several languages. At 19 he published a pamphlet in defense of Dublin's apprentices, and the officials issued a warrant for his arrest. Carey managed to escape to Paris, where he was befriended by Benjamin Franklin and the Marquis de Lafayette.

When he returned to Dublin, Carey published articles supporting Ireland against the harshness of British rule. After spending a short time in Newgate prison, he escaped to America, disguised as a woman.

In Philadelphia, his money soon ran out, but Marquis de Lafayette gave him $400. In 1789, Carey established himself in the printing business. One of his earliest ventures shows Carey's courage. He decided to publish a Rheims-Douai, or Catholic English translation of the Latin bible. There was little demand for such a volume, and there was much intolerance of Catholics, yet Carey managed to get 491 subscriptions for his Bible. In 1790, Carey published the first Catholic Bible in America. Its cost was $6.00.

With the persuasion of his bookseller Parson Weems, who gave us the story of Washington chopping down the cherry tree, Matthew Carey also began publishing the King James Version of the Bible for Protestants. Carey pioneered mass production and distribution of the Bible, publishing over sixty-five editions. He offered Bibles in a wide range of sizes, quality, and prices, and for twenty years he was the dominant producer of Bibles in America.

And that gift Lafayette had given him? Carey later repaid the money when General Lafayette's own finances were failing.

… thank we God without ceasing, because when ye received the word of God which ye heard of us, ye received it not as the word of man, but as it is in truth, the word of God, which effectually worketh also in you that believe.
—I Thessalonians 2:13—

ISAIAH THOMAS

Isaiah Thomas was an early Massachusetts printer who revealed his patriotism in numerous ways, including printing Bibles. Before the American Revolution broke out, Thomas published a Boston newspaper called the *Massachusetts Spy*, which the British authorities tried to suppress for its support of the American cause. For a time, Thomas also published the *Royal American Magazine*, which often contained engravings by Paul Revere. When it appeared that the British were preparing a military movement against the colonists, Isaiah moved his printing presses and type out of Boston to Worcester, Massachusetts. Three days later he was among the militiamen resisting the British on the green at Lexington and the Concord Bridge.

Thomas published over 400 books printed in thousands of copies. He became known for the excellent quality of his work, which included religious, educational, and historical books as well as many children's books. Thomas thought the new country should be called "The United States of Columbia," and he printed that as the country's name on a number of his books!

As the new country became established in peace and prosperity, Thomas thought the country should not have to import fine quality books from abroad. Fifteen years after the Declaration of Independence, he printed an exquisite Bible. In the preface, he noted the Bible was the foundation of the Christian religion, which itself was the moral support of the new nation. He commissioned four artists to make fifty copperplate engravings to illustrate the Bible. The frontispiece pictured the Triumph of the Gospel throughout the world, with people costumed from every land seeking the Scriptures.

Printing the Bible was an expensive undertaking, and Thomas followed the normal practice of taking subscriptions before beginning his printing. The cost for each Bible was $7.00, but money was scarce. To be accommodating, Thomas accepted half of the sum, the initial subscription price, in "wheat, rye, Indian corn, butter, or pork, if delivered at his store."

All the ends of the earth shall remember and turn to the Lord,
and all the families of the nations shall worship before you.
—Psalm 22:27—

THE AMERICAN STORY AND THE EXODUS

Many of the lives of the early colonists to America were permeated with the Scriptures, and they easily found analogies in their own lives to the Biblical events. As they fled from political and religious restrictions in England across the vast Atlantic to a wilderness world in America, they frequently saw similarities to the Israelites who were delivered from Pharaoh and bondage in Egypt by the hand of God, as they crossed the Red Sea, endured hardships in the wilderness, yet found new homes in a land of Promise.

This image of America as the New Israel gained new force during the American Revolution. The great seal Franklin and Jefferson proposed for the new United States, showing the crossing of the Red Sea, used this image. Washington was often compared to Moses or to Joshua as he led the American forces to liberty and freedom. The first great epic poem written in America, Timothy Dwight's *The Conquest of Canaan,* was dedicated to Washington, the American Moses.

As the nation of Israel's prosperity in the land was dependent on the people's adherence to God's covenant with them, so the success of the new United States was often seen as dependent on adherence to the morality of God's laws. The Hebrew tribal organization seemed to parallel the federal organization of the states under the Constitution. Jethro's advice to Moses was seen as an example of the kind of division of power important in good government: "Moreover, look for able men from all the people, men who fear God, who are trustworthy and hate a bribe, and place such men over the people as chiefs of thousands, of hundreds, of fifties, and of tens. And let them judge the people at all times." (Exodus 18:21-22) Virtue and morality were important to good government, as Washington himself testified in his Farewell Address.

I have done what is just and right;
do not leave me to my oppressors.
—Psalm 119:121—

JULY 20
THE BOOK DIVINE

Converted at the age of sixteen under the preaching of George Whitefield, John Fawcett (1739-1817) went on to become a Baptist minister. He was the author of a number of works on practical divinity as well as hymns and poetic works. After pastoring the Baptist Church near Bradford, Yorks for some years, he was invited to pastor Carter's Lane Church in London. Though he was prepared to make the move, at the last moment, he could not part with his dear congregation at Bradford and wrote the hymn "Blessed be the Tie that Binds."

Here is one of Fawcett's hymns which continued in use for many years:

How precious is the Book divine,
  By Inspiration given!
Bright as a Lamp its Doctrines shine
  To guide our Souls to Heaven.

Its light, descending from above,
  Our gloomy world to cheer,
Displays a Saviour's boundless love,
  And brings his glories near.

It Shews to man his wand'ring ways
  And where his feet have trod;
And brings to view the matchless grace
  Of a forgiving God.

When once it penetrates the mind,
  It conquers ev'ry sin;
Th'enlighten'd soul begins to find
  The path of peace divine.

It sweetly cheers our drooping Hearts
  In this dark Vale of tears;
Life, Light, and Joy, it still imparts,
  And quells our rising Fears.

This Lamp, thro' all the tedious Night
  Of Life, shall guide our Way.
Till we behold the clearer Light
  Of an eternal Day.[19]

When I think of your rules from of old, I take comfort, O Lord.
—Psalm 119:52—

PITCAIRN ISLAND AND THE *BOUNTY* BIBLE

Mutiny on the *Bounty* has been the source of numerous poems, plays, novels, and at least five films. The story of the mutiny aboard the British ship in 1789 has become a part of the popular culture. Though the story of the mutiny is fascinating as well as Captain Bligh's amazing return to England after being left adrift on a raft at sea, the story of the conversion of one of the mutineers is even more wonderful. After capturing the *Bounty*, the mutineers at first took the ship to Tahiti. After several months, Fletcher Christian and eight of the mutineers, along with 18 Tahitians, set sail again, eventually settling on the then-uninhabited island of Pitcairn. This island paradise was soon marred by the Englishmen's mistreatment of the Tahitians. The Tahitians rebelled, killing all but four of the English. One Englishman then learned how to distill liquor from the ti plant, and drunkenness became a way of life. One Englishman jumped off a cliff in a drunken stupor; another became insane and was killed in order to prevent him from killing others. Alexander Smith and Ned Young then destroyed the still and all the liquor on the island. Smith then discovered a Bible and a *Book of Common Prayer* from the remains of the *Bounty*. Smith was illiterate, but before his death in 1801, Young taught Smith to read. Smith kept reading the Bible, and gradually his life was transformed by what he read. He began teaching the Tahitian children and some of the mothers how to read, with the Bible and the prayer book as their only texts. Smith taught the Tahitians about the Christian faith, established a daily time of prayer, grace before meals, and worship on Sundays.

In 1808, Mayhew Folger, captain of the American ship *Topaz*, landed on Pitcairn island and was amazed to find 35 English-speaking Polynesians practicing the Christian faith and living very orderly lives. When British ships later visited the island, they too were amazed by the Christian lives of the people. A church and school were built on the island, and Alexander Smith continued to take a personal responsibility in the Christian nurture of the people until his death at the age of 70 in 1829. Reading the Bible had not only converted a drunken sailor to become a vibrant Christian, it had transformed a people and a culture. The Word of God is indeed alive and powerful.

For the word of God is living and active, sharper than any two-edged sword,
piercing to the division of soul and of spirit, of joints and of marrow,
and discerning the thoughts and intentions of the heart.
—Hebrews 4:12—

JULY 22

PRESIDENTIAL OATHS

New York City was the capital of the young United States when George Washington was inaugurated as the country's first President. Federal Hall on Wall Street was already crammed with congressmen and foreign ambassadors when Washington arrived for the ceremony on April 30, 1789. As Washington prepared to take the oath, they suddenly discovered that no Bible was present, and it was impossible to take the oath without a Bible! New York State Chancellor Robert Livingston remembered that the Masonic Lodge just down the street had a beautiful Bible, and it was quickly brought so the ceremony could begin. The Bible was placed on a red velvet cushion and opened at random to Genesis 49-50. (Americans later considered it Providential that the bible opened to Genesis 49-50, chapters in which Jacob reassured his sons of their promise to a new land.) Washington placed his hand on the open Bible and recited the Presidential oath, adding the words, "I swear, so help me God!" He then bent down and kissed the open Bible. By adding the words and kissing the Bible, he was following a practice used in royal coronations and in British and colonial courts of the day. Later Presidents have followed the precedent Washington established.

Many Presidents have chosen to use their own personal or family bibles for the oath taking, often opening the bible to a particular passage of Scripture meaningful to them, and since the Civil War a record has been kept of their choices. U.S. Grant, whose father's name was Jesse, chose Isaiah 11:1-3, a Messianic passage which begins, "And there shall come forth a rod of the stem of Jesse, and a branch shall grow out of his roots ...." Both William McKinley and William Howard Taft used passages from Solomon's prayer before his coronation, found in II Chron. 1:10 and I Kings 3:9-11: "Give me now wisdom and knowledge, that I may go out and come in before this people. For who can judge this thy people, that is so great?" In his first inauguration, Woodrow Wilson, the son of a Presbyterian minister, chose Psalm 119. For his second inauguration, with World War I raging, Wilson chose Psalm 46 "God is our refuge and strength: a very present help in trouble ...." Dwight Eisenhower used the Bible he had at West Point for his two inaugurations. The verses Eisenhower chose were Psalm 127:1: "Except the Lord build the house, they labor in vain that build it ...," and Psalm 33:12: "Blessed is the nation, whose God is the Lord: and the people, whom he hath chosen for his own inheritance."

I have sworn an oath and confirmed it, to keep your righteous rules.
—Psalm 119:106—

RICHES OF GOD'S WORD

When he was thirty-one, Samuel Stennett (1727-1795) succeeded his father as minister of Little Wild Street Baptist Church in London. He followed his grandfather in the writing and publishing of hymns. The most famous is "On Jordan's Stormy Banks I Stand," which became a favorite at American Methodist camp meetings. Five of Stennett's hymns were published in John Rippon's *A Selection of Hymns from the best Authors, Intended to be an Appendix to Dr. Watts' Psalms and Hymns.* Among them was "The Riches of God's Word":

Let Avaris[20] from Shore to Shore
    Her fav'rite God pursue;
Thy Word, O Lord, we value more
    Than India or Peru.

Here Mines of Knowledge, Love, and Joy
    Are open'd to our Sight:
The purest God without Alloy,
    And Gems divinely bright.

The Counsels of redeeming Grace
    These sacred Leaves unfold:
And here the Saviour's lovely Face
    Our raptured Eyes behold.

Here Light descending from above
    Directs our doubtful Feet:
Here Promises of heavenly Love
    Our ardent Wishes meet.

Our num'rous Griefs are here redrest,
    And all our Wants supplied:
Nought we can ask to make us blest,
    Is in this Book denied.

For these inestimable Gains
    That so enrich the Mind,
O may we search with eager Pains,
    Assur'd that we shall find![21]

In your steadfast love give me life, that I may keep the testimonies of your mouth.
—Psalm 119:88—

JULY 24
THE VALLEY OF GRACE

Herrnhut, Count Zinzendorf's community of Moravian Brethren in Saxony, was a leader in its day in sending out missionaries to other nations. In 1728, George Schmidt was sent to Bohemia as an evangelist. He was soon imprisoned for violating the Roman Catholic laws in the country and spent six years incarcerated. In 1736, after his release, Schmidt was sent to evangelize the Khoi or Hottentots in South Africa.

Schmidt went to the Valley of Baboons and began evangelizing the natives. He read the Dutch Bible to the people, established a school, and taught the people how to read and write. Four men, two women, and four children regularly attended the school. In 1742, five years after coming to the Valley of Baboons, Schmidt baptized five people who had believed the Gospel message. The Dutch, however, did not approve of Schmidt's evangelization and educational work among the Khoi, and in 1744, he was forced to leave the country.

In 1792, almost fifty years later, Moravian missionaries were allowed to return to the country. They wondered if there would be any remnant left from Schmidt's earlier Gospel work. They were amazed when they met an older woman who called herself Magdalena, which was her baptismal name. After Schmidt had left, Magdalena regularly sat under the tree near Schmidt's house and read the New Testament to the people. She had taught her daughter and granddaughter to read, and they carried on the practice of reading the Scriptures. Magdalena's faith in the Scriptures and in Jesus remained constant, even without outside missionary support or encouragement. The Valley of Baboons was renamed the Valley of Grace, which is its name today.

To the teaching and to the testimony!
If they will not speak according to this word,
it is because they have no dawn.
—Isaiah 8:20—

THE USEFULNESS OF SCRIPTURES

Though originally Benjamin Beddome (1717-1795) was apprenticed to a surgeon, he decided to become a minister rather than a physician. After training at the Baptist college in Bristol and Moorfields Academy in London, he became pastor of the Baptist church in Bourton-on-the-Water in Gloucestershire. He pastored the church for forty-five years, faithfully preaching the Word of God to his congregation. Beddome composed over 800 hymns during that time, often writing one each week to match the Scripture theme of the Sunday sermon. 830 of the hymns were published posthumously, and many were part of 18th- and 19th-century hymn collections. One of his hymns, after a sermon on Psalm 19, was "The Usefulness of the Scriptures":

When Israel thro' the desert pass'd
A fiery pillar went before,
To guide them thro
The dreary waste,
And lessen the fatigues they bore.

Such is thy glorious Word, O God,
'Tis for our light and guidance given;
It sheds a lustre all abroad,
And points the path to bliss and heaven.

It fills the soul with sweet delight,
And quickens its inactive powers,
It sets our wandering footsteps right,
Displays thy love, and kindles ours.

Its promises rejoice our hearts,
Its doctrines are divinely true;
Knowledge and pleasure it imparts,
It comforts, and instructs us too.

Ye British Isles, who have this Word,
Ye saints, who feel its saving power,
Unite your tongues to praise the Lord,
And his distinguish'd Grace adore.[22]

Let the words of my mouth and the meditation of my heart be acceptable in your sight, O Lord, my rock and my redeemer. —Psalm 19:14—

JULY 26

AUTHENTICITY AND AUTHORITY OF THE SCRIPTURES

When Timothy Dwight (1752-1817) became President of Yale in 1795, the intellectual climate was far different from when his grandfather Jonathan Edwards had entered Yale almost 80 years earlier. Several of the faculty no longer supported Christian beliefs, and the Enlightenment's skepticism was rampant. But under Dwight's Presidency, the campus had a revival of Christian faith. Students began again to rest their faith on biblical truth.

Dwight had read the Bible since he was four, and he had a life-long passion for the Bible. He was skilled in Latin and Greek and well-versed in biblical and ancient history. Entering Yale at age thirteen, he graduated at seventeen, giving his first public address at the 1771 commencement, "A Dissertation on the History, Eloquence, and Poetry of the Bible." During the American Revolution, Dwight was a chaplain and wrote a patriotic poem, *The Conquest of Canaan*, dedicated to George Washington. After the war, Dwight pastored a church in Connecticut before becoming President of Yale in 1795.

As President, Dwight challenged the ideas of French rationalism. In his first year, the students debated "Are the Scriptures of the Old and New Testament the word of God?" All the students argued the Bible was not God's word, and Dwight demolished all their arguments. For six months he preached in the chapel services on the authority of Scripture. He wrote *Young Man's Manual: The Genuineness and Authenticity of the New Testament*, a strong apologetic for the historicity, reliability, and authority of the Scriptures. He concluded his study by noting:

> No question, perhaps can be of more importance to the Divine Authority of the sacred Volume than this. If its Genuineness and Authenticity be established, its Authority is also established.

> If there was such a person as Jesus Christ; if he was so born; if he so lived; if he was so attested; if he so preached, wrought miracles, died, rose from the dead, ascended to heaven, commissioned his Apostles, and enabled them to preach, work miracles in his name, and erect his kingdom through the world, in the manner which they have related; then he was the Son of God; his Doctrines were true; his Apostles were inspired; and his Religion is of Divine Original, and of Divine Authority. Mankind are, of course, bound to receive and obey it. Those who reject it, reject it at their peril; and those who sincerely embrace it, are secured, beyond a hazard, in the certain future possession of its invaluable and immortal blessings.[23]

This is the disciple who is bearing witness about these things,
and who wrote these things, and we know that his testimony is true.
—John 12:24—

JULY 27
WHAT'S IN A NAME?

As colonists settled in America, they often named places after cities and places in their home country—or after places familiar to them from the Bible. In California, the land of the 1840's Gold Rush, there is an Ophir, Ophir City and a Mount Ophir, all named after the place the Bible mentioned as the source of King Solomon's fine gold. In the United States there are 10 towns named Palestine, after the name the Romans gave to the province which merged Judea and Syria. Twelve U.S. towns are named Goshen, after the area where Joseph had the Jews settle when they came to Egypt.

When Jacob dreamed of seeing the ladder to heaven with angels ascending and descending, he named the place Bethel, meaning "House of God." Thereafter Bethel is mentioned frequently in Scripture. There are at least eight Bethels in the United States. Other Biblical place names in the U.S. include Hebron, Lebanon, Bethlehem, Antioch, Bethany, Zion and Shiloh.

Probably the most frequent biblical place name found in the U.S. is Salem, after the city of Melchizedek, later called Jerusalem. There are at least thirty-eight cities or towns named Salem, including towns in Massachusetts, Connecticut, Alabama, New Jersey, New York, North Carolina, Oklahoma, Virginia, and Wisconsin, Oklahoma, and Texas.

Of course, biblical names were not only given to places, but to people. Names of people from the Bible continue to be popular and never go out of style—from Abigail, Mary, Deborah, Elizabeth, and Anna for girls to Aaron, Peter, John, Paul, and Matthew for boys—and many more.

Agree with God, and be at peace;
thereby good will come to you.
Receive instruction from his mouth,
and lay up his words in your heart.
—Job 22:21-22—

THOMAS CHARLES SEEKS WELSH BIBLES

At the age of seventeen, Thomas Charles (1755-1814) was converted through the preaching of Daniel Rowland during the revival in the latter part of the 18th century. He went on to study at Jesus College, Oxford and under the evangelical John Newton at Olney. Settling at Bala in Wales, he was concerned about the biblical ignorance of many in Wales, and he began establishing schools to teach children to read the Bible. Older people were also invited to the schools if they wished to learn to read. Boys and girls learned entire books of the Bible from memory, and often their parents recited with them. One five-year-old girl could recite one hundred Bible chapters, and she kept learning a chapter a week.

Yet there was a shortage of Welsh Bibles. Twelve peasant families subscribed to purchase a Bible together, agreeing to pass the Bible around so that each family had the Bible one month. The last subscriber was an older man, who wept bitterly when the Bible arrived—for, if he had to wait eleven months for the Bible, he would likely have died and left this world before it was his turn to have it. One young girl walked seven miles each week to read a Bible in a neighboring farmhouse.

With stories such as these, Thomas Charles enlisted organizations in London, such as the Religious Tract Society and the Society for the Promotion of Christian Knowledge, to provide Welsh Bibles. Eventually his efforts led to the formation of the British and Foreign Bible Society in 1804 "to encourage the wider circulation and use of the Scriptures."

Let those who fear you turn to me,
that they may know your testimonies.
—Psalm 119:79—

JULY 29
WALKING BY FAITH

Mary Jones (1784-1864) was born in the Welsh village of Llanfihanel-y-pennant. Her father, a weaver, died when Mary was four, and Mary's mother struggled to support herself and Mary. When Mary was about eight, a school was established in the village, a one hour walk from Mary's house. Daily Mary eagerly walked the two hour round trip to the school and learned to read.

About the same time, Mary professed her faith in Christ. She longed to have a Bible to read of her own, but her mother said it was too expensive. Mrs. Evans, a neighbor lady two miles away, did have a Bible, and every Saturday Mary walked to her house to read the Bible for several hours. One day, as she washed her family's clothes in the river, Mary had the idea that she could earn money for a Bible by washing other people's clothes. Mrs. Evans learned of her plan and gave Mary some chicks to raise; Mary cared for the chicks and when they became hens began selling eggs. Mary also earned money by caring for children, weeding gardens, and knitting socks. Mary saved her money for six years before she finally had enough funds for a Bible. The nearest place to purchase a Bible was in Bala, over twenty-five miles away. When she was not yet sixteen, in the summer of 1800, Mary set out on the walk to Bala. Sometimes she took off her shoes and carried them so that they would not wear out!

When Mary reached Bala and found Thomas Charles, who had the Bibles, he said he had only one left, and it was promised to someone else. Mary burst into tears. She had waited so long and walked so far and was so eager to have her own Bible! When Thomas Charles heard Mary's story, he gave her the Bible. He said the other person could wait a little longer.

Thomas Charles was deeply moved by Mary's story. In 1802, he laid before a committee of the religious Tract Society the need for Bibles in the Welsh language and told Mary Jones's story. Months later, in 1804, the British and Foreign Bible Society was formed "for the wider distribution of Scriptures." For over 200 years the Society has been a major impetus for the spread of the Scriptures around the world. What a mission young Mary Jones inspired!

Your testimonies are righteous forever;
give me understanding that I may live.
—Psalm 119:144—

A BOOK FOR CHILDREN

Fisher Ames (1758-1808), one of the lesser known of the "Founding Fathers" of the United States, was part of the Massachusetts convention which approved the United States Constitution in 1789. He went on to be elected to the United States Congress, serving four terms. He was active in all the debates and legislative action and was responsible for the wording of the religion clause in the First Amendment, "Congress shall make no law respecting an establishment of religion, or prohibiting the free exercise thereof..." Ames did not seek reelection to a fifth term in Congress but returned to the private practice of law in Dedham, Massachusetts. In 1805, Ames was offered the Presidency of Harvard University, but he declined because of his failing health.

In 1801, Ames wrote an article for *The Mercury and New England Palladium* in which he discussed the type of children's books available. He noted the growing trend to place in children's hands books of fables with moral lessons. He found many of these books "injudiciously compiled." How the morals related to the fables were not always clear or where the moral rules actually came from. Many of the fables "abound with a frothy sort of *sentiment*. He felt the "object of education" should be to properly direct emotions rather than simply cultivate a sentimental feeling. Ames then made an appeal for the Bible to be the book which would most impress a child and cultivate his mind:

> Why then, if these books for children must be retained, as they will be, should not the bible regain the place it once held as a school book? Its morals are pure, its examples captivating and noble. The reverence of the sacred book, that is thus early impressed, lasts long; and, probably, if not impressed in infancy, never takes firm hold of the mind. One consideration more is important. In no book is there so good English, so pure and so elegant; and by teaching all the *same* book, they will speak alike, and the bible will justly remain the standard of language as well as of faith. A barbarous provincial jargon will be banished, and taste ... will be restored.[24]

Teach me, O Lord, the way of your statutes;
and I will keep it to the end.
—Psalm 119:33—

WILLIAM CAREY: MISSIONARY AND BIBLE TRANSLATOR

A cobbler by trade, William Carey (1761-1834) had a gift for languages. While repairing shoes, he often had a grammar propped up nearby as he taught himself numerous languages—Greek, Hebrew, Italian, Dutch, and French. He joined with a local association of Particular Baptists and in time was pastor of the local church. After reading Jonathan Edwards' *Life of the Late David Brainerd*, the missionary to the native Americans, Carey became increasingly concerned with spreading the gospel throughout the world. Through his encouragement, writing, and preaching, in 1792, the Baptist Missionary Society was founded. The following year Carey and his family sailed for India.

The British East India Company opposed missionary work in India, fearing it would interfere with trade. So, the Careys relocated to Serampore, a region controlled by the Danish. Other missionaries joined them there, including printer William Ward and schoolteacher Joshua Marshman.

On the boat to India, Carey had been studying Bengali and beginning a translation of the Scriptures into that language. A printing press was acquired by the Serampore missionaries, and by the spring of 1800, the first printed Scriptures in Bengali were produced, which included the Gospel of Matthew and a selection of Old Testament prophecies concerning Christ. By the next year, the Bengali New Testament was completed and printed. William Ward said by this publication there were now 2000 more missionaries in India!

With the Bengali New Testament as an example of his scholarship, Carey was appointed a professor of the newly founded Fort William College. This gave him access to pundits who would help him in improving the Bengali translation and developing translations in other Indian dialects. Carey spent 41 years in India without a furlough. He established schools and wrote textbooks for young people. Most importantly, he provided Bible translations in Bengali, Oriya, Marathi, Hindi, Assanese, Sanskrit, and 30 other dialects. Carey and his fellow missionaries believed

> The translation of the Sacred Scriptures into those languages in which a translation of them does not exist, is perhaps one of the most important objects which can engage the attention of the Christian public. Schemes of temporal relief, however praiseworthy, can only extend their beneficial influence through the term of human life; but to impart the World of Life to those who have it not, is an exercise of benevolence as far transcending in importance all inferior plans of charity, as the interests of eternity outweigh those of time.[25]

And the gospel of the kingdom will be proclaimed throughout the whole world as a testimony to all nations, and then the end will come.
—Matthew 24:14—

AUGUST 1
WORDS ABOUT THE WORD, 19TH CENTURY

Thomas Jones (1754-1837), Scottish minister: "In matters of religion, all the doctrines which men are required to believe, and all the duties which they are commanded to perform, are contained in the Bible; and if anything is taught or enjoined which is not found in, or fairly deducible from, the doctrines and precepts of the sacred volume, it is an imposition and ought to be rejected."[1]

Robert Haldane (1764-1842), Scottish evangelist: "All religions but that of the Bible, share the glory of recovering men to happiness between God and the sinner. All false views of the gospel do the same thing. The Bible alone makes the salvation of guilty men terminate in the glory of God as its chief end. Can there be a more convincing evidence that the Bible is from God?"

Thomas Chalmers (1780-1847), Scottish preacher: "I would learn of Thy holy oracles. I would take the sayings of the Bible simply and purely as they are, and exercise myself on the trueness of these sayings."

Rev. Edward Payson (1783-1827), American Congregationalist pastor: "By opening this volume we may at any time walk in the garden of Eden with Adam, sit in the ark with Noah, share the hospitality or witness the faith of Abraham, ascent the mount of God with Moses, unite in the secret devotions of David, or listen to the eloquent and impassioned address of Paul. Nay, morel we may here converse with him who spake as never man spake, participate with the just made perfect in the employment and happiness of heaven, and enjoy sweet communion with the Father of our spirits through his Son Jesus Christ. Such is the society to which the Scriptures introduce us, such the examples which they present to our imitation."[2]

Sir Walter Scott (1771-1832), historical novelist and poet: "The most learned, acute, and diligent student cannot, in the longest life, obtain an entire knowledge of this one volume. The more deeply he works the mine, the richer and more abundant he finds the ore. New light continually beams from this source of heavenly knowledge to direct the conduct and illustrate the works of God and the ways of men; and he will, at least, leave the world confessing, that the more he studied the Scriptures the fuller convictions he had of his own ignorance and of their inestimable value." On his death, Scott said to his son-in-law, "Read to me." Mr. Lockhart said, "What book shall I read?"—"What book!" replied Sir Walter, "there is but one book,—the Bible!"

My soul keeps Your testimonies, And I love them exceedingly.
—Psalm 119:167—

READ THE BIBLE!

In 1784, 26-year-old William Wilberforce (1759-1833) was traveling in Europe and reading Philip Doddridge's *Rise and Progress of Religion in the Soul.* He later credited his faith in Jesus Christ and the great change in his life to Doddridge's work. A member of Parliament since he was twenty-one, when not attending to his Parliamentary duties, Wilberforce spent time drinking and gambling. After his conversion, his life changed. He regularly rose early to spend time in Bible study and prayer. Wondering whether he should remain in public life, Wilberforce sought advice from minister John Newton, who advised him to remain in politics and use his position for the public good.

Wilberforce was most concerned to reform the morals of England to reflect the morals delineated in Scripture. He was active in numerous societies to further Christian causes. He was a founding member of the Church Missionary Society and the British and Foreign Bible Society, of which he was Vice President from 1805 until his death in 1833. In Parliament, Wilberforce championed reform legislation. For twenty years, Wilberforce yearly introduced legislation to abolish the slave trade, and his tireless efforts succeeded in 1807. Wilberforce then worked for the abolition of slavery itself.

Wilberforce's Christian faith shaped his life. He wrote a work, which was very popular, showing the importance of biblical truth and doctrine in practical Christianity. The work's lengthy title tells its aim: *A Practical View of the Prevailing Religious System of Professed Christians, in the Middle and Higher Classes in this Country, Contrasted with Real Christianity.*

The work is filled with Scripture and shows the fruit of Wilberforce's daily Bible studies.

One of Wilberforce's friends recorded some of his last words:

> I never knew happiness till I found Christ as a Saviour. Read the Bible! read the Bible! Let no religious book take its place. Through all my perplexities and distresses, I never read any other book, and I never knew the want of any other. It has been my hourly study; and all my knowledge of the doctrine, and all my acquaintance with the experience and realities of religion, have been derived from the Bible only.[3]

You have dealt well with your servant, O Lord, according to your word.
—Psalm 119:65—

AUGUST 3
CHARLES THOMSON'S BIBLE TRANSLATION

When Charles Thomson's mother died in 1739, his father left Ireland and sailed for America with Charles and his brothers. Before the ship reached Philadelphia, Charles' father died and was buried at sea, leaving the eleven-year-old Charles an orphan. The boys were separated, and a blacksmith cared for Charles. But Charles ran away when the man planned to legally apprentice him as a blacksmith. A lady found him walking along a road and asked him what he wanted to do with himself. When he said he wanted to be a scholar, she took him to her home and began to give him an education. Charles excelled at Latin and Greek, and in a few years became a tutor in Latin. One day Charles saw a portion of a Greek text for auction and bought it, not knowing what it was. He soon discovered it was the Septuagint, the Greek translation of the Hebrew Scriptures made in the second century B.C. Amazingly, a few years later, he found the rest of the text for sale and was able to buy it also.

Thomson established an import business which did quite well until the Stamp Act began restricting colonial trade. He soon became a leader of the colonial cause in Philadelphia. He was chosen as Secretary of the Continental Congress, a position he held throughout the American Revolution and the writing of the Constitution. His name, along with that of President of Congress John Hancock, was printed on the first published Declaration of Independence.

During the American Revolution, Thomson began translating the Greek Septuagint into English. He believed it was important, because the New Testament writers' Old Testament quotes usually came from the Septuagint rather than the Hebrew. Thomson went on to translate the entire Bible, which was published in four volumes in 1808. His translation was the first English New Testament to be translated and published in America and the first English translation of the Septuagint. Thomson wrote about his translation, saying,

> I have sought for truth with the utmost ingenuity, and endeavored to give a just and true representation of the sense and meaning of the Sacred Scriptures; and in doing this, I have further endeavored to convey into the translation, as far as I could, the spirit and manner of the authors, and thereby give it the quality of an original.[4]

... you have been born again, not of perishable seed but of imperishable,
through the living and abiding word of God;
—I Peter 1:23—

JOHN Q. ADAMS' LETTER TO HIS SON

In 1811, John Quincy Adams, American diplomat and later Secretary of State and President of the United States, wrote a letter to his son encouraging him in his Bible reading. He wrote,

> In your letter of the 18th January to your mother, you mentioned that you read to your aunt a chapter of the Bible or a section of Doddridge's *Annotations* every evening. This information gave me real pleasure; for so great is my veneration for the Bible, and so strong my belief, that when duly read and meditated on, it is of all books in the world, that which contributes most to make men good, wise, and happy—that the earlier my children begin to read it, the more steadily they pursue the practice of reading it throughout their lives, the more lively and confident will be my hopes that they will prove useful citizens of their country, respectable members of society, and a real blessing to their parents ...
>
> I have myself, for many years, made it a practice to read through the Bible once every year ... My custom is to read four to five chapters every morning immediately after rising from my bed. It employs about an hour of my time ...
>
> It is essential, my son, in order that you may go through life with comfort to yourself, and usefulness to your fellow-creatures, that you should form and adopt certain rules or principles, for the government of your own conduct and temper... It is in the Bible, you must learn them, and from the Bible how to practice them. Those duties are to God, your fellow-creatures, and to yourself. 'Thou shalt love the Lord thy God, with all thy heart, and with all thy soul, and with all thy mind, and with all thy strength, and thy neighbor as thy self.' On these two commandments, Jesus Christ expressly says, 'hang all the law and the prophets'; that is to say, the whole purpose of the Divine Revelation is to inculcate them efficaciously upon the minds of men ...[5]

Blessed is the man
who walks not in the counsel of the wicked,
nor stands in the way of sinners,
nor sits in the seat of scoffers;
but his delight is in the law of the Lord,
and on his law he meditates day and night.
—Psalm 1:1-2—

AUGUST 5
THE BIBLE IN PERSIAN

Longing to bring the Gospel of Christ to lost souls around the globe, Henry Martyn (1781-1812) became a chaplain for the British East India Company. He had been inspired by the missionary work of William Carey, who had gone to India ten years earlier. Martyn had a gift for languages and soon was proficient enough in the local dialects to preach to the natives in their own language. He revised the Hindustani New Testament begun by William Carey's associates, and also translated the New Testament into Urdu and Persian, as well as the Psalms into Persian. Martyn, suffering from tuberculosis, which had earlier killed his parents and sister, was advised to take a sea voyage for his health. Martyn took the opportunity to travel to Persia, planning to improve his Persian New Testament.

In Persia he met Mollah Mahomet Ramah. Ramah describes the meeting with Martyn and his gift of a Persian New Testament:

> There came to Persia, an Englishman, who taught the religion of Christ, with a boldness we had never seen, in the midst of much scorn and ill-treatment from the rabble. He was young, and feeble with disease. I was then a decided enemy to infidels, and I, too, visited this teacher to treat him with scorn and contempt. These evil feelings left me beneath the influence of his gentleness; and before I quitted Shiraz, I paid him a parting visit. The memory of our conversation will never fade from mind: it sealed my conversion. He gave me a book; it has ever been my constant companion,—the study of it my most thoughtful occupation. On one of the blank leaves was written, "There is joy in heaven over one sinner that repenteth." (signed) *Henry Martyn.*[6]

As Martyn weakened and suffered from fever, he planned to return to England. At Tokat, Turkey, he breathed his last and entered eternity. He was only 31, but he had given the Word of God to many in the east.

... man does not live by bread alone,
but man lives by every word that comes from the mouth of the Lord.
—Deuteronomy 8:3—

BRINGING THE SCRIPTURES
TO THE PRISONERS

In 1813, Elizabeth Fry (1780-1845) visited Newgate prison in London and was horrified at the condition of the prisoners. Three hundred women and children were living, sleeping, and eating in four overcrowded rooms suitable for half that number. There was no order, and bullies ran the place. Elizabeth used her own funds and donations to begin to reform the prison. She brought in clothes and started classes to teach the women sewing and knitting. By selling their productions, they could earn money for food and soap.

Elizabeth began to visit the prison daily to read the Scriptures to the women. She usually began her reading with Isaiah 53:6-7, "All we like sheep have gone astray; we have turned everyone to his own way; and the Lord hath laid on him the iniquity of us all ..." She frequently read Psalms 24 and 27, which showed God sustaining faith. Psalm 69, a prayer under great affliction, was also regularly read. The Sermon on the Mount and the Parable of the Vineyard in Matthew 20 were also among Elizabeth's favorite readings. From these the women could learn that holiness, justice, and strength were all from God.

When John Randolph of Virginia visited London, he thought all the magnificent London sites could not compare with seeing Elizabeth Fry among the prisoners at Newgate. Under her Christian influence, the most wretched prisoners were transformed. Elizabeth Fry knew that only the Scriptures could change a human heart, and a real personal reformation was possible only through the truths of the Word of God.

I am severely afflicted; give me life,
O Lord, according to your word!
—Psalm 119:107—

AUGUST 7
NOTHING MORE PRECIOUS OR OF GREATER VALUE

"The Defense of Fort McHenry" was the original name of Francis Scott Key's poem which became the United States' national anthem, "The Star-Spangled Banner." During the War of 1812, Key had been in the Baltimore harbor watching the bombardment of Fort McHenry eagerly looking to see if the US flag continued to fly over the fort, a sign of American victory.

Fort McHenry was named after James McHenry (1753-1816), a medical doctor who served in the army during the American Revolution on George Washington's and then General Lafayette's staff. He represented Maryland at the Constitutional Convention and went on to serve as Secretary of War under Presidents George Washington and John Adams. In 1813, McHenry was elected President of the Bible Society of Baltimore. In an address written for the society, McHenry emphasized the importance of distributing God's Word:

> All Christians allow that the Old and New Testaments taken together, are the only books in the world which clearly reveal the nature of God, contain a perfect law for our government, propose the most powerful persuasions to obey this law, and furnish the best motives for patience and resignation, under every circumstance and vicissitude of life.

McHenry noted that there is a public utility in the distribution of the Scriptures to all:

> The doctrine they preach, the obligations they impose, the punishment they threaten, the rewards they promise, the stamp and image of divinity they bear, which produces a conviction of their truths, can alone secure to society, order and peace, and to our courts of justice and constitutions of government purity, stability, and usefulness. In vain, without the Bible, we increase penal laws and draw entrenchments around our institutions. Bibles are strong entrenchments. Where they abound, men cannot pursue wicked courses, and at the same time enjoy quiet conscience .... the rich do not possess aught more precious than their Bible, and ... the poor cannot be presented by the rich with anything of greater value .... It is an estate, whose title is guaranteed by Christ, whose delicious fruits ripen in every season, survive the worm, and keep through eternity.[7]

Great peace have those who love your law; nothing can make them stumble.
—Psalm 119:165—

BENJAMIN RUSH: THE BIBLE IN SCHOOLS

Though today few in America know his name, at the time of his death in 1813, Dr. Benjamin Rush was considered one of the three most notable Americans, along with Benjamin Franklin and George Washington. A medical doctor and patriot, Benjamin Rush published the first American chemical textbook and was a signer of the Declaration of Independence. For sixteen years he served as Treasurer of the U. S. Mint. Dr. Rush was also a Christian and founder of the Philadelphia Bible Society, the first Bible Society in America. Dr. Rush believed the Bible should be used in the schools to instruct the young, and his "Defense of the Use of the Bible in Schools" was distributed by the American Tract Society for many years.

Dr. Rush unhesitatingly stated that Christianity is the only true religion and can be learned best by reading the Bible. He was convinced that early instruction in the Bible is most important, for young people are most open to religious instruction and their memories are most ready to receive it. Rush believed the Bible contains more truth than any book in the world, and it is only proper that young people learn of their Creator and His providence through the Bible's pages. The Bible's truths are needed by the elderly as well, but if taught in youth, these truths will best be remembered in old age when most needed.

Rush wrote that morals alone cannot improve the lot of mankind. If that were true, the mission of Jesus into the world to suffer and die for man's sin would be unnecessary. Rush wrote that true ethics come from "the vicarious life and death of the Son of God. From this we have the principle of love Jesus taught: 'A new commandment I give unto you, that ye love one another, even as I have loved you.'" [8]

Rush concluded that teaching the Bible in schools would also support the political institutions of the United States: "we waste so much time and money in punishing crimes and take as little pains to prevent them ... we neglect the very means of establishing and perpetuating our republican forms of government; that is, the universal education of our youth in the principles of Christianity by means of the Bible." [9]

A new commandment I give to you, that you love one another:
just as I have loved you, you also are to love one another.
—John 13:34—

AUGUST 9

NAPOLEONIC WARS AND THE SPREAD OF BIBLES AMONG THE NATIONS

When Napoleon seized power in France, he brought some order to the chaotic conditions in France brought on by the French Revolution. Crowning himself emperor in 1804, Napoleon centralized the government and brought about important reforms in banking, education, and law; the Napoleonic Law is still the foundation of French civil law today. Napoleon's efforts to expand his empire led to a series of wars against other European nations opposing such expansion. Britain was one of the important opponents against French expansionism; the conflicts continued sporadically for a decade and a half.

During the Napoleonic Wars, the British took numerous prisoners. 1700 Spanish and 5000 French prisoners were kept in Plymouth, England. The British and Foreign Bible Society had French and Spanish Bibles printed to distribute among the prisoners. One person distributing the Bibles wrote,

> Many sought the books with tears and entreaties, and received the words of eternal life; since which, I have witnessed the most pleasing sight that my eyes ever beheld—nearly one thousand poor prisoners sitting around the prison walls, reading the word of God, with an apparent eagerness that would have put many professing Christians to the blush.[10]

When prisoners were exchanged or the war ended, they crossed the waters with their Bibles, and brought the Gospel to their homeland. These returning prisoners, now made new creatures in Christ, helped establish churches and furthered the distribution of the Bible once the wars had ended.

I write to you, young men, because you are strong,
and the word of God abides in you,
and you have overcome the evil one.
— I John 2:14—

IN GOD IS OUR TRUST

As he negotiated an exchange of prisoners, lawyer Francis Scott Key (1779-1843) was kept behind British lines during the fighting at Fort McHenry during the War of 1812. Watching the bombardment and the bombs bursting in air, he kept his eye on the large American flag flying at the fort, wondering if it would be still flying there in the morning. He wrote his thoughts in poetry on the back of a letter; the poem, "The Defence of Fort McHenry" later became the national anthem, "The Star Spangled Banner." The last verse especially reflected Key's Christian faith and gave the nation its national motto:

O thus be it ever, when freemen shall stand
Between their loved homes and war's desolation.
Blest with vict'ry and peace, may the Heav'n rescued land
Praise the Power that hath made and preserved us a nation!
Then conquer we must, when our cause it is just,
And this be our motto, 'In God is our trust."

Key was a devout Christian who at one time considered becoming a minister. Though he continued in his law practice, his Christian faith radiated through all he did. Twice a day he had Bible reading and prayer with his family. He was active in the American Bible Society and numerous Christian charity causes.

When Key was 32, he made his will and wrote letters for his wife and children, which were not to be opened until his death. To his children he wrote:

O my children, you, too, will die, you also will all stand before God! You have read your Bible; how God made us, what he requires of us, how Christ died for us, how we must pray and strive to do everything right and shun everything wrong. I have endeavored to instruct you. Never forget this, my dear children, and remember that we cannot serve and please God of ourselves, but we must pray to Him to help us for Christ's sake. "Watch and pray, and it shall be given unto you." Read your Bibles every morning and evening. Never neglect private prayers, both morning and evening, and throughout the day strive to think of God often and breathe a sincere supplication to Him for all things. Join also in family prayers—sometimes instead of your mother, one of you, by turns, should read prayers. Go regularly to church, plainly dressed, and behave reverently. Do all possible good to all—to your mother, to each other, to your relatives, to the poor and everybody within your reach. Do not love or indulge yourselves; learn and practice self-denial, and do everything for God's sake, and consider yourselves always in His service. Remember that you do not belong to yourselves, Christ has bought you, and His precious blood was your price.[11]

Though the cords of the wicked ensnare me, I do not forget your law.
—Psalm 119:61—

TO THE GLORY OF GOD ALONE

Heir to the extensive estate at Airthrey, near Stirling, Scotland, Robert Haldane (1764-1842) converted to the evangelical church in 1795. He had a great interest in evangelism and mission work. Hearing of the work of William Carey in India, he even proposed selling his estate and setting up a large mission in Bengal, but the East India Company didn't want missionaries interfering with business. Haldane did sell his estate in 1798, using funds to help establish the Society for Propagating the Gospel at Home in Edinburgh. The funds were used to build chapels and support missionary evangelists throughout Scotland. Haldane also promoted theological training among young men.

In 1815-1816, Robert visited Europe. In Geneva he met a group of theology students who seemed totally ignorant of basic biblical truth. Rather than studying the Scriptures in theology school, their main sources had been Plato, Cicero, and Seneca! Robert began a Bible study in his apartment on Romans. For the next five months, on Thursday and Monday evenings, Haldane met with 25 theology students, studying Paul's epistle to the Romans. Many of the students came to faith in Christ and went on to become evangelical leaders throughout Switzerland and France. The students asked Haldane later to publish a commentary on Romans, and Haldane's commentary on Romans remains an important commentary today.

When asked what had brought about this evangelical awakening among the students, Haldane said that nothing more brought about this turn from philosophy and vain deceit to the truth of the Gospel than Romans 11: 33-36,

> Oh, the depth of the riches and wisdom and knowledge of God! How unsearchable are his judgments and how inscrutable his ways! "For who has known the mind of the Lord, or who has been his counselor?" "Or who has given a gift to him that he might be repaid?" For from him and through him and to him are all things. To him be glory forever. Amen.

The students became aware of the "sublime view of the majesty of God" in Scripture, and that "the manifestation of the glory of God is the great end of creation ..."[12]

Your testimonies are wonderful;
therefore my soul keeps them.
—Psalm 119:129—

AUGUST 12

ADVICE TO A YOUNG PHYSICIAN

John Abercrombie (1780-1844) was one of Scotland's most noted physicians. Becoming a fellow of the Royal College of Physicians of Edinburgh in 1824 Abercrombie soon after appointed the king's physician in Scotland. Besides his private practice of medicine, he was one of the medical officers at the Royal Public Dispensary, providing medical treatment to the poor of Edinburgh. He wrote important scientific works on the diseases of the brain and spinal cord as well as on diseases of the stomach, intestines, and abdomen. The son of a parish minister, Abercrombie's Christian faith formed his character throughout his life. In the last decades of his life, he wrote several works of philosophy, morals, and a work of instruction for the young, *Elements of Sacred Truth*.

In 1816, Abercrombie wrote a lengthy letter of advice to a young physician just entering upon his career. Abercrombie recognized that character was of the utmost importance if the young man was to be held in high esteem. But, even more important than the esteem of men was the "approbation of God." Life should be lived with an eye on eternity, with the

> recollection of that Almighty Being who sees you every moment, before whose penetrating eyes your most secret thoughts are naked and open, and who has appointed a day in which he will judge the world in righteousness.... each man has his place and his duties assigned him, and the eye of the eternal God is over all. Cultivate an acquaintance with these important truths, by a daily and careful study of the Sacred Scriptures. By daily prayer to God, seek for the pardon of your daily sins and shortcomings, through Jesus Christ, the only Mediator, and for the Holy Spirit of God to enlighten and to purify you, to conduct you safely through this world, and to give you an inheritance in his heavenly kingdom. ... Let it be your study, then, my dear friend, in all your ways to set God before you. Study to fortify your mind against the sophistry of sinners, by a diligent study of the Word of God, and by daily prayer for the Holy Spirit to guide you in all your ways. Think of that pure and holy Being who is every moment at your right hand; think of that eternal world to which every day brings you nearer and nearer ... when in doubt with regard to any piece of conduct, try it by this test—'Is it agreeable to the law of God? ... living under the eye of the Almighty, you may look for a peace of mind which cannot be enjoyed in any other way. You will exhibit a firmness and uniformity of character which cannot be derived from any other source. You may look for the blessing of God upon all your concerns, and through Jesus Christ, an inheritance in the resurrection of the just ... Thus thinking and thus acting, it will be of comparatively little

moment what may be your lot in this world: that is in the hand of God, and will be ordered by his infinite wisdom as shall be best for you …[13]

… whoever keeps his word, in him truly the love of God is perfected.
By this we may know that we are in him.
—I John 2:5—

AUGUST 13
THE AMERICAN BIBLE SOCIETY

Founded May 8, 1816, the American Bible Society (ABS) grew up with the United States and throughout its 200 year history has played an important role in Bible distribution and translation. In 1816, Elias Boudinot called for a general meeting in New York of representatives from local Bible Societies. James Fennimore Cooper, the novelist, was among the approximately 60 attendees. The American Bible Society was founded with the sole object "to encourage a wider circulation of the Holy Scriptures, without note or comment." Elias Boudinot, former President of Congress and Director of the U.S. Mint, was elected the first President.

The American Bible Society was one of the first religious non-profit organizations in the United States and was an outgrowth of the Second Great Awakening, the spiritual revival that transformed much of American society in the first half of the nineteenth century. Many notable Americans were part of the Society's early years. John Jay, first Chief Justice of the Supreme Court and signer of the Declaration of Independence and the Treaty of Paris, became President of the ABS after Boudinot. Francis Scott Key, author of the "The Star Spangled Banner," was Vice-President from 1817 to 1843.

The ABS distributed copies of Bibles in prisons, to seamen and boatmen (such as workers on the Erie Canal), and Sunday Schools. European immigrants were given Bibles in their native languages when they arrived in America, and sometimes even at the port of embarkation. The Bible was foundational to the American republic, and it was important that every American know the Scriptures. In its first thirty years, the ABS printed over 6 million Bibles; by 1862 it was selling a million copies a year. Four times in its history, in 1829, 1856, 1866, and 1882, the ABS sought to ensure every family in America had a Bible, sending out representatives to visit every village and farm. In 1890, the ABS sought to make certain every child under fifteen who could read had a Bible. 200 years after its founding, the American Bible Society's aim continues: "that all men and women may read and hear the saving word of God and find life in Jesus Christ." [14]

... you have exalted above all things your name and your word.
—Psalm 138:2—

ELIAS BOUDINOT AND CONTINUING
WORK OF THE AMERICAN BIBLE SOCIETY

Elias Boudinot (1790-1821) was elected the first President of the American Bible Society. Boudinot was descended from French Huguenots who came to America in the 17th century. Born in Philadelphia, he was a neighbor and friend of Benjamin Franklin. Baptized by evangelist George Whitefield during the Great Awakening, Boudinot's faith in Christ was central to his life. He became a lawyer in New Jersey. He served as President of the Second Continental Congress and signed the Peace Treaty ending the American Revolution. With the adoption of the Constitution, Boudinot served three terms in the U.S. Congress from New Jersey. George Washington then appointed him Director of the U.S. Mint, where he served from 1795 to 1805. Boudinot resisted the ideas of the Enlightenment and Deism and wrote *Age of Revelation* as a reply to Paine's *Age of Reason*. Yet, with all his accomplishments, Boudinot considered his election as President of the American Bible Society as his highest honor; he donated $10,000 (no mean sum in 1816!) to help establish the Society.

Over its two-hundred-year history, the American Bible Society has provided Bibles to the military and translations throughout the world. In 1817, the ABS provided 654 Bibles to sailors on the *U.S.S. John Adams,* and since then has provided nearly 60 million free Bibles and resources to military members and their families. During the Civil War, the ABS supplied Bibles for both North and South. 7,420,910 Bibles were distributed to soldiers during World Wars I and II, and with the collapse of the Soviet Empire, the ABS made a commitment of $23.5 million to provide Bibles to the former Communist countries. The ABS also issued Bibles translated into the various Native American languages as well as helped finance William Carey's translation work in India. Working closely with the influential American Board of Commissioners for Foreign Missions, the ABS helped finance or provided Bibles throughout the world. The ABS also published the first Bibles for the visually impaired.

The ABS has a strong presence in our digital age, supporting the Digital Bible (digitalbible.org) which has the Scriptures in over 1000 languages.

... so shall my word be that goes out from my mouth;
it shall not return to me empty, but it shall accomplish that which I purpose,
and shall succeed in the thing for which I sent it.
—Isaiah 55:11—

AUGUST 15

JOHN JAY: FIRST CHIEF JUSTICE
OF THE UNITED STATES

John Jay (1745-1829) was one of the Founding Fathers of the United States who had multiple roles in the founding of the new country. From a wealthy merchant family in New York, Jay early joined the resistance to the British commercial policies that led to the American Revolution. Elected to the Second Continental Congress, Jay served as President of the Congress. Towards the end of the Revolution he was an ambassador to Spain and also served as a negotiator of the Treaty of Paris, which ended the War with Britain recognizing American independence. Jay was a strong supporter of the U.S. Constitution, and co-authored *The Federalist Papers* with James Madison and Alexander Hamilton in support of the new government. Once the new government was formed under the Constitution, George Washington appointed John Jay the first Chief Justice of the Supreme Court, a position he held from 1789 to 1795, when he resigned to serve as Governor of New York.

When the American Bible Society was organized in 1816, Jay was its vice-president; he served as president of the Society from 1821-1827. In an address to the annual meeting of the American Bible Society in 1824, Jay stated that by bringing the Bible to those ignorant of God's revealed will,

> We thereby enable them to learn, that man was originally created and placed in a state of happiness, but, becoming disobedient, was subjected to the deg-radation and evils which he and his posterity have since experienced. The Bible will also inform them, that our gracious Creator has provided for us a Redeemer, in whom all the nations of the earth should be blessed—that this Redeemer has made atonement "for the sins of the whole world," and thereby reconciling the Divine justice with the Divine mercy, has opened a way for our redemption and salvation and that these inestimable benefits are of the free gift and grace of God, not of our deserving, nor in our power to deserve. The Bible will also animate them with any explicit and consoling assurances of the Divine mercy to our fallen race, and with repeated invitations to accept the offers of pardon and reconciliation. The truth of these facts and the sin-cerity of these assurances being unquestionable, they cannot fail to promote the happiness of those by whom they are gratefully received, and of those by whom they are benevolently communicated.[15]

I rejoice at Your word as one who finds great treasure.
—Psalm 119:162—

NOAH WEBSTER DEFINES FAITH

In his 1828 *American Dictionary of the English Language*, Noah Webster's definitions frequently included Scripture references or quotes from Christian authors. His definitions for "faith" are examples. After defining faith as "belief; the assent of the mind to the truth of what is declared by another, resting on his authority and veracity …" Webster added:

> *In theology*, the assent of the mind or understanding to the truth of what God has revealed. Simple belief of the scriptures, of the being and perfections of God, and of the existence, character and doctrines of Christ, founded on the testimony of the sacred writers, is called *historical or speculative faith*; a faith little distinguished from the belief of the existence and achievements of Alexander or of Caesar.

He further defined Evangelical, justifying, or saving faith as
> The assent of the mind to the truth of divine revelation, accompanied with a cordial assent of the will or approbation of the heart; an entire confidence or trust in God's character and doctrines of Christ, with an unreserved surrender of the will to his guidance, and dependence on his merits for salvation. In other words, that firm belief of God's testimony, and of the truth of the gospel, which influences the will, and leads to an entire reliance on Christ for salvation.

Quotations he gives of this use of faith are the following:
> Being justified by *faith*. Rom. xv
> For we walk by *faith*, and not by sight. 2 Cor. v
> With the *heart* man believeth in righteousness. Rom. x
> The *faith* of the gospel is that emotion of the mind, which is called trust or confidence, exercised towards the moral character of God, and particularly of the Savior. *Dwight*
> *Faith* is a firm, cordial belief in the veracity of God, in all the declarations of his word; or a full and affectionate confidence in the certainty of those things which God has declared, and because he has declared them. *L. Woods*

Webster gives other nuances of the meaning of faith as
> Shall their unbelief make the *faith* of God without effect? Rom. iii
> An open profession of gospel truth.
> Your *faith* is spoken of throughout the whole world. Rom. i[16]

Hear the word of the Lord of hosts …
—Isaiah 39:5—

AUGUST 17

THE BIBLE'S BROAD INFLUENCE ON AMERICAN CIVILIZATION

After visiting the young United States in the 1830s, the Frenchman Alexis de Tocqueville wrote,

> Upon my arrival in the United States, the religious aspect of the country is the first thing that struck my attention; … The Americans combine the notions of Christianity and of liberty so intimately in their minds that it is impossible to make them conceive the one without the other … In the United States the sovereign authority is religious … There is no country in the world where the Christian religion retains a greater influence over the souls of men than in America, … [17]

Some examples of the Bible's influence in America:

- Columbus set sail in 1492, convinced from a reading of Scriptures that the Gospel would be brought to the far reaches of the world and then Christ would return.

- Puritan colonists came to America to establish a "City on a Hill" (Matthew 5:14), an example for the world of a Christian society.

- Beginning with John Eliot, missionaries translated the Bible into many Native American languages.

- Harvard, Princeton, Yale, and many other American colleges were established to train ministers of the Gospel.

- American schoolbooks from the early *New England Primer* to textbooks by Noah Webster and William McGuffey educated children in Biblical truths.

- Political speeches from William Penn to Benjamin Franklin to Abraham Lincoln to Martin Luther King, Jr. have been full of quotes and images from the Bible.

- Inventors such as Samuel Morse and George W. Carver studied the Bible and believed God directed them in their inventive ideas.

- The works of many American artists, authors, and song writers—including Francis S. Key, Fanny Crosby, Herman Melville, Harriet B. Stowe, and Lew Wallace- have strong Biblical themes.

- The spirituals of the African–American slaves, a genuine American contribution to the world's musical culture, have Biblical images woven throughout.
- Entrepreneurs such as J.C. Penney and the Tappan brothers, who founded Dun & Bradstreet, looked to the Bible for their business ethics.

Great is your mercy, O Lord; give me life according to your rules.
—Psalm 119:156—

THE NEW TESTAMENT IN HAWAIIAN

Hiram Bingham and Asa Thurston were among 14 missionaries the American Board of Commissioners of Foreign Missions sent to Hawaii in 1820. Hiram and Sybil Bingham settled in Honolulu; Asa and his wife Lucy settled in Kailua-Kona. Diligently learning the Hawaiian language, Hiram and Asa planned to translate the Bible into Hawaiian, which did not then have a written language. Hiram developed an alphabet and wrote a grammar for the written language. By 1828, the team had translated and printed the Gospel of Matthew in Hawaiian. Mark, Luke, and John followed in 1829-1830, and the rest of the New Testament was completed in 1832. The early translations were printed in New York, but by 1830, the missionaries had their own printing press on Oahu.

The Hawaiian Queen Ka'ahumanu was very receptive to Christianity. She encouraged her people to embrace Christianity and established laws based upon the Ten Commandments and Christian ethics. She faced opposition for this, largely from foreign traders who saw some of their lucrative practices restricted. Bingham's history of what were then called the Sandwich Islands was published in 1855. In his history, Bingham noted it was the privilege of the missionaries "to bring the Bible to the whole people"; it was the people's privilege "to bring themselves, by the blessing of God, to the Bible."[18] Bingham recounted that

> [Queen] Kaahumanu and [Chief Officer] Kalanimoku, and others most fully published their views of God's Word, and regarded His statutes as binding on all, without any civil, secular, or ecclesiastical enactment to make them so… Kalanimoku expressed his desire to see the laws of God observed, and the people conforming their lives to his will; and both he and the queen seemed determined to maintain the Christian ground they had taken in interdicting crime, and to persevere in their efforts to bring the people to respect, not only their own authority, but also the authority of God. [19]

Turn to me and be saved, all the ends of the earth!
For I am God, and there is no other.
— Isaiah 45:22—

AUGUST 19

NOAH WEBSTER'S BIBLE AND ITS STORY

Many recognize Noah Webster as the compiler of the first American dictionary as well as the author of the blue back speller, used in American schools for decades. But, few are aware that Webster also published a Bible. In his 1833 edition of the Bible, Webster was most concerned with modernizing the King James Version, which then was over two centuries old. Many words had changed their meanings or were no longer in use, and Webster sought to provide a translation which could be understood by common readers.

In 1842, Noah and his wife Rebecca celebrated their Golden Wedding anniversary. One of Noah's daughter's, Eliza Webster Jones, described the event:

> All the children, grandchildren, and great-grandchildren of the dear, dear old Patriarch and his wife Rebecca were invited to gather at brother Goodrich's…35 of us were there … We felt that God was with us and it was a cheerful meal … 21 of us were professedly children of grace, and the others— may they too come to the cross of Christ and find in Him their everlasting portion! At five we all went to Father's and took our tea in the home of our early days. In the evening before we parted, our beloved and revered parent called our attention, and kneeling, as we all did, fervently implored the blessing of heaven upon us, our children and our children's children to the last generation. Oh shall not that prayer be heard? Then rising, he said, it was the happiest day of his life to see us all together; so many walking in the truth and the other, children of promise … Then he presented each of us with a Bible, his last gift, with our names written by his own trembling hand; and we closed our meeting by singing "Blest be the tie that binds.' Shall we ever forget it? Oh No! the youngest there received some deep impression of the blessedness of nurturing a family in the fear of God. The little Bibles are cherished gifts.[20]

These words that I command you today shall be on your heart. You shall teach them diligently to your children, and shall talk of them when you sit in your house, and when you walk by the way, and when you lie down, and when you rise.
—Deuteronomy 6:6-7—

VALUE OF THE BIBLE

Noah Webster, author of the first American dictionary, believed the Bible and its teachings are foundational to the flourishing of individuals and nations. In *Value of the Bible and the Excellence of the Christian Religion*, he summarized the Bible's story and reflected on its importance and applicability:

The first and most essential advantage of the religion of the Bible, is, that it proceeds from God himself by revelation. It has God for its author, and truth for its basis. No other system of religion has even a plausible claim to a divine origin. Men without revelation wander in darkness; they have no just notions of the creator of all things; they know not who made the world and themselves, nor why they were made; … They have some crude notion of a superior power, but where he is, or what his character, they are utterly ignorant; hence they frame deities in their imaginations, and worship them; … and making images of their deities, they worship stocks and stones, of any and every monstrous form. Thus they live without a knowledge of God, in ignorance and beastly vices, and die without hope, like the brutes. Such has been the condition of most nations from the earliest ages.[21]…

> In the scriptures only can we obtain a knowledge of God's spiritual essence, his purity, holiness, truth, justice and benevolence. … [Only there] can we learn for what purposes we were made, what God requires us to *be* and to *do*, to obtain his favor and protection in this life, and what is to be our fate after death.[22] …

> As the will of God is our only rule of actions, and that will can be fully known only from revelation, the Bible must be considered as the source of all the truths by which men are to be guided in government …. Other books, if in accordance with the Bible, may be read with advantage. But a large proportion of the books which fill our libraries have little or no bearing on the sound principles of morals and religion…The first and most important duty of man is to furnish his mind with correct notions respecting God, his laws, and human duty, and then to … [work to] make others wiser and better. It was for these purposes, the revelation of God was given to men; revelations preserved in the Bible, the instrument of all reformation in morals and religion."[23]

In the way of your testimonies I delight as much as in all riches.
—Psalm 119:14—

AUGUST 21
THE BOOK OF HEAVEN

After the purchase of the Louisiana Territory from France in 1803, President Thomas Jefferson sent an expedition led by Meriwether Lewis and William Clark to map the region, study its animal and plant life, and establish trade with the natives. In their dealings with the Nez Percé, Lewis and Clark told them about the wider world, including something about the Bible. The Nez Percé called the Bible the Book of Heaven. They waited several years for the white men to return and bring them this book, but no one ever came. Finally, the tribal council decided to have a delegation find the book and bring it back to them. The delegation, consisting of Black Eagle, Man of the Morning, Rabbit Skin Leggins, and No Horns on the Head, traveled about 1500 miles and reached St. Louis, Missouri in October 1832. They found William Clark and asked him to tell them about his God and give them the Book of Heaven. Clark eagerly sought a Bible for them, but there was none available in a language they could understand. Black Eagle and Man of the Morning died that winter. Before returning to his people, No Horns on the Head gave a speech at a farewell dinner and said,

> I came to you over the trail of many moons, from the setting sun. I came with one eye partly open for my people who sit in darkness. I go back with both eyes closed. How can I go back blind to my blind people? … When I tell my poor blind people after one more snow, in the big council, that I did not bring the Book, no word will be spoken by our old men or by our young braves. One by one they will rise up and go out in silence. My people will die in darkness and they will go on a long path to other hunting grounds. No White Man will go with them, and no White Man's Book of Heaven will make the way plain. I have no more words.[24]

Word of the Nez Percé plea spread, and in 1836 the American Board of Commissioners of Foreign Missions sent out five missionaries to the Oregon Territory. Narcissa and Eliza Spalding settled among the Nez Percé and began translating the Bible for them. Over thirty years after the Lewis and Clark expedition, the Nez Percé had at least portions of the Book of Heaven.

… and many peoples shall come, and say: "Come, let us go up to the mountain of the Lord, to the house of the God of Jacob, that he may teach us his ways and that we may walk in his paths." For out of Zion shall go forth the law, and the word of the Lord from Jerusalem.
—Isaiah 2:3—

SHAPING MINDS ON THE FRONTIER

From the earliest settlers in Jamestown, through the founding of Massachusetts and the expansion of the country westward, the Bible has had an important influence on the thoughts and culture of the American people. Historian T.R. Fehrenbach ably summarized the role of the Bible in early Texas and on the frontier:

The historical role of the English Bible in this Texas has increasingly been overlooked. But the King James Version afforded this stultified civilization on the fringes of the 19th century Western world with a great part of the basic culture it required. It gave the frontier farmer ... a basic folklore, philosophy, and literature. It was, in fact, almost the only literature most families possessed.

The Old Testament fitted easily into the 19th-century Texas world. Its revelations of the human condition were held, even by the nonreligious, to be entirely valid and timelessly true. The young Texan read of evil that was ancient and ever-present, requiring eternal discipline of man; he learned of false prophets and lying sycophants, of licentious Jezebels and foolish kings, of mighty warriors and wise men. He absorbed an unflattering impression of such intellectual tribes as Scribes and Pharisees. And although few could articulate it or explain it, Texans gained a timeless portrait of man's world, of the rise and fall of peoples, of bondage and deliverance, of God's patience and wrath, and man's enduring inhumanity to man. Visitors were often surprised to find Texans, who had no apparent cultivation, able to strip vanities and euphoric philosophies from better-educated men. As a cultural, folkloric instrument the Holy Bible played its part, in a way no official history or intellectually fabricated philosophy ever could ....

The frontiersmen were Old Testament-oriented. The land they lived in had many parallels with the land of Canaan, and they themselves with the children of Israel. They were beset with dangerous heathen enemies. The land was scourged by ravaging insects and burning drouth; the imagery of the Israelite deserts struck home in the Texan heart. The farmer endured plagues of grasshoppers; he lost sheep and cows to cats and wolves; he saw green crops die and wells run dry. The Old Testament had a relevance it would have for no later American generations. The lives of the farmers hung on acts of God, who made rain fall from the heavens and the rivers swell. Their best-loved hymns... of cool and beautiful rivers they would someday cross, and of glorious showers of blessing upon the land[25]

You rebuke the insolent, accursed ones,
who wander from your commandments.
—Psalm 119:21—

AUGUST 23
SCHOOLMASTER OF AMERICA— WILLIAM HOLMES MCGUFFEY

Over 122 million copies of *McGuffey's Readers* were distributed between 1836 and the 1920's, making them the most published books in America, after the Bible. At least half of America's schoolchildren during that period learned from the famous readers. The books gave American youth a sense of common experience, a common body of literary allusions, and an acquaintance with the great writers of both England and the United States. The social and moral teachings of the readers affected students throughout their lives and shaped the moral fiber of the United States throughout the nineteenth century.

The McGuffey's Readers were among the first textbooks in the country to be used sequentially, with each text more difficult than the last. Students stayed in a text until they mastered the material, regardless of their age. Many students only completed the first two readers, equivalent to an elementary education today.

William Holmes McGuffey, the writer of the textbooks, was a Presbyterian minister and educator who believed, as did many of America's Founding Fathers, that religion and morality were necessary to preserve republican institutions

McGuffey wrote many of the stories for the 1836 readers. The readers also included excerpts from the Bible. Both the Bible readings and stories reinforced character traits of honesty, truthfulness, obedience, kindness, thrift, industry, and patriotism. McGuffey's texts were full of moral lessons showing that evil never pays. Students read of a world in which God reveals Himself through both nature and the Bible as Creator, Preserver, and Governor of all life. Throughout, the stories were concerned with the character and nature of God and His relationships with men and His world.

The McGuffey Readers went through many revisions over the years. Though the 1879 revision, made after William's death, included new illustrations, it had a less Biblical worldview. Christianity's influence in America was eroding. In the last revision of the *Readers*, God was mentioned only once, and the Bible stories disappeared. Gone was the emphasis on salvation and piety, though the strong moral emphasis remained.

The unfolding of your words gives light;
it imparts understanding to the simple.
—Psalm 119:130—

EXCERPT ON THE BIBLE FROM
MCGUFFEY'S READER

The Readers written by William H. McGuffey were used in schools throughout the United States for a century and are still in print today. Lessons 18-19 of the *Third Eclectic Reader* (1837) were on the Bible. Following are excerpts from these chapters (the vocabulary is quite advanced for our day but was expected to be understood by elementary students of the 19th century!):

The word Bible means book, and the sacred volume is so called because it is the book of books—the best book. The word Scriptures signifies writings. The Bible was not written at one time, or by one person, but consists of various parts, written at different times by different men. It is divided into two Testaments, called the Old and the New, chiefly with reference to the time when they were published. The Old was published before the coming of Christ, and the New after His death. The excellency of the Bible might be proved sufficiently from its sanctifying and transforming influence upon the minds of all who read it with a proper spirit. This is manifest more especially from the fact of its having God for its author. That God is its author is evident from its being the only book which teaches everything that our Creator requires of us, either to know, or believe, or do, that we may escape his deserved displeasure, obtain his sovereign favor, and dwell forever in the bliss of his immediate presence. It opens to us the mystery of the creation, the nature of God, of angels, and of men, the immortality of the soul, the end for which man was created. It teaches the origin of evil, and the inseparable connection between sin and misery, the vanity of the present world, and the glory reserved in a future state for the pious servants of God. Although many hundreds of thousands of books have been written in different ages by wise and learned men, even the best of them will bear no comparison with the Bible, in respect either of religion, morality, history, or purity and sublimity of composition …

The design of the Bible is evidently to give us correct information concerning the creation of all things by the omnipotent word of God, to make known to us the state of holiness and happiness of our first parents in paradise, and their dreadful fall from that condition by transgression against God, which is the original cause of all our sin and misery. It is also designed to show us the duty we owe to Him, who is our almighty Creator, our bountiful Benefactor, and our righteous Judge, the method by which we can secure His eternal friendship and are prepared for the possession of everlasting mansions in His glorious kingdom. The scriptures are especially designed to make us wise unto salvation through faith in Christ Jesus, to reveal to us the mercy of the Lord in Him, to form our minds after the likeness of God our Savior, to build up our souls in wisdom and faith, in love and holiness, to make us thoroughly furnished unto good works, enabling us to glorify God on earth, to lead us to an imperishable inheritance among the spirits of just men made perfect, and finally to be glorified with Christ in heaven. If such be the design of the Bible, how necessary must it be for everyone to pay a serious and proper attention to what it reveals. The word of God invites our attentive and prayerful regards in terms the most engaging and persuasive. It closes its gracious appeals by proclaiming, "Whosoever will, let him take the water of life freely." The infinite tenderness of the divine compassion to sinners flows in the language of the inspired writers, with which they address the children of men, and the glory of the most gracious promises of the Lord of glory accompany the divine invitation.

His divine power has granted to us all things that pertain
to life and godliness, through the knowledge of him
who called us to his own glory and excellence,
by which he has granted to us his precious and very
great promises, so that through them you may become
partakers of the divine nature, having escaped from the
corruption that is in the world because of sinful desire.
—II Peter 1:3-4—

EDUCATION FOR WOMEN

In 1837, Mary Lyon (1797-1849) founded Mount Holyoke as an institution of higher education for women, a rather innovative venture in her day. Lyon wanted a school for women which would provide an education equivalent to the men's colleges such as Harvard and Yale. A devout Christian, Lyon designed life at Mount Holyoke to encourage the ladies in their Christian faith and provide them with biblical resources and habits they could use in the service of Christ upon graduation. Psalm 144: 12 expressed the founding goal of the school, "that our daughters may be as corner stones, polished after the similitude of a palace."

Mary Lyon regularly taught the Bible to the students in the thrice weekly chapel meetings, and the ladies especially appreciated her lectures from Proverbs, providing timeless spiritual advice and wisdom. She and her teachers prayed for the conversion of each student and met with the students for devotions throughout the day. Lyon read Jonathan Edwards' *History of Redemption* with the students, giving them a grasp of God's plan of salvation. As one student wrote:

> In her teachings, we found Christ on every page of the Old Testament. She led us on from that first promise to Adam lying so low in his fall, through types and shadows pointing to the Messiah, till, with Isaiah, we stood on the mountain-top, and could see the desire of all nations coming to his holy temple. We discovered then a fullness in Christ, not before understood, and we sang the hymn of our childhood with new delight:—"Holy Bible, book divine, Precious treasure" [26]

Whoever despises the word brings destruction on himself,
but he who reveres the commandment will be rewarded.
The teaching of the wise is a fountain of life,
that one may turn away from the snares of death.
—Proverbs 13:13-14—

AUGUST 26
THE SOUTH PACIFIC FOR CHRIST

The voyages and exploits of Captain James Cook captivated 18th century Europeans. Cook's explorations and mapping of the islands of the Pacific awakened in many a desire for adventure in the newly discovered lands. William Carey first desired to become a missionary to Tahiti before he went to India. However, John Williams (1796-1839) did make the Pacific his mission field.

Williams, who had a Christian mother and an unbelieving father, had a period of disinterestedness in Christianity during his youth, loving pleasure more than loving God. January 30, 1814, a sermon Williams heard at Moorfield's Tabernacle on Matthew 16:26—"For what will it profit a man if he gains the whole world and forfeits his soul? Or what shall a man give in return for his soul?"—brought conviction. Williams forsook his worldly companions, became a teacher in a Sabbath school, and began growing in the grace of Christ.

Frequently Williams thought about the heathen and the debt of love owed to God for His goodness. With a desire to bring the Gospel to the lost, Williams became a missionary with the London Missionary Society. He first went to Tahiti and spent several months in language study.

Williams built a boat he called *The Messenger of Peace* to travel around the islands, preaching and establishing churches led by native converts. His favorite Scripture was I Timothy 1:15, "The saying is trustworthy and deserving of full acceptance, that Christ Jesus came into the world to save sinners, of whom I am the foremost."

In 1823, Williams discovered the island of Raratonga. He established missions there and translated the Bible into the Raratonga language. Wherever he went, Williams developed native leaders for the churches; in 1838 he began to establish a college for the pastors. In 1839, Williams visited the island of Erromango in the New Hebrides, which no missionary had ever visited. He was attacked by the cannibals on the island, was clubbed to death, and eaten by the cannibals. Williams' death was mourned by people throughout the Pacific Islands.

For I delivered unto you first of all that which I also received,
how that Christ died for our sins according to the scriptures.
—I Corinthians 15:3—

ESSENTIAL TO HUMAN FLOURISHING

William Seward (1801-1872) held numerous offices during his political career—state senator, U.S. Senator from New York, Governor of New York, and Secretary of State under Presidents Lincoln and Johnson. He was targeted in the assassination plot against Abraham Lincoln and seriously injured but recovered. As Secretary of State under Andrew Johnson, he negotiated the purchase of Alaska from Russia in 1867, a transaction which became known at the time as "Seward's Folly." Seward believed that the Scriptures are essential to human advancement:

> They describe the Creator and man more accurately according to the standard of enlightened reason, and define the relations between them more justly according to the suggestions of the human heart. ... I do not believe human society, including not merely a few persons in any state, but whole masses of men, ever has attained, or ever can attain, a high state of intelligence, virtue, security, liberty or happiness without them; and that the whole hope of human progress is suspended on the every-growing influence of the Bible.[27]

In an address to the American Bible Society in 1839, when he was Governor of New York, Seward asserted that the government of the people established in the United States would not have come into existence without the Bible's influence, and he questioned whether a republican government of the people "could flourish among a people who had not the Bible." As a census was made among the country each decade, he thought efforts each decade to distribute the Bible among every family would ensure the continuance of the republican institutions.

You have appointed your testimonies
in righteousness and in all faithfulness.
—Psalm 119:138—

AUGUST 28
ADONIRAM JUDSON'S BURMESE BIBLE TRANSLATION

Christianity came to the people of Burma (now Myanmar) via Adoniram and Ann Judson. In 1812, the Judsons became the first missionaries from the United States to a foreign land. Until they came to Burma, there were no Christians in Burma. Friendless in a foreign culture, they struggled against melancholy, disease, and opposition. It was seven years before the Judsons saw the first Burmese convert to Christ. But they persevered, convinced of the Bible's truthfulness. During his 38 years in Burma, Judson suffered imprisonment, the threat of execution, and the death of three successive wives. Yet he persisted in his efforts to bring the Gospel to the Burmese people. Skilled in Latin, Greek, and Hebrew, Judson learned Burmese and spent 24 years in translating the Bible into that language. He printed the New Testament in 1837, and two editions of the complete Bible in 1840.

One of Judson's first converts was Shwe Ngong, a teacher dissatisfied with Buddhism and attracted to Christianity. When Ngong said he was ready to believe in God and Jesus Christ, Judson asked him if he believed that Jesus the son of God had died on the cross, as he had read in the Gospel of Matthew. Ngong said he believed Jesus died, but couldn't believe that it was such a shameful death as a cross. Later, he came to say, "I have been trusting in my own reason, not the word of God ... I now believe the crucifixion because it is contained in scripture."[28]

Because of the climate, as well as political and religious oppression, none of Adoniram Judson's original works could be found in Myanmar today. From overseas sources, missionaries are finding tracts and other works written by Judson long ago. They are discovering that Judson's works show great wisdom in reaching out to the Buddhist people, and today's pastors in Myanmar are fascinated to see copies of these original texts so important to their Christian heritage. In nearby Thailand, teams are typesetting and printing Burmese Christian literature, while teams in the USA are scanning material to produce a digital research archive for the pastors and people. Foremost is a digitized copy of Judson's Burmese Bible.

... in Christ God was reconciling the world to himself, not counting their trespasses against them, and entrusting to us the message of reconciliation.
—II Corinthians 5:19—

THE MENDI BIBLE

In 1839, a group of West African natives was kidnapped to be sold illegally as slaves. When the ship resumed its voyage after docking in Cuba, the Africans rebelled and took over the ship, killing the captain and the cook. The Africans directed the ship navigators to return to Africa, but they sailed north. When the ship, *La Amistad* was apprehended off the coast of Long Island, New York, the ship and captives were taken into custody. The captives' case ultimately went to the U.S. Supreme Court, where John Q. Adams, former President and Secretary of State argued for their freedom. The Court decided that the Africans were illegally captured and were by right free.

While in the United States, the 39 Africans were cared for, educated in English, and, most importantly, given the Gospel of Jesus Christ. When they returned to Africa in 1841, they gave Adams a letter of appreciation and a Bible. Here is their letter:

> *Most respected Sir:*—The Mendi people give you thanks for all your kindness to them. They will never forget your defence of their rights before the great court at Washington. They feel that they owe to you in a large measure their deliverance from the Spaniard, and from slavery or death. They will pray for you as long as they live, Mr. Adams. May God bless and reward you.
>
> We are about to go home to Africa, we go to Sierra Leone first, and then we reach Mendi very quick. When we get to Mendi we will tell the people of your great kindness. Good missionary go with us. We shall take the Bible with us. It has been a precious book in prison, and we love to read it now we are free! Mr. Adams, we want to make you a present of a beautiful Bible! Will you please accept it, and when you look at it, or read it, remember your poor and grateful clients? We read in this Holy Book, 'If it had not been the Lord who was on our side, when men rose up against us, then they had swallowed us up quick, when their wrath was kindled against us.' [Psalm 124:2] Bless be the Lord, who hath not given us up a prey to their teeth. Our soul is escaped as a bird out of the snare of the fowler; the snare is broken, and we are escaped. Our help is in the name of the Lord, who made Heaven and Earth.
>
> For the Mendi people,
> Cinque, Kina, Kale.
> Boston, November 6, 1841.[29]

Uphold me according unto thy word, that I may live:
and let me not be ashamed of my hope. —Psalm 119:116—

AUGUST 30

HEZEKIAH AND ARCHAEOLOGY

Hezekiah, the 13th king of Judah, ruled in a tumultuous time. In 721 B.C. Assyria had captured Israel's capital of Samaria and carried the Israelites into captivity. When Hezekiah came to the throne six years later, at the age of twenty-five, he sought to strengthen the kingdom of Judah. He began his reign by purifying and repairing the Temple, reforming the priesthood, and removing idols from the kingdom. He also refused to pay tribute to the Assyrians. Sennacherib responded by attacking Judah and laying siege to Jerusalem. The events of this period are recorded in II Kings 18-20; II Chronicles 29-32; and Isaiah 28-39. Several archaeological finds relate to the events of Hezekiah's reign.

When Sennacherib moved against Judah, he conquered many of the cities in his path, including Lachish. After the conquest of Lachish, Sennacherib sent messengers to Hezekiah warning him that Jerusalem would be next. In 1845-47, Austen Layard discovered carvings about the conquest of Lachish on the walls of Sennacherib's west palace in Nineveh. Today these bas-reliefs are in the British Museum in London. They show the brutality of the siege, with Assyrians even flaying captives alive.

As Sennacherib moved against Judah, Hezekiah took defensive measures to protect Jerusalem. He repaired the broken sections of the wall and built towers upon it. Part of these fortifications have been uncovered. The wall was originally 27 feet high and 23 feet thick, made to withstand the Assyrian battering rams. Hezekiah also took steps to make certain Jerusalem would have a fresh water supply, by creating a conduit for the Gihon spring into a reservoir within the city. This amazing tunnel is 1777 feet long, carved from solid rock. An inscription inside the tunnel commemorated when the two groups of workmen from the two ends of the tunnel met to complete the work. The inscription was discovered in 1880 by a young boy swimming in the tunnel.

In 1830, a prism was discovered in Nineveh recording Sennacherib's campaign in Israel. Sennacherib boasts of conquering 46 of Hezekiah's cities and shutting up Hezekiah in Jerusalem "like a bird in a cage." However, he could not boast of the conquest of Jerusalem. The Bible says the angel of the Lord struck down 185,000 in the Assyrian camp, causing Sennacherib to leave off the siege and go home. Archaeology provides vivid evidence for the Bible's record of Hezekiah's reign.

... this is the one to whom I will look: he who is
humble and contrite in spirit and trembles at my word.
— Isaiah 66:2—

PRIZE THE WORD

Though his life was brief, Robert Murray McCheyne (1813-1843) shone brightly with a love for the Savior. McCheyne's health was never robust, and he was only pastor of St. Peter's Church, Dundee for seven years, but his fame as a preacher spread throughout Scotland. His pastoral heart and love for the Scriptures drew many to Christ and a closer walk with Him. McCheyne also wrote hymns, including "Thy Word is a Lamp unto my Feet." Its stanzas recount the guidance of the Word for Israel in the desert and for Paul in his missionary journeys and Stephen in his martyrdom. The hymn begins:

When Israel knew not where to go,
God made the fiery pillar glow;
By night, by day, above the camp
It led the way—their guiding lamp;
Such is Thy Holy Word to me
In day of dark perplexity.
When devious paths before me spread,

And all invite my foot to tread
I hear Thy voice behind me say—
"Believing soul, this is the way,
Walk thou in it." O gentle Dove,
How much Thy holy law I love!
My lamp and light
In the dark night ....[30]

The Scriptures not only guide believers but are important in sanctifying the Christian. In an 1841 sermon on Christ's love for the Church, McCheyne noted that

> Christ's work is not done with a soul when He has brought it to pardon—when He has washed it in His own blood. Oh, no! the better half of salvation remains—His great work of sanctification remains…. When Jesus makes holy, it is by writing the Word in the heart: "sanctify them through thy truth." [John 17:17] When a mother nurses her child, she not only bears it in her arms, but holds it to her breast, and feeds it with milk of her own breast; so does the Lord. He not only holds the soul, but feeds it with the milk of the Word. The words of the Bible are just the breathings of God's heart. He fills the heart with these, to make us like God. When you go much with a companion, and hear His words, you are gradually changed by them into His likeness; so when you go with Christ, and hear His words, you are sanctified. Oh, there are some whom I could tell to be Christ's, by their breathing the same sweet breath! … Oh, believers, prize the Word![31]

My soul is consumed with longing for your rules at all times.
—Psalm 119:20—

SEPTEMBER 1
THUMB BIBLES AND MINIATURE BOOKS

Miniature books have been printed since the earliest days of printing. Their small size makes them convenient to carry in a pocket or handbag, and they are also perfect prizes and gifts for children. In the 19th century, miniature Bibles came to be called Thumb Bibles, after the famous midget Tom Thumb (also because some of them are barely bigger than a person's thumb!). The first English Thumb Bible, printed in 1614, contains a paraphrase in verse of both testaments by the English poet John Taylor (1578-1653). His stated purpose of the work:

> With care and pains out of the Sacred Book,
> This little Abstract for thee took:
> And with great reverence have I cull'd from them,
> All things that are of Greatest consequence.

One of the most famous Thumb Bibles, *The Bible in Miniature, or a concise history of the Old and New Testaments* was printed by Elizabeth Newbery in 1780. Elizabeth was the niece of John Newbery, the first publisher in England to focus on the publication of children's books and the one for whom the annual Newbery Medal in children's literature is named. The preface to her 1780 miniature Bible notes how sad it is that in a country where the Bible is readily available, so many are ignorant of its first principles. In 256 miniature pages, the book summarizes the Old and New Testaments, hoping to give a taste of the wisdom of God and how all ages find their completion in Jesus Christ.

In 1847, the American Tract Society printed a little Thumb book called *Dew Drops*, which included one Bible verse for each day of the year. When printer David Bryce printed *The Holy Bible* in 1854, he advertised it as the "smallest complete Bible." The 876 photographically reduced pages, 1 ⅝" x 1 ⅛," were printed on thin India paper. A small magnifying glass was included to aid in reading the Bible!

The Child's Bible, a Thumb Bible printed in 1834, stated the purpose for the little Bible in its preface:

> The Bible is the best book in the world ... We have made this small book, dear children, on purpose for you ... After you read this through, you will wish to know more about the Bible ... Your mama will get you one or let you take hers, and you will learn much more than we had room to tell you.

I find my delight in your commandments, which I love.
—Psalm 119:47—

FOOD FOR THE INNER MAN

Evangelist George Müller (1805-1898) was noted for his life of prayer and close dependence on the Lord. His orphanage in Bristol became a model for Christian care and education. Müller never solicited funds but prayed that God would touch the hearts of His people to give to the work. Funds always were provided, often in amazing ways. Müller's life of prayer was closely linked to his study of the Scriptures. In his *Autobiography*, he wrote of his discovery of the importance on meditating on the Scriptures for his personal prayer life and spiritual strength:

> I saw more clearly than ever that the first ... business to which I ought to attend every day was, to have my soul happy in the Lord. The first thing to be concerned about was not how much I might serve the Lord, how I might glorify the Lord; but how I might get my soul into a happy state, and how my inner man might be nourished. For I might seek to set the truth before the unconverted, I might seek to benefit believers, I might seek to relieve the distressed, I might in other ways seek to behave myself as it becomes a child of God in this world; and yet, not being happy in the Lord, and not being nourished and strengthened in my inner man day by day, all this might not be attended to in a right spirit. Before this time my practice had been, at least for ten years previously, as an habitual thing to give myself to prayer, after having dressed myself in the morning. Now, I saw that the most important thing I had to do was to give myself to the reading of the word of God, and to meditation on it, that thus my heart might be comforted, encouraged, warned, reproved, instructed; and that thus, by means of the word of God, whilst meditating on it, my heart might be brought into experimental communion with the Lord.

> I began therefore to mediate on the New Testament from the beginning, early in the morning, The first thing I did, after having asked in a few words the Lord's blessing upon his precious word, was, to begin to meditate on the word of God, searching as it were into every verse, to get a blessing out of it; not for the sake of the public ministry ..., but for the sake of obtaining food for my own soul. The result I have found to be almost invariably this, that after a very few minutes my soul has been led to confession, or to thanksgiving, or to intercession, or to supplication; so that, though I did not, as it were, give myself to *prayer*, but to *meditation*, yet it turned almost immediately more or less into prayer. When thus I have been for a while making confession, or intercession, or supplication, or have given thanks, I go on to the next words or verse, turning all, as I go on, into prayer for myself or others, as the word may lead to it, but still continually keeping before me that food for my own soul is the object of my meditation. ...

... my heart being nourished by the truth, being brought into *experimental* fellowship with God, I speak to my Father and to my Friend (evil though I am, and unworthy of it) about the things that he has brought before me in his precious word ... the first thing the child of God has to do morning by morning is, to *obtain food for his inner man*. ... How different, when the soul is refreshed and made happy early in the morning, from what it is when, without spiritual preparation, the service, the trials, and the temptations of the day come upon one.[1]

Why do you spend your money for that which is not bread,
and your labor for that which does not satisfy? Listen diligently to me,
and eat what is good, and delight yourselves in rich food.
Incline your ear, and come to me; her, that your soul may live.
—Isaiah 55:2-3—

ELECTRIFYING COMMUNICATION

In 1825, while he was painting the Marquis de Lafayette's portrait in Washington, D.C., Samuel Morse (1791-1872) received a letter that his wife was sick in New Haven, Connecticut. By the time Morse reached New Haven, his wife had died and been buried. Grief-stricken, Morse vowed to develop a way to send messages faster.

Morse, an artist and portrait painter, traveled to Europe in 1830 to study and improve his painting skills. Crossing the Atlantic on his return home in 1832, Morse met Charles Jackson and learned some principles of electromagnetism. Morse had become interested in electricity while a student at Yale, and with additional information on electromagnetism, developed the idea of the telegraph, which he patented in 1837. Morse had many disappointments as he tried to secure finances to develop his telegraphic system, but he relied on God's Providence to direct and provide. Congress finally appropriated $30,000 to construct a telegraph to prove its worth. The first telegraph line was between Washington, D.C. and Baltimore and formally opened May 24, 1844. Morse had Anna Ellsworth, a young daughter of a friend, send the first telegraph message. She chose the verse from Numbers 23:23, "What hath God wrought!"

Morse lived to see the telegraph connect cities all along the East Coast as well as see the overland telegraph connect the west and east coasts in 1861. In 1868, as he neared the end of his life, Morse wrote his grandson:

> The nearer I approach to the end of my pilgrimage, the clearer is the evidence of the Divine origin of the Bible, the grandeur and sublimity of God's remedy for fallen man are more appreciated, and the future is illumined with hope and joy.

To his brother he wrote:

> The Saviour daily seems more precious, his love, his atonement, his divine power, are themes which occupy my mind in the wakeful hours of the night, and change the time of 'watching for the morning' from irksomeness to joyful communion with him.[2]

My soul melts away for sorrow;
strengthen me according to your word!
—Psalm 119:28—

SEPTEMBER 4
OLD HICKORY

Andrew Jackson (1767-1845), or "Old Hickory" as he came to be known, was a general who became a hero after the Battle of New Orleans in the War of 1812. The United States' victory over the British at New Orleans ushered in a period of over two centuries of peace between the two countries. Jackson had been a frontier lawyer in Tennessee and later had represented Tennessee in the House of Representatives and Senate. After the War of 1812, he led U.S. troops in the First Seminole War, leading to the annexation of Florida from Spain. Jackson returned to the Senate with presidential ambitions, and was elected President of the United States, serving from 1829-1837.

Jackson's victory in being elected President was tempered with sorrow, as his dear wife Rachel died three weeks after the election and before Jackson's inauguration. Rachel was a devout Christian who had often encouraged Jackson to consider seriously the need of his soul for salvation in Jesus Christ, but he never committed his life to Christ. After he had left office, however, and attended church services, Jackson was convicted of his sin and came to faith in Christ. In1838, he made a profession of faith in the church on his plantation. Everyone noticed the change in Jackson's manner. He held daily prayer and Bible readings with his family, and regularly studied his Bible, especially valuing the commentaries of Thomas Scott.

In his final days, as he lay dying, Jackson repeatedly expressed his faith in Jesus and the Scriptures:

> I am in the hands of a merciful God. I have full confidence in his goodness and mercy. My lamp of life is nearly out, and the last glimmer has come. I am ready to depart when called. The Bible is true. ... Upon that sacred volume I rest my hope for eternal salvation, through the merits and blood of our blessed Lord and Saviour, Jesus Christ.

In his last hours, Jackson spoke and said,

> My dear children, do not grieve for me; it is true, I am going to leave you; I am well aware of my situation; I have suffered much bodily pain, but my sufferings are but as nothing compared with that which our blessed Saviour endured upon that accursed cross, that we might all be saved who put their trust in him.[3]

I entreat your favor with all my heart;
be gracious to me according to your promise.
—Psalm 119:58—

SEPTEMBER 5
A LAMP FOR OUR FEET

A simple and amiable man, Bernard Barton (1784-1849) earned his living as a clerk in a bank while also publishing poetry, gaining the nickname of "The Quaker Poet." When British Prime Minister Sir Robert Peel read Barton's *Household Verses,* published in 1845, Peel granted Barton a pension of £100 per year. One of the poems in *Household Verses* was a reflection on Hebrews 13:8, "Jesus Christ is the same yesterday and today and forever." Another poem, "The Bible," is a reflection on Psalm 119:105, "Your word is a lamp to my feet and a light to my path."

The firmest friends may change,
 The best beloved may leave us,
Familiar ones—grow strange,
 Or death of all bereave us.

Where is the love undying?
 The Friend who never fails?
In whom the heart, relying,
 May trust—when grief assails!

Behold the Lamb! Who beareth
 Believers' sins away:
For each He ever careth—
 And now! As yesterday![4]

 — — —

Lamp of our feet, whereby we trace
 Our path when wont to stray;
Stream from the fountain of heavenly grace,
 Brook by the traveler's way.

Word of the ever-living God;
 Will of His glorious Son;
Without thee how could earth be trod,
 Or heaven itself be won?

Yet, to unfold the hidden worth,
 The mysteries to reveal,
That Spirit which first gave thee forth
 Thy volume must unseal.[5]

In the second poem, Barton expressed the truth that it is the Spirit of God who gives an understanding for the Word of God He has revealed.

You shall therefore keep the whole commandment that
I command you today, that you may be strong ...
— Deuteronomy 11:8—

SEPTEMBER 6
EDUCATION FOR THE HEART

Many leaders in the early days of the United States recognized the importance of the Bible for the formation of the character of the people. Among those was Lewis Cass (1782-1866), second governor of Michigan, Senator, Ambassador to France and Secretary of War under President Andrew Jackson, and Secretary of State under President James Buchanan. In 1846, in response to a gentleman from New York who asked Cass's views on the Bible and the Christian Sabbath, Cass wrote:

> That we are *fearfully* and *wonderfully* made [Psalm 139:14], we learn equally from the book of nature and from the Book of Revelation. Our faculties and our moral perceptions are in strange combination; and any system of education which confines its efforts to the head, and leaves the heart untouched, will be faithless of the great purposes of human discipline. And what can touch the heart like the plan of redemption, and the revelation of the designs of God for the progress of man in knowledge and happiness, commencing here, and continuing, but never terminating, hereafter? It is vain to expect that the impulses and passions, which make part of our moral and physical constitutions, can be regulated and restrained by the cool deductions of reason … Experience shows that the improvement of the intellectual powers has no necessary connection with the heart and conscience. God, in his providence, has given us the Book of his revealed will to be with us, at the commencement of our career in life, and at its termination; and to accompany us during all … its trying and fitful progress, to control the passions, to enlighten the judgment, to guide the conscience, to teach us what we ought to be here, and what we shall be hereafter, and to show the inseparable union which exists between our duty and our destiny.
>
> To send this Book to all, and to persuade all to read, to study, and to believe it, is worthy of our age and country, and is worthy of the zealous co-operation of every man interested in the improvement and moral advancement of the human family.
>
> The youth of America have a glorious theatre of exertion before them. That they may appreciate its duties and its rewards, and may be prepared for its offers and demands, by the lessons of the Sabbath and of the Bible, must be the sincere wish of every one interested in the progress … of our country … I earnestly hope that God's Day may be hallowed, and his Word studied through this whole land, till their obligations are felt and acknowledged by all its people.[6]

I understand more than the aged, for I keep your precepts.
—Psalm 119:100—

THE BIBLE FOR THE CHILDREN

Born on the eve of the American Revolution, John Cotton Smith (1765-1845) served his state of Connecticut and his nation in many capacities, including representative, Speaker of the House, and Governor. The son of a Puritan minister, Smith's entire life was informed by his Christian faith. Daily he read his Bible, reading through it at least once a year. He eventually had the entire New Testament memorized. He was active in numerous civic and Christian organizations, serving as the first President of the Connecticut Bible Society, President of the American Board of Commissioners of Foreign Missions from 1826 to 1841, and President of the American Bible Society from 1831 to 1845.

He once expressed the wish that a history of the American Revolution could be written by one who had experienced the events and who could also learn the Bible's influence on the people—of George Washington's daily Bible reading, of Congress's concern for the Bible among the people, and the patience produced under times of deprivation. The founders of the country

> placed the Bible in all their schools as an essential element of education—an indispensable preparative for usefulness in this life, as well as for the joys of the life to come; and what was the result? Clear views of duty to God, and a just estimate of individual and social rights and obligations, the only sure basis of private prosperity and national greatness.[7]

Smith believed the Bible should be restored to the schools to preserve the America established by the Founders:

> We must restore the Bible to the schools. Who can tell how much of the delinquency which stains our judicial records may be attributed to ignorance of its divine precepts and sanctions? ... establish it as an exercise in the common schools. And you make every child and youth in the public acquainted, of course, with a book which of all others it behooves them to know—a book whose divine origin, if there were no other proof, is demonstrated by its perfect adaptation to every capacity, the humblest and the highest; to the condition of man through every stage and vicissitude of his earthly existence as well as to his immortal destiny. Who can withhold such a book from the children of our country, and be blameless?[8]

I have more understanding than all my teachers,
for your testimonies are my meditation.
—Psalm 119: 99—

SEPTEMBER 8

FAMILY BIBLES

Once the Bible was available in printed form and ordinary people could purchase their own copy, reading the Bible together as a family became a daily activity for many. The family was considered a little church, and the father was responsible for leading his family in worship. Many had the habit of reading through the Bible together every year.

Bibles began to be produced especially for the family—with notes to help explain the Scriptures and special pages for the family to keep a record of births, marriages, and deaths. The family record pages were usually placed between the Old and New Testaments. This seemed the perfect place for genealogical records. The last verse of the Old Testament read, "And he will turn the hearts of the fathers to their children and the hearts of the children to their fathers ..." (Malachi 4:6), and the New Testament began with Matthew's genealogy of Jesus.

In 1846, Harper & Brothers printed a Bible which became the model for the large Family Bibles popular in the late 19th century. The advertisement for *Harper's Illuminated Bible* read, "the most splendidly elegant edition of the Sacred Record ever issued." The Bible was described as a "New Pictorial Bible embellished with Sixteen Hundred Engravings." The pictures were based on historical fact, not simply artistic imagination. Because of the new printing process of electrotyping, pictures and text were printed on the same page, rather than on separate sheets. Artists were engaged for more than six years in preparing the designs and engravings in the Bible, at a cost of $20,000 (about $2 million in today's dollars). Because of the expense, the publisher sold the Bible in 54 parts to subscribers from 1843 to 1846, at 25 cents each. The *Harper's Illuminated Bible* is almost like an encyclopedia and includes numerous supplemental materials—tables of weights, lists of names, a concordance, marginal notes, and an index.

Family Bibles were considered so much a part of the home that in the 19th century, home decorating books even included design suggestions for how the family Bible was to be displayed in the parlor.

Through your precepts I get understanding;
therefore I hate every false way.
—Psalm 119:104—

SIMON GREENLEAF AND BIBLICAL EVIDENCE

Simon Greenleaf (1783-1853) was a noted jurist who joined Judge Joseph Story at Harvard Law School in 1833 and succeeded Story as head of the Law School on Story's death. Greenleaf's *Treatise on the Law of Evidence* became the standard textbook in American law during the 19th century and remains a classic of American jurisprudence.

Greenleaf decided to take the legal rules of evidence and cross-examination and apply them to the Gospels. Would the Gospels stand up to the rules of evidence? Are they trustworthy witnesses to the truth of Jesus and His resurrection? Greenleaf wrote his conclusion in another noted work, *Testimony of the Evangelists*, published in 1846. He examined the Gospels according to the standards of evaluating ancient documents and determined they could be received in a court of law as genuine documents. In examining the testimony of the evangelists about the death and resurrection of Jesus, Greenleaf found compelling evidence of their truthfulness by the transformed characters of the apostles after Jesus' resurrection and their unanimity in proclaiming the risen Christ, even in the face of persecution and death.

For many years, Greenleaf was President of the Massachusetts Bible Society. In a letter to the American Bible Society, Greenleaf gave testimony to his belief in the trustworthiness of the Bible and its importance for salvation:

> Of the Divine character of the Bible, I think, no man who deals honestly with his own mind and heart can entertain a reasonable doubt. For myself, I must say, that having for many years made the evidences of Christianity the subject of close study, the result has been a firm and increasing conviction of the authenticity and plenary inspiration of the Bible. It is indeed the Word of God. It opens up to our view the only true source of moral obligation, or of public and private duty, and enforces these with the only sanctions that can affect the mind and reach the conscience of man: namely, the omniscience and goodness and mercy of God, and the certain retributions of the life to come. Without these sanctions, the laws are no longer observed, oaths lose their hold on the conscience, promises are violated, frauds are multiplied, and moral obligation is dissolved. And these securities natural religion does not furnish: they are found in the Bible alone. ... The Holy Bible is not even approached by any human composition. It is only this that can make men wise unto salvation.[9]

... from childhood you have been acquainted with the sacred writings,
which are able to make you wise for salvation through faith in Christ Jesus.
—II Timothy 3:15—

SEPTEMBER 10

A BIBLE-READING AMERICAN STATESMAN

One of the most noted American statesmen of the 19th century was Daniel Webster (1782-1852). Born at the end of the American Revolution and dying before the Civil War tore the nation asunder, Webster's political acumen and eloquent, principled oratory did much to shape the young nation. As a constitutional lawyer, Webster argued over two hundred cases before the Supreme Court. He held numerous government positions, including U.S. Representative for both Massachusetts and New Hampshire, U.S. Senator from Massachusetts, and Secretary of State for Presidents Harrison, Tyler, and Fillmore. Webster's speeches, which are among the greatest in America's history, gain their eloquence in part by the biblical phrases embedded in them.

Webster could not remember a time when he could not read, and the book he read most was the Bible. From an early age, he began memorizing Scripture, especially the psalms. One evening when friends stopped by to visit, they were out gazing at the night sky; Webster movingly recited Psalm 19. Scripture was the frequent subject of his conversation. On another occasion, when friends were visiting, Webster laid his hand on the Bible and said

> *This is the Book.* I have read through the entire Bible many times. I now make it a practice to go through it once a year. It is the Book of all others for lawyers as well as divines; and I pity the man that can not find in it a rich supply of thought, and of rules for his conduct. It fits man for life—it prepares him for death ... The Gospel is either true history, or it is a consummate fraud; it is either a reality or an imposition. Christ was what he professed to be, or He was an imposter. There is no other alternative.[10]

In his address on the dedication of the Bunker Hill Monument June 17, 1843, as Webster reviewed the history and foundation of the nation, he noted that the early settlers brought with them the riches of the past:

> ...in science, in art, in morals, religion and literature. The Bible came with them. And it is not to be doubted, that to the free and universal reading of the Bible, is to be ascribed in that age, ascribed in every age, that men were much indebted for right views of civil liberty. The Bible is a book of faith, and a book of doctrine; but it is also a book, which teaches man his own individual responsibility, his own dignity, and his equality with his fellow man.[11]

My lips will pour forth praise, for you teach me your statutes.
—Psalm 119:171—

DANIEL WEBSTER'S GREAT ORATORY

Daniel Webster (1782-1852) was a leading politician of the early nineteenth century, serving as a Congressman, Senator, and Secretary of State for three presidents. Webster was known for his oratorical skills, and his impassioned speech on the preservation of the Union in the face of impending secession has been a model of oratory for ensuing generations.

Webster's rhetorical skills were molded in part by his Bible reading as a child. Even as a child he read the Bible with passion and expression, so much so that teamsters stopping to water their horses would call for "Webster's boy" to come and read the Bible to them under the shade of the trees. Webster's mother also had him memorize Scripture. In later life he could keep people spellbound by his recitation of the Hebrew prophets or the Psalms. One man said he never received such an idea of the majesty of God as on one night when he heard Webster recite Psalm 8.[12]

When Webster was once asked what was the greatest thought he ever had, he replied after a solemn pause, "the greatest thought I ever had, or can have, is a *sense of my accountability to God.*"[13]

In its *Annual Report* for 1912, the American Bible Society quoted Webster on the foundational importance of the Bible in America:

If we abide by the principles taught in the Bible, our country will go on to prosperity; but if we and our posterity neglect its instructions and authority, no man can say how sudden a calamity may overwhelm us and bury all our glory in profound obscurity.

The ABS *Report* further claimed that "The Bible is America's standard of citizenship, the people's Magna Charta, and its transforming, enlightening power is her only hope ... for the Bible is not only the book of our nation, but the basic text-book of the world's education."[14]

For whatever was written in former days was written or our instruction,
that through endurance and through the
encouragement of the Scriptures we might have hope.
—Romans 15:4—

SEPTEMBER 12
MORAL FOUNDATION FOR A NATION

Robert Charles Winthrop (1809-1894) was a descendant of that John Winthrop who was a founder of the Massachusetts Bay Colony back in 1630. He studied law with Daniel Webster, then established his law practice in Boston. Winthrop also served in the Massachusetts House of Representatives as well as the U.S. Congress, serving as Speaker of the House for the 30th Congress, 1847-1849. In 1849, Winthrop gave an address to the Massachusetts Bible Society in which he spoke of the importance of the Bible for the country:

> The world, which seems to outgrow successively all other books, finds still in this [Bible] an ever fresh adaptation to every change in its condition and every period in its history. Now, as a thousand years ago, it has lessons alike for individuals and for nations; for rulers and for people; for monarchies and for republics; for times of stability and for times of overthrow; for the rich and the poor; for the simplest and the wisest ....

> ... how impossible it is to separate the influence of the Bible as a mere book, from that which it owes to its divine character and origin. And they ought not to be separated. Unquestionably, it is as containing the word of God, the revelation of immortality, the gospel of salvation, that the Bible presents its preeminent title to the affection and reverence of the world. And it is in this view above all others, that its universal distribution becomes identified with the highest temporal and eternal interests of the human race ...

> Everything in the immediate condition of our own country, calls for the most diligent employment of all the moral and religious agencies within our reach, and particularly for increased activity in the distribution of the Bible ...

> All societies of men must be governed in some way or other. The less they may have of stringent State Government, the more they must have of individual self-government. The less they rely on public law or physical force, the more they must rely on private moral restraint. Men, in a word, must necessarily be controlled, either by a power within them, or by a power without them; either by the word of God, or by the strong-arm of man; either by the Bible, or the bayonet. It may do for other countries and other governments to talk about the State supporting religion. Here, under our own free institutions, it is Religion which must support the State.[15]

I shall not be put to shame, having my eyes fixed on all your commandments.
—Psalm 119:6—

A MORAL LAW FOR THE NATION

John McLean (1785-1861) served in Congress, then was an Associate Justice of the Ohio Supreme Court, then Postmaster General under Presidents Monroe and John Quincy Adams. Finally, he was a Justice of the United States Supreme court for over thirty years. At the same time, he was President of the American Sunday-School Union from 1848 until his death in 1861. McLean believed the Sunday-School Union was vital for maintaining the United States as a free republic. McLean recognized that the Scriptures are the basis of the inner moral law needed for the preservation of free government in the United States:

> For many years my hope for the perpetuity of our institutions has rested upon Bible morality and the general dissemination of Christian principles. This is an element which did not exist in the ancient republics. It is a basis on which free governments may be maintained through all time ... A free government can have no other than a moral basis; and it requires a high degree of intelligence and virtue in the people to maintain it ... Our mission of freedom is not carried out by brute force, by canon law, or any other law except the moral law and those Christian principles which are found in the Scriptures.[16]

In an 1852 letter to the American Bible Society, McLean spoke of the Bible bringing light to a dark world:

> No one can estimate or describe the salutary influence of the Bible. What would the world be without it? Compare the dark places of the earth, where the light of the Gospel has not penetrated, with those where it has been proclaimed and embraced in all its purity. Life and immortality are brought to light by the Scriptures. Aside from Revelation, darkness rests upon the world and upon the future. There is no ray of light to shine upon our pathway there is no star of hope. We begin our speculations as to our destiny in conjecture, and they end in uncertainty. We know not that there is a God, a heaven, or a hell, or any day of general account, when the wicked and the righteous shall be judged. The Bible has shed a glorious light upon the world. It shows us that in the coming day we must answer for the deeds done in the body. It has opened to us a new and living way, so plainly marked out that no one can mistake it. The price paid for our redemption shows the value of our immortal souls.[17]

I have chosen the way of faithfulness; I set your rules before me.
—Psalm 119:30—

SEPTEMBER 14
A SONG FOR THE RAGGED SCHOOLS

During the early Industrial Revolution in England, children, often as young as four, were employed to work in the factories. Two thirds of the workers in the cotton mills in England and Scotland were children. Robert Raikes (1736-1811), a newspaper publisher, was concerned about the children who were not getting an education or any moral training. Since the children worked in the factories six days a week, Raikes began to establish schools on Sunday to teach the children to read (there were no public schools at the time). The textbook in Raikes's school was the Bible, and the lessons from the catechism provided basic instruction in the Christian faith. The school also included regular church attendance. Some criticized the schools, mockingly calling them "Ragged Schools," and said they desecrated the Sabbath. Yet Raikes's schools were forerunners of the English public schools and began the important Sunday School movement, providing Christian instruction for many in churches today.

John Burton (1803-1877) was a teacher in the Sunday schools who wrote hymns for children, knowing that music could reinforce the lessons being taught. His most popular hymn was "Holy Bible, Book divine." In it, Burton sang of the many values and uses of the Bible for the Christian:

Holy Bible, book divine,
Precious treasure, thou art
   mine!
Mine, to tell me whence I came;
Mine to teach me what I am.

Mine to chide me when I rove;
Mine to show the Savior's love;
Mine thou art, to guide and guard;
Mine to punish or reward.

Mine to comfort in distress,
If the Holy Spirit bless;
Mine, to show, by living faith,
Man can triumph over death.

Mine to tell of joys to come.
And the rebel sinner's doom;
O thou Holy Book divine,
Precious treasure, thou art mine![18]

I am small and despised, yet I do not forget your precepts.
—Psalm 119:141—

SEPTEMBER 15
CHARLES HADDON SPURGEON'S CONVERSION

An attraction to visitors to London at the end of the 19th century was a visit to the Metropolitan Tabernacle, where Charles Spurgeon (1834-1892) was preacher. Spurgeon's oratory kept his audience spellbound, causing many admirers to call him the "Prince of Preachers."

As a teenager, Charles Spurgeon had an interest in spiritual things and read from the Puritan books in the family library. Seeking to find salvation and relief from the guilt of sin, he read John Bunyan's *Pilgrim's Progress*, Dr. Doddridge's *Rise and Progress of Religion in the Soul* and other works. Though these books were helpful, it was the preached Word which removed the blindness from Spurgeon's spiritual eyes. He had resolved to attend services at every church in his city, and one cold Sunday morning in January he made his way through the snow and stopped at a little Primitive Methodist Chapel. There were only 13-15 people there, and the snow had even prevented the preacher from showing up. A thin-looking man rose to preach, and Spurgeon described the scene:

> This man was really stupid. He was obliged to stick to his text, for the simple reason that he had little else to say. The text was, "Look unto Me, and be ye saved, all the ends of the earth." [Isaiah 45:22]. He did not even pronounce the words rightly, but that did not matter. There was, I thought, a glimpse of hope for me in that text. The preacher began thus:—"My dear friends, this is a very simple text indeed. It says. 'Look.' Now lookin' don't take a deal of pains. It ain't liftin' your foot or your finger; it just says 'Look.' Well, a man needn't go to College to learn to look. You may be the biggest fool, and yet you can look ... Anyone can look; even a child can look. But then the text says, 'Look unto *Me.*" Ay!" said he in broad Essex, "many on ye are lookin' to yourselves, but it's no use lookin' there. You'll never find any comfort in yourselves... Jesus Christ says, 'Look unto *Me.*' ...

The preacher noticed the young Spurgeon and said, "Young man, you look miserable ... Young man, look to Jesus Christ. Look! Look! Look! You have nothin' to do but to look and live." Spurgeon at once saw the way of salvation. Spurgeon looked, and "there and then the cloud was gone, the darkness had rolled away, and that moment I saw the sun."[19]

So faith comes by hearing, and hearing by the Word of Christ.
—Romans 10:17—

SEPTEMBER 16
HARRIET BEECHER STOWE AND THE BIBLE

The best-selling novel in 19th century America was *Uncle Tom's Cabin*, written by Harriet Beecher Stowe. The novel contains nearly 100 biblical references and reflects an evangelical perspective on slavery. Themes of sin, suffering, repentance, and salvation are woven throughout the powerfully influential book. It is from the Bible that the slave named Tom receives his comfort, strength, and true freedom. He does not let his heart be troubled, for he knows in his Father's house are many mansions and Jesus had gone to prepare a place for him (John 14:1-6). With Paul, Uncle Tom had learned to be content in whatever condition he found himself. When threatened by the evil Simon Legree, Tom remembered Isaiah 43:1, "Fear not! For I have redeemed thee. I have called thee by name. Thou art MINE!" When beaten so harshly that death was certain, Tom forgave his persecutors and prayed for their salvation. When death came, Tom's last words were those from Romans 8, "Who shall separate us from the love of Christ?" Harriet wrote that the story of Uncle Tom was "to show how Jesus Christ, who liveth and was dead, and now is alive and forever-more, has still a mother's love for the poor and lowly, and no man can sink so low but that Jesus Christ will stoop and take his hand."[20]

Harriet was a member of a prominent Christian family. Her father Lyman Beecher and brothers Henry Ward, Charles, and Edward were all famous preachers, as was her husband, Calvin Stowe. Harriet wrote thirty books, all reflecting her Christian faith. One of her earliest works, published in 1834, was *The Child's Bible*. This miniature book tells the Bible's story, with illustrations, from the creation through Jesus and the beginning of the Gospel spreading to the world. In the preface, Harriet wrote, "The Bible is the best book in the world...We have made this small book, dear children, on purpose for you … After you read this through, you'll wish to know more about the Bible … Your mama will get you one or let you take hers, and you will learn much more than we had room to tell you." Harriet wrote other books with a biblical focus. In 1873 she published *Woman in Sacred History: A Series of Sketches Drawn from Scripture, Historical and Legendary Sources*, a work beautifully illustrated with chromo-lithographs. Harriet described her purpose in the book was "to show, in a series of biographical sketches, a history of Womanhood Under Divine Culture, tending toward the development of that high ideal of womanhood which we find in modern Christian countries."

Sanctify them in the truth; your word is truth.
—John 17:17—

AN APPEAL TO CLEAVE TO THE BIBLE

Exeter Hall, located north of the Strand in London, was for many years the English headquarters of the Y.M.C.A. The regular lectures there were widely attended, and later published and widely read. In his December 1850 lecture, "National Obligation to the Bible," Rev. Robert Bickersteth traced England's obligations to the Scriptures in advancing intellectual, social, and spiritual progress. He concluded with an appeal:

> The Bible reveals a method of salvation so plain, that all may comprehend; so plenteous, that none are excluded from the offer of its benefits—so free, that all may partake without money and without price. The Bible is in itself a fountain of spiritual blessing. It is the revelation of God as a reconciled Father in Christ, long-suffering to all men not willing that any should perish, but that all should come to repentance. The Bible points to an eternity of which time is the vestibule; to an endless existence upon which we must enter, when this life is over. It proclaims to every human being …—you have an immortal soul to be saved or lost; Jesus died and rose again for its redemption …be wise for eternity. Born for immortality, fritter not away your majesty of being by living only for time; ransomed by the blood of Jesus, glorify God in your body and spirit, which are God's.

> Would you know how to pass securely through life, and to inherit a blissful eternity? God's Word is a lamp to the feet, and a light to the path. Cleave, to the Bible. It is the only safe chart. Here there is truth, without intermixture of error. Here there is guidance which cannot mislead. It is the voice of God that speaks in this volume. Its utterance, "Thus saith the Lord," can neither change nor deceive. Study prayerfully and diligently at this source, and you shall find truth to enrich you for all time and gladden you to all eternity. Drink in from this fountain, and you shall find relief from anxious care, and fretting toil, and weary disappointments. Men of every rank, of every clime, and of every occupation, have found in this volume the knowledge without which they must have everlastingly perished ….

> Surely such a volume bears the impress of Divinity. It carries with it its own witness … It is the oil on the troubled waters of human life. It is the chart of navigation to the haven of eternal glory.[21]

… holding fast to the word of life, so that in the day of Christ I may be proud that I did not run in vain or labor in vain.
—Philippians 2:16—

SEPTEMBER 18
THE BIBLE—GOD'S GIFT FOR MEN

In 1853 the American Tract Society first published in three volumes a Family Bible with notes and instructions to assist the reader in understanding the Scriptures. The preface to the Bible encouraged the reading of the Scriptures as God's Word: [22]

This book is the word of God. In it he makes known to men his character and will. It is all given by inspiration of the Holy Ghost, and is profitable; teaching men what to believe; showing them in what they are wrong; instructing them in what is right; and leading them, through the grace of God, to do it [II Timothy 3:16-17]. Although written by men, God directed them what to write and how to write it, that as a rule of human faith and conduct it might be perfect [II Peter 1:21] ... it is "perfect, converting the soul; sure, making wise the simple; and right, rejoicing the heart" [Psalm 19:7-8] ... knowledge of this book is more to be desired than gold, even much fine gold; because in understanding, believing, and obeying it, there is a great present and a great future reward [Psalm 19:10-11].

Hence, every person who can, should own a copy of it, and should read it every day; asking God to teach him, by his Spirit, rightly to understand, cordially to believe, and faithfully to obey it [John 16:13-14]. It will then be spirit and life to his soul, and make him wise to salvation [II Timothy 3:15]. It will be a lamp to his feet, and a light to his path [Psalm 119:105]; guiding him in the way of righteousness, that way of pleasantness and path of peace [Proverbs 3:17] Through it he will get understanding and will hate every false way; and by it he will be furnished thoroughly for every good work ....

Reader, make this book your own. By it try your faith, and your practice. Hearken to it daily, as the voice of God speaking to you, telling you words by which you may be saved, and by which you may also be instrumental in saving others. Follow its heavenly teachings, and all things shall work together for your good [Romans 8:28]. God will guide you by his counsel through life; he will support and comfort you in death; and after death he will receive you to glory [Psalm 73:24]; where with him, and all his people, you will rise from glory to glory for ever and ever [II Corinthians 3:18; Daniel 12:3].

And he [Nehemiah] read from it ... from early morning until midday,
in the presence of the men and the women and those who could understand.
And the ears of all the people were attentive to the Book of the Law.
—Nehemiah 8:3—

A CITY BROKEN DOWN AND WITHOUT WALLS

The life of Sam Houston (1793-1863) was filled with adventure, daring, and important contributions to the westward expansion of the United States, as well as with moral failures and disappointments. Born in Virginia, Houston moved to Tennessee, practiced law, served in the U.S. House, and became governor in 1827. When his wife left him shortly after their wedding, he resigned as governor and went to live among the Cherokees. He took a Cherokee wife and began drinking heavily. The Cherokees called him "Big Drunk." In 1832, Houston went to Texas and became involved in Texas' independence movement from Mexico. He signed the Texas Declaration of Independence on March 2, 1836 and became the Texas forces' Commander-in-Chief. Houston's victory at the Battle of San Jacinto on April 21 secured Texas' independence, but he was injured in the battle. When he went to New Orleans for treatment, he met Margaret Lea, a devout Christian, whom he later married. Margaret encouraged Houston to stop drinking and to yield his life to Christ.

Houston became President of the Republic of Texas and then U.S. Senator and Governor after Texas became a state. As Senator, he was often in Washington, D.C., separated from Margaret, but the two kept up a warm and beautiful correspondence. In Washington, he began attending East Street Baptist Church, at first out of respect for Margaret, but soon he was absorbed by the sermons. A sermon, on Proverbs 25:28, "He that hath no rule over his own spirit is like a city that is broken down, and without walls," convicted Houston of his sinfulness. Later Sunday sermons from Hebrews 11 on the patriarchs, the judges, and the origin of the Hebrew nation resonated with Houston as he saw an analogy with the young United States in "the story of the settlement of a new land, of the conquest of heathen tribes, of fratricidal strife among the jealous states not yet consolidated into nationality."[23] He asked the pastor for a book to help him with the doubts he had about the Christian faith. The pastor gave him Nelson's *Cause and Cure of Infidelity*. Houston studied it carefully and bought copies for friends. He attended church in Washington faithfully, using Sunday afternoons to write a summary of the sermons to Margaret back in Texas. On November 19, 1854, Sam Houston made a formal profession of faith in Christ and was baptized at Rocky Creek in Independence, Texas. It was an answer to years of prayers by Houston's faithful wife Margaret.

My soul clings to the dust; give me life according to your word!
—Psalm 119:25—

SEPTEMBER 20

GORDON OF KHARTOUM

One of the most admired leaders of Victorian England was major-general Charles Gordon (1833-1885). He was in the Crimean war, then gained the nickname "Chinese Gordon" for his actions in China helping to put down the Taiping Rebellion. He served the Khedive of Egypt and was Governor-general of Sudan. When he met his death during Muhammad Ahmad's siege of Khartoum in 1885, all of Britain mourned. Gordon was noted not only for his military ability, but also as a charitable man of integrity and a devout Christian. Gordon's sister, Mary Augusta Gordon, presented Queen Victoria with Gordon's Bible—well-used, with many markings and notes by Gordon, who spent at least two hours in Bible study and prayer every morning. The queen placed it in an ornate crystal display case in the Grand Corridor of Windsor Castle.

Throughout his travels, Gordon and his sister had corresponded concernring the spiritual life. In the letters, Gordon wrote the following about the Bible:

> The chief proof, after all, the Bible is good food is the eating of it; the healing efficacy of a medicine, when it is used, is a demonstration that it is good. I believe the origin of evil is disclosed in the Bible.[24]

> The secret of reading the Bible is, abiding in Him who is "the way, the truth, and the life." "Ye need not that any man teach you." "I will instruct and teach thee in the way that thou shalt go, I will guide thee with mine eye." "Love not the world," for it passes away. "Pray without ceasing." If we keep these words in mind, we shall find the very greatest peace.[25]

> My belief is, that whenever we are in doubt about anything, we should place the matter before God by prayer, then take the Bible wherever we may be reading, and having our attention fixed on the subject of our prayer, seek to get the answer and take it in just the same way as if we heard God's voice. Saul inquired of the witch of Endor, while David kept asking God (I Samuel xxiii.2,4, 9-11; xxx.7,8).[26]

> …the Scripture contains the mind of Christ, and is when illuminated with the Spirit, as if Christ was ever talking to us. Now, we should think that if Christ was ever near to talk with us, *that* should suffice us.[27]

With my whole heart I cry; answer me, O Lord! I will keep your statutes.
—Psalm 119:147—

THE BOOK OF GOD

Adolphe Monod (1802-1856), one of the greatest of French preachers, was bedridden the last several months of his life, but he continued to reflect on Scripture and encouraged his companions with him to devote their lives to the reading and study of the Scripture. These reflections, published posthumously as his *Farewell,* continue to encourage us in the Scripture:

> What are the Holy Scriptures? Men can never precisely explain the manner in which they were composed, nor, in particular, how the Spirit of God and the spirit of man are combined in them so as to make them at the same time Divine and human—a Divine word, reaching to heaven, and at the same time, human and quite near to us. This is not less difficult to explain than the manner in which the Divine and human natures were united in Jesus Christ. This parallel is not mine, for Scripture calls itself the written Word, and it calls Jesus Christ the "Word made flesh." But however the Holy Scriptures may have been composed, "they literally are heaven speaking upon earth;" they are the maxims of the kingdom of heaven communicated to men in human language, as if the invisible world were come down amongst them, and placed before their eyes. There is no other book, even among the best, which makes known to us the mysteries of the kingdom of heaven. All are more or less tainted human errors: this alone is exempt from them. It is the book of God, full of the truth of God; in it we hear God speak by the Holy Spirit. We see God, man—the present, the future—time and eternity, described such as they are.
>
> For any one who has thus understood what Scripture is, it will not be difficult to confess the use to which he ought to make of it. We ought to interrogate the Scriptures just as we would an angel from heaven sent by God at this very moment in order to instruct us; or, what is still better, as we would question the Lord Jesus Christ if we could speak to Him and hear Him. And, in fact, we do speak to Him and hear Him when we read the Holy Scriptures, and through Him they reveal all things by His Spirit.
>
> Oh! how can we sufficiently love and venerate this book? It is true it is not the book that saves us, but it is the book that reveals the way of salvation without which we could never have known it; and by which, the better we know it, the better we shall know Jesus the Saviour of our souls.[28]

I keep your precepts and testimonies, for all my ways are before you.
—Psalm 119:168—

SEPTEMBER 22
THE PONY EXPRESS BIBLE

Though the Pony Express existed for only 18 months, it has become an important part of American history and folklore. With the motto of "The mail must go through," the company of Russell-Majors & Waddell contracted to carry mail the 1,996 miles from St. Joseph, Missouri to Sacramento, California in record time. A schedule as exacting as a railroad timetable was set up. Horses traveled 8-10 miles per hour and were changed every 10-15 miles. Delivery of Lincoln's Inaugural Address in 1861, was made to the west coast in a record 7 days and 17 hours. The total number of known Pony Express riders was 183, with rider Buffalo Bill later becoming famous.

The American Bible Society gave Russell-Majors & Waddell 300 Bibles for the riders. Engraved with gold on the cover was "Presented by Russell, Majors & Waddell, 1858." Every rider had to swear on a Bible an oath which in part said. "before the great and living God, that during my engagement, and while I am an employee … I will, under no circumstances, use profane language. I will drink no intoxicating liquors; I will not quarrel or fight with any other employee of the firm, and that in every respect, I will conduct myself honestly, faithful to my duties, and so direct my acts as to win the confidence of my employers. So help me God."[29] The rider then signed the oath, which was inside the front cover of the Bible. After signing the oath, riders were given the Bible, which they took with them on their trail. Only twelve copies of the Pony Express Bibles are known to exist today.

This Book of the Law shall not depart from your mouth, but you shall meditate on it day and night, so that you may be careful to do according to all that is written in it. For then you will make your way prosperous, and then you will have good success.
—Joshua 1:8—

PRECIOUSNESS OF THE WORD OF GOD

The Precious Things of God by Octavius Winslow (1808-1878) has a chapter on the preciousness of God's Word. In it he notes that though nature displays the power and wisdom of God, it does not tell us about the moral problems of the universe; only divine revelation can reveal and disclose the Savior. All that is precious for the believer is bound up in the Scriptures. The Scriptures, as the Word of the Lord, reveal His perfections, His mind, and His will. God's character as holy, wise, merciful, and sin-pardoning, is known only through His revealed Word. Here we learn of the love of God. Nowhere in the heavens above or in the earth beneath do we learn of the precious Gospel announced in God's Word:

> As testifying to Jesus and His activities, the Word of God must ever be transcendently precious to the believer. The Bible is, from its commencement to its close, a record of the lord Jesus. Around Him the divine and glorious Word centers; all its wondrous types, prophecies, and facts gather. His Promise and Foreshadowing, His holy Incarnation, Nativity, and Baptism, His Obedience and Passion, His Death, Burial and Resurrection, His Ascension to heaven, His Second Coming to judge the world, are the grand and touching, the sublime and tender, the priceless and precious truths interwoven with the whole texture of the Bible, to which the Two Witnesses of Revelation, the Old and the New Testaments, bear their harmonious and solemn testimony. Beloved, let this be the one and chief object in our study of the Bible—the Knowledge of Jesus. The Bible is not a history, a book of science, a poem,—it is a record of Christ. Study it to know more of Him,—His nature, His love, His work. With the magnanimous Paul, "count all things but loss for the excellency of the knowledge of Christ Jesus your Lord." [Philippians 3:8] Then will God's Word become increasingly precious to your soul, and its truths unfold. In every page you will, trace the history of Jesus, see the glory of Jesus, admire the work of Jesus, learn the love of Jesus, and hear the voice of Jesus. The whole volume will be redolent of His name, and luminous with His beauty ....

> Do we study the "Word of Christ" spiritually and honestly, as those whose souls hunger and thirst for this the bread and water of life? Do we search it diligently and earnestly as for hidden treasure; treasure beyond all price? ... Do we read it with a child like mind, receive it with reverence of soul, and receive its decisions in all questions of faith and practice as decisive and ultimate? In a word, do we search the Scriptures humbly, prayerfully, depending upon the guidance of the Spirit, to find Jesus in them? Of these Scriptures He

is the Alpha and the Omega, the substance, the sweetness, the glory, the one, precious, all absorbing theme. Yes, Lord! Your word is precious to our souls, because it reveals to us Your glory and tells us of Your love![30]

... the word of the Lord remains forever.
And this word is the good news that was preached to you.
—I Peter 1:25—

BIBLE WOMEN

Ellen White Raynard (1809-1879) cared about the poor even as a teenager. She and a friend frequently visited the poor and shared the Gospel with them, working with the Bible Society to supply the poor with Bibles. Ellen married Benjamin Ranyard in 1839 and had one son, who later became a noted astronomer. Ellen's marriage did not stop her visitation among the poor, and in 1859 she formally organized the Bible and Domestic Female Mission. The Mission was to help supply Bibles to the poor while also teaching them to become productive and help themselves. "Bible Women" from among the poor were trained to first read the Scriptures with the poor women. They could also teach the women to read and supply inexpensive copies of the Scriptures, which the people could purchase on installment if necessary. Ellen believed that having the people purchase the Scriptures rather than simply giving them out free made the people value them more. Bible Women also could take subscriptions for clothing and bedding and provide instructions in cleanliness, cooking, and needlework. Ellen believed that improving the lives of the mothers was most important in helping the poor. Within ten years, there were 234 Bible women working in London, the first paid social workers in the city.

Ellen's organization of Bible Women became a pattern used in foreign missions. Missionaries enlisted native women to go among the people and read the Scriptures in their homes. They could then provide further instruction in the Scriptures as well as lessons in cleanliness and work habits which would improve their lives.

Ellen believed the Word of God is foundational to improving the lives of the poor. She was most concerned about providing the Scriptures to them: "Let us sow wherever we are able the imperishable seed of the word broadcasting it in humble faith and prayer."[31]

... devote yourself to the public reading of Scripture,
to exhortation, to teaching.
—I Timothy 4:13—

SEPTEMBER 25
ELEMENTS OF SUCCESS

Born in New Jersey, William Bross (1813-1890) grew up on a farm in Pennsylvania. He worked his way through Williams College, where he was deeply influenced by the Christian faith of college President Mark Hopkins. After teaching several years in New York and Pennsylvania, Bross went west to the new town of Chicago, where he became active in politics and publishing. In 1852, he began *The Democratic Press*, which six years later merged with the *Chicago Tribune*, where Bross served as editor. Opposed to slavery, Bross became a supporter of Abraham Lincoln and the new Republican Party, often speaking on the same platform with Lincoln. After the Civil War, Bross served as Lieutenant Governor of Illinois for a term.

When asked what teachings had a strong influence in his own life and helped his success, Bross replied, "The Proverbs of Solomon and other Scriptures ... They were quoted a thousand times by my honored father, and caused an effort to do my whole duty each day, under a constant sense of my duty to my Maker and my fellow-men." Bross said a person's lack of success in life could be ascribed to a lack of integrity, a carelessness of the truth, a recklessness in thought and expression, bad company, bad morals, and a "want of trust in God and disregard for the teachings of his Word." He advised young people to cultivate a "Sterling, unflinching integrity in all matters, public and private. Let everyone do his whole duty each day both to God and man. Let him follow earnestly the teachings of the Scriptures and eschew infidelity in all its forms."[32]

In Chicago, Bross was often known as "Deacon Bross." He was a faithful member of Second Presbyterian Church and active in Christian affairs. He concluded an 1876 address n "The History of Chicago" with the admonition for the churches to work for the conversion and moral upbringing of the people. He encouraged the people to vote for honest and respectable men, "let us all do our whole duty as citizens and as ever acting upon the Divine maxim that "Righteousness exalteth a nation" (Proverbs 14:34) and "Godliness is profitable for all things." (I Timothy 4:8).

Teach me good judgment and knowledge,
for I believe in your commandments.
—Psalm 119:66—

ABRAHAM LINCOLN AND THE BIBLE

Any true consideration of Lincoln must include something of the Bible's influence on his life and thought. In her 1909 book *Lincoln's Use of the Bible*, S. Trevena Jackson tells the story of a school located across the fence from the White House:

> The President often watched the children play. One morning the teacher gave them a lesson in neatness and asked each boy to come to school next day with his shoes blacked. They all obeyed. One of them, John S., a poor, one-armed lad, had used stove polish, the only kind his home afforded. The boys were merciless in their ridicule. The boy was only nine years old, the son of a dead soldier, his mother a washerwoman, with three other children to provide for. The President heard the boys jeering Johnny and learned the facts about the boy.

> The next day John S. came to school with a new suit and with new shoes and told that the President had called at his home and took him to the store and bought two suits of clothes for him and clothes for his sisters and sent coal and groceries to the house. In addition to this the lad brought to the teacher a scrap of paper containing a verse of Scripture, which Mr. Lincoln had requested to have written upon the blackboard: 'Inasmuch as ye have done it unto one of the least of these my brethren, ye have done it unto me.'

> Some weeks after, the President visited the school, and the teacher directed his attention to the verse, which was still there. Mr. Lincoln read it, then, taking a crayon said: 'Boys, I have another quotation from the Bible, and I hope you will learn it and come to know its truth as I have known and felt it.' Then below the other verse he wrote: 'It is more blessed to give than to receive.' A. LINCOLN.[33]

Lincoln was often found immersed in his Bible reading while President. In 1864, when a group of black pastors gave Lincoln a Bible, he wrote them a thank you note in which he said,

> It [the Bible] is the best gift which God has ever given to man. All the good from the Saviour of the world is communicated to us through this book. But for that book, we could not know right from wrong. All those truths desirable for men are contained in it.[34]

Teach me your way, O Lord, that I may walk in your truth;
unite my heart to fear your name.
—Psalm 86:11—

SEPTEMBER 27
THE FATHER OF ELECTRICITY ON THE SCRIPTURES

Albert Einstein had a portrait on the wall of his study of the man he said laid the foundation for his own studies—Michael Faraday (1791-1867). Largely self-educated, Faraday became one of the leading scientists of his day. He discovered principles underlying the electromagnetic field and the laws of electrolysis, and his inventions made the production of electricity practical. The terminology he developed of electrode, ion, anode, and cathode became standard, and he provided the research and experimentation for the electric motor, the dynamo, the transformer, and the generator. He can fittingly be called the "Father of Electronics." He also could clearly present his ideas, and his scientific lectures were well attended.

Though highly esteemed in his own day, Faraday remained a humble man. Offered a knighthood for his scientific work, he refused. The Bible warned against pursuing worldly rewards, and Faraday preferred to remain "plain Mr. Faraday."

Faraday was a member of the Sandemanian church, which sought to pattern itself on the primitive church of the New Testament. An avid Bible student, his favorite book was the book of Job. Though in his scientific work, Faraday, was trying to understand the organization of God's creation, he also realized, as Job realized, that God cannot be understood by man's reason, but only through God's revelation in Scripture. Faraday wrote that

> ... the Christian ... is taught of God (by His Word and the Holy Spirit) to trust in the promise of salvation through the work of Jesus Christ. He finds his guide in the Word of God and commits the keeping of his soul into the hands of God. He looks for no assurance beyond what the Word can give him. And if his mind is troubled by the cares and fears which may assail him, he can go nowhere but in prayer to the throne of grace and to Scripture.[35]

By the word of the Lord the heavens were made,
and by the breath of his mouth all their host.
—Psalm 33:6—

SEPTEMBER 28
"I AM WITH YOU ALWAYS"

Missionary and explorer David Livingstone (1813-1873) was a legend in his own lifetime. His devout Christian parents encouraged Livingstone in his Christian faith and his early desire to become a missionary and a doctor, to bring both physical and spiritual healing to the people. As a university student, Livingstone wrote an essay in which he summarized the importance of faith and reliance on Scripture:

> The first inquiry which ought to engage the attention of every candid searcher after truth, in coming to the Bible, ought to be Is This The word of God? Let him ascertain that it is so, and then every statement contained therein ought to be received with perfect confidence; although it may not coincide with what he should have expected to find ...; And every precept it enjoins ought to be received with ready obedience, although it may not accord with his preconceived ideas of right and wrong; And though he cannot understand its mysteries, or compass them within ... [his limited mind], all ought to be received on the ground of the divine Testimony, and relied on with implicit confidence.[36]

Livingstone had hoped to go to China as a missionary, but the Opium Wars restricted missionary activity there. After he met Robert Moffat, a missionary to South Africa, Livingstone eagerly set off for Africa. He went where no missionary had ever been, bringing the truth of the Gospel to the natives and exploring the unmapped African continent. He was appalled and dismayed by the Arab slave trade that captured Africans from the interior and drove them to the coasts to be sold.

In his extensive African explorations, Livingstone encountered many difficulties. He was attacked by a lion that bit into his shoulder and shook him "as a terrier does a rat." Livingstone had followed Jesus' command to "Go therefore and make disciples of all nations ..." and through all his difficulties, he clung to Jesus' promise, "I am with you always" (Matthew 28:19-20).

One day, Livingstone's servants found him dead, on his knees in prayer. They buried his heart in Africa and embalmed his body for return to Britain, where it was buried in Westminster Abbey. Inscribed below his epitaph is "Other sheep I have which are not of this fold; them also I must bring (John 10:16)."

All the kings of the earth shall give you thanks, O Lord,
for they have heard the words of your mouth.
—Psalm 138:4—

SEPTEMBER 29
QUEEN VICTORIA AND THE SCRIPTURES

An 1861 painting by Thomas Jones Barker in the National Portrait Gallery, titled "The Secret of England's Greatness," shows a young Queen Victoria in the audience chamber of Windsor Castle presenting a Bible to a kneeling African chief. Colored lithographs based on the painting ended up in homes across England and the British Empire. Though the scene probably never actually occurred, there is a similar idea in a letter from the Queen to Sagbua and other chiefs of Abeokuta, who had sent a petition against slavery to the Queen, and also thanked her for the commerce with England and the good the people received from Christian missionaries. The Queen replied:

> The Queen and the people of England are very glad to know that Sagbua and the chiefs think as they do upon this subject of commerce. But commerce alone will not make a nation great and happy like England. England has become great and happy by the knowledge of the true God and Jesus Christ. The Queen is, therefore, very glad to hear that Sagbua and the chiefs have so kindly received the missionaries, who carry with them the Word of God, and that so many of the people are willing to have it. In order to show how much the Queen values God's Word, she sends this, as a present to Sagbua, a copy of this work in two languages—one the Arabic, the other the English.[37]

The Bible was a constant source of strength, wisdom, and comfort for Victoria. When in London, the Queen conducted a Bible Class for her servants' children. She had each child read one verse of a selected Scripture, and then she explained the more difficult passages and the lesson to be learned.

Late in her life, Victoria learned of a mother who was seriously ill in a little cottage in Windsor. She began visiting the lady, and on the first visit told the family not to be put out; she came as a Christian, not as a queen. She took the lady's hand and told her, "Put your trust in Jesus, and you will soon be in a land where there is no pain. You are a widow, so am I; we shall soon meet our beloved ones." Victoria then read her the comforting words from John 14, knelt on the floor, and prayed for the lady. She visited the lady once or twice a week, and always read the scriptures and prayed with her.[38]

When he sits on the throne of his kingdom, he shall write for himself in a book a copy of this law ... And it shall be with him, and he shall read in it all the days of his life, that he may learn to fear the Lord his God by keeping all the words of this law and these statutes ...
—Deuteronomy17:18-19—

SEPTEMBER 30
AMERICAN SOLDIERS' BIBLES

The American Bible Society (ABS) and local Bible societies were active in distributing New Testaments and Bibles to soldiers in the Mexican War and every American war thereafter. During the Civil War, the ABS distributed Bibles to both the North and South. During the Spanish-American War, nearly 75,000 Bibles were sent to the front lines. The Bibles and Testaments distributed to the soldiers during World War I were a witness to the diverse immigrant population of the United States. Scriptures were distributed in Armenian, Chinese, Czech, French, Greek, Italian, Lithuanian, Polish, Portuguese, Rumanian, Russian, Spanish, Swedish, Yiddish and other languages, as well as English! A letter of commendation from President Wilson was reproduced in the front of Pocket New Testaments distributed during World War I:

> The Bible is the word of life. I beg you will read it and find this out for yourselves, read,—not little snatches here and there, but long passages that will really be the road to the heart of it. You will find it full of real men and women not only but also of the things you have wondered about and been troubled about all your life, as men have always, and the more you read the more it will become plain to you what things are worthwhile and what are not, what things make men happy—loyalty, right dealing, speaking the truth, readiness to give everything for what they think their duty, and most of all, the wish they may have the approval of the Christ, who gave everything for them,—and the things that are guaranteed to make men unhappy,—selfishness, cowardice, greed, and everything that is low and mean. When you have read the Bible you will know that it is the Word of God, because you will have found it the key to your own heart, your own happiness, and your own duty.

World War II was the first time that the U.S. government made the Bible part of the general issue to servicemen. Different Bibles were given according to the religious preference of the soldier—Jewish, Protestant, or Catholic. A letter from President Roosevelt, "To the Armed Forces" was printed in the front of the Bibles. Roosevelt wrote,

> As Commander-in-Chief I take pleasure in commending the reading of the bible to all who serve in the armed forces of the United States. Throughout the centuries men of many faiths and diverse origins have found in the Sacred Book words of wisdom, counsel, and inspiration. It is a fountain of strength and now, as always, an aid in attaining the highest aspirations of the human soul.

When Eddie Rickenbacker and his seven companions had to abandon their aircraft and drifted on three rafts in the Pacific for weeks, a Bible was their comfort. Rickenbacker wrote:

> With the New Testament as an inspiration, we held morning and evening prayers. The rafts were pulled together making a rough triangle. Then, each in turn, one of us would read a passage. None of us, I must confess, shewed himself to be very familiar with them, but thumbing the books we found a number that one way or another bespoke our needs.[39]

Most appreciated were Psalm 23 and Jesus' Sermon on the Mount.

Therefore, take no thought, saying What shall we eat?
Or what shall we drink? Or wherewithal shall we be clothed?
… for your heavenly father knows that you have need of all these things.
But seek you first the kingdom of God, and his righteousness,
and all these things shall be added to you.
—Matthew 6:31-33—

THE BIBLE AND ASTRONOMY

Ormsby MacKnight Mitchel (1810-1862) had many talents. A West Point graduate and a major general during the American Civil War, he also was a lawyer, surveyor, professor and astronomer. He wrote on astronomy, and even has a crater and region on Mars named after him! A sincere Christian, Mitchel's series of lectures on the Bible and astronomy were popular and published in 1863, after his death from yellow fever. In *The Astronomy of the Bible*, he discussed the vastness of the expanse of the universe, then wrote,

> The Bible ... furnishes the only fitting vehicle to express the thoughts that overwhelm us; and we break out involuntarily in the language of God's own inspiration: "The heavens declare the glory of God, the firmament showeth his handywork. Day unto day uttereth speech, and night unto night showeth forth knowledge." [Psalm 19:1-2] "When I consider thy heavens the work of thy fingers, the moon and the stars which thou hast ordained, Lord, what is man, that thou art mindful of him, or the son of man that thou visitest him." [Psalm 8:3-4] "If I take the wings of the morning and fly to the uttermost parts of the earth, lo! Thou art there;if I ascend to the heaven of heavens, lo! Thy presence filleth immensity. Thou, and thou alone art God over all, and blessed forever!" [Psalm 139:8-9] ... The glory of an earthly monarch is derived from the extent and variety of his empire, ... the perfection of his laws and perfect manner in which they are administered, ... and ... the consequent happiness and prosperity of his subjects. God's empire as displayed in the material universe, is thus far immeasurable. ...
>
> In the Milky Way we have one hundred millions of suns, and in deeper space we find even other milky ways. ... "The heavens, then, in their vast, incomprehensible dimensions, and in the uncounted millions of their clustering orbs, proclaim the glory of God's empire." All these are governed by God's perfect laws, perfectly administered. These laws reflect God's wisdom and power ... These results are not ... [by] accident, they are not the evolutions of blind fatality, they are the arrangements of an ever-living omnipotent, omniscient power, who can be none other than God the Creator. Wisdom infinite is written all over the universe ... so hath the finger of inspiration written—"while as yet He had not made the earth nor the fields. When He prepared the heavens I was there ..." [Proverbs 8] The wisdom of God reigns supreme throughout the manifold works of His creation. Thus is it written in the word of God, and thus is it recorded in the celestial machinery which is recoded on high."[1]

Lead me in the path of your commandments, for I delight in it.
—Psalm 119:35—

OCTOBER 2

PROTECTED BY THE WORD

The Union surgeon examining the young Confederate thought the femoral artery was hit, and left him on the battlefield of Shiloh to die. A chaplain, later passing by, saw the scattered contents of the soldier's pack and picked up a Bible which was inscribed, "Sam Houston, Jr, from his Mother, March 6, 1862." The chaplain had known Sam Houston Jr.'s father in the Senate and called the surgeon back to have a closer look at the soldier. On closer examination, it was determined the artery was not severed, Sam Jr. received further treatment, eventually recovered, and was taken to the Confederate Prisoner of War Camp Douglas near Chicago.[2]

Sam Jr.'s Bible had saved him in a previous engagement. After that earlier battle was over, he discovered a bullet which had entered his Bible, stopping at Psalm 70. The Psalm reads

> Make haste, O God, to deliver me!
>   O Lord, make haste to help me!
> [2] Let them be put to shame and confusion
>   who seek my life!
> Let them be turned back and brought to dishonor
>   who delight in my hurt!
> [3] Let them turn back because of their shame
>   who say, "Aha, Aha!"
>
> [4] May all who seek you
>   rejoice and be glad in you!
> May those who love your salvation
>   say evermore, "God is great!"
> [5] But I am poor and needy;
>   hasten to me, O God!
> You are my help and my deliverer;
>   O Lord, do not delay!

After the war, Sam Jr. gained a medical degree and practiced medicine in Texas for a time. He later spent time writing poetry and short stories.

Look on my affliction and deliver me,
for I do not forget your law.
—Psalm 119:153—

JESUS CHRIST OUR ADVOCATE

One of the comforting truths of Scripture is that Jesus is at the right hand of God interceding for us and nothing can separate us from His love (Romans 8:34-39). In 1863, when she was twenty-two, Charitie Smith wrote a poem she titled "The Advocate" expressing the truth that Jesus "ever lives to make intercession for us." (Hebrews 7:25). The hymn is rich in biblical allusions, showing Charitie's familiarity with the Scriptures. Some of the biblical references are here placed to the side of her hymn:

Before the throne of God above	*Hebrews 4:15-16*
I have a strong and perfect plea.	
A great High Priest whose name is Love	*Hebrews 4:14*
Who ever lives and pleads for me.	*Hebrews 7:25*
My name is graven on His hands,	*Isaiah 49:6*
My name is written on His heart.	
I know that while in Heaven he stands	
No tongue can bid me thence depart.	*Romans 8:34*
When Satan tempts me to despair	*Luke 22:31-32*
And tells me of the guilt within,	
Upward I look and see Him there	*Acts 7:55-56*
Who made an end of all my sin.	*Colossians 2:13-14*
Because the sinless Saviour died	
My sinful soul is counted free.	
For God the just is satisfied	*I John 2:1-2*
To look on Him and pardon me.	*Romans 3:24-26*
Behold Him there the risen Lamb,	*Revelation 5:6*
My perfect spotless righteousness,	*I Cor. 1:30; I Peter 1:18-19*
The great unchangeable I AM	*Hebrews 13:8; John 8:58*
The King of glory and of grace,	*Psalm 24:8*
One with Himself I cannot die.	
My soul is purchased by His blood	*Hebrews 9:11-12; Rev. 5:9*
My life is hid with Christ on high,	*Colossians 3:3*
With Christ my Saviour and my God!	*Titus 2:13*

I wait for the Lord, my soul waits, and in his word I hope.
—Psalm 130:5—

OCTOBER 4
THE CHURCH'S ONE FOUNDATION

In the mid-19th century, controversy stirred in the Church of England as some questioned key articles of the Christian faith as well as the authenticity of portions of the Old Testament Scriptures. Samuel Stone (1839-1900), an Anglican clergyman, defended the Biblical teachings against the critics in 1866 by publishing *Lyra Fidelium: Twelve Hymns on the Twelve Articles of the Apostles' Creed.*

The Church's one foundation	*I Cor. 3:11;Eph. 2:20*
Is Jesus Christ her Lord,	
She is His new creation	*II Corinthians 5:17*
By water and the Word;	*Ephesians 5:26-27*
From heav'n He came and sought her	*Luke 19:10*
To be His holy Bride;	*Ephesians 1:4; 5:26-27*
With His own blood He bought her,	*Ephesians 1:7*
And for her life He died.	*Romans 5:6*
Elect from every nation,	*Ephesians 3:14-20*
Yet one o'er all the earth,	*I Corinthians 12:12*
Her charter of salvation,	
One Lord, one faith, one birth,	*Ephesians 4:5*
One holy Name she blesses,	*Acts 4:12*
Partakes one holy food,	*John 6:51*
And to one hope she presses,	*Ephesians 4:4*
With very grace endued.	*Ephesians 4:7*
'Mid toil and tribulation	*John 16:33; Acts 4:23*
And tumult of her war,	
She waits the consummation	
Of peace for evermore,	
Till, with the vision glorious,	*Revelation 21:10-20*
Her longing eyes are blest,	
And the great Church victorious	*I Corinthians 15:54*
Shall be the Church at rest.	*Hebrews 4:9-21*

Christ loved the church and gave himself up for her, that he might sanctify her, having cleansed her by the washing of water with the word, so that he might present the church to himself in splendor, without spot or wrinkle or any such thing, that she might be holy and without blemish.
—Ephesians 5:25-27—

THE CINCINNATI BIBLE WARS

In the mid-1800's Cincinnati was a burgeoning city of the west, with a population of a quarter million people, including immigrants from across the United States as well as Europe. Religiously, the population was a mixture of Roman Catholics, Protestants, free thinkers, and Jews. The Northwest Ordinance of 1787, which outlined the organization of the territories including Ohio, had specified that "Religion, Morality and knowledge being necessary to good government and the happiness of mankind, Schools and the means of education shall forever be encouraged."[3] The state constitution of Ohio had incorporated similar language, requiring religious instruction, necessary to morality, in the schools.

The Cincinnati school board had a regulation that "The opening exercise in every department shall commence by reading a portion of the Bible by or under the direction of the teacher and appropriate singing by the pupils."[4] The Catholics had established Catholic schools for their students, and the number of Catholic students was approaching those in the common schools. Wanting public support for their schools, the Catholics suggested a merger with the common schools. The Catholics were opposed to the practice of Bible reading from the King James Bible, and the compromise reached was that a merger would be agreed to. The Catholics would not have religious instructions in their schools, and there would no longer be Bible reading in the common schools. The vote for the merger by the school board greatly divided the city, with opposing sides organizing mass meetings and petition drives sponsoring their views. One side noted the long history of Bible reading and moral instruction in the schools; the other argued for a secular state and school without religious instruction.

The issue finally made its way to the Ohio Supreme Court, which ruled unanimously that the Bible reading could be cancelled in the schools. The arguments made in Cincinnati in the 19th century, would be played out again a century later, in the 1963 Supreme Court case of *Abington School District v. Schempp*, ruling school-sponsored Bible reading in the schools unconstitutional.

... take not the word of truth utterly out of my mouth,
for my hope is in your rules.
—Psalm 119:43—

OCTOBER 6
CHRIST THROUGHOUT THE SCRIPTURES

In his book *Emmanuel or the Titles of Christ*, 19th century preacher Octavius Winslow (1806-1878) encouraged Christians to see Jesus throughout the Scriptures:

Christ is the Alpha and Omega, the first and the last of the inspired Scriptures of truth. He is the sum and substance both of the law and the gospel. He is the one great theme both of the Old Testament and the New. The whole Bible is designed to testify of Christ, "Search (or, as the word means, 'excavate, dig into') the Scriptures, for in them you think you have (or in them you have) eternal life. These Scriptures point to Me.[5]" In Christ the Messiah, in Jesus the Savior, in the Son of God the Redeemer, all the truths of the Bible center; to Him all the types and shadows point; of Him all the prophecies give witness; while all the glory of the Scriptures, from Genesis to Revelation, culminates at the cross of Christ. The Bible would be an inexplicable mystery from first to last but for Christ, who unfolds and explains it all. He is the one, the golden Key which unlocks the divine arcade of revelation. ...

Who, as he opens the 'typical' Scriptures, and reads of the applied blood of the Paschal Lamb, thinks not of the "blood of sprinkling," ... the blood of "Christ our passover, sacrificed for us"?[6] Who, as he beholds the scapegoat let go into the wilderness, thinks not of Christ "bearing our sins in His own body on the tree"?[7] Who, as he studies the mystery of the "Tabernacle of Testimony in the wilderness"- its construction and its furniture: the showbread, the golden candlestick, the veil, the altar of burnt-offering, the pure olive oil, the laver, the incense-altar, the sacred fire, the priesthood, the holy garments- sees not the Lord Jesus as the significance, the beauty, and the glory of it all? When Jesus "spoke of the tabernacle of His body,"[8] He, as it were, pointed to Himself as the "Tabernacle of Witness," all whose mysteries find their full explanation and deep meaning in Him, the true Tabernacle of the Church. Who can read of the manna falling from heaven around the camp, thus daily, amply, and freely supplying the needs of the whole host of Israelites, and not recall the words of Jesus, "I am the Bread of life. Your fathers ate manna in the wilderness, and died. This is that bread which comes down from heaven, that a man may eat thereof, and not die. I am the living Bread which came down from heaven: if a man eat of this bread he shall live forever."[9] ... "To Him give all the prophets witness."[10] "The testimony of Jesus is the spirit of prophecy."[11] And, as we revel in the narratives of the evangelists, and unfold the epistles of the apostles, and close our research with the sublime Apocalypse of the apostle John, we read these titles of our Lord in a light which renders divinely luminous and savingly intelligible every word and syllable- "I am Alpha and

Omega, the first and the last."[12] Thus Christ is the sum and substance of the Scriptures. Speak we of the *law?* Christ fulfilled every precept, kept every command in behalf of His people, and thus He became the "end of the law for righteousness to every one that believes."[13] Speak we of the *gospel?* Christ is the substance of the whole. All its divine doctrines, its holy precepts, its gracious instructions, its precious promises, its glorious hopes, meet, center, and fill up their entire compass in Jesus. He is the Alpha and the Omega of the Bible, from the first verse in Genesis to the last verse in Revelation. Oh, study the Scriptures of truth with a view of learning Christ. Do not study the Bible as a mere history; do not read it as a mere poem, do not search it as a book of science; it is all that, but infinitely more. The Bible is the Book of Jesus- it is a Revelation of Christ. Christ is the golden thread which runs through the whole. ... The Old Testament predicts the New, and the New fulfils the Old, and so both unite in testifying, "Truly, this is the Son of God!"[14]

Winslow concluded with a prayer:

Blessed Lord Jesus! I will read and study and dig into the Scriptures of truth to find and learn more of You! You, Immanuel, are the fragrance of this divine box of precious ointment. You are the beauteous gem sparkling in this divine cabinet. You are the Tree of life planted in the center of this divine garden. You are the Ocean whose stream quickens and nourishes all who draw water out of this divine well of salvation. The Bible is all about You.[15]

To him give all the prophets witness, that through his name
whosoever believeth in him shall receive remission of sins.
—Acts 10:43—

OCTOBER 7
THE POWER OF THE LIVING WORD

Martin Luther said, "The Bible is alive, it speaks to me; it has feet, it runs after me; it has hands, it lays hold of me."[16] He claimed that a simple layman, armed with Scripture, had more credibility than any pope or cardinal without it. In his introduction to his translation of the Old Testament, Luther wrote,

> These are the scriptures which make fools of all the wise and understanding, and are open only to the small and simple, as Christ says in Matthew 11:25. Therefore dismiss your own opinions and feelings, and think of the scriptures as the loftiest and noblest of holy things, as the richest of mines which can never be sufficiently explored, in order that you may find that divine wisdom which God here lays before you in such simple guise as to quench all pride.[17]

The Victorian preacher Charles Haddon Spurgeon spoke similarly:

> Why, this Book has wrestled with me; the Book has smitten me; the Book has comforted me; the Book has smiled on me; the Book has frowned on me; the Book has clasped my hand; the Book has warmed my heart, The Book weeps with me, and sings with me; it whispers to me; and it preaches to me; it maps my way, and holds up my goings; it is the Young Man's Best Companion, and it is still my morning and evening Chaplain.[18]

Spurgeon noted that some people spend a lot of time defending the Bible, which is a right thing to do, but if more strength were spent in simple exposition of the Bible and spreading its truth, the Bible would defend itself:

> Suppose a number of persons were to take it into their heads that they had to defend a lion, a full-grown king of beasts! There he is in the cage, and here come all the soldiers of the army to fight for him. Well, I should suggest to them … that they should kindly stand back, and open the door, and let the lion out! I believe that would be the best way of defending him, for he would take care of himself; and the best "apology" for the gospel is to let the gospel out … preach Jesus Christ and him crucified. Let the Lion out and see who will dare to approach him. The Lion of Judah will soon drive away all his adversaries.[19]

This God—his way is perfect; the word of the Lord proves true;
he is a shield for all those who take refuge in him.
—II Samuel 22:31—

OCTOBER 8
RESTORING THE BANISHED

September 11, 1870, Charles Spurgeon, the "prince of preachers" in Victorian England, preached a sermon on II Samuel 14:14, "Neither doth God respect any person; yet doth he devise means, that his banished be not expelled from him." In the sermon, Spurgeon explained how the wandering, wayward soul can be restored, most often by the preaching of the gospel. Even when the gospel is mocked or presented by an unfaithful witness, God can use His Word to bring salvation:

> There have been cases of persons who have heard the gospel ...even by blasphemy and profanity, yet, strange to say it, God's all-conquering grace has made even this to be the way by which his banished ones should be brought back to him. The memorable case of Mr. Thorpe, a noted preacher of the gospel, rises to one's mind here. He was, before his conversion, a member of an infidel club; ... and this sceptical society took the name of the "Hell Fire Club." Amongst their amusements was that of holding imitations of religious services, and exhibiting mimicries of popular ministers. Young Thorpe went to hear Mr. Whitefield [George Whitefield was a dramatic, powerful evangelist of the 18th century], that he might take him off before his profane associates; he heard him so carefully that he caught his tones and manner and somewhat of his doctrines. When the club met to see his caricature of the great preacher, Thorpe opened his Bible that he might take a text to preach from it extempore after the manner of Mr. Whitefield; his eye fell on the passage, "Except ye repent, ye shall all likewise perish." As he spoke upon that text he was carried beyond himself, lost all thought of mockery, spoke as one in earnest, and was the means of his own conversion. He was wont to say in after years, "If ever I was helped of God to preach, it was that very day when I began in sport but ended in earnest." He was carried by the force of truth beyond his own intention, like one who would sport in a river, and is swept away by its current .... the scoffer may be reached by the arrows of truth. Where shots are flying, the most careless may be wounded. God who makes use of his ministers as he wills, can bring his banished home by it. Even a minister's failures may be a part of God's ordained scheme of salvation.[20]

Spurgeon's sermon noted other means God uses other means God uses to bring the "banished" to Himself: reading words of Scripture, reading Christian books, casual remarks of earnest Christians, sickness and suffering: "Songs eternal shall celebrate the wisdom of God which achieved his purposes of love."

It is good for me that I was afflicted,
that I might learn your statutes.
—Psalm 119:71—

OCTOBER 9
MY MOTHER'S BIBLE

A Bible which belonged to a loved one often becomes a precious item after the loved one has died. The worn pages, underlinings or notes attest to a soul intimately reading the Word of God and communing with its Giver. George Pope Morris (1802-1864), a poet and journalist most known for his poem "Woodman, Spare that Tree," captured some of that in his poem "My Mother's Bible":

This Book is all that's left me now, —
    Tears will unbidden start, —
With faltering lip, and throbbing brow
    I press it to my heart.
For many generations past
    Here is our family tree;
My mother's hands this Bible clasped,
    She, dying, gave it me.

Ah! Well do I remember those
    Whose names these records bear;
Who round the hearthstone used to
    close,
    After the evening prayer,
And speak of what these pages said
    In tones my heart would thrill;
Though they are with the silent dead,
    Here are they living still!

My father read this Holy Book
    To brothers, sisters dear;
How calm was my poor mother's look,
    Who loved God's Word to hear!
Her angel face, —I see it yet!
    What thronging memories come!
Again that little group is met
    Within the halls of home.

Thou truest friend man ever knew,
    Thy constancy I've tried;
When all were false, I found thee true,
    My Counsellor and guide.
The mines of earth no treasure give
    That could this Volume buy;
In teaching me the way to live,
    It taught me how to die![21]

The Lord is my portion;
I promise to keep your words.
—Psalm 119:57—

THE ABIDING WORD

Sir Henry Williams Baler (1821-1877), Vicar of Monkland, was among the nineteenth century writer of popular hymns. Among his most beautiful was his poetic arrangement of Psalm 23:

The king of love my shepherd is,
whose goodness faileth never.
I nothing lack if I am his,
and he is mine forever.

Where streams of living water flow,
my ransomed soul he leadeth;
And where the verdant pastures
grow, with food celestial feedeth.

Perverse and foolish, oft I strayed,
but yet in love he sought me;
And on his shoulder gently laid,
and home, rejoicing, brought me.

In death's dark vale I fear no ill,
with thee, dear Lord, beside me;
Thy rod and staff my comfort still,
thy cross before to guide me.

Thou spreadest a table in my sight;
thy unction grace bestoweth;
And oh, what transport of delight
from thy pure chalice floweth!

And so through all the length of days,
thy goodness faileth never;
Good Shepherd, may I sing thy praise
within thy house forever.[22]

Over thirty of Baker's hymns appeared in *Hymns Ancient and Modern*. His "Lord, Thy Word abideth" beautifully speaks of the light and guidance the Word of God brings, the cheerful consolation in times of darkness, the help in living and strength in dying, all because the Word brings us near to the Lord:

Lord, Thy Word abideth,
And our footsteps guideth;
Who its truth believeth
Light and joy receiveth.

When our foes are near us,
Then Thy Word doth cheer us,
Word of consolation,
Message of salvation.

When the storms are o'er us.
And dark clouds before us,
Then its light directeth,
And our way protecteth.

Who can tell the pleasure,
Who recount the treasure,
By Thy Word imparted
To the simple-hearted?

Word of mercy, giving
Succour to the living;
Word of life, supplying
Comfort to the dying!

Oh, that we discerning
Its most holy learning,
LORD, may love and fear Thee,
Evermore be near Thee! Amen.[23]

I call to you; save me, that I may observe your testimonies.
—Psalm 119:146—

OCTOBER 11
A UNIQUE AMERICAN MUSICAL FORM

The spirituals of the African-American slaves are a unique American contribution to the world's musical culture. Africans brought to America as slaves for the first time encountered Christianity and learned something of the Bible. The Bible's history of Israel's deliverance from bondage in Egypt especially appealed to the slaves' longing for freedom and liberation. Other stories and Scriptures spoke of the new life and future which Christianity promised. The slaves wrote songs from the Biblical narratives which included features from their African roots, especially a call and response style and syncopation. These songs came to be called "spirituals" from the term "spiritual songs" used in Ephesians 5:19, "Speaking to yourselves in psalms and hymns and spiritual songs, singing and making melody in your heart to the Lord."

In the 1870s, a group of African American singers from Fisk University, known as the Jubilee Singers, brought the spirituals to a wider audience. The spiritual "Go Down, Moses" tells of Israel's deliverance from Egypt and the spiritual deliverance brought by Christ, while also reflecting the longing for freedom among the American slaves:

When Israel was in Egypt's land,
    Let my people go,
    oppressed so hard they
    could not stand,
    Let my people go.

Refrain:
    Go down, Moses,
    way down in Egypt's land,
    tell old Pharaoh:
    Let my people go.

2 The Lord told Moses what to do,
    Let my people go,
    to lead the Hebrew children
    through,
    Let my people go. [Refrain]

3 As Israel stood by the waterside,
    Let my people go,
    at God's command it did
    divide,
    Let my people go. [Refrain]

4 When they had reached the
    other shore,
    Let my people go,
    they let the song of triumph
    soar,
    Let my people go. [Refrain]

5 Lord, help us all from bondage flee,
    Let my people go,
    and let us all in Christ be free,
    Let my people go. [Refrain][24]

Now these things happened to them as an example, but they were written down for our instruction, on whom the end of the ages has come.
—I Corinthians 10:11—

BRINGING THE BIBLE TO KOREA

Robert Jermain Thomas (1839-1866) had a passion for others to come to know Jesus Christ, and in 1863 went to China as a missionary with the London Missionary Society. In 1865, he met two Koreans who were members of the Catholic Church, who had sent missionaries to Korea in the 1700s. Learning that these Koreans had never even seen a Bible, Thomas longed to bring the Scriptures to the Korean people. Since Koreans could read Chinese characters and the Chinese Scriptures, Thomas planned to visit Korea with Bibles to distribute. Korea, however, was known as the Hermit Kingdom since it cut itself off from the world and forbade all foreigners from entering. The government saw all missionary work as trying to establish foreign control in the kingdom. Such opposition did not deter Thomas. He was able to secure a vessel and reach some islands on the west coast of Korea, but then returned to China. In 1866, Thomas became a translator on the merchant ship *The General Sherman,* which planned a trip to Korea to try and open the country for trade. As *The General Sherman* sailed up the Tai Tong River towards Pyengyang, it stopped along the way at several places. At each stop, Thomas gave out Bibles or left copies along the banks. When near Pyengyang, the Koreans set boats on fire in the river to head towards *The General Sherman.* The ship caught fire, and the crew and all on board plunged into the river to escape; the Koreans were waiting on shore with swords and pistols and killed them all. Thomas came to shore with his arms full of Bibles, which he thrust into the hands of the Koreans as he was clubbed to death. Some became Christians from reading these Scriptures. One person used the pages of the Bibles as wall paper! People later came to the home to read the Scriptures, and some of these also became Christians.

Today, Bibles are again restricted in North Korea, which continues to be a hermit kingdom, and Bibles are smuggled into North Korea with balloons!

Is not my word like fire, declares the Lord,
and like a hammer that breaks the rock in pieces?
— Jeremiah 23:29—

OCTOBER 13
OUR GREAT HERITAGE

By the nineteenth century, rationalism had penetrated the Lutheran church in Denmark, and few pastors remained faithful to their biblical faith. While Nikolai Grundtvig's (1783-1872) father was one of the few pastors true to his Christian faith, Nikolai himself was influenced by the "New Theology" when he attended the University of Copenhagen and lost any interest in Christianity. He became more interested in poetry and Norse mythology, publishing *Mythology of the North* in 1808. However, when Nikolai's father became ill, he asked Nikolai to come and be his pastoral assistant. By then, Nikolai saw that the decline in morality and spiritual indifference among the people was due to the declining influence of the Scriptures. His probation sermon on "Why has the Lord's Word disappeared from His House?" criticized the rationalism which prevailed among the Danish pastors. The ecclesiastical authorities were not pleased with Nikolai's sermon and withheld ordination from him for a time.

Nikolai wrote numerous works on Norse folklore and Anglo-Saxon literature as well as several histories on changing views of God in human history. Active in politics, Nikolai was influential in establishing free public high schools and in introducing parliamentary government in Denmark. Nikolai's influence continues in the thousands of hymns he wrote, many of which emphasized the Word of God as the rule and guide for the Christian. Among his most popular hymns is "God's Word is Our Great Heritage":

> God's Word is our great heritage
> And shall be ours forever;
> To spread its light from age to age
> Shall be our chief endeavor.
> Through life it guides our way,
> In death it is our stay.
> Lord, grant, while worlds endure,
> We keep its teachings pure.
> Throughout all generations.[25]

Now those who were scattered went about preaching the word.
—Acts 8:4—

BENEATH THE CROSS OF JESUS

When "Beneath the Cross of Jesus" was published in *The Family Treasury* in 1872, editor William Arnot introduced the hymn with these words:

> These lines express the experiences, the hopes, and the longings of a young Christian lately released. Written on the very edge of this life, with the better land fully in the view of faith, they seem to us footsteps printed on the sands of Time, where these sands touch the ocean of eternity. These footprints of one whom the Good Shepherd led through the wilderness into rest may, with God's blessing, contribute comfort and direct succeeding pilgrims.[26]

Elizabeth Clephane (1830-1869) wrote the hymn a year before her death at the age of thirty-nine. Though suffering ill health most of her life, Elizabeth regularly visited the sick and dying, bringing them the joy and comfort of Christ through the Scriptures. Elizabeth's deep love of the Scriptures is evident from the numerous Biblical references and allusions in the hymn:

Beneath the cross of Jesus I fain would take my stand,	*Isaiah 32:2*
The shadow of a mighty rock within a weary land;	*Psalm 63:1*
A home within the wilderness, a rest upon the way	*Jeremiah 9:2; Isa. 28:12*
From the burning of the noon day heat and the burden of the day.	*Isa. 4:6; Matt. 11:30*
O safe and happy shelter! O refuge tried and sweet!	*Isa. 4:6*
O trysting place where Heaven's love and Heaven's justice meet!	*Psalm 85:10*
As to the exiled patriarch that wondrous dream was given,	*Genesis 28:10ff.*
So seems my Savior's cross to me—a ladder up to heaven!	*John 3:51*

There lies beneath its shadow, but on the further side,	*Psalm 36:7*
The darkness of an open grave, that gapes both deep and wide;	
And there between us, stands the cross, two arms outstretched to save,	*Ex. 6:6*
Like a watchman set to guard the way from that eternal grave.	

Upon that cross of Jesus mine eye at times can see
The very dying form of One who suffered there for me;
and from my smitten heart with tears two wonders I confess—
The wonders of redeeming love, and my own worthlessness.

He remembers his covenant forever,
the word that he commanded, for a thousand generations.
—Psalm 105:8—

OCTOBER 15
IT IS WELL WITH MY SOUL

"Saved alone" were the heart-wrenching words which began Anna Spafford's telegram to her husband Horatio. Horatio, a prominent Chicago lawyer and friend of Dwight L. Moody, had lost sizeable investments in the Chicago fire of 1871. The Spaffords' four-year-old son then died of scarlet fever. By 1873, Horatio decided the family needed a holiday and arranged for a trip to England, where Moody would be preaching. He sent his wife and four daughters ahead while he wrapped up business, but as the family crossed the Atlantic, the steamship was struck by an iron sailing ship, and 226 people drowned. Anna Spafford survived, but not their four daughters. Later, crossing the Atlantic to meet his wife, Horatio wrote a beautiful hymn as he was over the Atlantic where the ship went down. Several Scripture passages are reflected in the hymn:

When peace, like a river, attendeth my way,	*Isaiah 48:18*
When sorrows like sea billows roll;	
Whatever my lot, Thou has taught me to say,	
It is well, it is well with my soul.	
Though Satan should buffet, though trials should come,	*II Corinthians 12:7*
Let this blest assurance control,	
That Christ hath regarded my helpless estate,	
And hath shed His own blood for my soul.	*Mark 14:24*
My sin, oh the bliss of this glorious thought!	
My sin, not in part but the whole,	
Is nailed to His cross, and I bear it no more,	*Colossians 2:4*
Praise the Lord, praise the Lord, O my soul!	
And Lord haste the day, when the faith shall be sight,	*II Corinthians 5:7*
The clouds be rolled back as a scroll;	*Isaiah 34:4*
The trump shall resound, and the Lord shall descend,	*I Thessalonians 4:15-18*
Even so, it is well with my soul.	

Horatio and Anna went on to have three more children. In 1881 they moved to Jerusalem where they were engaged in philanthropic work among the people.

Trouble and anguish have found me out,
but your commandments are my delight.
— Psalm 119:143—

BLESSED BIBLE!

When she was eleven, Phoebe Palmer (1807-1874) composed and wrote a poem inside a New Testament presented to her:

> This Revelation—holy, just, and true—
> Though oft I read, it seems forever new;
> While light from heaven upon its pages rest,
> I feel its power, and with it I am blest.
> Within its leaves it grace divine displays,
> Makes known the Almighty's will in various ways;
> Justice it speaks to those who heaven defy,
> And with ungracious lips its truths deny.
>
> 'Tis here the wearied one, in sin's rough road,
> May find the path mark'd out that leads to God;
> And when oppressed by earth, *all* here may find
> Sweet promises of peace to cheer the mind.
>
> To this blest treasure, O my soul, attend,
> Here find a firm and everlasting friend—
> A friend in all life's various changes sure,
> Which shall to all eternity endure.
>
> Henceforth I take thee as my future guide.
> Let naught from thee my youthful heart divide;
> And then, if late or early death be mine,
> All will be well, since I, O Lord, am Thine.[27]

Years later, Phoebe wrote another poem about the Bible which her daughter, Phoebe Knapp, put to music. Here is part of it:

> Yes, sweet Bible! I will hide thee
>   *Deep*, yes, *deeper* in this heart;
> Thou, through all my life will
>   guide me,
>   And in death we will not part.
> Part in death? No! never! Never!
>
> Through death's vale I'll lean
>   on thee;
> Then, in worlds above, forever,
>   Sweeter still thy truths shall be![28]

In your steadfast love give me life, that I may keep the testimonies of your mouth.
—Psalm 119:88—

OCTOBER 17
HISTORICAL CORROBORATION OF THE BIBLE

The Bible is a book of history, telling the story of God's providential working in the affairs of men for His glory. Though some have asserted the Old Testament stories are simply legends, archaeology repeatedly brings to light artifacts which in some way confirm the biblical narrative. The Moabite stone, Merneptah Stele, Tel Dan Stele and Black Obelisk of Shalmaneser are four examples.

Sir Henry Layard discovered the Black Obelisk of Shalmaneser III in Iraq in 1846. The obelisk includes both an inscription and a carving, showing Israel's King Jehu (II Kings 10) bowed down to the ground in front of the Assyrian King Shalmaneser, as 13 Israelites bring tribute of gold and silver. The obelisk provides the only known likeness of an Israelite king.

In 1868 an inscribed stone was found in Jordan which seems to refer to an event in II Kings 3:4-8, around 840 B.C., when Moab revolted against Israel's rule. Israel under King Jehoram was able to defeat the Moabite army, but unable to capture the capital. The Moabite Stone mentions specific cities referenced in the Bible and contains the earliest known inscription mentioning a king of Judah or Israel, Omri. The Moabite Stone also contains the earliest reference outside the Bible to Yahweh, Israel's God.

The Merneptah Stele, discovered in Egypt in 1896 and dating from around 1210 B.C., contains the earliest extra-biblical record of Israel. The inscription lists city-states and nations defeated by Pharoah Merneptah. That Israel was included in the list, indicates that Israel had well established settlements in the land of Canaan by the 13th century B.C.

Fragments of a stele found at Tel Dan, in northern Israel, were discovered in 1993-94. The Aramaic inscription commemorates Hazael's defeat of Kings Joram and Ahaziah at Ramoth Gilead, described in II Kings 8:28-29. The inscription, dating from around 841 B.C., is the earliest extra-biblical reference to the House of David. Before the discovery of the Tel Dan Stele, some had contended David was a legendary figure and that there had not been a united kingdom under David and Solomon. Archaeology attests to the truthfulness of the biblical record.

The Lord has done what he purposed;
he has carried out his word,
which he commanded long ago ...
—Lamentations 2:17—

MATTHEW FONTAINE MAURY:
PATHFINDER OF THE SEAS

Matthew Maury (1806-1873) was the first to extensively study ocean and wind currents, publishing his findings in *The Physical Geography of the Sea* in 1855. In 1825, Maury had obtained an appointment to the navy through the influence of family friend Sam Houston, then a Tennessee Representative. His first voyage, aboard the *Brandywine*, carried the Marquis de La Fayette back to France after his visit to the United States. On that voyage, midshipman Maury began studying the seas and recording navigation methods. He continued his studies in future voyages and developed international contacts to further spread an understanding of the ocean and wind currents vital for shipping. He was encouraged in his study by Psalm 8:8-9, which spoke of "The fowl of the air, and the fish of the sea, and whatsoever passeth through the paths of the seas. O LORD, our Lord, how excellent is thy name in all the earth!" Maury had been raised in a Christian home. Daily, morning and evening, the family gathered to read the Psalter for the day. Maury came to know the Psalms so well he could cite a quotation by chapter and verse.

In 1855, Maury wrote a letter in which he expressed some of his views on the "harmony of science and revelation." Isaiah 44:2 speaks of "the circle of the earth" before most people accepted that the earth was a round globe. Job 26:7, "He stretches out the north over empty space And hangs the earth on nothing," implies gravity important in the position of the earth. Job 28:25, "To make the weight for the winds; and he weigheth the waters by measure," shows an understanding of air pressure. Ecclesiastes 1:7, "All the rivers run into the sea; yet the sea is not full; unto the place from whence the rivers come, thither they return again," shows an awareness of the circulation of the atmosphere. Maury wrote of

> … a rule of conduct which I have adopted in order to make progress with these physical researches …. The rule is, never to forget who is the Author of the great volume which Nature spreads out before us, and always to remember that the same Being is the Author of the book which revelation holds up to us, and though the two works are entirely different, their records are equally true, and when they bear upon the same point, as now and then they do, it is as impossible that they should contradict each other as it is that either should contradict itself. If the two cannot be reconciled, the fault is ours, and is because, in our blindness and weakness, we have not been able to interpret aright either the one or the other, or both.[29]

Your promise is well tried, and your servant loves it..
—Psalm 119:140—

OCTOBER 19
LIKE A RIVER GLORIOUS

Victorian preacher Charles Haddon Spurgeon said Frances Havergal (1836-1879) sang like an angel. Though trained as a concert artist, she rejected worldly fame and chose to serve her savior. She loved the Scriptures, and by the time she was twenty-two had memorized the Gospels, Epistles, Revelation, Psalms, and Isaiah. Her rich knowledge of the Scripture is reflected in many of her poems and hymns.

In 1876, Frances suffered from typhoid fever, and her lungs became greatly inflamed. Though death seemed imminent, Frances had perfect peace, knowing that her death would only bring her into the glorious presence of her Savior. When she recovered from her illness, Frances wrote a beautiful hymn reflecting on God's perfect peace:

> Like a river glorious is God's perfect peace,
> Over all victorious in its bright increase;
> Perfect, yet it floweth, fuller ev'ry day;
> Perfect, yet it growth deeper all the way.
> > Stayed upon Jehovah,
> > Hearts are fully blest—
> > Finding as He promised,
> > Perfect peace and rest.

Two Scriptures especially were behind Frances' words. In Isaiah 40:18, God said, "Oh that you had paid attention to my commandments! Then your peace would have been like a river, and your righteousness like the waves of the sea." Isaiah 26:3 is reflected in the chorus: "You keep him in perfect peace whose mind is stayed on you, because he trusts in you."

Bless the Lord, O you his angels,
you mighty ones who do his word,
obeying the voice of his word!
— Psalm 103:20—

THE MOST VALUABLE PURCHASE

John Wanamaker (1838- 1922) was a most successful businessman who transformed marketing and sales techniques in America. He began his business by founding Oak Hill, a men's clothing store, in Philadelphia. In 1876, he purchased the abandoned Pennsylvania railroad station and transformed it into one of the country's first department stores. Before the store opened, Wanamaker allowed evangelist Dwight L. Moody to use the Depot for his meetings. The refurbished Grand Depot included men's and women's clothing as well as dry goods, and Wanamaker introduced many innovations. Price tags were placed on all items, and printed advertisements guaranteed the quality of merchandise, which could be returned for a cash refund. Wanamaker's store was also the first to have electric lights and a telephone. Wanamaker treated his employees with respect and provided free medical care, pensions, and profit-sharing plans before this became a corporate practice.

In 1889, Wannamaker began a Penny Savings Bank to encourage thrift and was appointed U.S. Postmaster General by President Benjamin Harrison. In this position he laid plans for a free rural postal service and introduced the first commemorative stamp.

In remarks made to the Pocket Testament League, Wanamaker noted that as Postmaster-General, he had made contracts involving millions of dollars, arranging for mail to foreign countries to be carried in four ships built in Cramp's Shipyard in Philadelphia. In his own business, he had made purchases of buildings and grounds worth millions of dollars. Yet, he noted that the most important purchase he ever made was when he was twelve years old. He then purchased a little red leather Bible, about eight inches long and six inches wide, from his Sunday School teacher, for $2.75. Looking back over his life, he said that this book was the foundation of all he later did in life. This was the most important investment he ever made; all other purchases were secondary.[30]

Blessed be the Lord who has given rest to his people Israel,
according to all that he promised. Not one word has failed of all his
good promise, which he spoke by Moses his servant.
—I Kings 8:56—

OCTOBER 21
HOW TO READ THE BIBLE

The religious leaders of Jesus' day were meticulous readers of Scripture. They could tell you what the middle verse of the Scripture was and how many times each letter or word occurred. Yet, Jesus challenged them "Have you not read?… Have you not read?" (Matt. 12:3-7). In 1879, Charles Spurgeon preached a sermon on this very topic of how to read the Scriptures. He first emphasized that the Scriptures must be read with understanding, not simply counting the letters in a text:

> … when we come to the study of Holy Scripture *we should try to have our mind well awake to it* …. As you ask a blessing over your meat before you fall to it, so it would be a good rule for you to ask a blessing on the word before you partake of its heavenly food. Pray the Lord to strengthen your eyes before you dare to look into the eternal light of Scripture. As the priests washed their feet at the laver before they went to their holy work so it were well to wash the soul's eyes with which you look upon God's word, to wash even the fingers, if I may so speak the mental fingers with which you will turn from page to page—that with a holy book you may deal after a holy fashion. Say to your soul—"Come, soul, wake up; thou are not now about to read the newspaper thou are not now perusing the pages of a human poet to be dazzled by his flashing poetry; thou art coming very near to God, who sits in the Word like a crowned monarch in his halls. Wake up, my glory; wake up, all that is within me" … Scripture reading is our spiritual meal time. Sound the gong and call in every faculty to the Lord's own table to feast upon the precious meat which is now to be partaken of …

To read with understanding, you will need to *meditate* on the Scripture, thinking closely upon its spiritual truths. The Scripture should be read with *prayer*, looking to the author of the book to learn its true meaning:

> The Holy Spirit is with us, and when we take his book and begin to read, and want to know what it means, we must ask the Holy Spirit to reveal the meaning … he will elevate our minds, and he will suggest to us thoughts which will lead us on by their natural relation, the one to the other, till at last we come to the pith and marrow of his divine instruction. Seek then very earnestly the guidance of the Holy Spirit, for if the very soul of reading be the understanding of what we read, then we must in prayer call upon the Holy Ghost to unlock the secret mysteries of the inspired word. [31]

I incline my heart to perform your statutes forever, to the end.
—Psalm 119:112—

THE NAMING OF IVORY SOAP

William Proctor was a candlemaker from England; James Gamble was a soapmaker from Ireland. Both immigrated to the United States and settled in Cincinnati. They first met when they married sisters, Olivia and Elizabeth Norris. The girls' father encouraged his new sons-in-law to form a partnership, and thus Proctor & Gamble was born in 1837. The two families worked together for three generations, the Gambles running the production side of the company and the Proctors running the store or the office.

During the Civil War, P&G began making soap for the Union army. The soap was yellow, as was all soap made from household cooking fats, but after the war, P&G began experiments to see if they could make a white soap. Castile soap, made from olive oil, was white, but it was very expensive. By 1878, son James Gamble had developed a white soap, and "P&G Soap" made its debut.

The following year, Harley Proctor was sitting in the Church of Our Savior in Cincinnati one Sunday morning. The reading was from Psalm 45. When Proctor heard the words of verse 8, "All thy garments smell of myrrh and aloes and cassia out of ivory palaces whereby they have made me glad," the word "ivory" kept resonating through his mind. That was it—Ivory Soap! The following week, the name of the soap was changed. Ivory was registered as a trademark on July 18, 1879 and remains an important P&G product today.

John Wesley in 1778 was the first to use the phrase "cleanliness is next to godliness" which remained popular in the nineteenth century, The first ads for Ivory soap appeared in an 1882 edition of The Independent, a Christian weekly. There Harley Proctor stated, "Americans are the apostles of cleanliness ... and we continue in our belief that cleanliness is akin to godliness. Wherever there is stainless white cleanliness, there you may find Ivory soap.

Incline my heart to your testimonies, and not to selfish gain!
—Psalm 119:36—

OCTOBER 23
COMMUNION WITH CHRIST IN HIS WORD

Born in Switzerland, educated in Germany, and teaching in the United States, Philip Schaff (1819-1893) had a masterful grasp of the history of the Christian church and its theology, reflected in his seven-volume *History of the Christian Church* still studied today. Schaff wrote the importance of the Bible to the Church:

> The Bible occupies a conspicuous isolation among books, and is more indispensable to the moral welfare of mankind than all the libraries of genius and learning. It is not a book simply, but an institution...an all-pervading and perennial force in the Church; it is the voice of the living God; it is the message of Christ, whose divine-human nature it reflects; it is the chief agency of the Holy Spirit in illuminating, converting, warning, and cheering men. It rules from the pulpit, it presides at the family altar, it touches human life at every point from the cradle to the grave, and guides the soul on its lonely journey to the unseen world. It has molded the languages, laws, habits, and home-life of the nations of Europe, and inspired the noblest works of literature and art. The Bible retains with advancing age, the dew and freshness of youth, and readapts itself in ever improving versions to every age in every civilized land. It is now more extensively studied than ever before, and it will be the standard-bearer of true progress in all times to come.

Though in the early centuries of the church the Bible was swiftly translated into the language of the people—Greek, Syriac, Coptic, Latin, Gothic and others, during the Middle Ages the Church authorities withheld the Bible from the people. The sixteenth century Reformers again brought the Bible to the people, declaring

> ... the Scriptures to be the supreme and infallible rule of the Christian faith and life, which must guide the individual and the Church at large. They went to the fountainhead of truth and removed the obstructions which prevent a direct access of the believer to the word of God and the grace of Christ. They reconquered the liberty wherewith Christ has made us free ... The Christians of the present age are as near to Christ as the Christians of the first generation. In the Gospels he speaks to us now as he spoke to the Twelve, and in the Acts and Epistles his inspired apostles teach us the same truths with the same authority and force as they did on the day of Pentecost. This unspeakable privilege of direct communion with Christ and his Word can never be wrested from the Christian people. [32]

Hear my voice according to your steadfast love;
O Lord, according to your justice give me life.
—Psalm 119:149—

VALIANT FOR TRUTH

Charles Spurgeon called him "the best man of the age," exceeding all others in "usefulness and influence." Spurgeon said Anthony Ashley Cooper (1801-1885), the seventh Early of Shaftesbury,

> … was a man most true in his personal piety, as I know from having enjoyed his private friendship; a man most firm in his faith in the gospel of our Lord Jesus Christ; a man intensely active in the cause of God and truth … he was admirable: he was faithful to God in all his house, fulfilling both the first and second commands of the law in fervent love to God, and hearty love to man. He occupied his high position with singleness of purpose and immovable steadfastness: where shall we find his equal? … I rejoiced greatly in his integrity, his fearlessness, his adherence to principle, …

Shaftesbury had a difficult childhood, growing up in a rather cold and unloving home. The housekeeper, however, showed him the love of Christ, teaching him Bible stories and how to pray. As a young adult, he had a conversion to Christ after reading Philip Doddridge's *The Rise and Progress of Religion in the Soul* and studying Thomas Scott's Bible commentaries. When elected to Parliament, Shaftesbury worked tirelessly for the betterment of the poor and suffering. He worked for the reform of the lunacy laws and care for the mentally unbalanced and for the reform of child labor and factory laws He worked to outlaw women and children in the coal mines and favored laws prohibiting using boys as chimney sweeps. A diligent student of Scripture, Shaftesbury believed the second coming of Christ was imminent and worked for the restoration of the Jewish people to the Holy Land. He was also a leader in the Ragged School movement, establishing schools for the poor before there were public schools for all.

Shaftesbury was President of the British and Foreign Bible Society from 1851 until his death in 1885. He believed the remedy of people's ills around the globe is the spread of the Scriptures. Preaching Christ is the power of God unto salvation. As Spurgeon said, "in a day when revelation is questioned, the gospel explained away, and human thought set up as the idol of the hour," Shaftesbury "felt that there was a vital and eternal difference between truth and error."[33] Throughout his life, Shaftesbury was Valiant for Truth.

Do your best to present yourself to God as one approved,
a worker who has no need to be ashamed, rightly handling the word of truth.
—II Timothy 2:15—

OCTOBER 25
REASONS FOR SEARCHING THE SCRIPTURES

In his devotional *Morning and Evening*, preacher Charles Spurgeon commented on Jesus' words in John 5:29, "Ye search the Scriptures because you think that in them you have eternal life; and it is they that bear witness about me.:"

The Greek word here rendered *search* signifies a strict, close, diligent, curious search, such as men make when they are seeking gold, or hunters when they are in earnest after game. We must not rest content with having given a superficial reading to a chapter or two, but with the candle of the Spirit we must deliberately seek out the hidden meaning of the word. Holy Scripture *requires searching*—much of it can only be learned by careful study. There is milk for babes, but also meat for strong men. The rabbis wisely say that a mountain of matter hangs upon every word, yea, upon every tittle of Scripture. Tertullian exclaims, "I adore the fullness of the Scriptures." No man who merely skims the book of God can profit thereby; we must dig and mine until we obtain the hid treasure. The door of the word only opens to the key of diligence. The Scriptures *claim searching*. They are the writings of God, bearing the divine stamp and imprimatur—who shall dare to treat them with levity? He who despises them despises the God who wrote them. God forbid that any of us should leave our Bibles to become swift witnesses against us in the great day of account. The word of God *will repay searching*. God does not bid us sift a mountain of chaff with here and there a grain of wheat in it, but the Bible is winnowed corn[34]—we have but to open the granary door and find it. Scripture grows upon the student. It is full of surprises. Under the teaching of the Holy Spirit, to the searching eye it glows with splendor of revelation, like a vast temple paved with wrought gold, and roofed with rubies, emeralds, and all manner of gems. No merchandise is like the merchandise of Scripture truth. Lastly, *the Scriptures reveal Jesus*: "They are they which testify of me." No more powerful motive can be urged upon Bible readers than this: he who finds Jesus finds life, heaven, all things. Happy he who, searching his Bible, discovers his Saviour.[35]

I have seen a limit to all perfection,
but your commandment is exceedingly broad.
—Psalm 119:96—

CHRISTIANITY IN THE FACE OF MODERNISM

By the end of the nineteenth century, the influences of the Enlightenment, Darwinian evolution, and biblical higher criticism had undermined many people's belief in the Bible as a trustworthy historical record and an authoritative revelation of God. One man who mightily fought against these modernist influences was Abraham Kuyper (1837-1920). Kuyper was a man of amazing accomplishments. A pastor in the Netherlands, Kuyper was a noted theologian, but he also became active in the Anti-Revolutionary political party, opposing the ideas of the French Revolution. For over forty-five years he was editor of the major newspapers *De Standard* and *De Heraut*. In 1874, he was elected to Parliament, and he served as prime minister of the Netherlands from 1901 to 1905. In 1880 he founded the Free University of Amsterdam, which "took the Bible as the unconditional basis on which to rear the whole structure of human knowledge in every department of life."[36] In his inaugural address at the dedication of the University, Kuyper asserted that "There is not a square inch in the whole domain of our human existence over which Christ, who is Sovereign over all, does not cry: 'Mine!'"[37]

Kuyper believed that Christianity is a comprehensive worldview which should shape all the institutions and realms of life. He had one ruling passion in all his many endeavors:

> One high motive has acted like a spur upon mind and soul. And sooner than that I should seek escape from the sacred necessity that this is laid upon me, let the breath of life fail me. It is this: That in spite of all worldly opposition, God's holy ordinances shall be established again in the home, in the school and in the State for the good of the people to carve as it were into the conscience of the nation the ordinances of the Lord, to which the Bible and Creation bear witness, until the nation pays homage again to God.[38]

Turn away the reproach that I dread, for your rules are good.
—Psalm 119:39—

OCTOBER 27
A SLIPPERY DOWNHILL SLOPE

In the spring of 1887, Charles Spurgeon's *The Sword and Trowel* began publishing a series of articles warning of the slippery downhill slope many churches seemed to be on, drifting from Scripture and accepting modernist teachings. Truths about the deity of Jesus, the atonement, and the reality of hell were all being modified in various ways. Foundational to the "down-grade" was the attitude to Scripture:

> The first step astray is a want of adequate faith in the divine inspiration of the sacred scriptures. All the while a man bows to the authority of God's Word, he will not entertain any sentiment contrary to the teaching. "To the law and to the testimony" is his appeal concerning every doctrine. He esteems that holy Book, concerning all things, to be right, and therefore he hates every false way. But let a man question or entertain low views of the inspiration and authority of the Bible, and he is without chart to guide him and without anchor to hold him.

> In looking carefully over the history of the times, and the movement of the times … this fact is apparent: that where ministers and Christian churches have held fast to the truth that the Holy scriptures have been given by God as an authoritative and infallible rule of faith and practice, they have never wandered very seriously out of the right way. But, when, on the other hand, reason has been exalted above revelation, and made the exponent of revelation, all kinds of errors and mischiefs have been the result.[39]

In sounding the alarm to the growing accommodations with modernism in the churches, Spurgeon became the first to stand for biblical evangelical Christianity against the growing tide of liberalism. In the August issue of *The Sword and Trowel*, Spurgeon wrote,

> A new religion has been initiated, which is no more Christianity than chalk is cheese; and this religion, being destitute of moral honesty, palms itself off as the old faith with slight improvements, and on this plea usurps pulpits which were erected for gospel preaching.[40]

The church was being turned into a place for amusements. Churches were no longer having prayer meetings, and "God is being robbed of his glory, and many of his hope."

In spite of his great reputation, Spurgeon was severely criticized for raising the alarm in "The Down-Grade Controversy." His own health suffered under the strain of the debate, and many saw the controversy as contributing to his own early death. Yet throughout, Surgeon remained "Valiant for Truth," never wavering in his confidence in the truth and authority of Scripture.

I know, O Lord, that your rules are righteous,
and that in faithfulness you have afflicted me.
—Psalm 119:75—

OCTOBER 28
THE IMPREGNABLE ROCK OF SCRIPTURE

One of Britain's greatest leaders was William Ewart Gladstone (1809-1898). For over sixty years Gladstone was an important figure in British government, beginning with his first entering the House of Commons in 1832, then going on to serve many years as Chancellor of the Exchequer and twelve years as Prime Minister. Gladstone was raised in a family with strong evangelical beliefs, and he maintained his strong Christian faith throughout his life. In an age when historical and biblical criticism spawned a skepticism to the Bible's truthfulness, Gladstone retained a belief in the Bible's authority.

In 1890, Gladstone published *The Impregnable Rock of Holy Scripture* on the trustworthiness of Scripture. As the tide of historical criticism was coming in and its waves were beating against the Scripture, Gladstone says the Scripture is an impregnable rock which will stand against the attacks. Gladstone thought that even the recent attacks on the Scriptures were in God's Providence. The attacks helped dispel the lethargy of believers and motivated them to look at their faith, ejecting any human elements that had weakened the truth of Scripture. Gladstone examined the creation, the historicity of the Old Testament, and the nature of the Mosaic legislation. Perhaps his most powerful section is on the Psalms. With a thorough grounding in Homeric studies and the Greek and Roman classics, Gladstone noted the special uniqueness of the Psalms. There is a communion with God not found in any pagan prayers; the intercessory prayers found in the Psalms are unknown in other ancient writings. The affections which were alienated by sin are again aligned with God, and God's Word is the joy of the Psalmist, who desires God to be glorified on earth. The glory of God is of highest interest to the Psalmist.

With my whole heart I cry;
answer me, O Lord! I will keep your statutes.
—Psalm 119:145—

GEORGE MÜLLER ON THE SCRIPTURES

George Müller's life spanned almost the entire 19ᵗʰ century (1805-1898), and his influence continues into the 21ˢᵗ century. Müller's youth in Prussia was wayward. George's father was a tax collector, and even as early as 10, George was stealing money from his government funds. He became known for lying, drinking and careless living. When he was 20, someone invited him to attend a prayer meeting in a private home. Müller had never heard the Gospel and did not have a Bible, but that evening, a chapter of the Bible and a printed sermon were read. As he kept attending the prayer meetings, God's grace moved his heart. His life was transformed by the precious truth that "God so loved the world, that He gave His only begotten Son, that whosoever believeth in Him should not perish, but have everlasting life."

Müller came to realize the importance of the Scriptures for growth in the Christian life. He read the Bible though at least four times a year, so that eventually reading it through well over 100 times. In 1834 Müller founded the Scriptural Knowledge Institution for Home and Abroad (SKI), with the 3-fold purpose: "Support missionaries at home and abroad; provide a source of cheap Bibles and tracts; open and support Day- and Sunday-Schools for adults and children."[41] By the time of his death, SKI was supporting five orphanages in Bristol and had distributed 285,407 Bibles, 459,506 New Testaments and thousands of religious tracts in twenty languages.[42]

Müller encouraged systematic reading of all the Scriptures, so that we can discern the connectedness of God's Word. He taught the Scriptures should be read prayerfully, seeking the Holy Spirit's illumination as we read. We should also meditate on the Word, pondering its meaning, especially how it refers to our own heart: "If you merely read the Bible, and no more, it is just like water running in at one side and out at the other." Scripture reading should be mixed with faith, as the "revealed will of the Lord." Finally, Müller stressed the importance of being obedient to the Scriptures. "Accept the Word as His will and carry it into practice ... The Lord Jesus Christ says: 'If ye know these things, happy are ye *if ye do them.*'"[43]

You have commanded your precepts to be kept diligently.
—Psalm 119:4—

OCTOBER 30
LEANING ON THE WORD

In all of his charitable works and in the administration of his numerous orphanages and schools, George Müller made it a practice never to ask or advertise for donations, but always to seek the Lord in prayer for the provisions needed. When wrestling with the idea of starting an orphanage when he didn't have the funds, Müller was encouraged by reading Psalm 81:10, "Open thy mouth wide, and I will fill it." With the faith in that promise, Müller prayed for God to supply the funds for an orphanage. Within two days, gifts began arriving to begin this great orphanage work.

On several occasions, there was no food in the orphanage, but the Lord provided at just the right time. One morning, there was no food for breakfast. Yet, Müller and his wife sat the orphans down to eat and thanked the Lord for His provision for them. At that moment, a baker came to the door with bread enough to satisfy all. Shortly after, a milkman came to the door whose cart had broken down in front of the orphanage; he brought all the milk for the orphans. When confronted with so many mouths to feed, Müller regularly had faith that the Lord would provide and quoted Matthew 6:31,33, "Do not worry then, saying, 'What shall we eat?' or 'What will we drink?' or 'What will we wear for clothing?'... But seek first His kingdom and His righteousness, and all these things will be added to you."

His soul saturated with the Scripture from his frequent reading and prayerful meditation on the Word, Müller was strengthened by the Scriptures in all of life's circumstances. When his wife lay dying, he read her Psalm 84:11, "For the Lord God is a sun and shield; the Lord bestows favor and honor. No good thing does he withhold from those who walk uprightly." At his wife's funeral, Müller preached from Psalm 119:68, "You are good and do good ...." He was personally comforted that his wife was free of suffering and rejoiced in her happiness in the presence of the Lord.

O know, O Lord, that Your judgments are righteous,
and that in faithfulness You have afflicted me.
—Psalm 119:75—

OCTOBER 31
THE BOOK FOR MAN

The Bible's influence can be seen in literature and art, as well as the human heart. The 19th century pastor Dr. K.B. Tupper summarized this influence:

> Wonderfully is the Bible the book of God, and therefore gloriously is it the book for man, when man would rise to loftiest conceptions and grandest achievements. … Shakespeare … often goes to the shepherds and fishermen of the Bible for poetic inspiration. … [In his works are] no fewer than 550 quotations from, and references to, God's Word. Turn to Richard II, and you will find 40; to Richard III and you will find 49; to Hamlet and you will find 80. Sixty-six books there are in this divine library and Shakespeare quotes from fifty-four of them. No one of his fifty-four plays is without a Scriptural quotation, reference, or allusion. Nor is Shakespeare alone. The finest productions in literature, as in art, have caught their inspiration from the Bible: Milton's *Paradise Lost* and *Samson Agonistes*, Scott's *Rebekah*, Bunyan's *Progress*, Tasso's *Jerusalem*, the choices parts of Cowper's *Task* and Wordsworth's *Excursion*, Byron's *Hebrew Melodies*, and Burns' *Cotter's Saturday Night*. No wonder John Quincy Adams could exclaim, "In whatever light you view the Bible—whether with reference to revelation or history or morality—it is a mine of knowledge like which none other has ever been found in any land or any age." And why? Because God-breathed, it has an inspiration and doctrine surpassing all of man's creations, both in kind and degree. It came into the life of John Seldon, the learned lawyer, and made him say, "I have surveyed most of the world's learning, yet I can recall nothing in which to rest my soul but the Scriptures." It so comforted the historian, Hallam, that he could exclaim, "It fits every fold and crevice of the human heart." It so permeated the heart of the dramatist and novelist Charles Read, that it led him, before his death, to compose his own epitaph, thus, "I hope for holiness and happiness in a future life, not because of anything that I have said or done, but because of the merits and mediation of Jesus Christ, my Lord, for the propitiation of my sins." Yes, just here we find the strongest proof that the Word is from God, its perfect universal … adaptedness to all human conditions, answering man's deepest questions, enlightening his darkest hours, solving his hardest questions, and thrilling his soul with an ecstatic joy. "A personal experience of fifty years," recently wrote an ex-president of Harvard College, "gives me an absolute knowledge of the saving, uplifting power of Jesus. His word has a power to rebuke, to cleanse, to uphold, to comfort me, incomparably greater than that of any other word that has ever reached me." Ah! On this very ground we rejoice today in the inspiration and perpetuity of the Sacred Word.[44]

But be doers of the word, and not hearers only, deceiving yourselves.
—James 1:22—

NOVEMBER 1
'TIS GOD'S OWN WORD

Baptist minister Henry John Betts (1825-1898) was the son of a Baptist minister and pastored churches in London, Edinburgh, Bradford, Manchester, and Newcastle-upon-Tyne. He published a collection of hymns and poems as well as two volumes of sermons on Scripture localities. For several years Betts edited the *Primitive Church Magazine.* Among his hymns is the following hymn on the Bible:

> There is a lamp whose steady light
> Guides the poor traveler in the night:—
> 'Tis God's own word! Its beaming ray
> Can turn a midnight into day.
>
> There is a storehouse of rich fare,
> Supplied with plenty and to spare:—
> 'Tis God's own word! It spreads a feast
> For every hungering, thirsting guest.
>
> There is a chart whose tracings show
> The onward course when tempests blow:—
> 'Tis God's own word! There, there is found
> Direction for the homeward bound.
>
> There is a tree whose leaves impart
> Health to the burdened, contrite heart:—
> 'Tis God's own word! It cures of sin,
> And makes the guilty conscience clean.
>
> Give me this lamp to light my road;
> This storehouse for my daily food;
> Give me this chart for life's rough sea;
> These healing leaves, this heavenly tree.[1]

Oh that my ways may be steadfast in keeping your statutes!
—Psalm 119:5—

NOVEMBER 2

WISER THAN PLATO, SOCRATES, AND THE GREEK PHILOSOPHERS

When Paul went to Athens and spoke to the philosophers on the Areopagus, he clearly presented to them the glorious Gospel of Jesus and His resurrection, stating that God had overlooked their earlier "times of ignorance." (Acts 17:22-31). Implicitly, Paul was saying that the "golden era" of Greek philosophy was a time of ignorance; fullness of truth is found in Jesus Christ.

Classical scholar James Robinson Boise (1815-1895) similarly found the Greek philosophers like chaff compared to the value of knowing Christ. Boise had a distinguished academic career as a Greek scholar, professor of Greek at the University of Michigan and later the University of Chicago. He published translations of the Greek texts of Xenophon, Homer, and others and wrote texts on Greek grammar and syntax which went through numerous editions. For his work he even received an honorary Doctorate from the University of Tubingen. Yet, when he began to teach and study the New Testament, the Greek classics lost their appeal in the face of the truth that was to be found in Christ through the Scriptures:

> "Christ and the Bible!" What two words are more important and signify more to every human soul? I know of none.
>
> I was engaged for more than thirty years in teaching the Latin and Greek classics. I also edited portions of Homer, Herodotus, Thucydides, Xenophon, Plato, and Demosthenes. I have now for fifteen years been engaged in studying and teaching the Greek New Testament. And what is the result? I have almost lost my fondness for the classic authors. They seem to me so deficient in those spiritual truths which the human soul so much needs in this mortal life. Compared with the doctrines of the New Testament, they seem to me as chaff compared to the wheat. Beautiful chaff it may be, in the light of the sun, but they have nothing to nourish and satisfy the soul; whereas, the more one meditates on the inspired truths of the Bible, the more the spiritual nature, the God-like in man, grows, expands, is lifted up and strengthened. Experience alone confirms the truths of these statements to the human heart.[2]

O Lord God, you are God, and your words are true.
—II Samuel 7:28—

NOVEMBER 3
LIGHT IN A DARK PLACE

Robert Moffat labored as a missionary in South Africa for almost a quarter of a century. The British and Foreign Bible Society printed his translation of the Psalms and the New Testament into Setswana, and thousands of copies brought the light of the Gospel into Southern Africa. Moffat recounted one of his trips deep into the interior. Coming to one village where they hoped to stay for the night (there were lions out in the open country!), the villagers told them to halt and wouldn't allow them to enter. The villagers wouldn't allow them water or food, though Moffat and his companions were tired, thirsty, and hungry. Moffat recounted:

> When twilight drew on, a woman approached from the height beyond which the village lay. She bore on her head a bundle of wood, and had a vessel of milk in her hand. The latter, without opening her lips, she handed to us, laid down the wood, and returned to the village. A second time she approached, with a cooking vessel on her head, and a leg of mutton in one hand, and water in the other. She sat down without saying a word, prepared the fire, and put on the meat. We asked her again and again who she was. She remained silent, till affectionately entreated to give us a reason for such unlooked-for kindness to strangers. Then the tear stole down her sable cheek, and she replied, "I love Him whose servants you are; and surely it is my duty to give you a cup of cold water in his name. My heart is full; therefore I cannot speak the joy I feel to see you in this out-of-the-world place."

> On learning a little of her history, and that she was a solitary light burning in a dark place, I asked her how she kept up the light of God in her soul, in the entire absence of the communion of saints. She drew from her bosom a copy of the Dutch New Testament, which she had received from Mr. Helm, when in his school, some years before. 'This," said she, "is the fountain whence I drink; this is the oil which makes my lamp burn!"[3]

Moffat noticed the Testament was a publication of the British and Foreign Bible Society. It was a great joy to approach the heavenly Father in prayer with this solitary Christian lady.

The seed is the word of God ... As for that in the good soil,
they are those who, hearing the word, hold it fast in an honest and
good heart, and bear fruit with patience.
(from parable of the Sower) —Luke 8:12, 15—

THE WORLD'S SPIRITUAL LIGHT

In 1877, the Colgate Company introduced a toothpaste in a jar which became the best-selling dental cream in the world for the next 80 years. In 1896, the Company innovatively introduced the first toothpaste in a tube. The company first expanded into foreign markets in 1914, and today the Fortune 500 company is on over 200 countries.

William Colgate (1783-1857), founder of the company, was an English immigrant who established a soap and candle factory in New York in 1806. A devout Baptist, Colgate always used biblical principles and truths as guides for his business. When his first attempts at business failed, William took as his own Jacob's vow in Genesis 28: 20-21, "If God will be with me and will keep me in this way that I go and will give me bread to eat and clothing to wear…then the Lord shall be my God." His business grew, and he was active in numerous philanthropic enterprises, including the American Bible Society, the American Bible Union, the American and Foreign Bible Society, giving as much as 50 % of his income to Christian work.

William's son Samuel (1822-1897) followed his father in business and in Christian work. Samuel was President of the New York Baptist Educational Society and also active in the American Tract Society and the American Baptist Missionary Union. Samuel recognized that

> The only spiritual light in the world comes through Jesus Christ and the inspired Book; redemption and forgiveness of sin alone through Christ. Without His presence and the teachings of the Bible we would be enshrouded in moral darkness and despair. The condition of those nations without a Christ, contrasted with those where Christ is accepted, reveals so marked a difference that no arguments are needed. It is an object-lesson so plain that it can be seen and understood by all. May "the earth be full of the knowledge of the Lord, as the waters cover the sea."[4]

He sends out his command to the earth; his word runs swiftly.
—Psalm 147:15—

NOVEMBER 5
BUSINESSMEN DISTRIBUTING BIBLES

About 9 pm on September 14, 1898, traveling salesman John H Nicholson walked into the Boscobel Central House Hotel in Boscobel, Wisconsin. He had often stayed in the hotel during his travels, but this night the hotel was fully booked with a convention in the town. There was an extra bed in a room booked by another traveling salesman, Samuel E. Hill, and Nicholson agreed to take that. That evening, when Nicholson picked up his Bible, which he read daily as a promise to his mother twenty years before, Hill told Nicholson he was a Christian too and asked him to read to him. Nicholson read from John 15:1-16, and the two men prayed together and conversed about spiritual things into the early morning hours. As they conversed, they talked about the need for an association of travelling Christian businessmen. After more discussions, along with businessman William Knights, the three men on July 1, 1899, organized The Gideons International, taking the name of the Hebrew warrior of Judges 6-8. The purpose of the Association was to "band Christian commercial travelers together for mutual recognition, personal evangelism, and united service for the Lord."[5]

Since many of the early members were travelling businessmen, one trustee suggested a good witness would be to supply a Bible for each hotel room in the United States. This "Bible Project" was adopted in 1908. Churches soon supported the Gideons with funds for the project. The first Bible was placed in a hotel room in Montana. In the following century, over 2 billion Bibles and New Testaments were distributed through the Gideons. The Gideons not only place Bibles in hotel rooms, but also distribute Bibles in prisons, to the military, police, fire, and medical personnel, students, and people in shelters. Members personally witness to the saving power of Jesus as they distribute the scriptures and seek to "fulfill their God-given responsibilities as spiritual leaders in their homes and churches."

At midnight I rise to praise you,
because of your righteous rules.
—Psalm 119:162—

RED LETTER BIBLES

The idea for a Red Letter edition of the Bible, in which the words of Jesus are printed in red, was the idea of Louis Klopsch (1852-1910), a German immigrant and journalist. In 1890, Klopsch was the American editor of *The Christian Herald*, a British weekly, and distributed the sermons of Rev. T. Dewitt Talmage to newspapers. On June 19, 1899, when writing an editorial, Klopsch's eye fell on Luke 22:20, "This cup is the new testament in my blood, which I shed for you." Klopsch asked Rev. Talmage if Christ's words could be printed in red. Rev. Talmage replied, "It could do no harm and it most certainly could do much good." By the end of that year, Klopsch printed 60,000 copies of a New Testament with all the words of Jesus in red letters. The red letters were especially helpful in the King James Version which did not use quotation marks, and the response was very favorable. The King of Sweden sent a telegram praising the red-letter edition, and President Teddy Roosevelt invited Klopsch to dinner in the White House (Klopsch accepted). In his own day Klopsch was well known not only as American editor of *The Christian Herald*, but for his philanthropy and famine relief around the world. Today red-letter Bibles have become so accepted that some people may consider them part of the original Bible, as they do chapters and verses.

And we have something more sure, the prophetic word,
to which you will do well to pay attention
as to a lamp shining in a dark place,
until the day dawns and the morning star rises in your hearts.
— II Peter 1:19—

NOVEMBER 7

BIBLICAL APHORISMS

Many of the sayings used in every day speech come from the Bible, either referencing the Biblical idea or as direct quotes. Here are a few, along with their Scriptural location:

Earn living by the sweat of your brow	Genesis 3:19
Eat forbidden fruit	Genesis 2:17
Way of all flesh	Genesis 6:12
Eye for an eye and tooth for tooth	Exodus 21:24
Vale of tears	Psalm 84:7
Escape by skin of his teeth	Job 19:20
Sow the wind and reap the whirlwind	Hosea 8:7
Lick the dust	Psalm 72:9
Spare the rod and spoil the child	Proverbs 10:12
You can't take it with you	Eccl.5:14
Man proposes, God disposes	Proverbs 16:9
Nothing new under the sun	Eccl. 1:9
Your sin will find you out	Num. 32:23
Apple of his eye	Deut. 32:10
See eye to eye	Isaiah 52:8
No peace for the wicked	Isaiah 48:22
Out of the mouth of babes	Psalm 8:3
At death's door	Psalm 107:18
At their wit's end	Psalm 10:27

I hate the double-minded, but I love your law.
—Psalm 119:113—

THE CHURCH'S HERITAGE

Nineteenth-century clergyman Horatius Bonar (1808-1889) wrote over 140 hymns, the most well-known being "I Heard the Voice of Jesus Say" and "Blessing and Honour and Glory and Power." Following is his hymn on the Church's Heritage in the Scriptures:

Thy thoughts are here, my God,
    Expressed in words divine,
The utterance of heavenly lips
    In every sacred line.

Across the ages they
    Have reached us from afar,
Than the bright gold more golden they,
    Purer than purest star.

More durable they stand
    Than the eternal hills;
Far sweeter and more musical
    Than music of earth's rills.

Fairer in their fair hues
    Than the fresh flowers of earth,
More fragrant than the fragrant climes
    Where odors have their birth.

Each word of Thine a gem
    From the celestial mines,
A sunbeam from that holy heaven
    Where holy sunlight shines.

Thine, Thine, this book, though given
    In man's poor human speech,
Telling of things unseen, unheard,
    Beyond all human reach,

No strength it craves or needs
    From this world's wisdom vain;
No filling up from human wells,
    Or sublunary rain.

No light from suns of time,
    Nor brilliance from its gold,
It sparkles with its own glad light,
    As in the ages old.

A thousand hammers keen
    With fiery force and strain,
Brought down on it in rage and hate,
    Have struck this gem in vain.

Against this sea-swept rock
    Ten thousand storms their will
Of foam and rage have wildly spent;
    It lifts its calm face still.

It standeth and will stand,
    Without or change or age,
The word of majesty and light,
    The church's heritage.[6]

Seven times a day I praise you for your righteous rules.
—Psalm 119:164—

NOVEMBER 9
NEWS OF A KINGDOM OF RIGHTEOUSNESS

Henry Van Dyke (1852-1933) was a Presbyterian clergyman and professor of literature at Princeton University. Woodrow Wilson, a classmate and friend of Van Dyke's, later appointed Van Dyke ambassador to Luxembourg and the Netherlands. Best known today for his Christmas story "The Other Wise Man" and for the hymn lyrics "Joyful, Joyful, We Adore Thee," Van Dyke was a prolific author of essays, short stories and poems. In 1910 he authored "The Influence of the Bible in Literature" for *The Century Magazine* in which he wrote,

> Born in the East and clothed in Oriental form and imagery, the Bible walks the ways of all the world with familiar feet and enters land after land to find its own everywhere. It comes to the palace to tell the monarch that he is a servant of the Most High, and unto the cottage to assure the peasant that he can be a son of God. Children listen to its stories with wonder and delight, and wise men ponder them as parables of life.
>
> It has a word of peace for the time of peril, a word of comfort for the time of calamity, a word of light for the hope of darkness. Its oracles are repeated in the assembly of the people, and its counsels whispered in the ear of the lonely. The wicked and the proud tremble at its warnings, but to the wounded and penitent it has a mother's voice.
>
> No man is poor or desolate who has this treasure for his own. When the landscape darkens and the trembling pilgrim comes to the valley named of the shadow, he is not afraid to enter; he takes the rod and staff of Scripture in his hand, he says to his friend and comrade, "Goodbye, we shall meet again": and comforted by that support, he goes toward the lonely pass as one who walks through darkness into light ….
>
> The hunger for happiness which lies in every human heart can never be satisfied without righteousness; and the reason why the Bible reaches down so deep into the breast of man is because it brings news of a kingdom which is righteousness and the peace and joy in the Holy Spirit. It brings this news not in the form of a dogma, a definition, a scientific statement, but in the form of literature, a living picture of experience, a perfect ideal embodied in a Character and a Life.[7]

I will praise you with an upright heart,
when I learn your righteous rules.
—Psalm 119:7—

GREATEST DISCOVERY A PERSON CAN MAKE

September 5, 1901, President William McKinley came to Buffalo, New York to speak at the Pan-American Exposition, laying out plans for his second term in office. The next day, at a public reception, anarchist Leon Czolgosz fired two shots at point-blank range into McKinley's abdomen. The crowd grabbed Czolgosz, and McKinley urged them to not hurt the "misguided fellow," saying, "may God forgive him." The President apologized for being the "cause of trouble to the exposition." Surgeons operated but were unable to find the bullet. McKinley lingered for eight days as the nation prayed for a President they greatly admired and loved. As gangrene set into the wound, McKinley knew he was dying. McKinley said the Lord's Prayer, and whispered some words from the hymn "Nearer, My God to Thee." His last words were, "Good-bye all, good-bye. It is God's way. His will, not ours be done."

McKinley had a strong faith in the wisdom of God's Providence and considered the Presidency a responsibility God had given to him. He trusted in God's rule and oversight of the affairs of men, both in individual lives and in the lives of nations. In 1856, when he was a teenager, McKinley confessed at a Methodist youth meeting in Poland, Ohio, "I have not done my duty, I have sinned. I want to be a Christian ... I give myself to the Savior who has done so much for me." Days later he declared, "I have found the pearl of great price ... I love God."[8] McKinley's faith in Jesus Christ was central to his life. Daily Bible reading and prayer were constants throughout his life—whether as a soldier in the Civil War, a member of Congress, governor of Ohio, or President of the United States. McKinley stated that

> The greatest discovery a man or a nation can make is to find the truth of God's Word. More to be prized is it than the discovery of continents than the discovery of gold mines, than the marvelous discoveries being made in the physical and scientific laboratories of the day. When a man truly gives himself to the study of the Bible he discovers it to be God's great love story to man. The more profoundly we study this wonderful book, and the more clearly we observe its divine precepts, the better citizens we will become and the higher will be our destiny as a nation.[9]

They draw near who persecute me with evil purpose;
they are far from your law.
—Psalm 119:150—

NOVEMBER 11
TRUE HISTORY

Skeptics often claim that the Bible is a collection of stories and myths with no basis in history. Some claim Jesus never really lived but is a fabrication of the apostles, or that Adam and Eve are simply part of an interesting story. Yet, the truth and historical, factual reliability of the Scriptures can be repeatedly demonstrated. In the nineteenth century, one area for which scholars attacked the Bible as being unhistorical was the existence of the Hittites. Hittites are mentioned almost 50 times in Scripture, and they seem to be a people of power and influence. (Abraham's negotiations with Ephron the Hittite for the purchase of a burial site for Sarah, Genesis 23, is one of the earliest accounts of a commercial transaction.). Yet there was no extra biblical evidence for their existence. This began to change at the end of the 19th century.

William Wright (1837-1899) became a missionary to the Jews after hearing the preaching of Charles Spurgeon in Belfast. While traveling in the Middle East, Wright gained a knowledge of the customs and geography of the region. In Syria, he studied the monumental inscriptions at Hama and determined they were in an early Hittite script that predated the Phoenician. Assyriologist Archibald Sayce agreed with Wright's assessment. Wright later determined that the script in Hama matched that on a monument at Bogazköy in Anatolia. During excavations at Bogazköy beginning in 1906, Hugo Winckler found a royal archive with 10,000 tablets in Akkadian cuneiform and the script Wright had claimed as Hittite. Further excavations confirmed that the ruins at Bogazköy were the remains of Hattusa, the capital of the Hittite empire. It was determined that the Hittite Empire once rivaled the empires of Egypt and Mesopotamia, covering most of Anatolia and stretching into northern Syria. The Hittites were among the earliest workers in iron and successfully used chariots.

After archaeological discovery of the Hittites, skeptics could no longer claim the Bible's references to the Hittites were fabrications.

The wicked lie in wait to destroy me,
but I consider your testimonies.
—Psalm 119:95—

THE PRESENCE OF CHRIST

November 5, 1858, John Gibson Paton (1824-1907) and his wife landed on Tanna, one of New Hebrides islands, to bring the Gospel of Christ to the natives. When he first saw the people, Paton wrote that his "first impressions drove me to the verge of utter dismay. On beholding these Natives in their paint and nakedness and misery, my heart was as full of horror as of pity."[10]

Within a few months of his arrival, Paton's wife and infant son died, leaving him all alone—yet, he was not alone. Jesus' words from Matthew 28, "Lo, I am with you always!" were a source of comfort and strength. Paton wrote, "I was never altogether forsaken. The ever-merciful Lord sustained me."[11]

Paton would spend nearly half a century ministering to these people of New Hebrides (now called Vanuatu), known for their idolatry, cannibalism, and child sacrifice. Often during those years Paton faced danger and death. Once a chief followed him for hours with a musket aimed at him. Once his house was surrounded by armed men wanting to kill him. Another time, a man rushed him with an ax, but a Chief snatched a spade and defended Paton. Paton wrote,

> Life in such circumstances led me to cling very near to the Lord Jesus; I knew not, for one brief hour, when or how attack might be made; and yet, with my trembling hand clasped in the hand once nailed on Calvary and now swaying the sceptre of the Universe, calmness and peace and resignation abode in my soul.

For many years Paton worked on the island of Aniwa, teaching the natives, providing medicine, and establishing schools, always with the goal of spreading the truth of Christ. In 1899, Paton's translation of the New Testament into Aniwa was published, and the entire island professed Christianity.

When Paton died, his son had the Scripture "Lo, I am with you always" inscribed on his tombstone. It was the verse Paton quoted most often in his conversation and in his letters. The presence of Jesus with him had sustained him in all his missionary endeavors.

Your commandment makes me wiser than my enemies,
for it is ever with me.
—Psalm 119:98—

NOVEMBER 13
BY MY SPIRIT

Canadians Jonathan (1859-1936) and Rosalind Goforth set off as pioneer missionaries to China in 1888. They endured many hardships, including losing five of their eleven children to sickness. During the Boxer Rebellion in 1911, they fled many miles across China before reaching safety. Jonathan was attacked and injured with a sword but survived. News of the Christian revivals in Wales during 1904-1905 and in Korea in 1907, encouraged Jonathan with the example of the Spirit of God using the preaching of His Word to bring people to faith in Christ. As he preached in China, Zechariah 4:6 was a Scripture which strengthened him: "Not by might, not by power, but by my Spirit, says the Lord." In 1908, Goforth's preaching bore fruit in large numbers of conversions, often called the Manchurian Revival. Goforth later reflected on this outpouring of grace in his book *By My Spirit:*

> ... we can entertain no hope of a mighty, globe-encircling Holy Spirit revival without there being first a back-to-the Bible movement. The Author of the Bible is being greatly dishonored these days by the doubt cast upon His Word. It must, indeed, be a cause of intense grief to Him that the Book which alone testified of the Lord Jesus should be lightly esteemed by man. Unless the Bible is to us in very truth the Word of God, our prayers can be naught but sheer mockery. There never has been a revival except where there have been Christian men and women thoroughly believing in and wholeheartedly pleading the promises of God!
>
> The Sword of the Spirit, which is the Word of God, is the only weapon which has ever been mightily used in revival [Eph. 6:17]. Where it has been given for what it claims to be, the Word of God has always been like a sharp, two-edged sword, like fire, and like a hammer that breaketh the rock in pieces [Heb. 4:12; Jer. 23:29] ....
>
> In China I have often given from thirty-five to forty addresses in a week, practically all of them being simply Bible rehearsals. In fact, I think I can safely say that during the forty-one years that I have been on the foreign field, I have never once addressed a Chinese audience without an open Bible in my hand, from which I could simply say, "thus says the Lord!" I have always taken it for granted that the simple preaching of the Word would bring men to Christ. It has never failed me yet ... the call to revival must be a call to exalt Jesus Christ in our hearts as King of Kings and Lord of lords. He is like an Everest peak, rising from the level plain. There must be room only for Him, if we would have Him dwell with us at all.[12]

You spurn all who go astray from your statutes, for their cunning is in vain.
—Psalm 119:118—

PRESIDENT WOODROW WILSON
ON THE BIBLE IN AMERICA

In 1911, Woodrow Wilson, then Governor of New Jersey, but later to be President of the United States, gave addresses in Trenton, New Jersey and in Denver, Colorado in observance of the Tricentennial of the King James Bible. Wilson, son of a Presbyterian minister, thought a Bible-reading people was important to the American nation. In his address in Trenton, Wilson said:

> There are great problems, ladies and gentlemen, before the American people. There are problems which will need purity of spirit and integrity of purpose such as has never been called for before in the history of this country. I should be afraid to go forward if I did not believe that there lay at the foundation of all our schooling and of all our thought this incomparable and unimpeachable Word of God. If we cannot derive our strength thence, there is no source from which we can derive it.[13]

In Denver, Colorado, Wilson noted that

> America was born a Christian nation. America was born to exemplify that devotion to the elements of righteousness which are derived from the revelations of Holy Scripture.
>
> Ladies and gentlemen, I have a very simple thing to ask of you. I ask of every man and woman in the audience that from this night on they will realize that part of the destiny of America lies in their daily perusal of this great book of revelations—that if they would see America free and pure they will make their own spirits free and pure by this baptism of the Holy Scripture.[14]

If the foundations are destroyed, what can the righteous do?
—Psalm 11:3—

NOVEMBER 15
RESCUE THE PERISHING

April 12, 1912, there was great excitement among the over 2200 passengers and crew as the *Titanic* set off from Southampton, England for its maiden voyage to New York City. Some of the world's wealthiest were on board, as well as numerous poorer emigrants seeking a new life in America. Two days into her trans-Atlantic journey, the *Titanic* hit an iceberg. Water began to fill the compartments, and within a few hours the ship broke in two and sank. There were not enough lifeboats on the ship for all of the passengers, and the icy waters were lethally cold. Over 1500 died in the disaster; only 710 survived.

One of the passengers was Scottish Baptist pastor and evangelist John Harper, a widower travelling with his sister and his six-year-old daughter. Harper was pastor of Walworth Road Baptist Church in London and was travelling to America to lead evangelistic services at Moody Church in Chicago. When the iceberg hit, Harper placed his sister and daughter on a lifeboat. He went among the passengers witnessing to them and passionately telling them of the salvation which was to be found in Christ. When one man snubbed Harper's proclamation to "believe in the Lord Jesus Christ and thou shalt be saved" (Acts 16:31), Harper gave him his life vest, telling him, "you need this more than I do." Even when swimming in the frigid waters, Harper repeated to the people "believe in the Lord Jesus Christ and thou shalt be saved." Harper was intent in bringing as many as possible into Christ's kingdom, and then he himself drowned in the frigid waters.

Several years after the disaster, a *Titanic* survivors meeting was held in Ontario, Canada. One survivor told how, while he was clinging to some debris to stay afloat, Harper was swimming in the waters and challenged him to "believe in the Lord Jesus Christ and thou shalt be saved." The man rejected his plea. When Harper swam by again, he asked if he was now ready to believe in Christ. The man said that with miles of water beneath him, he gave his life to Christ. He was rescued by a lifeboat, while Harper went to his watery grave. The man said he was Harper's last convert.

… their heart is unfeeling like fat, but I delight in your law.
—Psalm 119:70—

STRENGTH FOR *ENDURANCE*

In August 1914, shortly after the beginning of what became known as World War I, Sir Ernest Shackleton began his Trans-Atlantic Expedition, seeking to cross Antarctica via the South Pole. He had been on two previous expeditions exploring Antarctica, unsuccessfully seeking to reach the South Pole; Norwegian Roald Amundsen did successfully reach the South Pole in 1911. Though Shackleton would no longer be a part of the race to reach the South Pole, there was still great interest in his new expedition. Over 5000 people applied to join the expedition. Shackleton chose the 56 crew members based on character, temperament and technical skills. The *Endurance* carried the main exploring party; the *Aurora* would provide supply depots during the trip.

In the Weddell Sea, ice slowed the progress of *Endurance*, and by January 1915, the ship was frozen in an ice floe. After months of drifting, the ice put such pressure on the ship that it began to break apart. On October 24, the ship was abandoned; provisions and equipment were transferred to the ice, where the party camped for several months. When the ice floe began to break, the men took to the lifeboats. After some time on Elephant Island, some took to the sea again seeking help and came to South Georgia. Whaling stations were on the other side of the island. Rather than take to the sea again, Shackleton and two of his men walked thirty-two miles over mountainous, frozen, dangerous terrain to reach the whaling stations. Help was then sent to the remaining crew on South Georgia and Elephant Island, where the men had been isolated for four and a half months.

Shackleton and his two companions said that during the march across the mountains and glaciers of South Georgia, it often seemed like there was another person with them—like the other person in the fiery furnace with Shadrach, Meshach and Abednego! In later speeches describing his march, Shackleton often noted, "As we made that journey over the icy ranges, we saw God in His splendors and heard the *text that Nature renders*."[15] A source of strength to him during the voyage in the open boats and the march, were words from Psalm 139, "If I take the wings of the morning, and dwell in the uttermost parts of the sea, even there shall Thy hand lead me and Thy right hand shall hold me."

Let your hand be ready to help me, for I have chosen your precepts.
—Psalm 119:173—

NOVEMBER 17

HISTORIAN OF THE FIRST RANK

Skeptics of an earlier century routinely ridiculed the truthfulness of the Bible's historical narratives. For example, many contended that Luke, the author of the Gospel bearing his name and Acts, wrote in the second century and made up many of the incidents in his account. One such skeptic was William Ramsay (1851-1939), a New Testament scholar educated at the universities in Aberdeen, Scotland and Tübingen, Germany.

Ramsay traveled extensively throughout Asia Minor to study Luke's accounts of Paul's missionary activities, rather expecting to find a lot of historical discrepancies in Luke's work, since Ramsay thought he wrote at least a century after Paul. However, the more he studied the topography and geography of Asia Minor, as well as the increasing archaeological discoveries, the more Ramsay realized the tremendous accuracy to detail in Luke's account. Luke mentions 32 countries, 54 cities, and 95 people by name, 62 of whom are not mentioned elsewhere in the New Testament. Ramsay repeatedly found Luke accurate in the names used. Luke also was accurate in describing the political situation of the first century. While many had been skeptical of Luke's identification of Sergius Paulus (Acts 13) as proconsul in Paphos on the island of Cyprus, thinking his title would have been "proprietor," an inscription was found describing Paulus as a proconsul. Luke was again doubted in his use of the term "politarch" for the ruler of a city, when no other known ancient writer used the term, but then nineteen inscriptions were found, five in Thessalonica, which used the exact term. Ramsay also found Luke accurate in describing the political positions and dates of various rulers, such as Tiberius, Claudius Felix, and Festus. Increasingly Ramsay came to admire the marvelous truth of Luke's writings, causing him to conclude, "Luke is a historian of the first rank; not merely are his statements trustworthy…this author should be placed along with the greatest historians."[16]

Your promise is well tried, and your servant loves it.
—Psalm 119:140—

THE BIBLE TEMPLE

A popular baseball player in the 1880's, Billy Sunday (1862-1935) left baseball for Christian ministry after his conversion. Sunday went on to become the most famous evangelist of the early 20th century. He once described reading the Bible as walking through a temple or palace:

> I entered through the portico of Genesis and walked down through the Old Testament's art gallery, where I saw the portraits of Joseph, Jacob, Daniel, Moses, Isaiah, Solomon and David hanging on the wall; I entered the music room of the Psalms and the Spirit of God struck the key-board of my nature until it seemed to me that every reed and pipe in God's great organ of nature responded to the harp of David, and the charm of King Solomon in his moods.

> I walked into the business house of Proverbs.

> I walked into the observatory of the prophets and there saw photographs of various sizes, some pointing to far-ff stars or events—all concentrated upon one great Star which was to rise as an atonement for sin.

> Then I went into the audience room of the King of Kings, and got a vision from four different points—from Matthew, Mark, Luke, and John. I went into the correspondence room, and saw Peter, James, Paul and Jude, penning their epistles to the world. I went into the Acts of the Apostles and saw the Holy Spirit forming the Holy Church, and then I walked into the throne room and saw a door at the foot of a tower and, going up, I saw One standing there, fair as the morning, Jesus Christ, the Son of God, and I found this truest friend that man ever knew; when all were false I found him true.

> In teaching me the way of life, the Bible has taught me the way to live, it taught me how to die.[17]

Whoever believes in me, as the Scripture has said,
"Out of his heart will flow rivers of living water."
—John 7:38—

NOVEMBER 19
A DECORATED HERO

Raised in a Christian family in the mountains of Tennessee, Alvin York (1887-1964) ran the family farm and blacksmith shop, taking care of his widowed mother and siblings after his father's death in 1911. On weekends he began to find escape in alcohol, so much so that people thought he was a drunk who would never amount to anything. However, at a New Year's Day church service in 1915, York accepted Jesus as his personal Savior. He later wrote,

> I truly felt as though I had been borned again. I felt that great power which the Bible talks about and which all sinners feel when they have found salvation. I felt in my soul like the stormy waters must have felt when the Master said, "Peace be still." I used to walk out in the night under the stars and kinder linger on the hillside, and I sorter wanted to put my arms around them-there hills. They was at peace and so was the world and so was I.[18]

York's life was transformed. He saw his struggle with alcoholism as building his character and helping him understand and love others. He became a leader in his church, teaching choir and Sunday school and even preaching as the pastor's assistant.

When the United States entered World War I, York was called up for the draft. Though he was very patriotic and wanted to serve his country, he believed the Bible was against killing. York was conflicted in how to be both a good Christian and a good American. He tried to register as a conscientious objector, but his appeals were not successful. York was assigned to the 82nd Division of the Army and sent to France with the rank of corporal. His commanding officers, Captain Danforth and Major Buxton, appreciated York as a model soldier and his Christian example. Both Christians, they spent time with York discussing the morality of a just war. When Captain Danforth read Ezekiel 33, York began to see that he could serve in the military as a "watchman on the wall."

In the fighting in the Argonne Forest, October 8, 1918, the Americans had a mission to take out machine guns aimed at the Americans. After several Americans were killed, York found himself in charge of his unit. In the ensuing fight, York amazingly killed 25 enemy soldiers and captured 132, forcing the enemy to retreat. York was awarded the Medal of Honor, but he always gave God the credit for his actions. When one of his officers asked York how he did this amazing feat, York later recalled telling him,

It was not man-power but it was divine power that saved me. I told him that before I went to war I prayed to God and He done gave me my assurance that so long as I believed in Him not one hair of my head would be harmed and even in front of them-there machine guns He knowed I believed in Him.

Before I was afflicted I went astray, but now I keep your word.
—Psalm 119:67—

NOVEMBER 20
A SCIENTIST LOOKING TO JESUS

He was born a slave in Missouri shortly before the Civil War. When he was an infant, George and his mother were stolen and sold in a neighboring state. Master Moses Carver was able to find only George and brought him back to Missouri, where he raised George as his own child. Susan Carver taught George to read, and the Carvers encouraged the young George in his schooling. When he was thirteen, George was given a Bible for Christmas, a book he cherished and read the rest of his life.

Working in various jobs and occupations, George steadily furthered his education in various schools open to those of his race. He was musically talented, learning to play the piano in church, as well as artistically gifted, developing an admirable skill as a painter. Yet, he also had a great interest in nature. George debated whether to be a scientist, a missionary, or an artist. In 1896, Booker T. Washington invited George Carver to head the Agriculture Department at Tuskegee Institute in Alabama. Carver remained at Tuskegee for forty-seven years, teaching farmers how to improve their agricultural output by developing new crops, and implementing crop rotation to enrich the soil. His laboratory at Tuskegee was full of samples collected from the surrounding woods which he analyzed for their productivity and usefulness. He regularly prayed as he began his work, "Open thou mine eyes, that I may behold wondrous things out of thy law. My help cometh from the Lord who made heaven and earth, and all that in them is."[19] Carver was especially interested in the many uses for the sweet potato and peanut, developing many uses for both and providing studies on their growth and benefits.

After speaking to the House Committee on Ways and Means on the many uses of peanuts to improve the southern economy, Carver was asked how he learned all things. Carver answered from an old book, the Bible. The questioner asked, "Does the Bible tell about peanuts?" Carver replied, "No sir, but it tells about the God who made the peanut. I asked Him to show me what to do with the peanut, and He did." [20]

I shall walk in a wide place, for I have sought your precepts.
—Psalm 119:45—

NOVEMBER 21

SEARCHING FOR OIL

As God's Word, the Bible's accuracy is evident not just in spiritual matters, but in its historical, geographical, and indeed geological references. Natural gas around the Dead Sea was discovered as some, reading Genesis 14:10 about the asphalt pits around the Cities of the Plain, recognized this was an area of petrochemical deposits. Others, reading about the blessings of Asher and Joseph in Deuteronomy 33:17-24 and Genesis 49: 22-26 have drilled for oil around Mt. Carmel, in the lands allotted to Joseph and Asher.

The reason Standard Oil Company began exploring for oil in Egypt in the early twentieth century has to do with a Bible-reading director. An article from the 1920s in *Oil and Gas News* tells the story:

> The fact that the Standard Oil Co. has discovered oil and is operating wells in Egypt is generally known, but the reason for its going to that ancient land to look for oil is probably not so well known. It is asserted that one of the directors of the company happened to read the second chapter of Exodus. The third verse immediately caught his attention. It is stated that the ark of bulrushes which the mother of Moses made for her child was 'daubed with slime and with pitch.' This acute gentleman reasoned that where there was pitch there must be oil, and if there was oil in Moses' time it is probably still there. So the company sent out Charles Whitshott, its geologist and oil expert, to make investigations, with the result that oil was discovered. Three wells are now in operation and others are to be opened.[21]

The wicked have laid a snare for me,
but I do not stray from your precepts.
—Psalm 119:110—

NOVEMBER 22
TEN REASONS TO BELIEVE THE BIBLE

Evangelist, pastor, and teacher Reuben Archer Torrey (1856-1928) believed firmly in the truth of the Scripture. A graduate of Yale University and Yale Divinity School, Torrey also studied at Leipzig and Erlangen Universities. He worked closely with Dwight L. Moody in Chicago, while serving also as pastor of the Chicago Avenue Church. He served as chaplain during the Spanish-American War and World War I, and conducted revival meetings throughout Great Britain, Australia and Asia. He then helped found the Bible Institute of Los Angeles and pastored the Church of the Open Door in Los Angeles. The author of over 40 books, Torrey consistently adhered to the truth and authority of Scripture, a theme developed in *Ten Reasons Why I Believe the Bible is the Word of God.*[22] The 10 reasons are:

1. From the testimony of Jesus Christ. Jesus Himself recognized the law of Moses, the Prophets, and the Psalms all were Scripture and spoke of the Holy Spirit who would further teach the Apostles, in what became the New Testament (Mark 7:13; Luke 24:27; John 14:26).

2. From the Bible's fulfilled prophecies, such as the prophecies of the Messiah (Isaiah 53; Micah 5:2; Daniel 9:25-27).

3. From the unity of the book. Though written over many centuries by different authors, yet it has the unified story of God's redemption.

4. From the Bible's superiority to any and all other books. Other books might contain truth, but they also contain error. The Bible contains truth unmixed with error.

5. From the history of the book and its victory over attack. Though often hated and sought to be destroyed, God's Word endures. "Heaven and earth shall pass away, but my word shall not pass away."

6. From the character of those who accept and those who reject the book. The stronghold of the Bible is "in the pure, unselfish happy home." The stronghold of infidelity is in "the gambling hall, the drinking saloon, and the brothel."

7. On the Ground of the Influence of the Book. "There is more power in that little Book to save men and purify, gladden and beautify their lives, than in all other literature put together—more power to lift men up to God....a Book that has a power to lift men up to God that no other book has, must have come down from God in a way that no other book has."

8. From the inexhaustible depth of the book.

9. From the fact that as we grow in knowledge and holiness we grow toward the Bible.

10. From the direct testimony of the Holy Spirit. "The Holy Spirit sets His seal in the soul of every believer to the Divine authority of the Bible. It is possible to get to a place where we need no argument to prove that the Bible is God's Word. Christ says, "My sheep know my voice."

But the Scripture imprisoned everything under sin,
so that the promise by faith in Jesus Christ
might be given to those who believe.
—Galatians 3:22—

NOVEMBER 23
WHAT GOD SAYS

When the Enlightenment elevated reason as the source of all truth, the Scriptures began to be ridiculed as unhistorical myths. A statue of the Goddess of Reason was set up in Notre Dame Cathedral, and the God of the Old Testament was repudiated as a god of wrath and vengeance. Biblical miracles were deemed irrational and impossible, and the Bible was no longer considered a source for morals. Christianity was seen as a relic of the past and not worthy of forward looking, enlightened and rational people.

An important leader in resisting this skepticism was Benjamin B. Warfield (1851-1921). A pastor and eminent biblical scholar, Warfield was a distinguished theology professor at Princeton from 1887 until his death in 1921. In seeing the authority of Scripture as foundational to the Christian faith, Warfield resisted the rationalism of the higher critics as well as the emotionalism of some of the revivalists. Warfield contended that the Bible was the Word of God, so that what the Bible said, God said. He showed that this attitude of trust in the authority of Scripture could be traced throughout the teachings of the Church—from Origen, Irenaeus, Augustine, to Martin Luther, John Calvin, Richard Baxter, and on to Charles Hodge.

When discussing the inspiration of the Scriptures, Warfield noted that the Holy Spirit influenced the human authors, so that the words of Scripture themselves are breathed out by God. The Bible does not just contain a message of God but contains the very words of God. Because these are the words of God, they reflect God's character and are powerful, true, and infallible. This was the view Jesus and the apostles had of the Old Testament Scriptures and this has been the teaching of the Church through the ages. Jesus similarly commissioned the New Testament Scriptures, and the Holy Spirit further works to bring the truth of the Scripture to our minds and hearts. These Scriptures are God's revelation to man, and the only way we can know of salvation. Warfield's writings on the truthfulness, sufficiency, preservation and transmission of the Scriptures to us continue to edify and build up Christians today. He clearly shows that what the Bible says is what God says.

It is time for thee, Lord, to work:
for they have made void thy law.
—Psalm 119:126—

CHRISTIANITY AND LIBERALISM

J. Gresham Machen (1881-1937), professor at Princeton Theological Seminary for twenty years, became increasingly concerned with the growing influence of liberalism within the seminary and the wider Christian community. Liberalism sought to modernize Christianity by emphasizing the Christian experience rather than the historic, biblical teachings. Machen's 1923 classic *Christianity and Liberalism* contended that liberalism and Christianity were entirely different religions. Liberalism was founded on man's will and emotions; Christianity was founded on the historic facts of Jesus' death for our sins, His burial, and resurrection. Machen devoted one chapter of his work to the Bible, noting that man cannot know of the salvation that is in Christ without God's revelation. Jesus' sacrifice for the sins of men is the central event in all of history. All of the Old Testament looks forward to that event, and it is central to the New Testament. The Christian life doesn't depend on personal experience, but upon the record of Scriptures. How can we know the Bible is true?:

> We know that the gospel story is true partly because of the early date of the documents in which it appears, the evidence as to their authorship, the internal evidence of their truth, the impossibility of explaining them as being based upon deception or upon myth.[23]

Through the inspiration of the Bible, "the Holy Spirit so informed the minds of the Biblical writers that they were kept from falling into the errors that mar all other books."[24] In the Bible, the Christian finds

> the very Word of God ... Dependence upon a word of man would be slavish, but dependence upon God's word is life. Dark and gloomy would be the world, if we were left to our own devices and had no blessed Word of God. The Bible, to the Christian is not a burdensome law, but the very Magna Charta of Christian liberty.

> It is no wonder, then, that liberalism is totally different from Christianity, for the foundation is different. Christianity is founded upon the Bible. It bases upon the Bible both its thinking and its life. Liberalism on the other hand is founded upon the shifting emotions of sinful men.[25]

Jesus said to them, "Is this not the reason you are wrong,
because you know neither the Scriptures nor the power of God?
—Mark 12:24—

NOVEMBER 25
WINSTON CHURCHILL ON MOSES

Winston Churchill, Prime Minster of Great Britain during World War II, first learned of the Bible from his nanny, Elizabeth Everest. It was she who first read the Bible to him and had him memorize Scripture. Churchill's affection for Mrs. Everest continued throughout his life; her photo along with his Bible were on his nightstand even in his last years.

Churchill came to see the rise of Hitler as a threat to Christian civilization itself. From his reading of Israel's wars in the Old Testament, he knew that God could fight for right in the 20th century as He had in the days of ancient Israel. The confidence and hope he gave Britain in its time of crisis had biblical roots.

In 1932, Churchill published "Moses: The Leader of a People," an essay in which he asserted his conviction in the truth and authenticity of Moses as in the biblical record:

> We reject with scorn all those learned and laboured myths that Moses was but a legendary figure upon whom the priesthood and the people hung their essential social, moral, and religious ordinances. We believe that the most scientific view, the most up-to-date and rationalistic conception, will find its fullest satisfaction in taking the Bible story literally, and in identifying one of the greatest human beings with the most decisive leap forward ever discernible in the human story. ... We may be sure that all these things happened just as they are set out according to Holy Writ. We may believe that they happened to people not so very different from ourselves, and that the impressions those people received were faithfully recorded and have been transmitted across the centuries with far more accuracy than many of the telegraphed accounts we read of goings on of today. In the words of a forgotten work of Mr. Gladstone, we rest with assurance upon *The Impregnable Rock of Holy Scripture*. Let the men of science and learning expand their knowledge and probe with their researches every detail of the records which have been preserved to us from these dim ages. All they will do is to fortify the grand simplicity and essential accuracy of the recorded truths which have lighted so far the pilgrimage of man.[26]

Give me understanding, that I may keep your law
and observe it with my whole heart.
—Psalm 119:34—

SCRIPTURE MEMORY
FOR SAILORS — AND OTHERS

Though Dawson Trotman (1906-1956) had been president and valedictorian of his high school class and had even led a Christian Endeavor group at his church, after graduating he fell into a Roaring Twenties lifestyle. In the era of Prohibition, Trotman was bootlegging liquor, and stealing became a way to finance his gambling habits. When he was arrested for drunkenness, Trotman realized his life was going the wrong direction. He went back to his old Christian Endeavor group at church, and he was challenged by the Scripture memorization contest they were having. In two weeks he memorized twenty verses, and the Word of God began to pierce his conscience. Two verses which particularly took hold of him were John 5:24, "Verily, verily, I say unto you, He that heareth my word, and believeth on him that sent me, hath everlasting life," and John 1:12, "as many as received him, to them gave he power to become the sons of God, even to them that believe on his name." Trotman prayed to receive Jesus.

After his conversion, Trotman continued memorizing Scripture, and he began sharing the gospel with those at work. In 1933, a friend introduced him to a sailor, Les Spencer, who wanted to know better how to share the gospel with others. Trotman spent a lot of personal time with Spencer teaching him how to share his faith through Scripture and how to be a productive Christian. Spencer went on his next six-week sea voyage, and there were a dozen new converts by the end of the voyage. On furlough, the new converts stayed with Trotman and received the same training Spencer had received. The Navigators were formed to evangelize and disciple fellow sailors, with the motto "To Know Christ and to Make Him Known." Spencer and his fellow sailors taught the Bible to the 125 men aboard the *USS West Virginia*, one of the ships hit a few years later in the attack on Pearl Harbor; hundreds of ships and army bases during World War II had Navigators memorizing Scripture.

While focusing on Scripture memorization and evangelism, the Navigators also developed resources and materials which helped train new converts in the Christian faith. Dawson Trotman worked closely with Billy Graham and Campus Crusade for Christ in developing material to help disciple young believers. Numerous other ministries have been influenced by Trotman's Navigators ministry. Foundational to all is the memorization of the Scripture.

Seek and read from the book of the Lord.
—Isaiah 34:16—

NOVEMBER 27

MONUMENTAL SCRIPTURES

The Scriptures' importance to the foundation of the government of the United States is reflected in many buildings and monuments in Washington, D.C. In the Capitol building, one of the eight paintings in the rotunda is the "Embarkation of the Pilgrims" showing the Pilgrims in prayer and William Brewster holding a book inscribed "New Testament of our Lord and Savior Jesus Christ." In the chapel of the House of Representatives, a stained-glass window shows George Washington in prayer with the words of Psalm 16:1, "Preserve me, O God, for in Thee do I put my trust."

The Washington Monument, built 1848-1884, contains a Bible in a capsule in the cornerstone. The capstone's east face says *"Laus Deo,"* Latin for "praise be to God." Several of the monument's stones are inscribed with Bible verses, including "Holiness to the Lord" (Exodus 28:26); "Search the Scriptures" (John 5:39); "The memory of the just is blessed" (Proverbs 10:7); and "Train up a child in the way he should go, and when he is old, he will not depart from it" (Proverbs 22:6).

The Library of Congress, built in 1897, has several Scriptures inscribed on its walls: "The light shineth in darkness, and the darkness comprehendeth it not" (John 1:5); "Wisdom is the principal thing; therefore, get wisdom, and with all thy getting, get understanding." (Proverbs 4:7; "What doth the Lord require of thee, but to do justly and to love mercy, and to walk humbly with thy God" (Micah 6:8); "The heavens declare the Glory of God, and the firmament showeth His handiwork" (Psalm 19:1).

The Lincoln Memorial, built in 1922, contains two Scriptures: "Woe unto the world because of offenses, for it must needs be that offenses come, but woe to that man by whom the offense cometh" (Matthew 18:7) and "the judgments of the Lord are true and righteous altogether" (Psalm 19:9).

The National Archives, built in the 1930s, has a bronze of the 10 commandments on the floor. The Supreme Court building, completed in 1935, has several images of Moses and the 10 commandments. The wooden doors of the main entrance to the court and the outer bronze doors have images of the ten commandments.

Assemble the people, men, women, and little ones, and the sojourner …,
that they may hear and learn to fear the Lord your God,
and be careful to do all the words of this law, and that their children,
who have not known it, may hear and learn to fear the Lord your God,
as long as you live in the land that you are going over the Jordan to possess.
—Deuteronomy 31:12-13—

MIRACLE AT DUNKIRK

In the summer of 1940, the British Expeditionary Force, which had been sent to help France in its resistance to Hitler, found itself trapped on the beaches of Dunkirk in the north of France. Belgian, French and English troops were cut off and surrounded by German troops in what Winston Churchill called "a colossal military disaster." King George VI called for a national day of prayer, and an entire nation prayed for the safety of their soldiers in France.

One British naval officer cabled three words to London: "But if not." What could that mean? In a day when Bible reading and chapel were a regular part of British education, the three words were instantly recognized as a quote from Daniel 3:17-18 and a declaration of total trust in God for deliverance. In Daniel 3, Shadrach, Meshach, and Abednego were before the Babylonian king Nebuchadnezzar and made to bow down and worship his golden image or be thrown into a fiery furnace. The three young men refused to worship the image saying, "If it be so, our God whom we serve is able to deliver us from the burning fiery furnace, and he will deliver us out of thine hand, O king. But if not, be it known unto thee, O king, that we will not serve thy gods, nor worship the golden image which thou hast set up." The men were thrown into the fiery furnace but were totally unharmed by the flames!

In what is often called the Miracle of Dunkirk, over 380,000 soldiers were evacuated from the "fiery furnace" under German attack. The British came with almost 700 private ships—merchant marine boats, fishing boats, pleasure cruisers—as well as 160 navy vessels to get the soldiers off the beaches. A violent storm over Dunkirk grounded the German planes, while a great calm on the English Channel such as is rarely seen allowed the evacuation. Many at the time called the evacuation a miracle.

I will keep your statutes; do not utterly forsake me!
—Psalm 119:8—

NOVEMBER 29

WYCLIFFE BIBLE TRANSLATORS

In 1917, when Cameron Townsend (1896-1982) was a missionary in Guatemala, a Guatemalan Indian asked him, "Why doesn't your God speak my language?" Convinced that every man, woman, and child should be able to read God's Word in their own language, in 1934, Townsend began a summer training program in linguistics with two students. Each year the number of students grew, so that today the Summer Institute of Linguistics has a staff of over 4800 in over 100 countries.

Townsend believed that "The greatest missionary is the Bible in the mother tongue. It needs no furlough and is never considered a foreigner."[27] In 1942, Townsend founded Wycliffe Bible Translators, named after the 14th-century scholar John Wycliffe, who was the first to translate the whole Bible into English. Believing the Bible is God's Word, Townsend wanted everyone to be able to hear or read the Bible in their own language.

Wycliffe translators completed their first translation in 1951, and in 2000 the 500th translation was completed. Over 1500 languages have the New Testament or some portion of Scripture; 650 languages have the complete Bible. Over 1600 languages are still needing a Bible translation. At least 1.5 billion people do not have the full Bible in their language, and over 110 million do not have a single verse of Scripture. With so many people around the globe still needing to hear the Gospel, Wycliffe has set the goal of having a Bible translation program begun by 2025 in the over 1600 languages still needing the Scripture.

Their voice goes out through all the earth,
and their words to the end of the world.
—Psalm 19:4—

THE GOOD SEED

Marianna Slocum (1916-2017) and her fiancé Bill Bentley had enjoyed some very special days together before their August 30 wedding. Both Marianna and Bill were missionaries with Wycliffe Bible Translators in Mexico. They had met in 1940 at the Summer Institute of Linguistics. Bill had been working with the Chol tribe and Marianna was assigned to the nearby Tzeltal tribe. Bill often visited Marianna to help her in her translation work, and soon the two planned to marry. They returned to the States in the summer of 1941, where Bill spoke at a Keswick center. The couple then enjoyed a day of sight-seeing in New York before going to Marianna's parents in Philadelphia for the wedding just six days away. When Bill did not come down for breakfast, Marianna's father went up to call him, and found him dead. He had died of previously unknown heart problems. Marianna was of course heartbroken.

Later in the day, when Marianna called Cameron Townsend, the founder of Wycliffe Translators, to tell him the news, she asked him if she could go to the Tzeltal tribe and finish the translation Bill had begun. As news of Bill's death spread, Marianna received a telegram quoting John 13:7, "Jesus answered him, 'What I am doing you do not understand now, but afterward you will understand.'" This Scripture continued to be Marianna's comfort in the months ahead.

Marianna and several helpers worked on the Tzeltal Bible translation for fifteen years. Since the Tzeltal did not have a written language, Marianna had to develop the written language as well as the vocabulary and grammar befo translating the Scriptures. Once the Tzeltal New Testament was complet Marianna spent eight years translating the New Testament into the Bach language, and then went to work among the Paez Indians in Colombia, S America. The Tzeltal had called the Bible the "Good Seed," and Ma faithfully sowed the Good Seed among the Tzeltal, Bachajon, and Paez, ing every man, woman and child should have their own Bible.

I do not turn aside from your rules, for you have taught me.
—Psalm 119:102—

DECEMBER 1
FROM VENGEANCE TO FORGIVENESS

December 7, 1941, Sgt. Jacob DeShazer was peeling potatoes in an army camp when he heard of the attack on Pearl Harbor. He threw a potato at the wall and shouted "The Japs are going to have to pay for this." Soon after, DeShazer volunteered for a special unit forming to attack Japan. The crews began intensive training with the B-25, and the team gained the name "Doolittle's Raiders" after their commander, Lt. Col. Jimmy Doolittle. De Shazer was a bombardier on one of the B-25s. The April 18, 1942, attack on Tokyo and military targets in Japan was successful, but returning from the bombing, the aircraft, running low on fuel, crash-landed on the China coast. Eight of the airmen, including Jacob DeShazer, were captured by the Japanese.

The men were treated as war criminals, and three were executed by firing squad. The sentences of the others were commuted to life imprisonment. They were severely beaten and malnourished; one died of starvation. At one point, DeShazer was able to have a copy of the Bible. DeShazer read the Bible several times through and the Prophets six times, tracing the fulfillment of biblical prophecies. He memorized the Sermon on the Mount, I John, and many other passages of Scripture. June 8, 1944, Romans 10:9 especially spoke to DeShazer: "If you confess with your mouth that Jesus is Lord and believe in your heart that God raised him from the dead, you will be saved." DeShazer did believe and trust Jesus as Savior. The hatred and bitterness he had towards the Japanese turned into a love for his enemies, and he began to show respect and kindness to his brutal prison guards. They recognized the change in DeShazer, and their treatment of him improved as well. The war ended in August 1945, and after 40 months in prison, DeShazer was released. The next month, DeShazer enrolled in Seattle Pacific College to train to become a missionary—in Japan.

DeShazer returned to Japan in December 28, 1948 and began to tell the Japanese about Jesus. Within his first year in Japan, it is estimated there were 30,000 Japanese conversions. DeShazer and his wife Florence were missionaries in Japan for thirty years, sharing the love of Christ with once bitter enemies.

Redeem me from man's oppression,
that I may keep your precepts.
—Psalm 119:134—

IN THE SHELTER OF THE MOST HIGH

In 1837, Willem ten Boom opened a watch shop in a 200-year-old house in Haarlem, Holland. His son Casper continued as a watchmaker and raised four children in the home. The youngest, named Cornelia but called Corrie, became the first licensed female watchmaker in the Netherlands. Even more than working as a watchmaker, Corrie enjoyed helping others in the name of Christ. She organized clubs for teenage girls, providing them Bible instructions as well as teaching them sewing and handicrafts. She raised foster children in the old home and started a church for the mentally disabled.

In the spring of 1940, when the Nazis invaded the Netherlands, Corrie's Bible studies were banned. When Jews began to be rounded up and arrested, the ten Booms hid them in a secret room in their house. Some have estimated that the family saved the lives of 800 Jews during the Nazi occupation.

However, February 28, 1894, the Gestapo raided the ten Boom home and arrested the family, taking them to Schevingen prison. Casper asked his son to read them Psalm 91, beginning "He who dwells in the shelter of the Most High will abide in the shadow of the Almighty, I will say to the Lord, 'My refuge and my fortress, my God, in whom I trust.'" This was the last time Corrie saw her eighty-five-year-old father, for he was separated from them and died nine days later. Psalm 91 continued to be a special source of courage and inspiration for Corrie throughout her own imprisonment in the concentration camps.

While in prison, Corrie and her sister Betsy had Bible studies for the prisoners. They wondered why the guards seemed to stay away from the Bible studies, then they learned that the guards stayed away because of the fleas that were in the room! Corrie and Betsy thanked God for the fleas as they continued to find the Lord their refuge.

... you know in your hearts and souls, all of you,
that not one word has failed of all the good things
that the Lord your God promised concerning you.
All have come to pass for you; not one of them has failed.
—Joshua 23:14—

DECEMBER 3
DIETRICH BONHOEFFER ON BIBLE MEDITATION

Dietrich Bonhoeffer (1906-1945) was a leader of the Confessing Church in Germany, which stood firm for the Christian faith against Hitler's anti-Semitism and attempts to mold the church into a Nazi framework. The Nazis banned Bonhoeffer from preaching, and he joined the resistance movement. His resistance connections were discovered, and Bonhoeffer was imprisoned for the last two years of World War II. On April 9, 1945, just two days before the end of the War, he was hanged. Bonhoeffer understood that such a death could be the cost of following Christ.

Bonhoeffer wrote much about meditating on the Scripture. He noted that

> It is not necessary for us to find new ideas in our meditation. Often that only distracts us and satisfies our vanity. It is perfectly sufficient if the Word enters in and dwells within us as we read and understand it, as Mary "pondered...in her heart" what the shepherds told her (Luke 2:19), as a person's words often stick in our mind for a long time—as they dwell and work within us, preoccupy us, disturb us, or make us happy without our being able to do anything about it—so as we meditate, God's Word desires to enter in and stay with us. It desires to move us, to work in us, and to make such an impression on us that the whole day long we will not get away from it. Then, it will do its work in us, often without our being aware of it ...[1]

> The Word of Scripture should never stop sounding in your ears and working in you all day long, just like the words of someone you love. And just as you do not analyze the words of someone you love, but accept them as they are said to you, accept the Word of Scripture and ponder it in your heart, as Mary did. That is all. That is meditation ... Do not ask 'How shall I pass this on?' but 'What does it say to me?' Then ponder this Word long in your heart until it has gone right into you and taken possession of you.[2]

> Every gift we receive, every new understanding, drives us still deeper into the Word of God. We need time for God's Word. In order to understand the commandments of God correctly we must meditate at length upon his Word.[3]

And I shall lift up my hands to Your commandments,
Which I love; and I will meditate on Your statutes.
—Psalm 119:48—

DECEMBER 4
BIBLES FOR JAPAN

September 2, 1945, General Douglas MacArthur formally accepted the Japanese surrender aboard the *USS Missouri*, ending the four years of World War II in the Pacific. In the ensuing four years, MacArthur was the Supreme Commander of Allied Powers overseeing the occupation of Japan. Under MacArthur's oversight, Japan was transformed into a parliamentary democracy, and economic stability was brought to the war-ravaged nation. Shintoism was abolished as the state religion, the emperor was no longer recognized as a god, and freedom of religion became part of the constitution.

MacArthur believed that its defeat in the war had left a spiritual vacuum in Japan, and he believed that Christianity was important in undergirding the new democracy. Like many earlier American leaders, he believed that democracy can succeed only with a moral and virtuous people. In a letter in 1948, MacArthur wrote, "I am absolutely convinced that true democracy can exist only on a spiritual foundation. It will endure when it rests firmly on the Christian conception of the individual and society."[4] MacArthur also thought that the Christian faith among the Japanese would be an antidote to the spread of communism in the ravaged country. Accordingly, MacArthur encouraged Christians to send missionaries, and he called for the importation of 10 million Bibles to Japan.

Even more than his numerous military accolades, MacArthur considered his "spiritual stewardship" of Japan his most important work. In one letter written as Supreme Commander on April 4, 1949, he wrote

> It gives me great pleasure to commend the reading of the Bible, God's immortal gift…In the Sacred Scriptures you will find the Saviour of the world Who is the chief cornerstone of all liberty, the basis of fair and honest government, and the foundation for a … faith in God Whose promises never fail.[5]

I hope for your salvation, O Lord,
and I do your commandments.
—Psalm 119:166—

DECEMBER 5
YEMINITE TORAH SCROLLS

Yemenite Jews are among the oldest of the Jewish communities outside of the land of Israel, claiming to have moved to the southern tip of the Arabian peninsula, the ancient land of Sheba, 42 years before the destruction of the First Temple in 586 BC. Relatively isolated from the larger Jewish Diaspora, the Yemenite Jews preserved the Hebrew punctuation and pronunciation similar to that used by Jews during the Babylonian captivity, which was different in many respects from that used by Sephardic (Spanish) and Ashkenazi (Central/Eastern European) Jews today.

For centuries the Yemenite Jews were the only minority in a Moslem country, and they endured regular periods of persecution and forced conversion. When the modern state of Israel was created in 1948, Moslem rioters in Yemen began a bloody pogrom of killing and rampage against the Jews. From 1948-1950 almost 50,000 Yemenite Jews, virtually the entire community, emigrated to Israel. Jews who had never seen an airplane before were airlifted back to their homeland, reminding them of God's description of that earlier Exodus, "I bare you on Eagles wings, and brought you unto myself." (Ex. 19:4). The emigration, often called "On Eagles Wings" or "Operation Magic Carpet," carried the Yemenite Jews not only thousands of miles, but seemingly thousands of years, as they were confronted with a totally different, technological way of life in their new land.

In their emigration, the Jews brought with them their Torah scrolls. The rabbis had implemented stringent rules for the copying of the Hebrew manuscripts. The rules required a scribe to pronounce every word out loud before writing it, not writing any word from memory but only while looking at another scroll, and counting each letter on a line and page to make certain nothing had been added. It would take a scribe one year to copy a Torah scroll. Though the Yemenite Jews were isolated for centuries from much of the rest of the Jewish people, a Yemenite scroll has only nine letter differences between it and European Jewish scrolls.

For truly, I say to you, until heaven and earth pass away,
not an iota, not a dot, will pass from the Law until all is accomplished.
—Matthew 5:18—

A PRAYER AT FOREST HOME

When Billy Graham (1918-2018) was only 30 years old, he had already pastored several churches. As an evangelist with the newly-formed Youth for Christ, he had preached across a post-World War II Europe. He became President of Northwestern College in St. Paul, Minnesota, the nation's youngest college President! He had held city-wide evangelistic campaigns in several U.S. cities, but, with meetings in Los Angeles looming, Graham was restless and depressed. His friend Charles Templeton, a founder of Youth for Christ, had enrolled at Princeton Divinity School and was telling Graham the Bible was filled with contradictions and flaws.

Henrietta Mears, a Christian educator, invited Graham to speak at Forest Home, a Christian camp and retreat center in the San Bernardino Mountains. Miss Mears met with him for Bible study and prayer, giving him much insight on the truthfulness of Scriptures. Graham had no doubts about Christ's deity or the Gospel, but was the Bible completely true? He knew that phrases such as "The Lord said" were in the Scriptures over 2000 times. Jesus loved the Scriptures and quoted from them constantly. If Graham couldn't trust the Bible, he couldn't continue as an evangelist. One night at Forest Home, he knelt by a tree stump, placed his open Bible on it, and prayed something like,

> O God! There are many things in this book I do not understand. There are many problems with it for which I have no solution. There are many seeming contradictions. There are some areas in it that do not seem to correlate with modern science. I can't answer some of the philosophical and psychological questions ... others are raising ... Father, I am going to accept this as Thy Word—by *faith!* I'm going to allow faith to go beyond my intellectual questions and doubts, and I will believe this to be Your inspired Word." [6]

When Graham preached in Los Angeles, the scheduled three weeks had to be extended to eight. Attendance was 350,000 people, and 3000 were converted to Christ. Graham became a national figure and proclaimed the Word throughout the world for the next sixty years.

With my whole heart I seek you;
let me not wander from your commandments!
—Psalm 119:10—

DECEMBER 7
FROM PEARL HARBOR TO CALVARY

Mitsuo Fuchida was facing difficult, despairing days. He had been exhilarated back in December 1941 when he successfully coordinated the Japanese attack on Pearl Harbor, leading the first wave of the attack. Fuchida became a national hero after the successful attack and even enjoyed a personal audience with Emperor Hirohito. Though Fuchida was later injured at the battle of Midway, he recovered and was promoted to the rank of captain. After the war, the Japanese forces were disbanded. Fuchida returned home to the village of Osaka and began farming, discouraged and unhappy.

Several times Fuchida was called by Gen. Douglas MacArthur to testify at the war crimes trials, though never accused himself. One day, getting off the train in Tokyo, he was given a pamphlet called *I Was a Prisoner of Japan.* The pamphlet was the story of Jake DeShazer's time as a prisoner of war of the Japanese, the bitterness he had against the Japanese, and the transformation he underwent as he read the Bible and gave his life to Christ, and how he learned to forgive his enemies. The pamphlet concluded with Jake returning to Japan as a missionary to share the love of Christ with the Japanese. Fuchida couldn't understand such forgiveness, but he decided he needed to read that book. Though a Buddhist, he found himself a Bible and began reading. When he came to the description of the Crucifixion and read Jesus' prayer in Luke 23:34, "Father forgive them; for they know not what they do," Fuchida realized Jesus was praying for him too and that he could have forgiveness in Christ. He understood Jesus had died for his sins, and he prayed that Jesus would give him a new purpose for living. On that day, April 14, 1950, Fuchida became a new person.

Fuchida became an evangelist presenting the Gospel of Jesus throughout Japan and the Orient. He recognized, "Though my country has the highest literacy rate in the world, education has not brought salvation. Peace and freedom—both national and personal—come only through an encounter with Jesus Christ."[7]

Let your hand be ready to help me,
for I have chosen your precepts.
—Psalm 119:173—

THE BIBLE AS A MARINER'S CHART

Pastor Arthur W. Pink (1886-1952) had a truly international ministry. Born in Nottingham England, he was raised in a Christian family. He flirted for a time with Theosophy, but in 1908 had a conversion to Christ. He studied briefly at Moody Bible Institute, married a lady from Kentucky, and pastored churches in Colorado, California, Kentucky, South Carolina, and Australia, before returning to Britain and devoting himself to writing. From 1922 to 1953 Pink published the monthly magazine *Studies in the Scriptures*. Pink's work was important in encouraging a resurgence of biblical exposition. In one issue, Pink described something of the importance of the Scripture for the individual Christian:

> The Bible is a book which calls not so much for the exertion of our intellect as it does for the exercise of our affections, conscience, and will. God has given it to us not for our entertainment, but for our education, to make known what He requires from us. Therefore, whenever we open the Bible, the all-important consideration for each of us to keep before him is, "What is there here for me today? What bearing does the passage now before me have upon my present case and circumstances—what warning, what encouragement, what information? What instruction is there to direct me in the management of my business, to guide me in the ordering of my domestic and social affairs, to promote a closer walking with God?" I should see myself addressed in every precept, included in every promise .... Nothing else will secure us from the infections of this world, deliver from the temptations of Satan, and be so effectual a preservative from sin, as the Word of God received into our affections. "The law of his God is in his heart; none of his steps shall slide" (Psalm 37:31) can only be said of the one who has made personal appropriation of that Law, and is able to aver with the Psalmist, "Thy word have I hid in mine heart, that I might not sin against thee"(Psalm 119:11). Just so long as the truth is actually working in us, influencing us in a practical way, is loved and revered by us, stirs the conscience, are we kept from falling into open sin—as Joseph was preserved when evilly solicited by his master's wife (Gen 39:9). And only as we personally go out and daily gather our portion of manna, and feed upon the same, will there be strength provided for the performing of duty and the bringing forth of fruit to the glory of God.[8]

... brothers, pray for us, that the word of the Lord may speed ahead
and be honored, as happened among you.
—II Thessalonians 3:1—

DECEMBER 9
GOD'S SMUGGLER

Andrew van der Bijl, born in the Netherlands to a poor blacksmith and an invalid mother, is known to many as Brother Andrew or "God's Smuggler" for his efforts to bring the Bible into forbidden areas. After World War II, Brother Andrew enlisted in the army of the Dutch East Indies where he suffered a period of great emotional distress and was wounded in the ankle. During his recuperation, he obsessively read the Bible and became a Christian.

Compelled by the Scripture in Revelation 3:2, "Wake up, strengthen what remains and is about to die," in 1955, Brother Andrew took his first trip into communist Poland to minister to the Christians there. In ensuing years, Brother Andrew travelled to other communist nations—including the Soviet Union, Czechoslovakia, Cuba, China, and some African countries where Christians were oppressed. Brother Andrew travelled with Bibles and Christian literature into many areas where it was forbidden. A prayer he began to say as he sought to enter the countries where Christians were persecuted was, "Lord, in my luggage I have Scripture I want to take to your children. When you were on earth, You made blind eyes see. Now, I pray, make seeing eyes blind. Do not let the guards see those things You do not want them to see."[9]

One of Brother Andrew's favorite stories was when he approached the Romanian border in his Volkswagen Beetle packed with illegal Bibles. He was in a line of cars, and he watched as each car in front of him had the drivers forced out and all the car's contents spread out on the ground. Sometimes the guards removed hubcaps, removed seats, and took apart the engine. Brother Andrew prayed and put some of the Bibles out in the open in the car for the guards to see. When he came to the check point, he gave the guard his papers and started to get out, but the guard had his knee against the door keeping it closed. The guard then just waved him on after looking at his papers. God had cleared the way to bring the Bibles into Romania.

Brother Andrew went on to found Open Doors, which supports persecuted Christians throughout the world.

It is the Spirit who gives life; the flesh is no help at all.
The words that I have spoken to you are spirit and life.
—John 6:63—

HELEN KELLER'S BIBLE

Helen Keller (1880-1968) became both blind and deaf from an illness contracted at 19 months. Yet she learned to speak and communicate. She learned to read books with raised letters and began reading the Bible.

In 1900, Helen was admitted to Radcliffe College. When she was graduated in 1904, Helen became the first blind person to earn a Bachelor of Arts degree. While at Radcliffe, the American Bible Society sent Helen portions of Scriptures in raised letters which she did not have. October 18, 1901, Helen typed out a letter of thanksgiving (without any typing errors) to Mr. Fox of the Bible Society:

> The volumes of the Old Testament, which you sent me by the Fall River Line several days ago, came today; and I want to thank you for them, and for your kind letter. I can never be grateful enough for the tokens of regard and interest that come to me so unexpectedly from friends whom I have never seen. Their pleasant words make every day of my life blossom with sweetest flowers. Will you kindly convey my grateful acknowledgments to the American Bible Society? They have lent me a helping hand when I needed it very much. I am studying the Bible in college this year and reading it with a delight that increases from day to day. Life grows richer and heaven nearer as God's great truths unfold themselves to me. With renewed thanks for your kindness, I am sincerely yours, Helen Keller.[10]

As she read through the Old Testament, her favorite verse became Isaiah 40:31, "But they that wait upon the Lord shall renew their strength; they shall mount up with wings as eagles; they shall run, and not be weary; and they shall walk, and not faint."

In 1931, the American Bible Society presented Helen with its first Braille Bible. She then gave them her older raised-letter Bible. With the thick paper and raised Braille markings, a complete Braille Bible is 21 volumes. Helen wrote,

> Unless we form the habit of going to the Bible in bright moments as well as in trouble, we cannot fully respond to its consolations because we lack equilibrium between light and darkness.[11]

Turn my eyes from looking at worthless things;
and give me life in your ways.
—Psalm 119:37—

DECEMBER 11
GOD IS NOT SILENT

In 1930, seventeen-year-old Francis Schaeffer (1912-1984) went to the bookstore to buy a beginner's reader to help him teach English to a Russian. He came home instead with a book on Greek philosophy! He was fascinated as he read, but he found that the philosophers asked a lot of questions without offering any answers about the human condition. The sermons he heard at church seemed as empty of meaning. Francis thought maybe he should just not call himself a Christian. However, as he thought, he realized he had never really read the Bible. Before discarding Christianity, maybe he should read the Bible. So, in the evenings he began reading Greek philosophy and the Bible. Gradually he put aside the Greek philosophy, but kept reading the Bible.

Schaeffer read the Bible as he read any other book, starting at Genesis and reading through to Revelation. In the flow of biblical history, with the accounts of the creation, fall of man, and redemption in Christ, he saw a view of life which fit the real world. In the Bible he discovered answers to life's questions. Christianity was not just an ethical system, as he had heard in church, but was an entire way of seeing. Within six months, Francis bowed before the God of Scriptures and accepted Christ as his Savior.

After college, Francis married Edith Seville, the daughter of missionaries to China, attended seminary, and became a pastor. In 1947, the Schaeffers went to Switzerland as missionaries; and in 1955, they established a Christian study center they named L'Abri, meaning "the shelter." At L'Abri, visitors could study and examine the relevance of Christianity to the issues of life, as well as enjoy the love and community the Schaeffers offered.

In Francis Schaeffer's lectures, discussions, and numerous books, he repeatedly proclaimed that God exists and is not silent. God is not a philosophical concept dreamed up by man, but He has spoken in the Bible. There He tells us about Himself, about us, and about our world. In the Bible we find truth which fits the real world. Schaeffer saw that all people have dignity, for all are created in God's image. While living a life of care and compassion for others, Schaeffer pointed them to the truth of the God who was there and encouraged them to look at all of life through the truth of the Scriptures.

Who among you fears the Lord and obeys the voice of his servant?
Let him who walks in darkness and has no light
trust in the name of the Lord and rely on his God.
—Isaiah 50:10—

DECEMBER 12
THE BIBLE AND SCIENCE

Werner von Braun (1912-1977) oversaw some of the leading technological developments of the twentieth century. Born in Germany, von Braun developed the V-2 rocket during World War II. At one point during the war, he was arrested by the Nazis for expressing reservations about the Nazi victory. He was released after a few weeks because he was considered indispensable for the V-2 rocket program. As the war wound down to its close, von Braun and his team considered whether to surrender to the Soviets or the Americans. Not wanting the world to endure another dreadful conflict, they thought it best to surrender to a country guided by the Bible. Von Braun came to the United States, bringing with him his rocket technology. Von Braun had long dreamed of sending men into space, even Mars, and establishing a station in space. He was director of NASA from 1960 to 1970, developing the Saturn rocket and overseeing the early Apollo moon flights.

Though raised in a Christian family, von Braun's Christian faith did not take root and grow until his time in the United States. He often would speak out about the compatibility of science and religion, affirming his belief that nature came into being through a Designer/Creator, not by chance. He stated that

> In this age of space flight, when we use the modern tools of science to advance into new regions of human activity, the Bible—this grandiose, stirring history of the gradual revelation and unfolding of the moral law—remains in every way an up-to-date book.

> Our knowledge and use of the laws of nature that enable us to fly to the moon also enable us to destroy our home planet with the atom bomb. Science itself does not address the question whether we should use the power at our disposal for good or for evil.

> The guidelines of what we ought to do are furnished in the moral law of God. It is no longer enough that we pray that God may be with us on our side. We must learn to pray that we may be on God's side.[12]

Von Braun is buried in Alexandria, Virginia. Psalm 19:1 is on his grave marker, "The heavens declare the glory of God; and the sky above proclaims his handiwork."

> *... the precepts of the Lord are right; rejoicing the heart;*
> *the commandment of the Lord is pure, enlightening the eyes.*
> —Psalm 19:8—

DECEMBER 13
SHOULD PEOPLE READ THE BIBLE?

During the Protestant Reformation, all Christians were encouraged to read the Bible and learn God's Word. As a result, literacy increased. The Roman Church, however, had a long history of prohibiting the Scriptures in vernacular translations. The 1407 Constitutions of Oxford prohibited the circulation of John Wycliffe's English translation, and no one was permitted to translate the Scriptures without the approval of the Archbishop. People were burned for possessing even portions of Wycliffe's translation. Behind such regulations was the belief that the Scriptures are too high a matter for ordinary people to inquire into. The Bible was not used to instruct either the clergy or the laity.

Though in the 9th century the Pope had given permission to Methodius to translate the scriptures into Slavonic for use by the Moravian church, by the 11th century, once the church had been established, Pope Gregory VII prohibited the use of the Slavonic Scriptures. If the Scriptures were easily available to all men, he said, they would become disrespected and falsely understood. In the 12th century the Waldensians had a vernacular Scripture, but Pope Innocent III decreed that the laity should not have the Scriptures, for they were difficult for even the most educated to fully understand; they were not to "cast pearls before swine." Many local church councils made similar restrictions, fearing that people would misinterpret them or become heretics.

The 1546 Council of Trent allowed Bibles in the vernacular, but only if accompanied by annotations approved by the Church. A papal decree in 1713 again condemned the Bible for everyone, but in 1757, Pope Benedict XIV stated the nations should have the Bible in their own languages. In the 19th century, several popes issued encyclicals against Bible societies and Bible distribution, especially if Bibles did not have Catholic annotations.

However, *Dei Verbum* (the Word of God) from the 2nd Vatican Council in the 1960s affirmed the importance of the Scriptures in the life of all Christians:

> Easy access to Sacred Scripture should be provided for all the Christian faithful. That is why the Church ... sees to it that suitable and correct translations are made into different languages, especially from the original texts of the sacred books .... The sacred synod also earnestly and especially urges all the Christian faithful ... to learn by frequent reading of the divine Scriptures the "excellent knowledge of Jesus Christ" (Phil. 3:8). "For ignorance of the Scriptures is ignorance of Christ."... Therefore, they should gladly put themselves in touch with the sacred text itself ... And let them remember that prayer should accompany the reading of Sacred Scripture, so that God and

man may talk together; for "we speak to Him when we pray; we hear Him when we read the divine saying." [13]

And now I commend you to God and to the word of his grace,
which is able to build you up and to give you the inheritance
among all those who are sanctified.
— Acts 20:32—

DECEMBER 14
THE BIBLE ON THE MOON

Apollo 8 was the first manned mission to orbit the Moon. On Christmas Eve, 1968, Apollo 8's crew of Frank Borman, Jim Lovell, and William Anders sent a message to "all the people on Earth." In a live television broadcast, they showed photos of the earth and moon as they read the first ten verses of Genesis, "In the beginning God created the heavens and the earth ... And God called the dry land Earth, and the gathering together of the waters he called Seas: and God saw that it was good."

In 1969, Apollo 11 became the first mission to land on the Moon. After completing all the landing chores, astronaut Buzz Aldrin celebrated communion, using a tiny communion chalice given to him for this occasion by his church. He read Jesus' words from John 15:5, "I am the vine; you are the branches. If a man remains in me, and I in him, he will bear much fruit. Apart from me you can do nothing." Later, during his Moon walk, Aldrin left on the Moon a portion of Psalm 8 he had written out, "When I consider thy heavens, the work of thy fingers, the moon and the stars which thou hast ordained; What is man, that thou art mindful of him?"

In 1971, Apollo 15 visited the Moon's highest mountains, the Appenine Mountains. The sun shining on the lunar scene brought Psalm 121 to Astronaut Jim Irwin's mind, "I look to the hills, from whence cometh my help? My help comes from the Lord who made heaven and earth." As exciting as walking on the moon was, back on earth Irwin frequently told people that, "Jesus Christ walking on the earth is more important than man walking on the moon."[14]

John Glenn, the first American in space in 1962, was able to be part of a space shuttle flight 36 years later, in 1998. He then said, "To look at this kind of creation out here and not believe in God is to me impossible. It just strengthens my faith."[15]

The heavens declare the glory of God,
and the sky above proclaims his handiwork.
—Psalm 19:1—

DECEMBER 15
THE TEN COMMANDMENTS
AND AMERICAN LAW

Above the seat of the Chief Justice in the Supreme Court building in Washington D.C. is a figure with a tablet with 10 Roman numerals on it, portraying Moses with the Ten Commandments. The doors of the U.S. Supreme Court building have a carving of the Ten Commandments, and a carving of Moses with the two tablets of the law can also be seen on the rear façade of the building. Moses' law and the moral teachings of the Bible have long been recognized as foundational to American morals and law. In his 1836 *A Course of Legal Study*, Professor David Hoffman noted that

> The purity and sublimity of the morals of the Bible have at no time been questioned; it is the foundation of the common law of every Christian nation. The Christian religion is a part of the law of the land, and, as such, should certainly receive no inconsiderable portion of the lawyer's attention.[16]

In a 1950 ruling, the Florida Supreme Court stated that

> A people unschooled about the sovereignty of God, the ten commandments, and the ethics of Jesus, could never have evolved the Bill of Rights, the Declaration of Independence, and the Constitution. There is not one solitary fundamental principle of our democratic policy that did not stem directly from the basic moral concepts as embodied in the Decalogue.[17]

The same year, President Harry S. Truman noted the importance of the Bible to America's laws:

> The fundamental basis of this nation's laws was given to Moses on the Mount. The fundamental basis of our Bill of Rights comes from the teachings we get from Exodus and St. Matthew, from Isaiah and St. Paul. I don't think we emphasize that enough these days. If we don't have the proper fundamental moral background, we will finally wind up with a totalitarian government which does not believe in rights for anybody except the state.[18]

… it is easier for heaven and earth to pass away
than for one dot of the Law to become void.
—Luke 16:17—

DECEMBER 16

A BIBLE-READING GENERAL

When he was a cadet at West Point, twenty-year old William K. Harrison (1895-1987) began a program of systematic Bible reading. He read the Old Testament through once a year and the New Testament through once every three months. He continued this practice throughout his busy life, so that his mind was informed by the Word of God. He brought the Scriptures to bear on every area of his life; people marveled at his knowledge of the Bible.

During World War II, Harrison was the most decorated soldier in the 30th infantry division, receiving the Distinguished Service Cross, the Bronze Star for Valor, and the Purple Heart. At the head of the Allied forces, he was the first American to enter Belgium during the war. In the Korean War, Harrison was Chief of Staff in the UN Command and headed the negotiations that led to the armistice.

When he retired from the army in 1957, Harrison was active in Christian service. He was executive director of the Evangelical Child Welfare Agency of Chicago for three years and served as president of the Officers' Christian Fellowship from 1954 to 1972. He was also on the board of Dallas Theological Seminary and a contributing editor of *Christianity Today*.

Even in the midst of a very busy and active life, Harrison maintained the pattern of daily Bible reading he had begun at West Point. Even during wartime, he would catch up on his Bible reading after days missed because of the ongoing battles. By the time he was 91, and his eyesight was failing, Harrison had read the Old Testament 70 times and the New Testament 280 times! His heart, mind, soul, and life had been shaped by the Word of God.

I hold back my feet from every evil way,
in order to keep your word.
—Psalm 119:101—

PRESIDENT GERALD FORD ON THE BIBLE

In a 1976 address to the Southern Baptist Convention, President Gerald Ford spoke of the importance of God's law and the Bible to the nation:

The American people have seen too much abuse of the moral imperatives of honesty and of decency upon which religion and government and civilized society must rest. To remedy these abuses, we must look not only to the government but, more importantly, to the Bible, the church, the human heart. We must look to the family for the instruction in righteousness and for the stabilizing influence so important in a complex, confusing, and ever-changing world. We must look to the faith of our fathers. The laws of God were of very special importance to our Founding Fathers and to the Nation they created.

I believe it is no accident of history, no coincidence that this Nation, which declared its dependence on God even while declaring its independence from foreign domination, has become the most richly blessed nation in the history of mankind and the world. For it is as true today as it was in the Old Testament times that "blessed is the nation whose God is the Lord." I believe that very deeply, and so do you.

In my own life and throughout my career in public service, I have found in the pages of the Bible a steady compass and a source of great strength and peace. As each of my predecessors in the Presidency has done, I asked for God's guidance as I undertook the duties of this office. I have asked for that guidance many times since …

As America enters its third century … we could ask no better inspiration than those words of a favorite passage of mine from the Book of Proverbs: "Trust in the Lord with all thine heart and lean not unto thine own understanding. In all thy ways acknowledge Him and He shall direct thy paths.[19]

Your faithfulness endures to all generations;
you have established the earth, and it stands fast.
By your appointment they stand this day,
for all things are your servants.
—Psalm 119:90-91—

DECEMBER 18
BIBLICAL INERRANCY

In 1977, The International Council on Biblical Inerrancy (ICBI) was founded to clarify and defend the inerrancy of the Scriptures. The Council held three summits. The 1978 summit developed a statement on Biblical inerrancy which is considered a landmark document—The Chicago Statement on Biblical Inerrancy. Signed by over 300 Christian leaders, representing a wide variety of denominations and backgrounds, the statement is one of the most comprehensive statements on the inspiration and authority of the Scripture in church history. The complete statement covers 19 articles, but "A Short Statement" provides a summary:

1. God, who is Himself truth and speaks truth only, has inspired Holy Scripture in order thereby to reveal Himself to lost mankind through Jesus Christ as Creator and Lord, Redeemer and Judge. Holy Scripture is God's witness to Himself.

2. Holy Scripture, being God's own Word, written by men prepared and superintended by His Spirit, is of infallible divine authority in all matters upon which it touches: it is to be believed, as God's instruction, in all that it affirms; obeyed, as God's command, in all that it requires; embraced, as God's pledge, in all that it promises.

3. The Holy Spirit, Scripture's divine Author, both authenticates it to us by His inward witness and opens our minds to understand its meaning.

4. Being wholly and verbally God-given, Scripture is without error or fault in all its teaching, no less in what it states about God's acts in creation, about the events of world history, and about its own literary origins under God, than in its witness to God's saving grace in individual lives.

5. The authority of Scripture is inescapably impaired if this total divine inerrancy is in any way limited, disregarded, or made relative to a view of truth contrary to the Bible's own; and such lapses bring serious loss to both individual and the Church.[20]

In 1982 and 1986, the ICBI held further summits on Biblical Hermeneutics and Biblical application and issued similar statements and publications on these Biblical issues. The ICBI disbanded in 1989.

Your righteousness is righteous forever, and your law is true.
—Psalm 119:142—

BIBLES IN CHINA

In 1966, Mao Zedong instituted the Great Proletarian Cultural revolution in China to preserve Chinese communism against the inroads of capitalism as well as to preserve traditional elements of Chinese culture. Part of the revolution was the outlawing of all religion in China. Bibles were confiscated and burned, churches were destroyed, and Christians were persecuted, tortured, and imprisoned. One pastor later told that during this period, he hid his Bible within the bricks of a wall to avoid its confiscation. When Bibles were unavailable, many carefully copied and hid portions of Scripture for their personal use. China was paralyzed economically for a decade as the Maoist policies of the Cultural Revolution continued, and many suffered persecution for their faith.

In 1979, the United States established diplomatic relations with the People's Republic of China. During Premier Deng Xiaoping's visit to the United States that year, President Jimmy Carter told Deng of his Christian faith and asked him to change the Chinese government's policies towards religion. Carter made three requests: guarantee freedom of worship, allow Bible distribution in China, and allow missionaries back into China. Before leaving the United States, the Premier said he would change the law for freedom of worship and allowing Bibles, but not allow missionaries, which the Chinese considered purveyors of western and foreign values. The next year, in 1980, churches were allowed to reopen in China.

In 1985, The Amity Foundation was established to provide Christian educational, medical, and social assistance. An important part of the Foundation is The Amity Printing Company, established in 1987. Amity has distributed 80 million Bibles in China, and today is the largest Bible printing press in the world. Amity has printed over 180 million Bibles in more than 90 different languages, including English, German, Spanish French and many African languages.

Contrary to the law, recently President Xi Jinping has implemented policies against Christians—shutting down churches, burning Bibles, persecuting Christians. Yet, Christianity continues to grow in China, with over one million becoming Christians each year.

All thy commandments are faithful:
they persecute me wrongfully; help thou me.
—Psalm 119:86—

DECEMBER 20
PRESIDENT RONALD REAGAN AND THE BIBLE

At his first inauguration, on January 20, 1981, Ronald Reagan chose to use his mother's worn Bible when taking the oath of office. He placed his hand on one of her favorite verses, II Chronicles 7:14: "If my people which are called by my name, shall humble themselves and pray, and seek my face, and turn from their wicked ways; then will I hear from heaven, and will forgive their sin, and will heal their land." Nelle Reagan had underlined the verse and wrote beside it, "A most wonderful verse for the healing of a nation."

Nelle Reagan's strong Christian faith profoundly influenced Ronald as a boy and throughout his life. With her he faithfully attended the Disciples of Christ church in Dixon, Illinois, where Nelle not only taught Sunday School and headed the Missionary Society, but let the light of her Christian faith shine by visiting the prisons, helping the poor, and by her dramatic readings of Scripture. Though the family was poor and went through many difficulties, Nelle believed that everything that happens does so for a reason, that God's Providence was working out His purposes, even if they were not understood at the time. Her son shared this trust in God's plan, purposes, and Providence throughout his life.

By the time he was fifteen, Ronald was teaching a Sunday School class of his own. Many in Dixon were convinced that the young Reagan had a call to the ministry; Nelle hoped her son would be a missionary. When Reagan spoke at his (public) high school commencement, he challenged the graduates to reflect on Jesus' words in John 10:10, "I have come that they may have life, and that they may have it more abundantly."

The rich grounding Reagan received in the Bible continued with Reagan throughout his adult life, shaping his character, his words, and even his vision for America. When asked his favorite Scripture, he usually quoted John 3:16, elaborating, "… having accepted Jesus Christ as my Savior, I have God's promise of eternal life in Heaven, as well as the abundant life here on earth."[21]

How can a young man keep his way pure?
By guarding it according to your word.
—Psalm 119:9—

YEAR OF THE BIBLE

The year 1983 was the 200ᵗʰ anniversary of the Paris Peace Treaty ending the American War for Independence and the beginning of the United States' 3ʳᵈ century as a nation. The United States Congress encouraged President Reagan to proclaim 1983 the "Year of the Bible." His proclamation said this:

> Of the many influences that have shaped the United States of America into a distinctive Nation and people, none may be said to be more fundamental and enduring than the Bible. Deep religious beliefs stemming from the Old and New Testaments of the Bible inspired many of the early settlers of our country ... These shared beliefs helped forge a sense of common purpose among the widely dispersed colonies—a sense of community which laid the foundation for the spirit of nationhood that was to develop in later decades.

> The Bible and its teachings helped form the basis for the Founding Father's abiding belief in the inalienable rights of the individual, rights which they found implicit in the Bible's teachings of the inherent worth and dignity of each individual ... For centuries the Bible's emphasis on compassion and love for our neighbor has inspired institutional and governmental expressions of benevolent outreach such as private charity, the establishment of schools and hospitals, and the abolition of slavery. ...

> The plain-spoken Andrew Jackson referred to the Bible as no less than "the rock on which our Republic rests."

> Today our beloved America, and indeed, the world, is facing a decade of enormous challenge. ... We will need resources of spirit even more than resources of technology, education, and armaments. There could be no more fitting moment than now to reflect with gratitude, humility, and urgency upon the wisdom revealed to us in the writing that Abraham Lincoln called "the best gift God has ever given to man. But for it we could not know right from wrong." ...

> NOW, THEREFORE, I, RONALD REAGAN, President of the United States of America, ... do hereby proclaim 1983 the Year of the Bible in the United States. I encourage all citizens, each in his or her own way, to re-examine and rediscover its priceless and timeless message.[22]

I will delight in your statutes; I will not forget your word.
—Psalm 119:16—

DECEMBER 22
THE BIBLE IN PUBLIC POLICY

Margaret Thatcher (1925-2013) was the first woman Prime Minister of the United Kingdom and the longest-serving Prime Minister in the twentieth century. A research chemist before studying law, Thatcher was a Member of Parliament and Secretary of State for Education and Science before becoming Prime Minister. The daughter of a Methodist lay preacher, Thatcher's Christian faith was important to her throughout her life and public career.

In a 1988 address to the General Assembly of the Church of Scotland, Thatcher noted:

> We are a nation whose ideals are founded on the Bible. Also, it is quite impossible to understand our history or literature without grasping this fact, and that's the strong practical case for ensuring that children at school are given adequate instruction in the part which the Judaic-Christian tradition has played in molding our laws, manners and institutions. How can you make sense of Shakespeare and Sir Walter Scott, or of the constitutional conflicts of the 17th century in both Scotland and England, without some such fundamental knowledge? But I go further than this ... The truths of the Judaic-Christian tradition are infinitely precious, not only, as I believe, because they are true, but also because they provide the moral impulse which alone can lead to that peace, in the true meaning of the word, for which we all long ... there is little hope for democracy if the hearts of men and women in democratic societies cannot be touched by a call to something greater than themselves. Political structures, state institutions, collective ideals—these are not enough.

The Bible itself was important to public policy:

> The Old Testament lays down in Exodus the Ten Commandments as given to Moses, the injunction in Leviticus to love our neighbour as ourselves and generally the importance of observing a strict code of law. The New Testament is a record of the Incarnation, the teachings of Christ and the establishment of the Kingdom of God. Again we have the emphasis on loving our neighbor as ourselves and to "Do-as-you-would-be-done-by." I believe that by taking together these key elements from the Old and New Testaments, we gain: a view of the universe, a proper attitude to work, and principles to shape economic and social life. [23]

And what great nation is there, that has statutes and
rules so righteous as all this law that I set before you today?
—Deuteronomy 4:8—

THE BIBLE AND AMERICAN LAW

America's Declaration of Independence states that individuals are endowed by their Creator with certain rights and that governments are instituted to secure or protect those rights. The country's founders, steeped in the legal thought of William Blackstone, recognized that God established a law for the nations and revealed His law in the Scriptures. Even today, when the authority of Scripture in our society is waning, the Bible's influence on the laws is still present, as noted by legal scholar John Witte:

> ... some of the Bible's basic laws are still at the heart of our legal system today. "Thou shalt not kill" remains at the foundation of our laws of homicide. "Thou shalt not steal" grounds our laws of property and theft. "Thou shalt not bear false witness" remains the anchor of our laws of evidence and defamation. The ancient laws of sanctuary still operate for fleeing felons, refugees, and asylum seekers. The ancient principles of Jubilee are at the heart of our modern laws of bankruptcy and debt relief. "Honor the authorities" remains the starting premise of modern constitutional law. Any good legal historian can show you the biblical genesis and Christian exodus of many of our modern rules of contract and promise, evidence and proof, marriage and family, crime and punishment, property and poverty, liberty and dignity, church and state, business and commerce. ... Western Christian teachings on law, politics, and society have made enduring contributions to the development of law as we know it today.

Witte further reflected:

> What would a legal system look like if we were to take seriously the final commandment of the Decalogue, "thou shalt not covet," especially when our modern systems of capitalism, advertisement, and wealth accumulation have the exact opposite premise? What would our modern law of torts and criminal law look like if we took seriously Jesus' command to "turn the other cheek"? What would our laws of civil procedure and dispute resolution look like if we took seriously the New Testament admonition for those with grievances against fellow believers to "go tell it to the church"? What would our system of social welfare, charity, or inheritance look like if we followed the Bible's repeated commands to tend to the poor, the widow, the orphan, the strangers—the "least" of society—knowing, as Jesus put it, that "as much as you do it to them you do it to me"? What would our public and private laws look like if we worked hard to make real and legally concrete the biblical ideals of covenant community or sacramental living? [24]

In all things I have shown you that by working hard in this way we must help the weak and remember the words of the Lord Jesus, how he himself said, "It is more blessed to give than to receive."
—Acts 20:35—

THE BIBLE LIFELINE

Theologian J.I. Packer notes that our modern world needs the hope that's in the Bible, a book of hope, a book looking forward to what God will do to restore the world and our lives through Jesus Christ:

> To moderns drowning in hopelessness, disappointed, disillusioned, despairing, emotionally isolated, bitter and aching inside, Bible truth comes as a lifeline, for it is future-oriented and hope-centered throughout. The God of the Bible, whom Christians know as the Father, the Son, and the Holy Spirit, united in a shared divine life, is both a very present help in trouble and a very potent hope in times of despair. The triune God, we might say, is the lifeguard, who ... comes in person to the place where we are drowning in order to rescue us; the holy scriptures are the lifeline God throws us in order to ensure that he and we stay connected while the rescue is in progress; and the hope that the Scriptures bring us arrests and reverses the drowning experience here and now, generating inward vitality and renewed joy and banishing forever the sense of having the life choked out of us as the waves break over us.

When the Scriptures are read, learned, and digested, they comfort and strengthen us with hope. The strong connection between Scripture and hope is made in a prayer Thomas Cranmer wrote for the Anglican *Prayer Book:*

Blessed Lord, who has caused all holy scriptures to be written for our learning Grant that we may in such wise hear them, read, mark, learn, and inwardly digest them. That by patience, and comfort of thy holy Word, we may embrace, and ever hold fast the blessed hope of everlasting life, which thou hast given us in our Saviour Jesus Christ.

Packer quotes the words from the British Coronation service when the new monarch is handed the Bible, which is called "the most valuable thing that this world affords,... wisdom ... the royal law ... the lively oracles of God." He dreams of

> Christianity freed from relativism, skepticism, anti-intellectualism, and antibiblicism: a Christianity whose adherents are all learning to testify to the truth and power of the Scriptures, and to stand together to proclaim biblical truth as it is in Jesus. [25]

You are good and do good; teach me your statutes.
—Psalm 119:68—

DECEMBER 25
THE MOST VALUABLE THING
THIS WORLD AFFORDS

Since the reign of King Henry VIII, the British monarch has been head of both the British government and the Church of England. The coronation of the British monarch, conducted in Westminster Abbey, is a religious service as a new monarch is established on the British throne. In the coronation of Queen Elizabeth II in 1953, the Queen entered the west door of the Church to an Anthem with words from Psalm 122:1-3, 6, 7. Part of the oath administered to the Queen was, "Will you to the utmost of your power maintain the laws of God and the true profession of the Gospel? Will you to the utmost of your power maintain in the United Kingdom the Protestant Reformed Religion established by law?" The Sword of State was presented to the Queen, and she took a solemn oath to observe those promises, placing her right hand on a Bible. After the Sword of State, a Bible was then presented to the Queen, and the Archbishop said, "Our gracious Queen: to keep your Majesty ever mindful of the law and the Gospel of God as the Rule for the whole life an government of Christian Princes, we present you with this Book, the most valuable thing that this world affords" The moderator than added, "Here is Wisdom; This is the royal law; These are the lively Oracles of God."

Scriptures read before the anointing focused on the godly role of government and included Psalm 84:9,10; I Peter 2:13; Psalm 141:2, and Matthew 22:15. During the actual anointing of the Queen, I Kings 1:39,40 was recited, "Zadok the priest and Nathan the prophet anointed Solomon king; and all the people rejoiced and said God save the king, Long live the king. May the king live for ever. Amen. Hallelujah." During the communion service, Scriptures focused on the salvation which is in Jesus: Matthew 11:28; John 3:16; I Timothy 1:15; I John 2:1. During the communion itself, Psalm 34:8 was sung.[26]

Queen Elizabeth has taken her Christian responsibilities seriously throughout her reign. In 2016, for the Queen's 90th birthday, the Bible Society published a book showing Queen Elizabeth's devotion to King Jesus, fitly titled *The Servant Queen and the King She Serves.*

Take away from me scorn and contempt,
for I have kept your testimonies.
—Psalm 119:22—

HE CALLS THEM ALL BY NAME

February 1, 2003, as the Space Shuttle *Columbia* reentered Earth's atmosphere after a sixteen-day scientific mission in space, it disintegrated, and all seven crew members on board died. For over twenty-two years *Columbia* had served as the flight vehicle for the Space Shuttle program; it was on its twenty-eighth mission when disaster struck. Debris was strewn across Texas and Louisiana, and a nation mourned the death of seven valiant astronauts.

Karen Hughes, counselor for President George W. Bush, turned to her Bible and the Psalms when the disaster occurred. What she at first read was too upbeat for the moment, but a Biblical cross-reference led her to turn to Isaiah 40:26. There she read, "Lift up your eyes on high, and behold who hath created these things, that bringeth out their host by number: he calleth them all by name by the greatness of his might, for that he is strong in power; not one faileth." It was the word of comfort that she and a hurting nation needed. Hughes shared the verse with President Bush, who read it to the nation as it grieved for those who had died in the disaster:

> My fellow Americans, this day has brought terrible news and great sadness to our country. At 9:00 a.m. this morning, Mission Control in Houston lost contact with our Space Shuttle Columbia. A short time later, debris was seen falling from the skies above Texas. The Columbia is lost; there are no survivors.

> On board was a crew of seven: Colonel Rick Husband; Lt. Colonel Michael Anderson; Commander Laurel Clark; Captain David Brown; Commander William McCool; Dr. Kalpana Chawla; and Ilan Ramon, a Colonel in the Israeli Air Force. These men and women assumed great risk in the service to all humanity. ...

> All Americans today are thinking, as well, of the families of these men and women who have been given this sudden shock and grief. You're not alone. Our entire nation grieves with you. And those you loved will always have the respect and gratitude of this country. ...

> In the skies today we saw destruction and tragedy. Yet farther than we can see there is comfort and hope. In the words of the prophet Isaiah, "Lift your eyes and look to the heavens. Who created all these? He who brings out the starry hosts one by one and calls them each by name. Because of His great power and mighty strength, not one of them is missing."

The same Creator who names the stars also knows the names of the seven souls we mourn today. The crew of the shuttle Columbia did not return safely to Earth; yet we can pray that all are safely home.

May God bless the grieving families, and may God continue to bless America.[27]

My eyes long for your promise; I ask, "When will you comfort me?
—Psalm 119:82—

DECEMBER 27

BE STRONG AND VERY COURAGEOUS

The evening before the launch of the *Columbia* space shuttle, the astronaut crew and their wives gathered together. Commander Rick Husband spoke a few words to the group, and with a voice full of emotion, quoted Joshua 1:7, "Only be strong and very courageous, being careful to do according to all the law that Moses my servant commanded you. Do not turn from it to the right hand or to the left, that you should have good success wherever you go." Commander Husband had wanted to be an astronaut since he was a small boy, but more important to him was his Christian walk and being a godly husband and father for his family. Whenever Husband autographed pictures for people, he always put "Proverbs 3:5-6" on the picture, the Scripture which says "Trust in the Lord with all your heart and lean not on your own understanding; in all your ways acknowledge him, and he will make your paths straight." In the funeral instructions Husband left in the event of a failure in *Columbia's* flight, he wrote, "Tell 'em about Jesus!—That He is real to me. Proverbs 3:5-6, Colossians 3:23."

After the *Columbia* disintegrated on re-entry February 1, 2003, and all the astronauts died, Evelyn Husband found comfort in the Scriptures. Isaiah 53:3 told her that Jesus was a Man of Sorrows and acquainted with grief. Psalm 147:3 re-assured her that God heals the brokenhearted and binds the wounds. From Revelation 21:4, she knew that her husband now was with Jesus where there were no tears, no death, no mourning. In the midst of losing her loving husband, the wonderful father of her children, and her best friend, Evelyn knew the truth Jesus spoke in Matthew 11:2, "Come to me, all you who are weary and burdened, and I will give you rest."[28]

The words from Joshua 1:7 with which Husband had challenged his crew before *Columbia's* launch continued to encourage the survivors. When the state of Israel issued a postage stamp in memory of Ilan Ramon, who was the first Israeli astronaut and made his first flight on *Columbia*, the Scripture from Joshua 1:7 was printed on the stamp.

Those who fear you shall see me and rejoice,
because I have hoped in your word.
—Psalm 119:74—

DECEMBER 28
OUT OF THIS WORLD

Job is one of the earliest books of Scripture written, yet its words speak truths which bring wonder in the modern space age. Space Shuttle Astronaut Col Jeffrey Williams formerly held the U.S. astronaut record for most days in space—534 days. Job 26, which speaks of God's greatness as seen in His creation, had always fascinated Col. Williams, and his space travels caused him to marvel at these Scriptures even more. Job 26: 7 says "God stretches out the north over the void and hangs the earth on nothing." How would anyone have known that 4000 years ago or so unless through God's inspiration? By having seen the earth from space, Williams could testify that the earth was indeed hanging on nothing—there are no strings attached!

Job further wrote that God "binds up the waters in His thick clouds, and the cloud is not split open under them" (26:8). From space especially, one can see the endless variations of the cloud formations over the earth. Job further gives an accurate description of what scientists call the terminator—the line on earth dividing day and night. God "has inscribed a circle on the face of the waters at the boundary between light and darkness." (26:10) The terminator cannot be seen on earth, but as the International Space Station orbits the earth every 90 minutes, the astronauts can clearly see the terminator from space. Williams asks, "How could the author of Job possibly describe the planet in that way several thousand years ago apart from supernatural inspiration?":

> Those verses in Job 26 provide an elegantly brief but accurate description of the planet we call home. But Job does not stop there. After his fascinating and beautiful description of the Earth in such an economy of words, he comes to the conclusion and declares that such beauty does not even begin to approach the fulness, majesty, and power of almighty God. "Behold, these are but the outskirts of His ways, and how small a whisper do we hear of Him!" (26:14). Creation, as observed and described by the biblical writer, points to a Creator, but, as amazing as it is, creation does not even begin to reveal who He is. No matter that the works of creation are so incredible. These works are on the *fringe*. Though the view shouts with beauty, it is but a *whisper*. Pondering that truth was humbling—more humbling than the view itself.[29]

For as the heavens are higher than the earth,
so are my ways higher than your ways and my thoughts than your thoughts.
—Isaiah 55:9—

SINGING PRAISE FOR GOD'S REVELATION

Following Paul in Romans 1, writers from the earliest days of the church wrote about the book of nature and book of Scripture as two types of divine revelation. The creation and nature itself reveal something of God's power and majesty, but the book of Scripture more specifically reveals the laws of God and the gospel of salvation. Famed hymn writer Isaac Watts wrote of these two modes of God's revelation of Himself in several hymns, including the following:

Behold the lofty sky,
Declares its Maker God.
And all his starry works on high
Proclaim his power abroad.

The darkness and the light
Still keep their course the same;
While night to day and day tonight,
Divinely teach his name.

In every different land
Their general voice is known;
They show the wonders of his hand,
And orders of his throne.

Ye Christian lands, rejoice,
Here he reveals his word:
We are not left to nature's voice
To bid us know the Lord.

His statutes and commands
Are set before our eyes;
He puts his gospel in our hands,
Where our salvation lies.

His laws are just and pure,
His truth without deceit,
His promises for ever sure,
And his rewards are great.[30]

As a preacher, Watts' sermons were saturated with Scripture, and in another hymn he wrote of his personal delight in God's Word:

Lord, I have made thy word my choice,
My lasting heritage;
There shall my noblest power rejoice,
My warmest thoughts engage.

I'll read the histories of thy love,
And keep thy laws in sight,
While trough the promises I rove
With ever fresh delight.

'Tis a broad land of wealth unknown,
Where springs of life arise,
Seeds of immortal bless are sown,
And hidden glories lies.

The best relief that mourners have,
It makes our sorrows blest;
Our fairest hope beyond the grace,
And our eternal rest.[31]

Accept my freewill offerings of praise,
O Lord, and teach me your rules.
—Psalm 119:108—

DECEMBER 30
A CALL TO PRAISE THROUGH THE CENTURIES

Psalm 103 is a moving hymn of praise in which David reflects on God's ways and works with His people. Beginning with "Bless the Lord, O my soul, and all that is within me," David recounts God's forgiveness of sin, His love, mercy, and care for the afflicted, and His sovereign rule over all. This psalm has inspired others throughout the centuries to write similar hymns of praise.[32] In 1525, early Reformation preacher Johann Graumann (1487-1541) wrote a hymn which, translated into English, begins,

> My Soul, now praise your Maker
> Let all within me bless His name,
> Who makes you full partaker
> Of mercies more than you dare claim
> Forget Him not whose meekness
> Still bears with all your sin,
> Who heals your ev'ry weakness,
> Renews your life within ...
> Praise Him forever reigning,
> All you who hear His Word—
> Our life and all sustaining
> My soul, O praise the Lord![33]

Over a century later the German Reformed pastor Joachim Neander (1650-1680) wrote the popular hymn "Praise to the Lord, the Almighty" based on Psalm 103:

> Praise to the Lord, the Almighty, the King of creation!
> O my soul, praise Him, for He is thy health and salvation!
> All ye who hear, now to His temple draw near;
> Praise Him in glad adoration.[34]

In England, Isaac Watts (1674-1748), who wrote some 800 hymns, put the psalms in verse form for congregational singing. His Psalm 103 began:

> O bless the Lord, my soul!
> let all within me join
> and aid my tongue to bless his name,
> whose favors are divine.
> O bless the Lord, my soul,

nor let his mercies be
forgotten in unthankfulness,
unsung by you, by me …[35]

More recently, Matt Redman (b. 1974) found inspiration for his "Ten Thousand Reasons" from Psalm 103:

Bless the Lord Oh My Soul, Oh my Soul,
Worship His holy name.
Sing like never before, Oh my soul
I worship Your holy name.

The sun comes up, it's a new day dawning
It's time to sing your song again.
Whatever may pass and whatever lies before me
Let me be singing when the evening comes ….

You're rich in love and you're slow to anger.
Your name is great and your heart is kind.
For all your goodness I will keep on singing.
Ten thousand reasons for my heart to find …

And on that day when my strength is failing
The end draws near and my time has come.
Still my soul will sing your praise unending
Ten thousand years and then forever more.[36]

---

*Moreover Hezekiah the king and the princes commanded the Levites to
sing praise unto the Lord with the words of David, and of Asaph the seer.
And they sang praises with gladness, and they bowed their heads and worshipped.*
—II Chronicles 29:30—

DECEMBER 31
JESUS THROUGHOUT THE BIBLE

Evangelist Billy Graham noted that:

> The Bible is concerned only incidentally with the history of Israel or with a system of ethics. The Bible is primarily concerned with the story of humanity's redemption through Jesus Christ. If you read Scripture and miss the story of salvation, you have missed the message and its meaning.

The story of Jesus can be traced through the Bible.

- In Genesis, He is the Seed of the Woman.
- In Exodus, He is the Passover Lamb.
- In Leviticus, He is the Atoning Sacrifice.
- In Numbers, He is the Smitten Rock.
- In Deuteronomy, He is the Prophet.
- In Joshua, He is the Captain of the Lord's Hosts.
- In Judges, He is the Deliverer.
- In Ruth, He is the Heavenly Kinsman.
- In 1 and 2 Samuel, 1 and 2 Kings, and 1 and 2 Chronicles, He is the Promised King.
- In Nehemiah, He is the Restorer of the Nation.
- In Esther, He is the Advocate.
- In Job, He is My Redeemer.
- In Psalms, He is My Song.
- In Proverbs, He is Wisdom.
- In Ecclesiastes, He is My Goal.
- In the Song of Solomon, He is My Satisfier.
- In the Prophets, He is the coming Prince of Peace.
- In the Gospels, He is God in Christ Jesus, come to redeem.
- In Acts, He is alive in the Church.
- In the Epistles, He is Christ at the Father's right hand.
- In Revelation, He is the Mighty Conqueror.

The message of Jesus Christ, our Savior, is the story of the Bible—it is the story of salvation it is the story of the Gospel; it is the story of life, peace, eternity and Heaven. The whole world ought to know the story of the Bible…

The story of the Scriptures is the story of your redemption and mine through Jesus Christ. The Scriptures teach the death, burial and resurrection of Christ. Jesus Christ is the Gospel. His death, burial, and resurrection is the Gospel story …

The Bible says the only way to bridge the gap between us and God is through Christ. Jesus said, I am the way, the truth, and the life. No one comes to the Father except through me." (John 14:6)[37]

... he greatly helped those who through grace had believed ...
showing by the Scriptures that the Christ was Jesus.
—Acts 18:27-28—

ENDNOTES

JANUARY

1   Genesis 15:4-5.

2   Isaiah 45:1.

3   Jeremiah 52.

4   Jeremiah 25:11.

5   Isaiah 23.

6   Erwin Lutzer. *Seven Reasons Why You Can Trust the Bible*. Chicago: Moody Press, 1998, 45-46.

7   Matthew 4:4; Deut. 8:3.

8   Matthew 5:18.

9   Luke 16:17.

10 John 10:35.

11 John 17:17.

12 Luke 11:51.

13 John 16:13-14.

14 J.C. Ryle. *Is All Scripture Inspired?* Edinburgh: The Banner of Truth Trust, 2017, 3-4, 6-11.

15 Thomas Boston, "The Scriptures: the Book of the Lord," *The Whole Works of Thomas Boston*, Vol. 1, ed. Samuel McMillan. Aberdeen: George & Robert King, 1848, 70, 75-76.

16 Parminder Summon. *Summon's Bible Miscellany*. Grand Rapids, MI: William B. Eerdmans Publishing Company, 2006, 21-23.

17 Barkay, Gabriel; Vaughn, Andrew G.; Lundberg, Marilyn J.; Zuckerman, Bruce "The Amulets from Ketef Hinnom: A New Edition and Evaluation," *Bulletin of the American Schools of Oriental Research,* May 2000, 334, p. 68.

18 Matthew Barrett. *God's Word Alone: The Authority of Scripture*. Grand Rapids, MI: Zondervan, 2016, 275-276.

19 John 5:39.

20 Luke 24:27.

21 Isaiah 7:14; Micah 6:2; Hosea 11:1; Isaiah 9:1-2.

22 Malachi 3:1; Isaiah 35: 5-6.

23 Psalm 41:8, Matt. 26:15, 49,50; Zech.11:12-13, Matt. 27, 5, 7.

24 Zech. 13:7, Isaiah 50:6, 53, Psalm 22:7-8, Mark 14:50; Matt. 26: 67, 27:12-19, 31.

25 Isaiah 53:12, Luke 23:34; Psalm 22:18, John 19:23, 24.

26 Psalm 22:16, Zech. 12:10, Isaiah 53:12, Matt. 27:38.

27 Psalm 69:21, Psalm 22:15, Matt. 27:34; Psalm 22:1. Matt. 27:46; Psalm 31:5, Luke 23:46.

28 Psalm 32:20, John 19:33; Psalm 31:5, Luke 23:46.

29 Amos 8:9, Matt, 27:45.

30 Isaiah 53:9, Matt. 27:57-60; Psalm 16:10, Acts 2:31, Luke 24:46.

31 Clement of Rome. ed. Anthony Uyl. *The Epistles of Clement.* Woodstock, Ontario: Devoted Publishing, 2017, vii.

[32] Tacitus. *The Annals* (trans. Alfred John Church and William Jackson Brodribb, 1876), XIV.44. (https://en.wikisource.org/wiki/The_Annals_(Tacitus)/Book_15#44).

[33] Paul L. Maier, ed. *Josephus: The Essential Works*. Grand Rapids, MI: Kregel Publications, 1994, 271-272.

[34] Bruce M. Metzger, Bart D. Ehrman, *The Text of the New* Testament, 4th edition, New York & Oxford: Oxford University Press, 2005, 56.

[35] Justin Martyr. *First Apology*, chapters xxxii-liii.

[36] Irenaeus. *Against Heresies* III.11.8-9 in Philip Schaff. *Ante-Nicene Fathers, Vol. 1* , 1885 , 428-*429 Christian Classics Ethereal Library,* http://www.ccel.org/ccel/schaff/anf01.toc.html.

[37] F.F. Bruce. *The New Testament Documents: Are They Reliable?* Wm. B. Eerdmans and InterVarsity Press, 1981, 22.

[38] Tertullian. *Against Praxeas* 15.

[39] Tertullian. *Against Marcion*, III. 14, http://www.newadvent.org/fathers/03123.htm.

[40] Lactantius. *Divine Institutes*, IV.20, *The Ante-Nicene Fathers*, vol. vii. New York: Chalres Scribner's Sons, 1913. http://www.ccel.org/ccel/schaff/anf07.iii.ii.iv.xx.html.

[41] Irenaeus, *Against Heresies* 3.12.12, as quoted in Michael J. Kruger, *Christianity at the Crossroads*. Downers Grove, IL: IVP Academic, 218, 118.

[42] Eusebius Pamphlius. *Church History* in *Nicene and Post-Nicene Fathers, Series 2, vol.1*, ed. Philip Schaff, chapter 15.

[43] Justin Martyr. *First Apology*, 67. *The Ante-Nicene Fathers*, vol. 1. New York: Charles Scribner's Sons, 1913.

[44] Tatian. *Address to the Greeks*, 29. *The Ante-Nicene Fathers*, vol. 3. New York: Charles Scribner's Sons, 1956.

[45] *Didascalia Apostolorum*, ed. R. Hugh Connolly. Oxford: Clarendon Press, 1929, 12.

[46] All quotations from Alphonsus de Liguo, ed. Eugene Grimm. *Victories of the Martyrs*. New York: Benziger Brothers, 1887, 90-92.

FEBRUARY

[1] Hippolytus, "Against the Heresy of One Noetus," 9, *The Ante-Nicene Fathers*, volume 5. Grand Rapids, MI, 1986, 227.

[2] "The Epistle of Theonas, Bishop of Alexandria, to Lucianus, the Chief Chamberlain," ix. *The Ante-Nicene Fathers,* volume 6. New York: Charles Scribner's Sons, 1899, 161.

[3] Athanasius, "Letter XXXIX," *A Select Library of the Nicene and Post-Nicene Fathers of the Christian Church*, Second Series, vol. 4. New York: Charles Scribner's Sons, 1907, 552.

[4] John Chrysostom. *Homilies on Colossians,* Homily 9, in *Nicene and Post-Nicene Fathers, First Series,* Vol. 13, ed. By Philip Schaff. Buffalo: New York: Christian Literature Publishing Col., 1889. At *New Advent,* http://www.newadvent.org/fathers/230309.htm.

[5] John Chrysostom, *On the Gospel of John,* Homily 37, *Nicene and Post-Nicene Fathers, First Series,* Vol. 14, ed. By Philip Schaff. Buffalo: New York: Christian Literature Publishing Col., 1889. At *New Advent, http://www.newadvent.org/fathers/240137.htm* .

[6] Augustine. *The Confessions of S. Augustine* in *A Library of Fathers of the Holy Catholic* Church, v. 1, Oxford: John Henry Parker, 1838, 153-154.

[7] Clement of Rome, "Letter to the Corinthians," 45, *New Advent,* http://www.newadvent.org/fathers/1010.htm.

8   Justin Martyr, *Dialogue with Trypho*, LXV.

9   Augustine to Jerome (A.D. 405), 3. *New Advent*, http://www.newadvent.org/fathers/1102082.htm.

10 "Bible Versions," *The New Schaff-Herzog Encyclopedia of Religious Knowledge, ed. Samuel Macauley Jackson.* New York and London: Funk & Wagnalls Co., 1908, vol.2, 124.

11 All quotes (some modernized for this book) are from Horatius Bonar, ed. *Words Old and New: Gems from the Christian Authorship of all Ages.* Edinburgh: The Banner of Truth Trust, 1994.

12 Simon Greenleaf. *A Treatise on the Law of Evidences*, vol. 1. Boston: Little, Brown, & Co., 1892, 506.

13 As quoted in Timothy Dwight. *Young Man's Manual: The Genuineness and Authenticity of the New Testament:* Hartford: Peter B. Gleason & Co., 1838, 77-80.

14 John Greenleaf Whittier. *The Writings of John Greenleaf Whittier: Narrative and legendary poems.* Cambridge: The Riverside Press, 1896, 17-19.

15 Samuel Parkes Cadman. *The Three Religious Leaders of Oxford and Their Movements.* New York: The MacMillan Company, 1916, 149, 157.

16 John Foxe. *The Acts and Monuments of the Church.* London: Scott, Webster, and Geary, 1838, 235.

17 John Clark Ridpath, ed. *The Ridpath Library of Universal Literature*, vol. 24. New York: Fifth Avenue Library Society, 1899, 288-289.

18 "Archbishop Thomas Arundel's Constitutions against the Lollards," http://www.bible-researcher.com/arundel.html.

MARCH

1   Christopher Columbus. *Christopher Columbus's Book of Prophecies* (trans. Kay Brigham). Madison: University of Wisconsin, 1991.

2   Fra Girolmo Savonarola. *The Triumph of the Cross* (trans. Rev. Father John Procter). London: Sands & Co., 1901, 58-59.

3   Roland Bainton. *Here I Stand: A Life of Martin Luther.* Nashville: Abingdon Press, 1978, 51.

4   Five Solas emerged: *Sola Scriptura* (Scripture alone), which has been called the formal principle of the Reformation; the principle which shaped Reformation convictions. The others are known as material principles (central teachings) of the Reformation: *Sola Gratia* (we're saved by grace alone), *Sola Fide* (we're saved by faith alone), *Solus Christus* (we're saved by Christ alone), *Soli Dei Gloria* (to God's glory), , alone). All five terms were used by the reformers, though they were not all used together until the 20th century.

5   Roland H, Bainton. *Here I Stand: A Life of Martin Luther.* Nashville: Abingdon Press, 1978, 107.

6   *Here I Stand*, 182.

7   Quoted in R.C. Sproul, Stephen J. Nichols, eds. *The Legacy of Luther*, Orlando, FL: Reformation Trust, 2016, 201.

8   From Erasmus' *Paracelsis*, as quoted in Philip Schaff, *History of the Christian Church*, vol. VI (by David Schaff). Grand rapids, Michigan: Wm. B. Eerdmans , 1991 reprint of 1910 edition, 723-724.

9   William Martin Conway. *Literary Remains of Albrecht Dürer.* Cambridge University Press, 1889, 134.

10 Ray Cameron-Smith, "Jacques Lefevre: A Reformer Before the Reformation," *Banner of Truth*, October 31, 2018, https://banneroftruth.org/us/resources/articles/2018/jacques-lefevre-a-reformer-before-the-reformation/.

11 Carlos M.N. Eire. *War Against the Idols: The Reformation of Worship from Erasmus to Calvin.* New York: Cambridge university Press, 1986, 170.

12 John Calvin. *Commentary on the Psalms,* volume 1. Grand Rapids, MI: Christian Classics Ethereal Library, 23. https://www.ccel.org/ccel/calvin/calcom08.pdf.

13 *Commentary on the Psalms,* volume 1, 24.

14 *Commentary on the Psalms,* volume 1, 406.

15 P.R. N. Carter, "Thomas Bilney," *Oxford Dictionary of National Biography.* http://www.oxforddnb.com/view/article/2400.

16 http://www.bl.uk/onlinegallery/sacredtexts/tyndale.html.

17 The language here has been modernized.

18 Jean Calvin. *Calvin: Commentaries* (trans. and ed. By Joseph Haroutunian). London & Philadelphia: S.C.M. Press & Westminster Press, 1958, 70-71.

19 Jean Calvin. "Epistle to the Reader," prefixed to the second edition, *Institutes of the Christian Religion* (trans. Henry Beveridge). Peabody, Massachusetts: Hendrickson Publishers.

20 A. Skevinton Wood, "Nicolas of Lyra," *Evangelical Quarterly,* 33.4 (October-December 1961), 205.

21 George Fox Bridges. *The Oxford Reformers and English Church Principles: Their Rise, Trial, and Triumph.* London: Elliot Stock, 1908, 283.

22 Paul O. Wegner. *The Journey from Texts to Translations: The Origin and Development of the Bible.* Grand Rapids, MI: Baker Academic, 1999, 297.

23 Christopher Anderson. *The Annals of The English* Bible, vol. I. London: William Pickering, 1845, 485.

24 *Lady Jane Grey Reference Guide,* http://www.ladyjanegrey.info/?page_id_2372.

25 James Townley. *Illustrations of Biblical literature exhibiting the history and fate of the Sacred Writings from the earliest period to the* present, volume 2. New York: Carlton & Porter, 1856, 355-356.

26 John Fox. *The Acts and Monuments of the Church.* London: George Virtue, 1851, https://www.exclassics.com/foxe/fox10pdf.pdf, 25-33.

27 *Elizabeth I: Collected Works.* (Leah Marcus, Janel Mueller, Mary Rose, eds.) Chicago & London: The University of Chicago Press, 2000, 319-321.

28 Brad Walton. "Elizabeth," *Handbook of Women Biblical Interpreters,* ed. Marion Ann Taylor. Grand Rapids, MI: Baker Academic, 2012.

29 Alfred Nevin. *Guide to the Oracles: Or, the Bible Student's Vade-mecum.* Lewisburg, PA: William Murray 1858, 28.

APRIL

1 Jane E.A. Dawson. *John Knox,* Yale University Press, 2016, 26.

2 Thomas Harriot. *A Brief and True Report of the New Found Land of Virginia.* London, 1588, 39-40.

3 Quotes from Cooper, Chemnitz, Hooker, Caryl, Milton and Romaine from Horatius Bonar, ed. *Words Old and New: Gems from the Christian Authorship of all Ages.* Edinburgh: The Banner of Truth Trust, 1994.

4 Quotes from Matthew Hale and Bishop Massillon from Samuel Bailey, ed. *Homage of Eminent Persons to the Book.* Boston: Rand, Avery, & Frye, 1870, 19, 3,331.

5 William Perkins. *How to Live, and That well in all estates and times,* in *The Workes of that Famous and worthy minister of Christ in the University of Cambridge, Mr. William Perkins,* Volume 1. London: John Legatt, 1635, 476- 477. Spelling has been modernized in this quote.

6   *The Autobiography of Charles H Spurgeon, Compiled from His Letters, Diaries, and Records by His Wife and Private Secretary*, vol. 4, 1878-1892. Curts and Jennings, 1900, 268.

7   Frederick F. Bruce. *History of the Bible in English*. Cambridge: Lutterworth Press, 2002, 96.

8   Nicholas Byfield. Matthew and Therese McMahon, eds. *The Promises of God*. Coconut Creek, FL: Puritan Publications, 2013, 27-29.

9   All quotes are from Leland Ryken. *World Saints*. Grand Rapids, MI: Academie Books, 1986, 139-143.

10   J.I. Packer. *A Quest for Godliness*. Wheaton, Illinois: Crossway Books, 1990, 11.

11   *A Quest for Godliness*, 12.

12   *A Quest for Godliness*, 105.

13   Francis Bacon. *The Works of Francis Bacon*, vol. 2. London: W. Baynes and Son, 1824, 485-487.

14   Isidore S. Meyer. "The Hebrew Preface to Bradford's History of the Plymoth Plantation," *Publications of the American Jewish Historical Society*, vol. 38, No. 4 (June 1949), 291.

15   As quoted in Dale L. McIntyre, "The Heavens and the Scriptures in the Eyes of Johannes Kepler," 13, https://acmsonline.org/home2/wp-content/uploads/2016/05/McIntyre2009.pdf.

16   As quoted in McIntyre, 8.

17   Robert Charles Winthrop. *Life and Letters of John Winthrop, from 1630 to 1649*, volume 2. Boston: Ticknor and Fields, 1867, 19-20.

18   Robert Bolton. *The Saints Sure and Perpetual Guide or A Treatise Concerning the Word*. London: printed by W. Purslow, for Rapha Harford, 1634, 44-45.

19   William Gouge. *A Guide to Goe to God: or, An Explanation of the perfect patterne of prayer, the Lord's Prayer*. London: Edward Brewster, 1636, 92-93.

20   Robert Boyle. *Some Considerations Touching the Style of the Holy Scriptures*. London: C. and J. Rivington, 1825, 85.

21   27.

22   138.

23   John Owen. "Of Communion with the Holy Ghost," *The Works of John Owen*, ed. Thomas Russell, vol. 10. London: Richard Baynes, 1826, 306.

24   Romans 2:14-15; 1:19-20; Psalm 19:1-4; Romans 1:32-2:1. The notations of Scripture are part of the *Westminster Confession*.

25   John 17:3; I Corinthians 1: 21; I Corinthians 2:13-14.

26   II Timothy 3:15; II Peter 1:19.

27   John 20:31; I Corinthians 14:37; I John 5:13; I Corinthians 10:11; Hebrews 1:1-2; 2:2-4.

28   II Peter 1:19-20; II Timothy 3:16; I John 5:9; I Thessalonians 2:13; Revelation 1:1-2.

29   I Corinthians 2:4-5, 9-10; Hebrews 4:12; John 10:35; Isaiah 55:11; Romans 11:36; Psalm 19:7-11; II Timothy 3:15; I Thessalonians 1:5; I John 2:20, 27; Isaiah 59:21. Scripture annotations are from the *Westminster Confession*.

30   II Timothy 3:16-17; Galatians 1:8-9; II Thessalonians 2:2.

31   John 6:45; I Corinthians 2:12, 14-15; Eph. 1:18; II Corinthians 4:6.

32   II Peter 3:16.

33   Psalm 119:1-5, 130; Deut. 30:10-14; Acts 17:11.

34   Matthew 22:29, 31; Acts 28:25; I John 4:1-6.

35 *The Westminster Directory, being a Directory for the Publique Worship of God in the Three Kingdoms,* 1645, https://reformed.org/documents/wcf_standards/index.html?mainframe=/documents/wcf_standards/p369-direct_pub_worship.html.

36 Hugo Grotius. *Grotius on the Rights of War and Peace: An Abridged Translation* (trans. William Whewell). Clark, N.J.: The Lawbook Exchange, Ltd., 2009, xxxix.

MAY

1 Robert Dingley. *Divine Optics, or a Treatise of the Eye discovering the Vices and Virtues thereof as also How That Organ May be Tuned, Chiefly Grounded in Psalm 119:37.* London: Printed by J.M. for H. Cripps, 1655, 71-73.

2 William Bridge, "Scripture Light the Most Sure Light," *The Works of the Rev. William Bridge*, vol. 1. London: Thomas Tegg, 1845, 403.

3 "Scripture Light the Most Sure Light," 411-413.

4 Edmund Calamy. *The Godly Man's Ark: or, City of Refuge in the Day of His Distress.* London: Theo. Parkhurst, 1709, 55-57.

5 Blaise Pascal. *Thoughts, Letters, and Opuscles*, trans. By O.W. Wight. New York: Hurd and Houghton, 1864, 334-335.

6 *The Works of George Swinnock.* London: James Nichol, 1868, 141-143. Spelling and wording have been modernized.

7 John Milton. *Protestant Union: A Treatise of True Religion, Heresy, Schism, Toleration.* London: F. and C. Rivington, 1826, 3-4.

8 Sir Matthew Hale. *Contemplations, Moral and Divine* in *The Works, Moral, and Religious* (ed. Rev. T. Thurlwall), vol. 2. London: R. Wilks, 1805, 316.

9 318.

10 Ralph Venning. *Venning's Remains, or, Christ's School: Consisting of Four Classes of Christians.* London: John Hancock, 1675, 67-68.

11 Mary Rowlandson. *Narrative of the Captivity and Restoration of Mrs. Mary* Rowlandson, W.W. Norton, 29. Other Scriptures which strengthened Mary during her trial included Psalm 119: 175; 46:10; 37:5; Isaiah 55:8. https://wwnorton.com/college/history/america-essential-learning/docs/MWRowlandson-Autobiography-1682.pdf.

12 C.H. Spurgeon. *Autobiography: Compiled from his Diary, Letters, and Records.* vol. 4. Chicago, New York: Fleming H. Revell, 1900, 268.

13 Christopher Nesse. *A Christian's Walk and Work on Earth until He Attain to Heaven.* London: Dorman Newman, 1678, 103-104.

14 Thomas Watson. *The Ten Commandments. http://www.monergism.com/thethreshold/sdg/watson/The%20 Ten%20Commandments%20-%20Thomas%20Watson.pdf*,273, 275.

15 Thomas Watson. "A Godly Man is a Lover of the Word," *The Godly Man's Picture*, 48-54. http://www.monergism.com/thethreshold/sdg/watson/The%20Godly%20Man%27s%20Picture%20-%20 Thomas%20Watson.pdf.

16 Thomas Gouge. *Christian Directions, Shewing how to Walk with God all the Day-long* in the *Works of the late Reverend and Pious Mr. Tho. Gouge.* London: Tho. Braddyll, 1706, 200-201. Spelling and grammar have been modernized.

17 Thomas Gouge, *Ibid.*, 198- 200. Spelling and grammar have been modernized.

18 The Puritans used the word *affections* for what we'd call the desires or emotions.

19   Joseph Hall. *The Works of the Right Reverend Father in God, Joseph Hall* (ed. Josiah Pratt), volume 7. London: C. Whittingham, 1808, 56.

20   J. Stephen Yuille. *Puritan Spirituality: The Fear of God in the Affective Theology of George Swinnock.* Eugene, Oregon: Wipf & Stock, 2008, 207.

21   Joel Beeke. *Puritan Reformed Spirituality: A Practical Biblical Study from Reformed and Puritan Heritage.* Evangelical Press, 2006, 79.

22   Thomas Brooks. *Precious Remedies Against Satan's Devices.* London: Religious Tract Society, 1986, v.

23   Francis Fane. *Reports on the Laws of Connecticut.* Tuttle, Morehouse & Taylor Press, 1915, 75.

24   James Hammond Trumbull, ed. *The True –Blue Laws of Connecticut and New Haven and the False Blue-Laws.* Hartford, Conn.: American Publishing Company, 1876, 58.

25   Henry Harrison Metcalf. *Laws of New Hampshire: Province Period, 1670-1702.* Manchester, N.H.: John B. Clarke Co., 1904, 62.

26   William Henry Foote. *Sketches of Virginia.* Philadelphia: William S. Martien, 1850, 48.

27   John Adams, Charles Francis Adams. *The Works of John Adams, Second President of the United States*, Volume 2. Boston: Charles C. Little and James Brown, 1850, 6-7.

28   *Records of the Governor and Company of the Massachusetts Bay in New England* (1853), II: 203.

29   Samuel Eliot Morison. *The Founding of Harvard College*, Cambridge, Massachusetts: Harvard University Press, 1968, 333.

30   Franklin Bowditch Dexter. *Biographical Sketches of the Graduates of Yale College.* New York: Henry Holt and Company, 1885, 348.

31   Verses 84, 90, 121, 122, 132.

32   Matthew Henry. *The Life of the Rev. Philip Henry* (ed. J.B. Williams). London: B.J Holdsworth, 1825, 247-248.

33   Matthew Henry. *Commentary on the Whole Bible*, Vol. III-1—Job to Psalm XC (ed. Anthony Uyl). Woodstock, Ontario, Canada: Devoted Publishing, 2017, 236.

34   Matthew Henry. *A Way to Pray* (ed. O. Palmer Robertson). Carlisle, PA: The Banner of Truth Trust, 2010, 162-163.

35   *The Spectator*, August 23, 1712, No. 465.

36   Daniel Defoe. *The Life and Adventures of Robinson* Crusoe. Chicago: Rand McNally & Co., 1914, 126-127. The next quotation is from p. 280.

37   As quoted in Harold B. Hunting. *The Story of Our Bible.* New York: Charles Scribner's Sons, 1918, 310-311. Language updated.

JUNE

1   John Locke. "Some Thoughts Concerning Reading and Study for a Gentleman," *The Works of John Locke*, vol. 2: *An Essay Concerning Human Understanding part 2 and Other Writings*. (London: Rivington, 1824, 12th ed.). http://oll.libertyfund.org/titles/762.

2   John Locke. *On the Understanding.* London: Thomas Allman, 1840, ix.

3   *Works of Jonathan Edwards, Letters and Personal Writings* (WJE Online Vol. 16), ed. George S. Claghorn. New Haven: Yale University Press, 793-794.

4   George Whitefield. Sermon 39 in *The Works of the Reverend George Whitefield*, Vol.VI. London: Edward and Charles Dilly, 1771, 123-124.

5   Isaac Watts. *Psalms, Hymns, and Spiritual Songs.* London, Thomas Ward and Co., 1837, (9).

6   *Psalms, Hymns, and Spiritual Songs*, 5.

7   Isaac Watts, "Shall Wisdom cry aloud," Hymnary.org, https://hymnary.org/text/shall_ wisdom_cry_aloud.

8   *A Collection of Psalms and Hymns: from Watts, Doddridge, and others,"* 4th edition. Philadelphia: R.& R. Bereford, 1846, 166. (*Psalms and Hymns of Isaac Watts* Hymns and Spiritual Songs in Three Books, Book 2, "Composed on Divine Subjects"), https://www.ccel.org/ccel/watts/psalmshymns.II.119.html).

9   *Baptist Hymnal.* Nashville, TN: Lifeway Wor-ship, 2008, 167.

10   *A Collection of Psalms and Hymns: from Watts, Doddridge, and others*, 4th edition. Philadelphia: R.&R. Bereford, 1846, 163.

11   Isaac Watts. *The Improvement of the Mind*, with corrections, questions, and supplement by Joseph Emerson (principal of the female seminary, Wethersfield, Conn.) Boston: Hickling, Swan and Brown, 1855. 33.

12   Isaac Watts. *The Improvement of the Mind*, 36.

13   Quotes of Edwards from Douglas A. Sweeney. *Edwards the Exegete: A Biblical Interpretation and Anglo-Protestant Culture on the edge of the Enlightenment.* Oxford University Press, 2016, 6-7.

14   From *Miscellanies* as quoted in Owen Strachan. *Always in God's Hands: Day by Day in the Company of Jonathan Edwards.* Tyndale Momentum, 2018, 18.

15   From *Sermons and Discourses, 1734-1738*, as quoted in *Always in God's Hands*, 20.

16   From *Sermons and Discourses, 1739-1742*, as quoted in *Always in God's Hands*, 193.

17   From *Miscellanies*, as quoted in *Always in God's Hands*, 204.

18   *An Abridged Memoir of the Rev. John Newton, late rector of the parish of St.Mary Woolnoth.* Cork: Richard Tuivy, 1821, 18.

19   *An Abridged Memoir of the Rev. John Newton, late rector of the parish of St.Mary Woolnoth.* Cork: Richard Tuivy, 1821, 21.

20   Jonathan Edwards. *The Life of the Rev. David Brainerd Missionary to the Indians.* London: Burton and Smith, 1818, 14.

21   Ralph Erskine. *The Poetical Works of the Late Reverend and Learned Mr. Ralph Erskine.* Glasgow: William Smith, 1778, 428-429.

22   Samuel Johnson. "Bible" *A Dictionary of the English Language: A Digital Edition of the 1755 Classic by Samuel Johnson.* Edited by Brandi Besalke. From page 240. https://johnsonsdictionaryonline.com/bible/, accessed July 20, 2018.

23   J.C. Ryle. *Christian Leaders of the Eighteenth Century*, 1885. https://www.crichbaptist.org/articles/augustus-toplady/ "Listeth" here means "wishes."

24   Augustus Toplady. "Poems on Sacred Subjects, written between fifteen and eighteen years of age," *The Works of Augusus Toplady.* London: J.J. Cidley, 1841, 903.

25   John Rippon. *A Selection of hymns from the best authors: intended to be an appendix to Dr. Watts' Psalms and hymns.* London: L. Wayland, 1790, xlvi.

26   Sir William Blackstone. *Commentaries on the Laws of England*, I.2.39-40.

27   Deuteronomy 1:9-18; 16:18-20 further elaborates on this organization of the tribes of Israel.

28   For a more detailed treatment and excellent analysis, see Daniel Dreisbach, *Reading the Bible with the Founding Fathers.* Oxford University Press, 2017.

29   "Francis Hopkinson, 1737-1791," *Library of Congress*, https://www.loc.gov/item/ihas.200035713/, accessed July 11, 2018.

30   *The Psalms of David, with the Ten Commandments, Creed, Lord's Prayer, etc. in metre...translated from the Dutch, for the use of the Reformed Protestant Dutch Church of the City of New York.* New York: James Parker, 1767.

31   Donald S. Lutz. "The Relative Influence of European Writers on Late Eighteenth-Century American Political Thought," *American Political Science Review.* Volume 78, Issue 1, 189-197.

32   Daniel L. Dreisbach. *Reading the Bible with the Founding Fathers.* Oxford University Press, 2017, 231.

33   Letter from Abigail Adams to John Adams, June 18, 1775, Massachusetts Historical Society, https://www.masshist.org/bh/aadams.html, accessed December 27, 2018. Quoting from Eccl. 9:11; Psalm 68:35; 62:8.

34   Louis Albert Banks. *Religious Life of Famous Americans.* Boston, New York, Chicago: American Tract Society, 1904, 202. Quoting from Matthew 6:28; 10:29-31.

35   *Religious Life of Famous Americans,* 206. Quoting from II Kings 3:8-9; Romans 14:19.

36   Letter from John Adams to Abigail Adams, 16 September 1774, *Adams Family Papers,* https://www.masshist.org/digitaladams/archive/doc?id=L17740916ja, accessed July 11, 2018.

37   William Wirt. *The Life of Patrick* Henry. McElrath, Bangs, & Herbert, 1834, 141.

38   John Witherspoon, "The Dominion of Providence Over the Passions of Men," *Political Sermons of the American Founding Era: 1730-1805* (ed. Elis Sandoz), 2nd ed. Indianapolis: Liberty Fund, 1988, Volume 1, 535.

JULY

1   *Journals of the American Congress from 1774-1788: Jan. 1, 1777 to July 31,* 1778, Vol. 2. Washington: Way and Gideon, 1823, 262.

2   George Washington. "Circular Letter to the States," 1783, http://www.mountvernon.org/education/primary-sources-2/article/circular-to-the-states-george-washington-to-the-states-june-8-1783/.

3   Benjamin Franklin. *Autobiography of Benjamin Franklin.* Boston & New York: Houghton Mifflin & Company, 1906, 5.

4   *Notes of Debates in the Federal Convention of 1787, reported by James Madison,* New York: W.W. Norton & Co., 1987, 209-210.

5   *A Collection of Psalms and Hymns: from Watts, Doddridge, and others,* 4th edition. Philadelphia: R. & R. Bereford, 1846, 162.

6   John Newton. "The Nature of Spiritual Revelation," *The Works of the Rev. John* Newton. Edinburgh: Ross & Co., 1839, 358-359.

7   John Lawson. *The Wesley Hymns as a Guide to Scriptural Teaching.* Grand Rapids, MI: Francis Asbury Press, 1987, 128-129.

8   John Lawson. *The Wesley Hymns as a Guide to Scriptural Teaching.* Grand Rapids, MI: Francis Asbury Press, 1987, 33-34.

9   I Kings 8:18.

10   Matt. 5:18.

11   John Newton. *Olney Hymns in Three Books.* London: W. Oliver, 1779, 165-166.

12   John Newton. *Olney Hymns.* London: W.Oliver, 1779, Book 2, Hymn lxiii, 256-258.

13   John Newton. *Olney Hymns.* London: W. Oliver, 1779, Book 2, Hymn lxii, 255-257.

14   Numbers 20:11

15   Joshua 6:20

16   John Newton. *Olney Hymns.* London: W. Oliver, 1779, 202-203.

17   *A Hieroglyphic Bible; or, Select Passages in The Old and New testaments, represented with Emblematic Figures, for the amusement and instruction of Youth.* London: Houlston and Son, 1830, vii-viii.

18   *Journals of the Continental Congress,* Philadelphia: David C. Claypole, September 12, 1782, 469.

19   Xliii. John Fawcett. *Hymns: Adapted to the Circumstances of Public Worship, and Private Devotion.* Leeds: G. Wright & Son, 1782, Hymn 41.

20   Capital of Egypt under the Hyksos.

21   John Rippon. *A Selection of hymns from the best authors: intended to be an appendix to Dr. Watts' Psalms and hymns.* London: L. Wayland, 1790, xlv.

22   John Rippon. *A Selection of hymns from the best authors: intended to be an appendix to Dr. Watts' Psalms and hymns.* London: L. Wayland, 1790, xliv.

23   Timothy Dwight. *Young Man's Manual: The Genuineness and Authenticity of the New Testament.* Hartford: Peter B. Gleason & Co., 1838, 85.

24   Fisher Ames. *Works of Fisher Ames, compiled by a number of his friends.* Boston: T.B. Wait & Co., 1809, 134-135.

25   W. Carey, J. Marshman, W. Ward. *College of the Instruction of Asiatic Christian and other Youth, in Easter Literature and European Science at Serampore,* Bengal. London: Black, Kingsbury, Parbury, and Allen, 1819, 28.

AUGUST

1   Quotes from Thomas Jones, Robert Haldane, and Thomas Chalmers from Horatius Bonar, ed. *Words Old and New: Gems from the Christian Authorship of all Ages.* Edinburgh: The Banner of Truth Trust, 1994.

2   Quotes from Edward Payson, William Wilberforce and Sir Walter Scott from Samuel Bailey, ed. *Homage of Eminent Persons to the Book.* Boston: Rand, Avery, & Frye, 1870, 14-15, 19-20, 40.

3   Alfred Nevin. *Guide to the Oracles: Or, the Bible Student's Vade-mecum.* Lewisburg, PA: William Murray, 1858, 101.

4   Lewis Reifsneider Harley. *Charles Thomson, Patriot and Scholar,* Morristown, PA: The Historical Society of Montgomery County, 1897, 34.

5   John Q. Adams. *Letters of John Quincy Adams, to his Son, on the Bible and its Teachings.* Auburn, N.Y.: Derby, Miller, & Co., 1848, 9-18.

6   L.N.R. *The Book and its Story: A Narrative for the Young, on occasion of the Jubilee of the British and Foreign Bible Society.* London: Samuel Bagster and Sons, 1853, 184.

7   Bernard Christian Steiner. *One Hundred and Ten Years of Bible Society Work in Maryland, 1810-1920.* The Maryland Bible Society, 1921, 13-14.

8   Benjamin Rush. *Essays, Literary, Moral and Philosophical.* Philadelphia: Thomas and William Bradford, 1806, 105.

9   Rush. *Essays,* 112.

10   L.N.R. *The Book and Its Story.* London: Samuel Bagster and Sons, 1853, 245.

11   "Old Letters Which Are New," *The Spirit of '76,* volume 1, September 1894, 6.

12   Robert Haldane. *Exposition of the Epistle to the Romans,* New York: Robert Caret & Brothers, 1949, 564.

13   "Dr. Abercrombie's Advice to a Young Physician," *The Leisure Home: a family journal of instruction and recreation. May 30, 1863, 349-350.*

14 Ernest S. Frerichs. *The Bible and Bibles in America*. Society of Biblical Literature, 1988, 21.

15 John Jay (Henry P. Johnson, ed.) *The Correspondence and Public Papers of John Jay, vol. 4, 1794-1826*, New York: G.P. Putnam's Sons, 1893, 494.

16 Noah Webster. *An American Dictionary of the English Language*. New York: S. Converse, 1828.

17 Alexis de Tocqueville. *Democracy in America*. Regnery Publishing, Inc., 2002, 241, 244-5.

18 Hiram Bingham. *A Residence of Twenty-One Years in the Sandwich Islands,* Hartford: Hezekiah Huntington, 1848,280.

19 *Twenty-One Years in the Sandwich Islands*, 281-282.

20 Eliza Webster Jones. "An Account of the Festival of the Golden Wedding" Bridgeport, May 1843, from *Notes on the Life of Noah Webster* compiled by Emily Ellsworth Fowler Ford, v. 2, New York, 1912, 359-361.

21 Noah Webster. *Value of the Bible, and Excellence of the Christian Religion. New Haven: Durrie & Peck, 1834,* 152.

22 154.

23 177.

24 "The Saint Louis Delegation of 1861," Baker City, OT: Bureau of Land Management, National Oregon Trail Interpretive Center, https://www.blm.gov/or/oregontrail/files/st-louis.pdf.

25 T.R. Fehrenbach. *Lone Star: A History of Texas and Texans*. New York: Collier Books, 1968, 304, 600-601.

26 Fidelia Fiske. *Recollections of Mary Lyon*. Boston: American Tract Society, 103-104.

27 *Testimony of Distinguished Laymen to the Value of the Sacred Scriptures*. New York: American Bible Society, 1853, 55-56.

28 Maung Shwe Wa, *Burma Baptist Chronicle* (Rangoon: University Press, 1963), 25.

29 Edward J. Giddings. *American Christian Rulers or Religion and Men of Government*. New York: Bromfield and Company, 1890, 11.

30 Robert Murray McCheyne, "Thy Word is a Lamp unto My Feet," 1838 *Robert Murray McCheyne Resource*, https://www.mcheyne.info/poems7.php.

31 Robert Murray McCheyene. *The Believer's Joy*. Greanies House, Fearne, Ross-shire Scotland: Christian Focus, 2018, 84-85.

SEPTEMBER

1 George Mueller. *The Autobiography of George Mueller*. Dallas, Texas: Gideon House Books, 2017, May 7, 1841.

2 Louis Albert Banks. *The Religious Life of Famous Americans*. New York: American Tract Society, 1904, 36-37.

3 James Parton. *The Life of Andrew Jackson*, volume 3. New York: Mason Brothers, 1860, 673, 677.

4 Bernard Barton. *Household Verses*. London: George Vertue, 1845, 207.

5 *Household Verses,* 57.

6 *Testimony of Distinguished Laymen to the Value of the Sacred Scriptures*. New York: American Bible Society, 1853, 27-28.

7 John Cotton Smith. *The Correspondence and Miscellanies of the Hon. John Cotton Smith* (William W. Andrews, ed.) New York: Harper & Brothers, 1847, 318.

8 *Testimony of Distinguished Laymen,* New York: American Bible Society, 1853, 15.

9   Samuel W. Bailey. *Homage of Eminent Persons to the Book*, New York, 1869, 55-56.

10   Charles Lanman. *The Private Life of Daniel Webster*. New York: Harper & Brothers, 1858, 104, 106.

11   Daniel Webster. *An Address Delivered at the Completion of the Bunker Hill Monument*, June 17, 1843. Boston: Tappan and Dennet, 1843, 17.

12   "Daniel Webster's Knowledge of the Bible," *The Old Testament Student*, February 1886, vol. 5, Issue 6, 276 (www.journals.uchicago.edu).

13   *Annual Report of the Board of Education*, volume 28, Boston: Wright & Potter, 1865, 96.

14   *Annual Report of the American Bible* Society, volume 96, New York: American Bible Society, 1912, 173.

15   Robert Charles Winthrop. *Address and Speeches on Various Occasions: 1835-1851,* Boston: Little, Brown, and Company, 1852, 168, 170, 172.

16   Benjamin Franklin Morris. *Christian Life and Character of the Civil Institutions of the United States, developed in the official and historical annals of the Republic*, Philadelphia: George W. Childs, 1864, 639.

17   Stephen Abbott Northrop, *A Cloud of Witnesses*. Fort Wayne, Indiana: The Mason Long Publishing Co., 1894, 314.

18   *Baptist Hymnal*. Nashville, TN: Lifeway Worship, 2008, 345.

19   Charles H. Spurgeon. *Charles Spurgeon: An Autobiography*. Harrington, Delaware: Delmarva Publications, 2013, chapter 11, "The Great Change Conversion."

20   Charles Edward Stowe. *Life of Harriet Beecher Stowe*. Boston and New York: Houghton, Mifflin & Co., 1891, 145.

21   Robert Bickersteth, "National Obligation to the Bible, *Twelve Lectures delivered before the Young Men's Christian Association in Exeter Hall, from December 1850, to February 1851.* London: Nisbet and Co., 1851.

22   *The Family Bible*. New York: American Tract Society, 1861.

23   Maquis James. *The Raven: The Story of Sam Houston, The Biggest Texan of them All!* New York: Ballantine Books, A Mockingbird Edition, 1975, 301.

24   Charles George Gordon. *Letters of General Gordon to His Sister M.A. Gordon*. London: MacMillan & Co., 1888, xiii.

25   13.

26   233.

27   279-280.

28   Adolphe Monod. *Farewell to the Friends and to the Church*. New York: Robert Carter & Brothers, 1858, 98-99.

29   William H. Hill. *The Pony Express Trail: Yesterday and Today*. Caldwell, Idaho: Caxton press, 2010, 19.

30   Octavius Winslow. *The Precious Things of God*. New York: Robert Carter and Brothers, 1867, 262-265.

31   E. Platt. *The Story of the Ranyard Mission, 157-1937*. London: Hodder and Stoughton, 1937, 1.

32   Wilbur Fisk Crafts. *Successful Men of To-day and what They Say of Success*. New York: Funk & Wagnalls Co., 1894. 232.

33   S. Trevena Jackson. *Lincoln's Use of the Bible*. Eaton & Mains, 1905, 29-31.

34   Abraham Lincoln. *Lincolnics: familiar Sayings of Abraham Lincoln*. New York: Gilbo & Co., 1901, 189-190.

35   Bence Jones. *The Life and Letters of Faraday*, volume 2. Philadelphia: J.P. Lippincott and Co., 1870, 431.

36 "The Divinity of the Holy Spirit, and his operation on the human heart," 1837. *Livingstone Online: Illuminating imperial exploration.* http://livingstoneonline.org/in-his-own-words/catalogue?view_pid=liv%3A000079&view_page=0 accessed July 14, 2018.

37 Walter Wash. *The Religious Life and Influence of Queen Victoria*, London: Swan Sonnenschein & Co., 1902, 55.

38 *Religious Life and Influence of Queen Victoria*, 182.

39 "Pacific Mission," *Life*, January 25, 1943, 94.

OCTOBER

1 Ormsby Macknight Mitchel. *The Astronomy of the* Bible, New York: Blakeman & Mason, 1863, 298-303.

2 "Saved by his Bible, Sam Houston, Jr.," Shiloh National Military Park, Facebook posting for June 10, 2014.

3 *Journals of Congress*, Volume 32, 340, Library of Congress - http://memory.loc.gov/cgi-bin/ampage?collId=lljc&fileName=032/lljc032.db&recNum=349.

4 Robert Michaelsen, "Common school, Common religion? A Case Study in Church-State Relations, Cincinnati, 1869-70. *Church History*, Vol. 38, No. 2 (June 1869), 201-217.

5 John 5:39.

6 I Corinthians 5:6-8.

7 Leviticus 16:10; I Peter 2:24.

8 John 2:19-22.

9 John 6:48-51.

10 Acts 10:43.

11 Revelation 19:10.

12 Revelation 1:8.

13 Romans 10:4.

14 Matthew 27:54.

15 Octavius Winslow, "Christ, the Alpha and Omega," *Emmanuel, or Titles of Christ*, 1869, http://www.gracegems.org/W/e10.htm.

16 *Westminster Collection of Christian Quotations*, 21.

17 Martin Luther, "Preface to the Old Testament," *Luther's Works*, vol. 35 (ed. E. Theodore Bachmann) Philadelphia: Muhlenberg, 1960), 236.

18 Charles Haddon Spurgeon, "The Word a Sword," *The Treasury of the Bible: The New Testament*, vol. 4 reprint; Grand Rapids: Zondervan, 1962, 40.

19 Charles Haddon Spurgeon, "Christ and His Co-Workers," preached June 10, 1886. In *Spurgeon's Sermons*, vol. 42, https://www.ccel.org/ccel/spurgeon/sermons42.xxii.html?highlight=let%20the%20lion%20out#highlight.

20 Charles Haddon Spurgeon, "Means for Restoring the Banished," *Metropolitan Tabernacle Pulpit*, volume 16, 508-509, 513, https://www.spurgeon.org/resource-library/sermons/means-for-restoring-the-banished#flipbook/7.

21 "My Mother's Bible," https://levysheetmusic.mse.jhu.edu/sites/default/files/collection-pdfs/levy-123-081.pdf.

22 "The King of Love my Shepherd Is," https://hymnary.org/text/the_king_of_love_my_shepherd_is.

23 William Henry Monk. *Hymns Ancient and Modern*. London: J. Alfred Novello, 1861, No. 201.

24 "When Israel was in Egypt's land," https://hymnary.org/hymn/LUYH2013/42.

25 "God's Word is Our Great Heritage," translator: O. G. Belsheim. *Hymnary.org*, https://hymnary.org/text/gods_word_is_our_great_heritage.

26 *The Family Treasury*, ed. Rev. William Arnot. London: Thomas Nelson and Sons, 1872,398-399.

27 Eva Munson Smith, ed. *Woman in Sacred Song: A Library of Hymns, Religious Poems and Sacred Music*, Oakland, CA: Arthur E. Whitney, 1888, 494.

28 Elon Foster. *New Cyclopedia of Poetical Illustrations: Adapted to Christian Teaching*. New York: W.C. Palmer, Jr. & Co., 1872, 61.

29 Nannie Corbin. *A Life of Mathew Fontaine Maury, U.S.N. and C.S.N., Author of Physical Geography of the Sea and Its Meteorology*. London: Sampson Low, Marston, Searle, & Rivington, 1888, 159-160.

30 James Gilcrhist Lawson. *Cyclopedia of Religious Anecdotes*. New York: Fleming H. Revell Co., 29-30.

31 Charles H. Spurgeon. "How to Read the Bible," *Metropolitan Tabernacle Pulpit*, vol. 25, 625-636. Accessed December 26, 2018 from The Spurgeon Center https://www.spurgeon.org/resource-library/sermons/how-to-read-the-bible#flipbook/12.

32 Philip Schaff. *A Companion to the Greek Testament and the English Version*. New York and London: Harper & Brothers Publishers, 1883, 305-307.

33 Charles Haddon Spurgeon. "Departed Saints Yet Living," *The Metropolitan Tabernacle Pulpit Sermons*, vol. 31. London: Passmore & Alabaster, 1884, 541-542.

34 "Winnowed corn" here means any kind of grain that has had the husks separated from it.

35 Charles Haddon Spurgeon. *Morning and Evening Daily Devotions*, June 9, as found in Christian Classics Ethereal Library, https://www.ccel.org/ccel/spurgeon/morneve.d0609pm.html.

36 Abraham Kuyper *Lectures on Calvinism,* Grand Rapids, MI: Wm. B. Eerdmans Publishing Co., 1931, i.

37 James D. Bratt, ed. *Abraham Kuyper: A Centennial Reader*. Grand Rapids, MI: Eerdmans, 1998, 488.

38 *Lectures on Calvinism*, iii.

39 "The Down Grade," *The Sword and Trowel*, April 1887.

40 "Another Word Concerning the Down-Grade," *The Sword and the Trowel*, August 1887.

41 "Müllers," www.mullers.org.

42 George Müller. *Autobiography of George Müller: A Million and a Half in Answer to Prayer*. Vestavia Hills, AL: Solid Ground Christian Books, 693.

43 "Address to Young Converts," a sermon preached at Mildmay Conference Hall, *The Writings and Teachings of George Müller of Bristol*, https://www.mullers.org/downloads/Muller%20Sermons%20pdf/The%20Writings%20and%20Teachings%20of%20George%20Muller%20of%20Bristol.pdf.

44 Rev. K.B. Tupper, "The Book for Man," *Record of Christian Work* (eds. Alexander McConnell, William Revell Moody, Arthur Percy Fitt), vol.11, 1892, 385.

NOVEMBER

1 Elon Foster. *New Cyclopedia of Poetical Illustrations: Adapted to Christian Teaching*. New York: W.C. Palmer, Jr. & Co., 1872, 62.

2 Stephen Abbott Northrop. *A Cloud of Witnesses: The Greatest Men in the World for Christ and the Book*. Fort Wayne, Indiana: The Mason Long Publishing Co., 1894, 35.

3   L.N. R. *The Book and Its Story*. London: Samuel Bagster and Sons, 1853, 347-348.

4   Stephen Abbott Northrop. *A Cloud of Witnesses: The Greatest Men in the World for Christ and the Book*. Fort Wayne, Indiana: The Mason Long Publishing Col, 1894, 93.

5   "The Gideons International" https://www.gideons.org/about.

6   Elon Foster. *New Cyclopedia of Poetical Illustrations: Adapted to Christian Teaching*. New York: W.C. Palmer, Jr. & Co., 1872, 61.

7   Henry Van Dyke, "The Influence of the Bible in Literature," *Century Magazine*, Volume 80, 1910, 890, 895.

8   *William McKinley: America as God's Instrument*, 2, https://www.visionandvalues.org/docs/William%20 McKinley%20-%20America%20as%20God%20s%20Instrument.pdf.

9   "William McKinley: America as God's Instrument," 3, quoted from an American Bible Society tract.

10 John Gibson Paton, James Paton. *Missionary to the New Hebrides: An Autobiography*, vol. 2. London: Hodder and Stoughton, 1889, 108.

11 *Missionary to the New Hebrides,* 130.

12 Jonathan Goforth. *By My Spirit. www.solidchristianbooks.com, 2015.* https://books.google.com/boo ks?id=uuGOCgAAQBAJ&printsec=frontcover&dq=Goforth,+By+My+Spirit&hl=en&sa=X&ved= 0ahUKEwiBr4yOxcPhAhUQXKwKHR1rCssQ6AEIKDAA#v=onepage&q=%22King%20of%20 Kings%22&f=false.

13 Arthur S. Link. *Wilson: The New Freedom, Volume II*. Princeton Legacy Library, 1956, 65.

14 Mario R. DiNunzio, ed. *Woodrow Wilson: Essential Writings and Speeches of the Scholar-President*. New York: New York University Press, 2006, 59.

15 Frank W. Boreham. *A Casket of Cameos: More Texts That Mae History*. New York: Abingdon press, 1924, 36.

16 William M. Ramsay. *The Bearing of Recent Discovery on the Trustworthiness of the New Testament*. New York: Hodder and Stoughton, 1915, 222.

17 Billy Sunday, William Thomas Ellis. *Billy Sunday, the Man and His Message: With His Own Words which Have Won Thousands for Christ*. Philadelphia: The John C. Winston Co., 1917, 259-260.

18 All quotes from Col. Douglas Mastriano, "Serving God or Caesar: Sergeant York and the Morality of War," *Providence*, Summer 2017, 23-30.

19 John Perry. *Unshakable Faith: Booker T. Washington & George Washington Carver*. Sisters, OR; Multnomah, 1999, 349; Psalm 119:18; 121:2.

20 William J. Federer. *America's God and Country*. Coppell, Texas: FAME Publishing, Inc., 1994, 96.

21 "Some Scriptural texts," *Oil and Gas News*, Vol. IX, No. 14, May 19, 1921, 1.

22 R.A. Torrey, *Ten Reasons Why I Believe the Bible is the Word of God* in Roger Martin. *R.A. Torrey: Apostle of Certainty*. Murfreesboro, TN: Sword of the Lord Publishers, 1976, 281 -293.

23 J. Gresham Machen. *Christianity and Liberalism*. Grand Rapids, MI: Wm. B. Eerdmans Publishing Co., 1923, 72.

24 74.

25 78-79.

26 Winston Churchill. *Thoughts and Adventures*. London: Thornton Butterworth, 1932, 293.

27 Knud Jorgensen. *Bible in Mission*. Eugene, Oregon: Wipf & Stock, 2013, 199.

1. Dietrich Bonhoeffer. *Life Together: Prayerbook of the Bible, Dietrich Bonhoeffer Works, Volume 5.* Minneapolis: Fortress Press, 1996, 88.

2. Dietrich Bonhoeffer. The *Way to Freedom: 1935-1939, from the Collected Works of Dietrich Bonhoeffer.* Harper and Row, 1966, 59.

3. Dietrich Bonhoeffer, trans. & ed. by David Gracie. *Meditating on the Word.* Lanham, MD: A Cowley Publications Book, 2000, 121.

4. John Gunther, *The Riddle of MacArthur: Japan, Korea and the far East.* London: Hamish Hamilton, 1951, 69.

5. Lawrence S. Wittner. "MacArthur and the Missionaries: God and Man in Occupied Japan," *Pacific Historical Review*, vol. 40, No.1 (February 1971), 89.

6. Billy Graham. *Just as I am: The Autobiography of Billy Graham.* Harper One/ Zondervan, 1999, 139.

7. Mitsuo Fuchida, "*From Pearl Harbor to Calvary*". *Christianity Today,* 2001 (1st ed. Published as *From Pearl Harbor to Golgotha*, 1953).

8. Arthur Pink, "The Application of the Scriptures," *Studies in the Scriptures,* Vol. XXXI, No. 10, October, 1952, 15.

9. Quoted in "Brother Andrew's Story," from *Open Doors* website, https://www.opendoorsusa.org/about-us/history/brother-andrews-story/, accessed June 25, 2018.

10. "Helen Keller's Bible," *The New York Times*, February 9, 1902.

11. Walter C. Knight. *Knight's Master Book of New Illustrations*, Eerdmans, 1956, 28.

12. Erik Bergaust. *Werner von Braun.* Stackpole Books, 2017, 116.

13. *Dei Verbum,* Vatican Archives, November 18, 1965, http://www.vatican.va/archive/hist_councils/ii_vatican_council/documents/vat-ii_const_19651118_dei-verbum_en.html. The two quotations in this selection are form Jerome's prologue to his commentary on Isaiah and Ambrose's *On the Duties of Ministers.*

14. Jim Irwin. *More than Earthlings: An Astronaut's Thoughts for Christ-Centered Living*, Nashville, TN: Broadman Press, 1983.

15. Roger D. Launius. *Frontiers of Space Exploration.* Greenwood Publishing Group, 2004, 181.

16. David Hoffman. *A Course of Legal Study*, vol. 1 Joseph Neel Publishers, 1836, 65.

17. State Ex Rel. Tampa v. City of Tampa, 48 So 2d 78 (1950), https://law.justia.com/cases/florida/supreme-court/1950/48-so-2d-78-0.html.

18. Harry S. Truman. "Address Before the Attorney General's Conference on Law Enforcement Problems," February 15, 1950, http://www.presidency.ucsb.edu/ws/?pid=13707.

19. *Public Papers of the Presidents of the United States: Gerald R. Ford, 1976-1977*, 1877-1880.

20. "The Chicago Statement on Biblical Inerrancy," *International Council on Biblical Inerrancy*, 1978, 2.

21. Mary Beth Brown. *The Faith of Ronald Reagan.* Thomas Nelson, 2011, xvi.

22. Ronald Reagan: "Proclamation 5018—Year of the Bible, 1983," February 3, 1983. Gerhard Peters and John T. Woolley, *The American Presidency Project.* http://www.presidency.ucsb.edu/ws/?pid=40728.

23. Margaret Thatcher. "Speech to General Assembly of the Church of Scotland," May 21, 1988, *Margaret Thatcher Foundation*, https://www.margaretthatcher.org/document/107246.

24. John Witte, "Foreword: What Does Christianity Offer to the World of Law?," *Journal of Law and Religion* 32(2017), 7-8.

25 J.I. Packer, "Our Lifeline," *ChristianityToday.com,* October 1996, http://www.christinaitytoday.com/holidays/nbw/features/ct6tc022.html.

26 "The Coronation of Her Majesty Queen Elizabeth II in the Abbey Church of St. Peter, Westminster, on Tuesday, the second day of June, 1953, *Oremus,* http://www.oremus.org/liturgy/coronation/cor1953b.html.

27 "President Addresses Nation on Space Shuttle Columbia Tragedy," https://history.nasa.gov/columbia/Troxell/Columbia%20Web%20Site/Documents/Executive%20Branch/President%20Bush/president1.html.

28 Evelyn Husband. *High Calling: The Courageous Life and Faith of Space Shuttle Columbia Commander Rick Husband.* Nashville: Thomas Nelson, 2003.

29 Jeffrey N. Williams. *The Work of His Hands: A View of God's Creation from Space.* Saint Louis: Concordia Publishing House, 2010, 46-49.

30 *A Collection of Psalms and Hymns: from Watts, Doddridge, and others*, 4th edition. Philadelphia: R. & R. Bereford, 1846, 159-160.

31 *Collection of Psalms*, 165-166.

32 John MacArthur, "Remembering All His Benefits, Psalm 103" *Grace to You* https://www.gty.org/library/print/sermons-library/81-25 is the source for the history of some of the hymns based on Psalm 103.

33 "My soul, now praise thy Maker," *Hymnary.org.* https://hymnary.org/text/my_soul_now_praise_thy_maker.

34 "Praise to the Lord, the Almighty," *Hymnary.org. https://hymnary.org/text/praise_to_the_lord_the_almighty_the_king.*

35 "O bless the Lord, my soul!" *Hymnary.org.* https://hymnary.org/text/o_bless_the_lord_my_soul_let_all_within#authority_media_flexscores.

36 "Ten Thousand Reasons," https://genius.com/Matt-redman-10000-reasons-bless-the-lord-lyrics.

37 Billy Graham, "The Bible: The Word of God," *Decision,* vol. 60, no. 3, March 2019, 18-19.

INDEXES

INDEX OF SUBJECTS

INDEX OF SCRIPTURES